New York and
the Lincoln Specials

ALSO BY JOSEPH D. COLLEA, JR.

*The First Vermont Cavalry in the Civil War:
A History* (McFarland, 2010)

New York and the Lincoln Specials

The President's Pre-Inaugural and Funeral Trains Cross the Empire State

Joseph D. Collea, Jr.

McFarland & Company, Inc., Publishers
Jefferson, North Carolina

ISBN (print) 978-1-4766-7075-1
ISBN (ebook) 978-1-4766-3324-4

LIBRARY OF CONGRESS CATALOGUING DATA ARE AVAILABLE

BRITISH LIBRARY CATALOGUING DATA ARE AVAILABLE

© 2018 Joseph D. Collea, Jr. All rights reserved

No part of this book may be reproduced or transmitted in any form or by any means, electronic or mechanical, including photocopying or recording, or by any information storage and retrieval system, without permission in writing from the publisher.

Front cover *top*: typical in appearance to the standard locomotives of the era, the Dean Richmond had the honor of pulling the "Lincoln Special" not only on the triumphant inaugural trip but again for the mournful post-assassination run from Rochester to Buffalo (courtesy of Edward L. May Memorial Collection)

Front cover *bottom*: christened the "United States," the specially-constructed coach on the left—originally intended to transport a living president in comfort—became instead the bearer of his coffin, while the one on the right—known as the "Officers' Car"—carried various dignitaries on the sad journey to Springfield (courtesy the Buffalo History Museum)

Printed in the United States of America

*McFarland & Company, Inc., Publishers
Box 611, Jefferson, North Carolina 28640
www.mcfarlandpub.com*

In memory of the late Harvey Mason Lincoln:
a connoisseur of life, proud relative of Abraham Lincoln,
and friend to three generations of my family

Table of Contents

List of Maps ix
Preface and Acknowledgments 1
Introduction 5

1. Welcome to the Empire State: The Journey Begins 9
2. An Overwhelming Reception: Western New York Is Lincoln Country 19
3. The Longest Day Begins: From Buffalo to Utica 29
4. Next Stop, Utica: Gateway to the Mohawk Valley 42
5. East Through the Valley: The Historic Route to the West in Reverse 53
6. Arrival in Albany: Political Considerations Rule the Day 66
7. The Last Leg Begins: Via an Improvised Route 83
8. Troy Rejoices: An Unexpected Visitor Is Readily Embraced 98
9. Down the Hudson Valley: The Run to New York City 107
10. New York City: The Last Stop in the Empire State 122
11. Final Hours in the Empire State: A Successful Stay Draws to an End 136
12. The Washington Years: When All the Joy Turned to Sorrow 150
13. Bringing the President Home: Funeral Arrangements Are Made 160
14. Return to New York: A City Pays Homage 166
15. Leaving the City: A Grand Procession to the Depot 181
16. Heading North: A Mournful Passage Up the Hudson Valley 192
17. Second Arrival in Albany: The State Capital Offers Its Last Respects 202
18. Into the Heartland: The Mohawk Valley Bids a Sad Farewell 220
19. From Utica to Syracuse: Places Large and Small Pay Homage 232

20. On Toward Buffalo: Western New York Offers Parting Tributes	242
21. Leaving the Empire State: The Long Goodbye Is Over	254
Appendix A: Presidents and Trains	265
Appendix B: Special Orders Governing the Safety of the Funeral Train	267
Chapter Notes	269
Bibliography	277
Index	281

List of Maps

Pre-Inaugural Tour Across New York	6
Visit to Buffalo: Inaugural Tour	20
Midtown Syracuse	40
Mohawk Valley	54
Arrival in Albany	71
Hannibal Hamlin's Route to New York City	85
Alternate Railroad Route: East Albany to Albany	87
Abraham Lincoln Passes Through Troy	104
President's Route: New York City	125
Funeral Processions: New York City	169
Hudson Valley	193
Passing Ilion	230
Downtown Utica, New York	233
Jordan, New York	246
Rochester	252
Route of Travel: Western New York	255

Preface and Acknowledgments

Growing up in Central New York's Mohawk Valley sixty-plus years ago laid the foundation for this book. While my family did not reside along railroad tracks, days and nights were still passed with the sounds of trains heading west to Chicago and east to New York City. Though our house was on the south side of the valley two miles from the New York Central's mainlines, rail traffic was clearly audible. During the night, comfort came from knowing that eventually a whistle would sound, announcing a locomotive's approach to the crossing just beyond the Mohawk River, one-tenth of a mile past the north end of town. Soon the engine's staccato blasts were followed by the rhythmic rattle of the trailing cars passing over joints in the tracks. On chilly winter nights, the trains sounded like they were outside my bedroom window, precursors of the yet-to-come *Polar Express*.

My dad and my grandfather fostered my interest in railroads by taking me to a parking area between the river and the tracks to "watch for trains." Each time the same tableau played out before my eyes: the gatekeeper popped out of his trackside shanty and cranked black-and-white safety barriers down, signaling that the show was about to start … somehow, he always knew when the time was right … and then the monstrous steam engines came thundering past … somehow, Dad and Grandpa always knew when a train was coming. They were usually passenger trains, but sometimes bonus freights would also rush past. Though I did not know it then, I would see the fabled *20th Century Limited* and the *Empire State Express* and, to my eternal chagrin, witness the passing of an era, as sleek diesels gradually became more prevalent—despised interlopers replacing my beloved steam engines. Without visible moving parts like the old locomotives had, these new kids on the block never appeared to be working hard. They did not chug noisily, pull mightily, or steam profusely. Instead they appeared to glide along, seemingly with little effort or sound. Not having whistles was hardly very endearing either—horns belonged on cars and trucks, not trains.

With my dad employed by the railroad in Utica, New York, a rare trip to his workplace situated amidst the busy yards was living the dream for me. I even got the rush that came with climbing into the cab of a big black wrecking crane that dad occasionally operated. As a bonus, working for the railroad entitled my father to a pass. Possession of this golden ticket made possible trips to Rochester, Albany, and New York City. To hear the conductor intone "Tickets, please" and call off at station stops at places of which I had never heard—Fonda, Poughkeepsie, and Ossining—was a thrilling experience. Christmas, too, became synonymous with trains—the Lionel variety. A complete set in 1955 and additions of cars, engines, and accessories occurred over the next several years. The centerpiece of the collection was of course a steam locomotive, and the most treasured car was a wrecking crane … Dad's sometimes wrecking crane.

But as befell "Puff, the Magic Dragon," the boy in me grew to a teenager and other interests evolved. Neatly boxed and safely stored, my train no longer made its annual holiday runs. Dad retired, and Grandpa passed away. No, the appeal of trains never left, for it was a passion too long nurtured and deeply imbedded. But its place in my life became relegated to that where fond memories reside.

In time, my calling became that of a history teacher, one whose passion was studying the Civil War. I was always interested in local and state connections to national events, and the role of my hometown's Remington Arms in the conflict was a source of continuing interest. By chance one day in Ilion's library, I noticed an old handbill calling upon village residents to meet and walk to the New York Central's tracks, there to pay homage as President Lincoln's remains passed on his funeral train. Further investigation led to the realization that the place where my forbearers had gathered was none other than the very same parking spot where Grandpa, Dad, and I had sat, watching for trains. Coincidentally, the time of our evening vigil was in the six-thirty to seven range, the same window during which nineteenth-century Ilionites had arrived in the gathering darkness on April 26, 1865, to see the Lincoln Special. We had parked on the very ground where they stood waiting, and, in the process, a family tradition had unknowingly shared the location with a historic event of national import.

That little spark of recognition brought my interests in trains, the Civil War, and New York State history together and resulted in the inspiration for the book which you now hold in your hands. My treasured Lionel train is still in the attic, the old gatekeeper has long since been outmoded by a bridge spanning both the river and the tracks, our viewing spot is now inaccessible by car … and Dad is gone now, too. But memories live in the heart forever. I can't pass across the new bridge without peering wistfully over its western railing and see that which no one else can … a 1953 Ford coupe parked facing the tracks, its three occupants watching for the next train … all the while surrounded by a somber, torch-bearing crowd of mourners, also waiting for a train…

* * *

One of the hidden pleasures in writing a book that has a national theme imbued with local ties is the opportunity afforded the author to interact with the dedicated folks who manage village, town, county, and state historical societies, associations, and libraries Tapping into the expertise of such people who reside at the grass roots level of preservation is to walk with knowledgeable individuals who are not only the proud guardians of the relics, artifacts, and documents from the past entrusted to their care and oversight, but also enthusiastic promoters willing to share their treasures and by so doing shine a spotlight on the special part their respective collections illustrate about the history of our country.

In some instances, my association with librarians, curators, and directors was only via electronic means, while in others it was an old-fashioned, face-to-face visit. Yet, regardless of the method of communication, my thanks to the following individuals for the willing, prompt, and accurate manner in which they so generously addressed my needs is indeed sincere: Jan Clough, Hastings Historical Society; Shari Golnits, McClurg Museum; William Keeler and Christie Zuhike, Rochester Historical Society; Sarah Komi, Onondaga Historical

Association; Thomas LaChiusa, representing his late mother and the Brighton Historical Society; Marled Leljedal, U.S. Army Heritage and Education Center; Norm MacDonald, Ossining Historical Society; Michael Maloney, Schenectady County Historical Society; Amy Miller and Cynthia Van Ness, Buffalo History Museum; John Nevin and Susan Young, Jordan Historical Society Museum; Susan Perkins, Herkimer County Historical Society; Richard Stoving, New York Central Railroad Historical Society; Krista Tandy, Indiana State Museum; Frank Tomaino, *Utica Observer-Dispatch*; and Michael VandeVelde, Mayor of Westfield, NY.

Special thanks also to Regina Nicolette and Diane Williams—former English teachers-deluxe at Ilion High—who ventured to provide some preliminary editing and proofing, thus giving me an idea of what needed to be addressed throughout the manuscript.

Moving to a larger venue, the resources and personnel of the New York State Library in Albany also proved to be invaluable. The Newspaper Project, which was undertaken several years ago to bring under one roof access to a statewide collection of primary source materials, is a researcher's dream. Access to this microfilm collection abetted by an efficient staff made the hours spent poring through the reels time well-spent.

Finally, I am deeply indebted to the same two talented folks who had assisted me with my first book. One is a former colleague and still a friend, Annie Boutin—she is a lady who possesses the knowledge and skill to unlock the mysteries of computer applications and employ them to properly format this book. Her assistance was invaluable. The other is my generous, unassuming son Bob, whose own wizardry with a computer produced both sharp pictures and cogent maps. I deeply appreciate his willingness to give of his time, patience, and expertise to help enhance yet another of his dad's projects ... none of which would have come to full fruition without him.

Introduction

During his lifetime, Abraham Lincoln experienced several significant relationships. The most cherished was formed in 1842 when Mary Todd became his wife, becoming a faithful spouse for twenty-three years. Then, in 1844, he entered a profitable law practice with William Herndon, a loyal individual who functioned not only as Lincoln's junior partner, but also as a close friend and confidant. A third association, one that ran contemporaneously with those of both his beloved consort and his professional colleague, served him equally as well, also remaining a part of his existence until the bitter end.

But rather than a living person, this last bond was with an ally made of wood and iron: the railroad. Through the symbiotic relationship that evolved, both parties profited handsomely. Lincoln earned a comfortable living, eventually handling over one hundred cases that involved some aspect of law as it applied to railroads, while the common carrier had a strong advocate who recognized their value to the growth of the country. Though he went to court as both their defender and prosecutor—for ultimately, he had bills to pay—he nevertheless believed that this burgeoning form of transportation represented the wave of the future—one he envisioned as a positive force for the development of both Illinois and the nation. The high point of Lincoln's support for railroads came with the signings of the Pacific Railroad Acts in 1862 and 1864, legislation that set the wheels in motion for constructing the transcontinental railroad.

As Lincoln had done much to back railroading, so also had the industry served him well. While he had ridden the rails across Illinois to keep his debating appointments with Stephan Douglas and later made an excursion east by train during his presidential campaign, his two most unforgettable associations with railroads did not occur until after his election to the presidency. The first was a pre-inaugural trip February 11 through February 23, 1861, a 1631-mile tour from Springfield to Washington. Not that Lincoln had any real choice but to go by rail. Coming from the farthest west of any previous president, train travel offered the only the sensible option to convey him over such a distance.

However, he did have choices. An itinerary would have been possible that took Lincoln's entourage directly to Washington, but the trade-off in such a pathway would have been the greatly reduced exposure that a more circuitous route afforded. Lincoln had to decide: fewer miles and fewer people or an extended journey and increased contact. He chose the latter. By stopping eighty-three times, the president-elect would be seen by a vast number of people. Since the reality of mid-nineteenth century politics were that candidates for national office did not campaign widely, the consequence was that ballots were cast without voters having heard or seen their aspirant of choice. Newspaper accounts, editorial opinions, political endorsements, and the back fence provided most voters their knowledge about national candidates. By opting for a post-election whistle-stop tour, Lincoln scored a public relations tour de force—one marred only by an unsettled situation in Baltimore that suddenly turned what had been a leisurely promenade-by-rail into a hurried, surreptitious dash to the safety of Washington.

Yet, as tense as the final fifty miles became, they did not erase the memory of the triumphant success that had hallmarked the previous twelve days. Appropriately, some of the high points of the journey came in New York. Since the chosen route passed across over 500 miles of the Empire State, Lincoln had many opportunities to greet constituents in this highly populated sovereignty, one which had given him 35 electoral votes. Though unnecessary then, the time was coming when New Yorkers would back Lincoln with more than just ballots, providing men and materiel in copious quantities for the war effort. The political capital that the new chief executive gained from living out of a suitcase those extra days of travel may well have proven worth the discomfort.

By war's end, contributions from the Empire State were indeed impressive. By any standard applied—men, materiel, or financing—New York was all-in with its backing of the war effort. Given the state's unwavering support, the relief that came with the end of hostilities was most welcomed. The knowledge that their boys would soon be returning gladdened the hearts of countless families. But their euphoria abruptly turned to anguish on April 14, 1865. Henceforth, not only would soldiers be returning home, but so also would

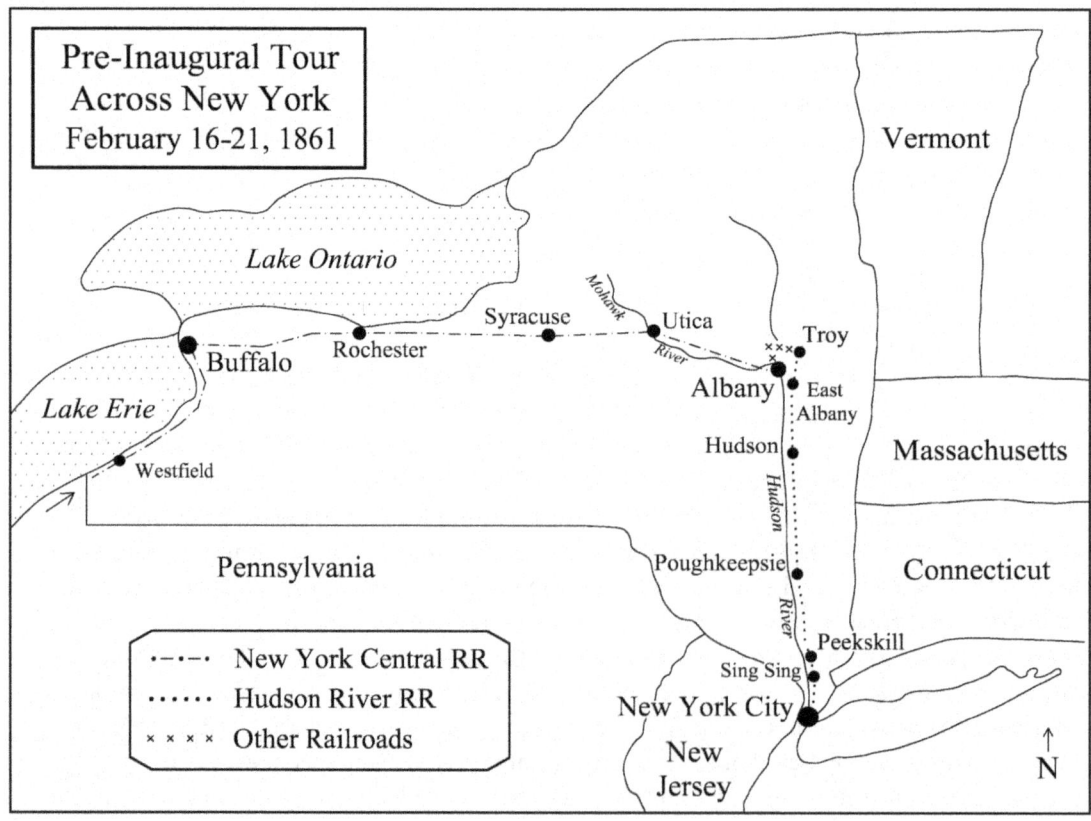

Drawn by Bob Collea.

Abraham Lincoln. However, unlike the joyous throngs that greeted his inaugural passage, the crowds this time would be somber. Once the determination was made to bury the martyred president in Springfield, the means and the route became paramount concerns. Here, as it had in 1861, the railroad stepped to the fore and helped coordinate the second major train trek of Lincoln's presidency. The final determination embraced transporting the president's remains by train, along with retracing virtually same route followed for the inaugural run.

Knowing that Empire Staters had warmly greeted Abraham Lincoln's previous statewide excursion and then steadfastly supported the war effort, no one was surprised that an outpouring of grief accompanied the funeral cortège as it slowly moved north from New York City to Albany and westward to Buffalo. For the second time in little more than four years, an iron horse conveyed Abraham Lincoln over New York soil. The uniqueness of both events and stark disparity in arrangements and emotions that sharply contrasted these epic runs make for the compelling story that is *New York and the Lincoln Specials*.

1

Welcome to the Empire State
The Journey Begins

When the *Rocket* left Erie, Pennsylvania, at 1:05 p.m. on February 16, 1861, the Buffalo-bound locomotive was making the most important run of its working life. In its service to the Buffalo and Erie Railroad, no previous passenger had ever approached the stature of a traveler currently onboard, for among those seated in a trailing coach was Abraham Lincoln. Scheduled to arrive in Buffalo at suppertime, he would first make whistle stops at Westfield, Dunkirk, and Silver Creek. As he rode along, Lincoln's mind was preoccupied with a myriad of pressing thoughts. Among his concerns were: the recent selection of Jefferson Davis to lead the newly constituted Confederacy; Southern demands that the federal government vacate Fort Sumter; intimations by Mayor Fernando Wood of New York that his city should also secede; the efforts of a Peace Convention in Washington to avert war; and the crafting of an inaugural speech.

Fortunately, one other anxiety had just been mercifully resolved. On February 13, Vice President John Breckinridge announced that "Abraham Lincoln of Illinois, having received a majority of the whole number of the Electoral votes, is duly elected President of the United States for four years, commencing the 4th of March, 1861."[1] Beyond making him officially the winner of the recent election, further relief came because the process was concluded without incident. In the days preceding the count, grave concerns had been harbored by federal authorities that armed pro-secessionists might attempt to disrupt the process. To thwart any hostile interventions, General Winfield Scott had posted guards at the Capitol's entrances, while "a regiment of army regulars roamed the floor, dressed in civilian clothes but armed with rifles, and an extra supply of arms and ammunition was locked in nearby conference rooms."[2]

One other worry still loomed, a concern not so much fretted over by Lincoln, but definitely a major anxiety shared by members of his entourage. This particular dark cloud involved the president's safety. Often the elephant in the room, the uncertainty of the times nevertheless precluded ignoring the possibility that someone might want to harm him. Ratcheting up his associate's anxieties was the complete transparency with which the entire trip was revealed. Lincoln's itinerary was published in newspapers across the state. Should an assassin lurk somewhere ahead, these disclosures made his task potentially that much easier.

Surprisingly, despite these fears, no one was assigned to coordinate efforts for Lincoln's protection, though several individuals on the train did have security-related assignments. One of the most conspicuous was Ward Hill Lamon. A burly mountain of a man, he traveled with an assortment of weapons concealed under his coat. They were long-time friends, and the president-elect had personally requested that Lamon accompany him to Washington. On his part, the devoted follower readily agreed, for "the fear that Lincoln would be assassinated was shared by very many of his neighbors at Springfield."[3] In effect, Lamon served 24/7 as the president's primary bodyguard.

Lamon's devotion to the future president was unsurpassed, but others aboard the train believed that they, too, carried the weight of his safety on their shoulders. The youngest was twenty-four-year-old Elmer Ellsworth. A self-appointed militia colonel and founder of Zouave units, Ellsworth came into Lincoln's orbit as a promising law clerk and later an indefatigable campaigner. A strong bond developed between these two men of disparate ages, eventually blossoming into that akin to a familial relationship. Of those providing security, Colonel Ellsworth had the best claim to operating in a sanctioned capacity. His mandate was a set of guidelines announced by William Wood, an individual appointed as the Superintendent of Arrangements for the entire trip.

Exercising full powers, he made the decisions regarding all stops and layovers. Local reception committees had to go through Mr. Wood to have their plans approved. Accordingly, he had promulgated a Circular of Instructions. With respect to safety, Wood's directives placed young Ellsworth in charge of crowd control. But without troops to deploy, Ellsworth's only power came from working with local authorities and whatever forces they could provide. In lieu of such support, he had the unenviable task of navigating the president through crowds, as not only the front man but at times the only man carrying out this critical assignment.

While Lamon and Ellsworth were committed to Lincoln's protection, others were equally intent upon exercising this same responsibility. Colonel William Sumner, Major David Hunter, and Captain John Pope were army officers detailed to look after the well-being of their future commander in chief. Additionally, two more of Lincoln's friends of long-standing—lawyers Norman Judd and David Davis—were members of the caravan, and, they too remained vigilant during the trip.

Given the passions aroused by the recent election, even the most optimistic of Lincoln's supporters had sufficient cause for concerns about his safety. That their fears were founded was given credence by a discovery arising very early in the journey. On Monday, February 18, 1861, an abortive attempt was made to derail the Lincoln Special, just as the train was poised to cross from Indiana into Ohio. But for the alertness of the engineer, a disaster could have befallen the inaugural express.

As the story was conveyed by a Lafayette newspaper, the engineer noticed "an obstruction on the track, and stopping his engine, found that a machine for putting cars on the track had been fastened upon the rails in such a manner that if a train at full speed had struck it, engine and cars must [sic] have been thrown off and many persons killed."[4]

Though the episode received only limited press exposure, a sobering awareness existed for those who cared to read the tea leaves: somewhere out there were evil-doers, men who possessed the motivation to harm Abraham Lincoln. Even more disconcerting, this foiled attempt occurred in a state adjacent to his home turf. If he wasn't safe in his own neighborhood, what was in store for the him farther down the tracks? Undoubtedly, this aborted sabotage attempt confirmed the fears held by many of Lincoln's associates. Since the worst might be yet to come, increased vigilance was clearly in order. Rumors, no matter how outlandish, could not be given short shrift. By the time the Lincoln cavalcade reached Albany, knowledge of a nascent plot to assassinate the president-elect in Baltimore had already begun to surface.

Upon reaching New York City, the evidence of nefarious undertakings waiting ahead mounted, as agents of the clandestine operative Alan Pinkerton began to supply an increasing volume of proof that a conspiracy was indeed gaining traction. Even though the president-elect had more pressing matters with which to concern himself, members of his party did not share those distractions. With each passing mile, at every upcoming station stop, and encompassing all future public interactions, their worries for their charge's safety were ever present.

Lincoln, however, would not let such thoughts deflect his focus from the tasks at hand. Having crossed into New York State, his train made good time as it passed along the shores of Lake Erie. Given the unpredictable nature of the weather there in late winter, with heavy lake-effect snow squalls liable to sweep in unexpectedly, railroad authorities had stationed locomotives with their steam up every twenty miles along the route to Buffalo. If the *Rocket* ran into trouble—be it mechanical or meteorological—assistance was readily available.

Coming up was the first stop in the president-elect's important five-day excursion through the Empire State, the small Chautauqua County community of Westfield.

Thirteen miles northeast of the Pennsylvania border, the hamlet's ideal location on the shores of Lake Erie and the banks of Chautauqua Creek provided it with three important assets: a transportation avenue for trade; a source of water power; and a moderate climate. By the time of Lincoln's arrival, Westfield was a growing community, its prosperity resting

As the late 1859 photograph on the left shows, Lincoln was elected with a clean-shaven countenance; then before leaving Springfield for Washington, he grew his famous beard, shown in an 1865 portrait (Library of Congress).

on an industrial foundation of mills and factories. Two years prior to Lincoln's arrival, the area's existing agricultural base was given a boost that would literally bear fruit and enhance its economy for decades to come with the introduction of grape-growing. Over time, the quality of the fruit, not only around Westfield but all along the lakeshore, caused an expansion into the business of wine production—a lucrative enterprise that continues to this day. But for the president-elect, his first stop in the Empire State held a personal significance that went beyond politics and economics. Here he was to meet an individual who unexpectedly helped shape his image for all time.

After leaving Pennsylvania, the Lincoln Special rolled into Westfield's little station and small rail yard at 1:32 p.m. Gathered at the depot, which was located on the western side of town just inland from the Great Lake, "a large multitude was assembled and a spacious banner was displayed, bearing 'Welcome to the Empire State.'"[5] Among the dignitaries onboard was George Patterson, an individual of considerable local stature. As one of the recurring practices on the journey, local VIPs were often taken aboard ahead of the president's appearance in their respective communities, hence Patterson's presence. A former state assemblyman and one-term lieutenant governor, Mr. Patterson was an ideal choice to accompany the president-elect, introduce him to officials waiting at the station, and then present the honored guest to the public.

Dutifully carrying out the last of his responsibilities, he eschewed holding the focus on himself and kept his remarks brief, after which the man of the hour stepped forward to

Lincoln was welcomed by an enthusiastic crowd in Buffalo that lined the parade route from Exchange Street Station to the hotel on Main Street (*Frank Leslie's Illustrated Newspaper*).

a rousing welcome. Lincoln spoke from the rear platform. By the time for his departure came, the good people of Westfield had two distinct memories of his visit—the first one they would come to share with other small communities like theirs across the state, while the second belonged uniquely to them.

Their collective experience was that of hearing a brief, folksy address containing the canned remarks that the president would repeat at many station stops on his passage across New York. During these brief orations, he would thank everyone for turning out, excuse himself for having no prepared speech, and compliment the ladies who gave him a better bargain to look at than he did them. By adhering to this simple template, Lincoln accomplished his primary goals of being seen and heard by his constituents, yet at the same time making no sweeping policy statements. While frustrating to many and even angering to others, he felt that it was the proper approach for a president-elect to take. The time and place for words of commitment would come at his inauguration.

But, where his words were decidedly pedestrian—muted to some extent by a hoarseness that was already weakening his voice—the closing minutes of his Westfield stop produced a unique, touching tableau, one which created an endearing story that became an integral part of both Lincoln lore and Westfield's history. The saga began inconspicuously enough months before. The father and brother of eleven-year-old Westfield resident Grace Bedell "returned from a trip to the West, and had brought her a portrait of the Republican nominee."[6] After studying the print, she was inspired to write the Republican candidate a letter.

But no idle fan mail was this earnest correspondence. Instead Grace offered her elder a piece of unsolicited advice:

> My father has just come home from the fair and brought home your picture and Mr. Hamlin's. I am a little girl only eleven years old, but want you should be President of the United States very much so I hope you will not think me very bold to write to such a great man as you are. Have you any little girls about as large as I am if so give them my love and tell her to write to me if you cannot answer this letter. I have got 4 brothers and part of them will vote for you anyway and if you let your whiskers grow I will try to get the rest of them to vote for you. You would look a great deal better for your face it is so thin. All the ladies like whiskers and they would make their husband's to vote for you and then you would be President. My father is going to vote for you and if I was a man I would vote for you to but I will and get everyone to vote for you that I can I think that rail fence around your picture makes it look very pretty. I have got a little baby sister she is nine weeks old and just as cunning as can be. When you write direct your letter direct to Grace Bedell Westfield Chautauqua County New York.[7]

The young lass's letter was dated October 15. Whether guided by luck or fate, the missive made it past Lincoln's secretaries, who customarily would have crafted a response on their boss's behalf. However, not only did the presidential candidate receive the child's note, but he also responded in two distinctly diverse ways, one immediately and the other in time. Lincoln's first reaction was to respond in his own hand. Written four days after receiving Grace's, his return correspondence was dated October 19, representing a quick a turnaround time. In his response, he told her: "Your very agreeable letter of the 15th was received. I regret the necessity of saying that I have no daughters. I have three sons—one seventeen, one nine, and one seven, years of age. They, with their mother, constitute my whole family. As to the whiskers, having never worn any, do you not think people would call it a piece of silly affectation if I were to begin it now?"[8]

That candidate Lincoln, during a hotly contested election, would take the time to quietly send a personal note to a child spoke volumes about the kind and thoughtful man that he was, along with revealing the soft spot in his heart for youngsters. Ward Hill Lamon confirmed this admirable trait possessed by Lincoln when he observed that "on making the acquaintance of a child he at once became its friend, and never afterward forgot its face or the circumstances under which the acquaintance was formed; for his little friends always made some impression on his mind and feelings that was certain to be lasting."[9] The ultimate effect of Grace Bedell's advice was, of course, Lincoln's decision to commence nurturing a crop of facial hair. He began transforming his appearance in late October, making him eventually stand out as the first of America's sixteen presidents to sport facial hair. For reasons of personal preference, Lincoln opted for what amounted to a half-beard, cultivating growth only along his lower jaws and chin, leaving his cheeks and upper chin and lip clean-shaven. Still the growth radically altered his appearance. Since his pre-election portraiture depicted a beardless visage, momentary confusion sometimes occurred at his whistle-stops across New York, simply because the crowd did not immediately recognize him.

For the people of Westfield, the Bedell-Lincoln exchange of letters was old news by the time of his arrival. After Grace received her return correspondence, word spread quickly, causing quite a stir locally. In fact, many people came to the Bedell home to see this unique document for themselves. Lincoln, meanwhile, had filed the whole account in his memory banks. In the vein of those gifted people who can readily access an appropriate information at the precise moment when needed, he recalled his connection to Grace Bedell on his way to New York, asking Patterson if he knew of the family. After his perfunctory remarks, Lincoln moved to the opposite side of the platform and confirmed with the crowd that he was in fact in Westfield. He then referenced his link to their community: "Some three months ago, I received a letter from a young lady here. It was a very pretty letter, and she advised me to let my whiskers grow, as it would improve my personal appearance. Acting partly upon her suggestion, I have done so, and now, if she is here, I would like to see her."[10]

Informed by a boy clinging to a lamp post that she was in fact present, the president-elect alighted from the train and looked in the direction to which the youngster pointed. The crowd obligingly parted and opened a pathway to the girl. Accompanied by members of her family and a neighbor, Grace came forward, clutching a bouquet of roses intended for Mr. Lincoln. Once they came face-to-face and had been introduced, the president-elect, who towered over the young lady, "took her by the hand and imprinted a kiss upon her

At the railroad station in Westfield, New York, the president-elect met young Grace Bedell on February 16, 1861, their introduction now immortalized by statuary in a town park (courtesy Village of Westfield, New York).

forehead and [then] stepped aboard the train."[11] The crowd cheered. Grace blushed. She was so flustered that she ran all the way home, still clutching the flowers that she had forgotten to give the president.

While never capitalized on by Lincoln, this spontaneous vignette could have been a public relations coup. Often disingenuously, politicians kiss babies, consume hot dogs, and wear cowboy hats—all in an attempt to establish a local connection, appear human, and garner favorable publicity. Lincoln, by being himself, had accomplished one of the most touching interactions with a constituent that any public official could ever hope to achieve. Today, reporters would be all over such a feel-good story. But 1861 was a different era. Correspondents did pick up on the event, and newspapers in various cities devoted limited coverage in sharing a heartwarming incident. But, then, the Abraham Lincoln who came to Westfield that day was but a president-elect. Whether he would succeed or fail was history yet unwritten. In time, he would come to be recognized as our country's greatest chief executives, and then all-things-Lincoln became of much greater interest than they had been before his inauguration.

The chronicle of the letters and the meeting between the two correspondents in Westfield was preserved for a time only in the yellowing pages of newspapers, on a couple of sheets of aging letter paper, in the memories of those who were at the station that day, and in the heart of Grace Bedell, which would beat until her death in 1936. Time, however, has elevated the account to a revered status. Preservation of the story has long since passed from the hands of those present and entrusted to posterity. Toward this end, their two letters now rest side by side in the Detroit Public Library. Clearly visible on Lincoln's letter are ink smears, caused by snowflakes that fell upon the paper as Grace read it on her way home from the post office. A pair of juxtaposed statues in a small downtown park—one of Abraham Lincoln and the other of Grace Bedell—commemorates their meeting at the Westfield depot. Of this unique episode, Lincoln would later speak with the wisdom that hindsight imparts: "How small a thing will sometimes change the whole aspect of our lives."[12]

Then, "after bidding the little miss good-by, and shaking hands with a good many within his reach, the president-elect stepped upon the platform of the car and the train moved off, he bowing to the crowd as it left the depot."[13] For the president-elect, his excursion across New York State had clearly opened on a high note. While there would be bumps along the way, events over the course of the next five days in the Empire State would provide a litany of largely positive experiences. The *Brockport Republican*, published in a community just to the west of Rochester, would later hail "Mr. Lincoln's journey as one continuous ovation."[14] With the warm feelings engendered by the Westfield experience setting the tone, Lincoln's next stop was Dunkirk.

Another lakeshore community, Dunkirk had recently enjoyed its own wave of prosperity following the completion of the Erie Railroad across New York's Southern Tier in the 1840s. As the carrier's western terminus, the railroad served to complement the town's already active port facilities, making Dunkirk an attractive site for industry. Passing under a ceremonial arch emblazoned with patriotic mottoes and accompanied by festive music filling the air, the Lincoln Special pulled in at 2:45 p.m., on a cold, clear Monday afternoon. As described in *The Centennial History of Chautauqua County*, "Lincoln from his car, which halted west of the Erie Depot and just east of Lion Street, made a short speech to those gathered there in which he impressively referred to the gathering storm about to burst upon the country."[15] To one witness, "it looked as if Chautauqua and all the surrounding country had poured its men, women, and children upon the place, [as] it was estimated that there were 10,000 people present."[16]

After greeting the turnout with but a few words, apologizing that the tightness of his schedule and the urgency of getting to Washington precluded lengthy orations at every stop, Lincoln impulsively launched into an unplanned discourse. Stepping from the train onto a red-carpeted platform, a relocation that was an unusual occurrence as he was repeatedly reluctant to leave the train for a stage, he found himself standing next to a flagstaff. Inspired by the vibrantly colored banner waving in the breeze, coupled with the enthusiastic demeanor of his audience, he impulsively placed his hand upon the pole from which Old Glory unfurled above his head and said: "I stand by the flag of the Union, and all I ask of you is that you stand by me as long as I stand by it."[17] The crowd's reaction to these stirring words was to burst forth with a frenzied approval.

To one onlooker, "the sentiment was electric, in its effect upon the multitude, which responded 'We will!' followed by shouts and cheers the most enthusiastic."[18] An embedded reporter for the *New York World* captured the scene for his readers: "It is impossible to describe the applause and the acclamation with which the Jacksonian peroration was greeted. The arches of the depot echoed and re-echoed with the ring of countless cheers. Men swung their hats wildly. Women waved their handkerchiefs, and, as the train moved on, the crowd, animated by a common impulse, followed, as if they intended to keep it company to the next station."[19]

Given their zealous reaction to Lincoln's plea for support, it is not surprising that Dunkirk's residents were equally responsive to Lincoln's call for troops two months later. As a later county history would proudly proclaim, "Dunkirk was not only the first town in the county to be awakened to the great danger that threatened the country, but the first to take action in support of the government."[20] Volunteers from Dunkirk quickly filled two companies in the 72nd New York Infantry and were off to war in June of 1861. During their three-year enlistment, the regiment was assigned to General Dan Sickles' Excelsior Brigade and saw action at Fredericksburg, Chancellorsville, and Gettysburg. Throughout the four years of conflict, a martial air pervaded the town, since the railroad made it a convenient staging area for troops heading to the battlefront.

As the Lincoln Special left Dunkirk, the president-elect stood on the rear platform, bidding his farewell to the exuberant crowd. Inside the train, elation also reigned supreme following the second triumphant stop in New York. Whatever fortunes lay ahead, the excursion into the Empire State had begun on a pair of decidedly uplifting receptions for Abraham Lincoln.

The next stop was Silver Creek, a small community that accrued a few minutes of Lincoln's time by default, for it was the location of a water tower and a wood pile. Since nineteenth century locomotives relied upon steam for propulsion, they could not travel far or long without replenishing the resources that produced their motive power.

While the resupply effort was in progress, the president-elect spoke to those folks who had come to see him. After his customary remarks, a young girl approached the train bearing a bouquet of roses. Unlike Grace Bedell, she successfully gave her floral presentation to the president and, like Grace Bedell, received a kiss on the forehead along with the great man's quaint appraisal that "you are a little rosebud yourself. I hope your life will open into perpetual beauty and goodness."[21] With that, the train again headed toward Buffalo. While the express passed through several more communities along the way, no stops were scheduled until reaching the Queen City of western New York. Nevertheless, even without the hope of a visit to spur them on, the ardor of the citizenry residing in the president's path was not dampened. As noted by an onboard correspondent, "all along the way, guns were fired, bands played patriotic airs, cheers were sent up, and handkerchiefs waved in honor of the illustrious passenger."[22]

Incorporated in 1825, the Buffalo which Lincoln rapidly approached was in the incipient stages of growth that would continue on well into the next century. From a population of only 1500 in 1810, the city was credited with just over 81,000 residents in 1860, an astounding growth rate that made it the tenth largest city in the country. Though setters had first populated the site in 1789, Buffalo's proximity to Canada turned out to be a temporary impediment to immediate development. With the advent of hostilities between the United States and Great Britain, the War of 1812 saw Buffalo become a jumping-off point for American forces invading their neighbor just across the Niagara River.

However, the military upside of this location proved to have a negative aspect too, for Buffalo, in turn, became a reachable target for invading enemy forces. British efforts were finally rewarded in 1814, when a raiding party captured the town. Buffalo was put to the torch, suffering the same ignominious fate at the hands of a vengeful foe as did the nation's capital. But, with the end of the conflict, Buffalo's location in a peacetime world again became advantageous. In 1825, the Erie Canal was opened, bringing boom times. As the waterway's western terminus, combined with Great Lakes' shipping using its port facilities and the New York Central and Erie Railroad tying it to eastern markets, Buffalo's destiny placed it at the hub of an important transportation network.

While Abraham Lincoln had passed through the city in several previous instances. he did so in relative anonymity, for he traveled as a private citizen. Though he had acquired a fair degree of regional acclaim over the previous two decades, his national stature built more slowly, only becoming full-blown in recent years. But when the Lincoln Special reached Buffalo's Exchange Street Station at 4:30 p.m., the city was primed to welcome him. His days of passing through unheralded were gone forever.

Though he was not the first president to grace the streets of Buffalo—Millard Fillmore was currently a resident—Lincoln's passage came at such a momentous time in the country's history that it warranted special attention. The editor of the *Buffalo Morning Express*, mincing no words, voiced his opinion on the import of the challenge Lincoln now faced: "The sun of the American Republic will either set in dishonor during the Presidential term of Mr. Lincoln, or the clouds that now dim its disk will be brushed away and it will shine upon the world with its accustomed splendor."[23] He therefore advised that "the people should remind him in a becoming manner that they look to him to save the nation and to show by proper tokens that they are with him on the side of the Union with their whole hearts, and ready hands."[24]

That the citizenry responded favorably to his clarion call that "the people of Buffalo, and the County of Erie, and for that matter of all Western New York should avail themselves of this occasion to tender him a hearty and cordial welcome to our State and its hospitalities" was clearly in evidence on Monday afternoon.[25] "When the looked-for hour of the president's coming had arrived," noted one observer, "the crowd, the bustle, the excitement which all day had grown, was at a climax which we think it perfectly safe to say never has been equaled in Buffalo."[26] The streets were inundated with a sea of people, all seeking desirable vantage points from which to catch a glimpse of the visiting dignitary. They were "packed upon the walks, clustered upon the roofs, crowded at the windows, clinging thickly to everything upon which man or boy could climb, heaped and overflowing everywhere within view of the route of the expected procession, such a swarming of humanity—of the rough and the genteel, of the masculine and the fair, of the old and the young, to the youngest, of every class and character—we never saw in our Queen City."[27]

Not surprisingly, the crush of spectators was greatest at the depot. Unfortunately, the civil authorities in charge of arrangements had not foreseen the magnitude of the reception which would welcome Mr. Lincoln. Though they did have the presence of mind to bar the public from the depot, they had not adequately gauged the enterprising nature of citizens on a mission. Temporarily frustrated, but equally determined not to be denied by the locked doors, the crowd gravitated around to the train entrance and gained access via that unintended means. The Buffalo station, like many kindred structures of that era, had long, high-roofed sheds under which the tracks were laid, thus offering passengers protection from the elements. With no guards at this inviting back door, the crowd took advantage of a golden opportunity. By the time the train hove into view, both the depot and the shed were densely packed with people, while others were strung out along the tracks.

Eagerly awaiting the president's arrival, they continued jostling for the most advantageous viewing positions. Normally, the sight of billowing smoke and the sound of a shrill whistle served ample notice that a train was approaching; however, on this day a local militia unit and then the crowd provided additional early warnings. After the boom from cannon fired by an artillery company had officially announced the sighting of the Lincoln Special, a continuous, rolling reverberation went up from the assembled mass. Starting first with those situated along the tracks, the sound wave produced by thousands of cheering people was picked up by those at the station and passed on to others lining the streets.

In the end result, "it became a roar mightier than and more majestic in sound than the boom of the cannon."[28] As the *Rocket* inched its way ever so slowly into the shed with its bell clanging an urgent warning, the dense horde in the path of the engine's unforgiving bulk made forward progress difficult and dangerous. Miraculously, no one was injured before the train halted. Once the hazard presented by the moving locomotive ceased to be a concern, people closed in tightly around the cars. Vying for position beside the rear coach became their prime objective, anticipating that its rear platform was the one onto which the president was expected to emerge. With an enthusiasm bordering on wild frenzy, the crowd swayed to and fro as more and more people tried to cram into a finite space. While no one in the crowd meant any harm, the scene that was about to unfold would hold many anxious moments for those charged with providing security for Mr. Lincoln.

2

An Overwhelming Reception
Western New York Is Lincoln Country

Even the weather helped make the day memorable, with early morning clouds eventually dissipating and allowing a late-winter sun to burst forth. Its warming rays melted the dusting of snow that had fallen during the night. Though the by-products of the heat and moisture were muddy roads, no one seemed to mind. Not to be outdone by the nature's glorious setting, Buffalonians added their own embellishments. Flags proliferated from businesses and homes on poles and railings. Banners hung in prominent locations. Tricolored bunting and streamers adorned porches and lampposts. The scene looked like a Fourth of July celebration.

People began gathering before noon. But, as the clock ticked toward the Lincolns' scheduled arrival, the "throng in the streets rapidly increased, country folks arriving in great numbers, from every part of the county, and the city inhabitants dropping their daily pursuits of business in holiday excitement."[1]

Once the engine halted, the challenge became moving the president from his coach through the station's lobby to the waiting carriages. Company D of the 74th Infantry Regiment took charge, forming two parallel lines and momentarily holding back the crowd. By passing between these military pickets, the presidential party could hopefully proceed unhindered to its carriages. However, before leaving, a bit of ceremonial etiquette was in order.

As the president stepped toward the stairs, he was accompanied by Almon M. Clapp, a local dignitary escorting Mr. Lincoln form Cleveland to Buffalo. This plum assignment came his way due to his elevated stature, for Clapp was the publisher of the *Buffalo Morning Express*, a former state assemblyman, and a delegate to the 1856 Republican National Convention.

As the two men were about to detrain, they were met by Buffalo's most distinguished resident. For standing at the bottom of the steps and offering Lincoln "a few words of congratulations on the safety of his journey and the preservation of his health" was none other than the city's first citizen, former president Millard Fillmore, accompanied by the city's acting mayor, John Bemis.[2] While the 13th president's presence was welcomed, that he paid Abraham Lincoln this honor was somewhat surprising, given that Fillmore was not a pre-election supporter of the Republican standard-bearer. More than likely, Fillmore's role in greeting the president-elect was a case where exercising the proper public protocol trumped personal political differences.

In an interesting turnabout, Lincoln soon had a chance to return the courtesy. At the time of his election, there were four living ex-presidents, with lame duck James Buchanan soon to join this esteemed fraternity which included Martin Van Buren, John Tyler, Millard Fillmore, and Franklin Pierce. Lincoln undoubtedly would have been equally willing to help any of them, but it is a revealing measure of the man that Lincoln was gracious enough to not let Fillmore's political animosities dissuade him from extending assistance when Fillmore asked. There was another unspoken bond which may have to some extent softened Lincoln's feelings toward his predecessor: both had suffered devastating losses in their respective families. Lincoln had to withstand the death of two sons, one in the 1841 and the other in 1862, while Fillmore's first wife passed away less than a month after he left office in 1853, and then his only daughter died the following year. While each man had reached heights of power and acclaim that few ever achieve, they had mutually experienced the depths of anguish from personal tragedies.

But on this glorious day in Buffalo, mournful thoughts were easily overcome by the enthusiastic welcome. At the Exchange Street Station alone, "the crowd in and surrounding the depot was dense, and numbered not less than 10,000 people."[3] Fortunately, none of the excited spectators meant any ill will toward the president. The local press concurred, noting that their behavior "certainly signified no disrespect towards the President, but rather the opposite feelings."[4] But in their collective desire to press as close to Mr. Lincoln as possible, the spontaneous crush precipitated a threat to his safety. Despite their best efforts, the mil-

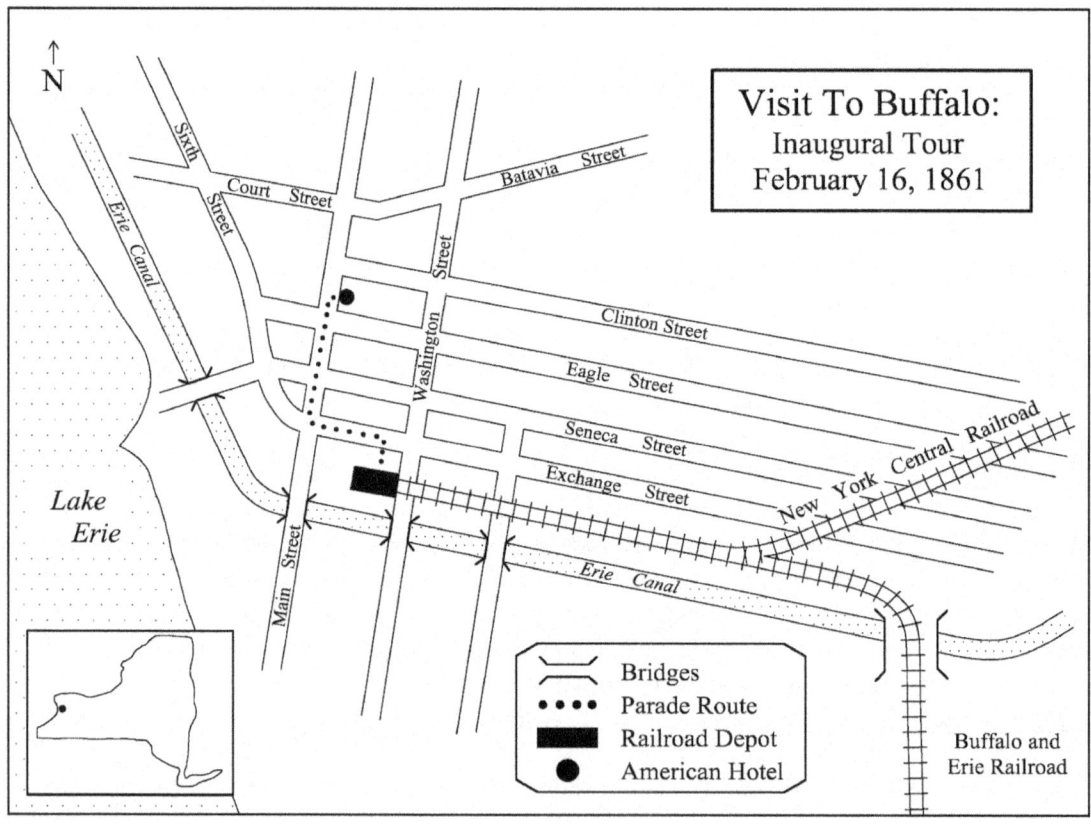

Drawn by Bob Collea.

itary guard was insufficient to stem the onrushing tide of humanity—the soldiers were simply overwhelmed. Unintentionally, the troops' awkward handling of their muskets almost resulted in citizens being impaled upon bayonets. "It seems like special providence that nobody was splitted [sic] open upon these death-dealing instruments," observed one eyewitness, "as the troops couldn't keep upright, much less preserve the perpendicular of their muskets."[5] In its post-mortem of the black-eye received by its city in the wake of this event, the *Buffalo Morning Express* offered that "decorous composure never can be expected from such a crowd of people; and, if order is to be had under circumstances like those of Saturday, it must be forcibly maintained."[6]

After much struggling, the president was extricated from the clutches of the crowd and gained the relative safety of his barouche. Seated with him were Millard Fillmore, Almon Clapp, John Bemis, and Ward Hill Lamon. All of these gentlemen had also survived the gauntlet unscathed. The same, however, could not be said for every member of Lincoln's entourage. The worst off was Major David Hunter. Violently pressed against a doorjamb at the station, he wound up with his arm in a sling, as the result of a severe shoulder sprain. Several members of Lincoln's party, including the injured Major Hunter, were involuntarily swept up in the flow of crowd, could not reach the waiting carriages, and were forced to walk to the hotel.

Once the guest of honor was seated, the remaining carriages filled in with a varied assortment of people: those who were a part of the traveling party, correspondents of the Fourth Estate assigned to report on the trip, members of various local committees charged to make arrangements for the day, and representatives of the city government. The honor of leading the procession went to the Union Cornet Band. Major Robert Wiedrich's artillery battery was slotted next. Then, in a second attempt to redeem itself, Company D marched protectively in front of and alongside the president's carriage.

Rooms for Lincoln's retinue in Buffalo were provided by the American Hotel, considered a topflight accommodation in its day (courtesy Buffalo History Museum).

Absent from the caravan was Lincoln's family, safely spirited along an alternate route. The destination in both instances was the American Hotel, only a half-mile along Exchange and Main Streets from the depot. Typical of big-city inns of that era—like the Delavan House in Albany and the Astor House in New York City where the presidential entourage would also stay—this facility outwardly appeared as a non-descript, multi-storied rectangular box.

Regardless of the abbreviated distance involved, the fiasco at the depot created apprehension about what kind of uproar might transpire along the parade route. The crowd that had assembled was indeed impressive. People were everywhere. Filling the streets, rooftops, balconies, and windows, they watched for the arrival of their new leader. Amicable and calm as they patiently waited, the crowd conveyed every impression of being under complete control of its faculties. But the minute the advancing cortège hove into view, their demeanor began ratcheting up. Its placid deportment morphed into a frenetic display of excitement. Loud cheers, thunderous applause, waving handkerchiefs, and a general surge forward all greeted the president. Though his convoy slowed to a crawl as it moved through the human maelstrom, progress continued without any incidents.

Upon reaching the American Hotel, the infantry again deployed in a double line to hold back onlookers, allowing Mr. Lincoln to proceed inside without incident. A few minutes later, in the company of the acting mayor, the president-elect appeared on a second-floor balcony. From this vantage point, he would speak to the people.

However, before the president was introduced, a curious incident occurred. A man drove up in front of the hotel with a wagon containing wood. Today, this intrusion would have galvanized the Secret Service into immediate action, but, in 1861, the arrival of the cart drew a fair amount of attention, but no challenges. As the crowd watched in anticipation, the driver announced that he had lost a bet with a friend over who would win the 1860 presidential election. As a staunch Douglas supporter, he was now obligated to saw up his load of wood. By speaking publicly at the hotel, an unsuspecting Lincoln provided the gentleman with a gift-wrapped opportunity to grandstand before a ready-made audience. So, while Lincoln spoke, the woodcutter toiled away. For some, the rasping sound interfered with their ability to hear Lincoln's speech, yet no one complained. Perhaps some degree of tolerance was extended because the wood was destined for one of the town's poor black families.

But distraction or not, the people expected the president-elect to speak. To Mayor Bemis belonged the pleasure of introducing the city's distinguished guest. Having gained this prized assignment due an illness temporarily incapacitating duly-elected Mayor Franklin Alberger, Bemis made the most it:

> Mr. Lincoln—In behalf of the good people of this city, I welcome you to Buffalo, and tender to you, and to the party accompanying you, the friendship and hospitality of our citizens. I also congratulate you, sir, that your progress thus far towards the Federal Capital has been without accident, or any circumstances to mar the pleasures of your journey. I wish, also, to express the high respect felt by our citizens for yourself as the Chief Magistrate-elect of these United States, as well as to bear testimony to their attachment and loyalty to the Union and Government over which you are soon to preside.
>
> Sir, this is the hour of our national disquietude, the eyes of all good citizens naturally turn with hope towards yourself, as the arbiter of peace that shall still the turbulent statements that threaten destruction to our beloved country. With confidence that your administration of the affairs of our national Government will be characterized by a spirit of equal rights and justice to all sections of our

Union, we look forward to the inauguration with serious thought, and shall hail its good results with pleasure.

Hoping, sir, that your visit—and that of your friends—to us on this occasion, may be as pleasant and agreeable as we desire it to be, I again bid you a hearty welcome to our city—and, with your permission, I will introduce you to the citizens of Buffalo.

Fellow citizens, I have the honor and pleasure of introducing to you the Hon. Abraham Lincoln, President-elect of these United States.[7]

Typical of many long-winded politicians whom Lincoln would encounter along the way, Mr. Bemis said more than most cared to hear. The sooner he stepped back and Lincoln forward, the happier the crowd would be. But, then, these few moments represented highlights in the man's life, so he could be given some slack for lingering a few extra seconds in the limelight.

When Bemis finished, Mr. Lincoln stood before a sea of upturned faces:

Mr. Mayor, and Fellow Citizens of Buffalo and the State of New York:—I am here to thank you briefly for this grand reception given not to me, but as the representative of our great and beloved country. [*Cheers*] Your worthy mayor has been pleased to mention in his address to me, the fortunate and agreeable journey which I have had from home on my rather circuitous route to the Federal Capital. I am very happy that he was enabled in truth to congratulate myself and companions on that fact. It is true we have had nothing, thus far, to mar the pleasure of this trip. We have not been met alone by those who assisted in giving the election to me—I say not alone—but by the whole population of the country through which we have passed. This as it should be.

Had the election fallen to any other of the distinguished candidates instead of myself, under the peculiar circumstances, to say the least, it would have been proper for all citizens to have greeted him as you now greet me. It is evidence of the devotion of the whole people to the Constitution, the Union, and the perpetuity of the liberties of this country. [*Cheers*] I am unwilling, on any occasion, that I should be so meanly thought of, as to have it supposed for a moment that I regard these demonstrations as tendered to me personally. They should be tendered to no individual man. They are tendered to the country, to the institutions of the country, and to the perpetuity of the country for which these institutions are made and created.

Your worthy mayor has thought fit to express hope that I may be able to relieve the country from its present—or should I say, its threatened—difficulties. I am sure that I bring a heart true to the work. [*Tremendous applause*] For the ability to perform it, I must trust in that Supreme Being who has never forsaken this favored land, through the instrumentality of this great and intelligent people. Without that assistance I shall surely fail. With it, I cannot fail.

When we speak of threatening difficulties to the country, it is natural that there should be expected from me something with regard to particular measures. Upon more mature reflection, however, others will agree with me that when it is considered that these difficulties are without precedent, and have never been acted upon by any individual situated as I am, it is most proper I should wait, see the developments, and get all the light that I can, so that when I do speak authoritatively I may be near right as possible. [*Cheers*] When I shall speak authoritatively, I hope to say nothing inconsistent with the Constitution, the Union, the rights of the States, of each State, and of each section of the country, and not to disappoint the reasonable expectations of those who have confided to me their votes.

In this connection allow me to say that you, as a portion of the American people, need only to maintain your composure. Stand up to your sober convictions of right, to your obligations to the Constitution, act in accordance with those sober convictions, and the clouds which now arise on the horizon will be dispelled, and we shall have a bright and glorious future; and when this generation has passed away, tens of thousands will inhabit this country where only thousands inhabit now.

I do not propose to address you at length—I have no voice for it. Allow me again to thank you for this magnificent reception and bid you farewell.[8]

After completing his remarks, Mr. Lincoln retired to his suite, hoping to rest his voice. For, while he tried his best to communicate to the crowd, "Lincoln spoke with the utmost difficulty being so hoarse from his frequent efforts as to be able to make himself heard."[9] While the people could not have known at the time, they had just been treated to one of the longest orations that he would deliver in the Empire State, vastly exceeding the very limited remarks that comprised most of his upcoming whistle-stop speeches. Still, his Buffalo discourse revealed little of his future intentions.

In hindsight, knowing the tumult that had engulfed them at the station, both the mayor and the president were very forgiving toward the people of Buffalo. However, taking the high road helped to achieve Lincoln's desire to make a positive impression on the people. Besides, the newspapers would readily handle the appropriate excoriation for the debacle at the station. Washington's *Evening Star* titled its column on the affair "A Rough Reception at Buffalo."[10] Locally, the *Buffalo Morning Express* summed up its low opinion of the event with its observation that "we never saw anything to compare with the fearful rush of the crowd after the President was leaving the depot. It was awful."[11]

Before trying to rest, the president-elect greeted several delegations who were waiting in the hotel's parlors. Six days now into their thirteen-day odyssey, the Lincolns were starting to feel the effects of being constantly on the go. In addition to a general weariness that pervaded his aging body, the president-elect was becoming hoarse. Since more people were likely to see than hear him, maintaining his appearance was an important consideration. As he proceeded deeper into the journey, the oft-made observation was that he looked haggard. Though the basis for fatigue was explainable, some observers still questioned if he was physically up to the difficulties that loomed before him. Having already won the election, those opinions would not have any detrimental outcome at the polls; nevertheless, his visible exhaustion was disconcerting to some.

While the Lincolns rested, the labors of the indefatigable Buffalo Police Department continued unabated. Beginning on Saturday afternoon with his arrival and lasting through the Monday evening after his departure, the local constabulary was busy rounding up pickpockets. Swarming thickly in public venues, these scoundrels had a field day as they preyed upon unsuspecting victims, people whose attention was intently focused on the Lincoln while their hands were occupied waving and clapping. Needing only an instant, these thieves managed to ruin the day for many people. They made off with amounts as small as four dollars on up to a thousand. That they were good at plying their trade, the newspaper did not quibble. In grudging admiration, its editor noted that "pockets of the most recondite were plundered and explored by the dexterous rogues."[12] While few valuables were recovered, the police did have the satisfaction of collaring a sizable lot of suspects, eventually arresting eleven of the slippery miscreants.

In order to apprehend as many of the miscreants as possible, the long arm of the law even extended beyond the city. Based on a tip that a contingent of pickpockets intended to slip out of town on Sunday evening's train, a squad of Buffalo policemen boarded the six-fifteen eastbound too. Almost immediately, the decision to ride the rails paid off. Three suspicious characters were immediately arrested. However, a bigger haul was yet to come. Suspecting that the police would be looking for them to catch a train from the downtown station, many of the more calculating crooks had moved their departure point to Lancaster station, fifteen miles outside of Buffalo. Staying concealed, "the strangers refrained from showing themselves until the cars commenced moving off, then, from every quarter appeared the rascals."[13]

Then, running alongside the train, they performed admirable acts of athleticism in leaping aboard. But the police were alert to this gambit. Further arrests ensued. Upon reaching Batavia, the officers took their haul of shackled prisoners to the local hoosegow for overnight detainment. The following morning all members of the party boarded a train bound for Buffalo. As of Tuesday, the police had twenty-two alleged pickpockets in custody. Unfortunately, as citizens in Albany and New York would come to rue, others escaped to continue their depredations.

Once the afternoon's brightness had mellowed into evening's shade, the Lincolns had ceremonial duties to perform. Each was hosting a public reception or levee. Because the expectation was that Mrs. Lincoln's crowd would be lighter, she was set up in one of the smaller first floor ladies' parlors. Meanwhile, arrangements for the president were made with an eye toward moving as many people past him as quickly as possible.

Luckily, the American Hotel had the perfect setting to expedite the anticipated turn out. Two stairways, one from the right and one from the left, led to a long hall on the second floor. The plan was for the visitors to go up on the right side, meet the president standing upon small platform near the other set of stairs, and then exit down and out via the second flight. Several members of the presidential party would flank Mr. Lincoln. Soldiers would keep well-wishers moving.

Despite misgivings harbored considering the earlier uproar, the lengthy reception went smoothly. The weather, which had turned cold and blustery, did not inhibit the turnout. For the most part, Lincoln bowed to each passer-by, usually accompanied by words of acknowledgment. He was given a pass when it came to handshaking, for extending this courtesy to the hundreds who filed past would have proven too taxing. However, being the gentleman that he was, Lincoln would not deny what the newspaper called "a manual greeting" to any ladies who came through the line.[14] When a few little girls materialized before him, he lifted them up for a peck on the forehead. Although noticeably fatigued, the president "wore, throughout the reception, which lasted for two hours, a most genial and pleasant smile upon his face, which bespoke real pleasure in meeting with such numbers of his fellow citizens, and responding to their individual greetings."[15] The man was clearly in his element.

Unlike upcoming receptions in other cities, the Buffalo affair was tightly controlled. Access was limited. This protocol in turn made closing the line much easier when the allotted two hours elapsed. Then, as if he really needed to extend his day any longer, Lincoln joined in on his wife's reception for another hour. He found Mary at the mid-point of two adjourning parlors, along the center line where a folding partition opened to create a double-sized space. Holding court in rooms decorated in a red, white, and blue theme, Mrs. Lincoln stood under a light canopy, accompanied by her son Robert. Throughout the evening, she met several hundred men and women, extending her hand in cordial greeting. Not accustomed to soloing on such public occasions, Mary nevertheless acquitted herself well. According to the Buffalo press, her future as a hostess looked bright: "we must be permitted to remark that she is a lady who will preside over the hospitalities of the Presidential mansion with a grace becoming to the exalted station."[16]

Viewed from 30,000 feet, the day had held contrasting tableaus. In an interesting juxtaposition of their respective turns as first ladies, Mrs. Lincoln's was in its ascendancy, just as her predecessor's was winding down. On this very day when Mary was preparing to greet hundreds of well-wishers at the start of what would be four years of such amenities, Harriet Lane was 800 miles away, basking in the afterglow of yet another successful White House reception. But as the *National Republican* pointed out, a bittersweet poignancy was attached to this levee: "Miss Lane's last reception took place at noon on Saturday, and was very largely attended. Everything went off very happily, and many cordial wishes for Miss Lane's future happiness were extended."[17]

As a gracious and charming hostess, Harriet Lane had set the bar high for her successors. Only twenty-six, Miss Lane was afforded a unique opportunity to function for four years as the first lady of the nation. Orphaned at age eleven, she was placed in her Uncle James' care. When her surrogate father was elected as the nation's 15th president in 1856, Harriet moved into the White House with him. Since James Buchanan was a bachelor, she served as her uncle's official hostess. In this capacity, Harriet Lane's performance for all White House social engagements represented one of the most memorable aspects of an otherwise dismal four-year term of office for Buchanan's administration.

The events over which Miss Lane presided were hallmarked by the planning and forethought that made them unforgettable occasions. "Lane entertained in a style," wrote biographer Milton Stern, "that would not be witnessed again until the Kennedy administration of the 1960s."[18] Being inordinately congenial, Harriet extended her successor an invitation for a get-acquainted visit to the White House upon her arrival in Washington. This gesture was commended by the press "as an act of courtesy on the part of Miss Lane which will distinguish her in the hearts of all intelligent classes, and will never be forgotten by the recipient of the courtesy."[19] It was well that Mrs. Lincoln had received high marks for one of her initial forays into public receptions, for Harriet Lane was leaving an enviable legacy for successors to match.

When 9:30 arrived, Mrs. Lincoln's levee concluded. But still, the day's obligations were not over. One last function had been scheduled for the presidential couple. Waiting for their own specially arranged audience was a German delegation. Not to be mistaken for

Serving as "First Lady" for her uncle, bachelor President James Buchanan, Harriet Lane—in the hoop skirt on the left—orchestrated many gala receptions in the East Room of the White House, the last coming on the same day that Mary Lincoln held one of her first in Buffalo (*Frank Leslie's Illustrated Newspaper*).

European visitors, these callers were German-Americans. Funneled first by the turnpikes, then the Erie Canal, and eventually the railroads, the lands of western New York became a destination of choice for many immigrants from Germany. Their strong suit tended to be in the area of light industry, taking up such occupations as brewers, bakers, and tanners. Claiming to represent these proud and industrious people, the committeemen wanted Mr. Lincoln to know that they were "all law-biding citizens, and loyal to the institutions of their adopted country."[20]

Lincoln responded, though in pointed fashion, saying: "I am gratified with this evidence of the feelings of the German citizens of Buffalo. My own idea about our foreign citizens has always been that they were no better than anyone else, and no worse. And it is best that they should forget that they are foreigners as soon as possible."[21]

For him to make this comment was not all out of character, for as one reporter noted: "It had always been his opinion that distinctions of nationality among citizens of the United States ought to be eliminated as soon as possible."[22] His plea was basically for assimilation, resistance to which is a bane that continues to plague America to this very day. Generations usually need to pass before any change in perspective occurs. However, for the German and the Irish immigrants of the Civil War era, allegiance was never a question, as these two ethnic strains populated the Union Army in droves.

When this brief engagement ended, the Lincolns retired to their suite. Though late in the evening of another long day, the public tributes kept coming. Continuing the Germanic theme, two different choral groups appeared in succession. The first, known as the Sangerbund, serenaded the hotel's guests from the street. Following its offerings, the Liedertafel gave a performance from inside the main hall. After appropriate thank-yous, the weary Lincolns finally could get some sleep.

Aside from the unexpected crush at the Buffalo depot, the day had unfolded smoothly. The president had every reason to be pleased with his reception in western New York.

Because February 17 was the Sabbath, no public functions were scheduled. As the Lord rested on the Seventh Day, so also would the Lincolns. The same was not true of the entire hotel, however, for various rooms and parlors in the establishment remained abuzz for some time. Even though late, pockets of people continued discussing the events of the day or matters of national import on into the wee hours, when observed a Rochester paper "most men are, or ought to be, in bed."[23]

That the president would attend church services should have surprised no one. In the fishbowl existence in which he now lived, such public appearances had were almost obligatory, for the criticism that might rain down on the head of one who was deemed less than pious was a consequence to be avoided. What was open to public conjecture, however, was which house of worship Mr. Lincoln would select. If local pastors had charged admission, many churches in downtown Buffalo would have realized windfall profits that Sunday. Since the president-elect's destination was unknown, many people guessed. As a result, pews were packed with worshipers, both the devout and the curious.

While the press and the public could only speculate as to his destination, one man who knew was Millard Fillmore. Continuing in his gracious role as an unofficial host, the ex-president and his second wife came by the hotel at ten o'clock to escort the president to Fillmore's church of preference, the First Unitarian, only a few blocks away. Like others in the vicinity that morning, the congregation's numbers were inflated—by opportunists who had speculated correctly. The service was conducted by the church's pastor, Dr. George Hosmer, who first offered up a stirring prayer beseeching God's blessings on the Lincoln administration and then followed it with a thoughtful sermon.

From the church, Mr. Lincoln and his hosts returned to the hotel where they picked up Mrs. Lincoln. The party then rode to Fillmore's downtown home for a quiet lunch. For Mary Lincoln, this dining experience was a special treat, since she had been a long-standing admirer of the former president. To his undying credit, the old gentleman had been the perfect host for the Lincolns. An affable, likeable man who was at his best in small-group gatherings, he did not let political differences with the president-elect cloud his personal treatment of his distinguished guests. He was cordial, garrulous, and entertaining.

After an enjoyable repast, the Lincolns returned to their hotel at approximately two o'clock. Most of the remaining day was spent relaxing. For the president, this downtime included occasional roughhousing with Tad and Willie. The only exception to the informal, sequestered nature of their activities was when Mr. Fillmore and acting-mayor Bemis came by after supper and escorted the president-elect to St. James Hall, where Father John Beeson was lecturing on the status of the American Indian. Having spent time among various western tribes, he could speak from first-hand observation about the depravities which these indigenous people suffered. Now he was touring the East, hoping to drum up support for legislative assistance to help these oppressed people. In addition to his humanitarian interest on behalf of Native Americans, Father Beeson had also espoused the abolition of slavery. Following his talk, Father Beeson offered a benediction on behalf of the president-elect.

After making his way slowly from the church, readily shaking hands with others in attendance, Lincoln was dropped off at his hotel and retired for the night. He would be leaving in the morning on the next leg of his journey, and departure was scheduled long before sunrise.

3

The Longest Day Begins
From Buffalo to Utica

Departure was scheduled for 5:45 a.m., which for the Lincolns meant arising at 4:30 a.m. Their exit was originally set for six, hoping to avoid the wild scene that had marred the president's arrival. However, any advantage gained through the altered schedule was negated by the presence of a band, whose sounds aroused people who might otherwise have slept through the president's exodus. The upshot was that a modest, but restrained crowd materialized at the station. Nevertheless, those present accorded Lincoln a cheerful farewell. He reciprocated by standing on the platform outside the rear coach and offering bows as the train moved away from the station.

In leaving Buffalo, the presidential party was now hosted by the New York Central Railroad. They had boarded at the same Exchange Street Station into whose shed their incoming train had entered two days ago. As Lincoln was headed for his inauguration in Washington, he and the New York Central shared a common status: both were in periods of ascendancy. In keeping with the desire of the railroad's management to put its best foot forward, no expense was spared in terms of the quality of equipment and degree of safety employed for this auspicious assignment. For its trip to the state capital, Lincoln's retinue was conveyed in a five-car consist—railroad terminology for the make-up of a train—that was comprised of a gleaming locomotive—the flag-decorated *Dean Richmond*—pulling a tender, baggage car, and two coaches. To have the locomotive in tip-top shape for this high-profile run, the *Dean Richmond* had been removed from service and "rebuilt and put in complete order" by mechanics in the railroad's Rochester maintenance shops.[1]

In curious juxtaposition, a portrait of Lincoln appeared in front of the engine's headlamp, while on either side was mounted a picture of Dean Richmond, the man for whom this particular iron horse was named. What made the pairing of these likenesses a decided oddity was Richmond's position as chairman of the state's Democratic Party, making him "the most efficient political opponent he [Lincoln] had in the state."[2] That this engine was selected was not lost on a discerning public, for it "created a great deal of amusement among the party, and was productive of much good-natured raillery at the expense of the Republican Party."[3]

Viewed in its entirety, the train appeared as one that "does full justice to the superb rolling stock of the New York Central." The first passenger car was occupied by about sixty-five people, the exception being the Lincoln family. This meant that the president's advisors, his protectors, the press, advanced delegations, and invited guests were crammed into this space.[4] Fortunately, since it was only a day-trip, no overnight accommodations were necessary. To provide a little extra room, part of the baggage car had been outfitted as a smoking area.

The second coach was reserved for the members of the Lincoln family: Abraham, Mary, Robert, Tad, and Willie—plus Mr. Lincoln's valet and the younger children's nurse. The family's car was "gorgeously fitted up, with sofas, chairs, mirrors, and carpets."[5] Various adornments in the way of festoons and banners added a patriotic touch. For those who had been onboard since Springfield, the absence of a third coach, detached at Cleveland, was most noticeable. However, the subtraction of this car had been ordered by Superintendent Wood, his rationale being to eliminate space for opportunists who eagerly sought a few moments of Lincoln's time.

Having by all accounts admirably seen to the president's comfort, the matter of his safety was given equal attention. Plans called for a pilot engine to make a run ten minutes ahead of the special, at best spotting some attempt to derail the president's train. At worst, the pilot engine would itself be thrown from the tracks, taking the hit in place of the tragedy befalling Lincoln's train. All switches were temporarily spiked in the open position, and a guard was posted to ensure they stayed that way until the presidential express passed over them. To maintain immediate communication with stations up the line, the train was equipped with a portable telegraph set. Should quick decisions need to be made, various regional superintendents were also aboard the train. Due to the level topography and straightness of the right of way, the engineer was able to keep the throttle wide open.

The first stop after Buffalo was Batavia. Remarkably, even in the face of a brisk headwind and wet snowfall, the thirty-seven-mile run between the two towns took only thirty minutes. While some might see such speed as too reckless with the president aboard, the converse thinking was that the accelerated rate might make the train less vulnerable to someone with malicious intent.

In reaching Batavia, the Lincoln Special achieved the halfway point in its early morning dash toward Rochester. Located in the geographic center of Genesee County, Batavia came into existence following the Revolutionary War, once land in western New York was opened for settlement. Like so many other communities across the east-west axis of the state, the Erie Canal and later the New York Central and Erie Railroads brought immediate prosperity to the town.

Though weather conditions were discomforting, in no way did they dampen the enthusiasm of Batavians, who turned out in force to see the people's choice. They greeted the train's arrival with wild cheers and booming cannon. While the stop only lasted five minutes, Lincoln did step out onto the back platform and spoke a few words. The people had hoped for more, but Lincoln told them that he did not wish to appear before them as a talker, much less gain a reputation as such. With that, he thanked them for coming out at such an early hour and then bade them farewell, bowing as was his custom while the train pulled away.

The next stop on the itinerary was Rochester. Like so many up and coming cities in western New York, the combination of water power—provided in this instance by the Genesee River and a multi-faceted transportation network consisting of Lake Ontario, the Erie Canal, and several railroads—again served as the impetus for agricultural and industrial growth and prosperity. By 1861, Rochester was the 18th largest city in America and known as the "Flour City" for all the grain which was processed and shipped from there.

Rochester had another claim to fame, one of which the president was undoubtedly aware. The area was a hotbed of abolitionist sentiment and a destination for many runaway slaves. Once reaching sanctuary at one of many Underground Railroad stations located in the vicinity, connections could be made for a boat ride to freedom in Canada. In addition to the presence of so many willing hands to help escapees, Rochester was the home of one of the country's most outspoken abolitionists—Frederick Douglass. From his office issued forth a weekly publication known as *The North Star*. Through the pages of this publication, and the companion *Douglass Journal*, the former slave denounced the slavery, issued clarion calls for action, and critiqued the efforts of those in power to help.

Among those who incurred jabs from Douglass' sharp pen was the incumbent president: "Much of the present trouble is owing to the doubt and suspense caused by the shuffling, do-nothing policy of Mr. Buchanan—no man has been able to tell an hour beforehand what to expect from that source."[6] While the incoming president and the crusading abolitionist did not meet until 1863, Douglass still offered his opinion of Lincoln's performance at the time of his abbreviated visit. Like many others, he too was disappointed, noting that "his speeches along the route are all of the same purport ... his short speech here did not touch on the great question of the day."[7]

However, Douglass harbored the hope that Lincoln, once in office, would do that which was expected of him:

> For the present, there is much reason to believe that he will not consent to any compromise which will violate the principle upon which he was elected; and since none which does not utterly trample upon that principle can be accepted by the South, we have double assurance that there will be no compromise, and that the contest must now be decided, and decided forever, which of the two, Freedom or Slavery, shall give law to the Republic. Let the conflict come, and God speed the Right, must be the wish of every true-hearted American, as well as of that of an onlooking world.[8]

Even as the special was leaving Batavia, a crowd of Douglass' fellow citizens had already begun to congregate in downtown Rochester. In the eyes of one who stood in the crowd, "at an early hour—long before the time announced for the arrival of the train bringing the president-elect and his party—our streets were thronged with people wending their way to the Central Station Depot, intent upon securing eligible places from which to see all that was to be seen, and hear all that was to be heard."[9] With the arrival drawing near, anticipation built, though the eager spectators had no way of knowing that the train's progress had been interrupted.

Alerted by the smell of burning wood and oil, the telltale sign of an overheated journal or "hot box," a temporary halt was necessitated. The problem was quickly located the under the first coach and fixed. Yet, despite the breakdown, the express still arrived in Rochester five minutes early. Along the way, manifestations of welcome and support were observable with every passing mile. In small villages through which the train slowed but did not stop, crowds were out in force, cheering and applauding. With flags waving and cannons booming, a festive air was in evidence for the few fleeting moments that the train rolled past. Outside the towns, at locations where country roads crossed the tracks, small knots of people gathered to witness the passage of the train bearing its important passenger. They also waved from the porches of their homes, from hilltops, and along the tracks bordering their farms.

Though Lincoln's expected arrival was not until 7:40 a.m., outsiders started streaming

The Rochester terminal of the 1860s featured an overarching shed, with the Lincoln Special pulling into the righthand portal—leaving only the last coach from which the president spoke protruding (courtesy Rochester Historical Society).

into the city well-beforehand, adding to the glut of locals. One area newspaper observed that in its community of Brockport—located nineteen miles west of Rochester—"early breakfasts were the order of the day on Monday last."[10] The reason for this was that over one hundred riders were catching a seven o'clock train for Rochester. At Spencerport, eight miles closer to the city, a similar number squeezed aboard the same run.

Beginning in the pre-dawn hours, the number of spectators increased until some 10,000 people had jammed themselves into the section of town where New York Central's tracks crossed State Street. That this spot became the prime destination for both the well-wishers and oglers was due to local papers, like the *Rochester Union and Advertiser*, that published a program, indicating that "Mr. Lincoln would leave the cars [at the crossing], go to the balcony of the Waverly Hotel, the best place in the city to be seen by a great multitude, and would there address the public."[11] After processing this information, people had to choose: should they position themselves near where Lincoln would leave the train, go over and stand in front of the hotel, or situate somewhere in-between? But, regardless of which choice was made, the outcome would be binding. For, once an option was selected, the tightly packed crowd would prohibit any relocation.

However, all the strategizing about early arrivals and vantage points went for naught—though the change in plans was not immediately ascertained. Rochesterians were certainly ready to greet the president. Once the train was sighted, a detachment of the Union Grays, posted over the river on Falls Field, commenced a thirty-four-round salute; though no one knew it then, the boys in this militia unit would soon be firing their cannons in earnest, for in eight months' time they would be mustered into federal service as Company L, Reynold's Battery of the 1st New York Light Artillery. Situated on the west side of the Genesee River which ran through the city, the New York Central's depot was adorned with several flags and topped off by a huge canvas banner emblazoned "Welcome to the President of the United States." The nearby Waverly Hotel, from whose upper balcony Lincoln was expected to speak, was also bedecked in hues of red, white, and blue. Further contributing to the festive atmosphere was a band—Perkins' Silver Cornets—which played a variety of appropriate airs from the hotel's lower balcony.

With bell clanging, the engine slowed its forward progress, as spectators crowded in dangerously close to the tracks. A densely packed throng had sandwiched itself in along the tracks and the streets between the crossing and the hotel. Altogether, an assembled mass of some 30,000 individuals had descending upon the downtown area.

As the train approached, thunderous cheers arose from excited throats. Then, much to everyone's astonishment, the train continued past the crossing for an additional block. Some of the spectators thought that the locomotive was just the pilot engine. But the special did not stop until it had entered under the shed of the depot. Most of the train was inside, with only a small portion of the last car protruding from under the roof. Still, even as they watched this unforeseen development, many fully expected to see the Lincolns' coach return. Content to await that development, most of the crowd remained patiently in place.

Unfortunately, what very few in the crowd apparently knew was that the site of the president's welcome had been changed. The revised arrangement called for Lincoln to speak from the train shed and not the Waverly Hotel, utilizing the last coach as his pulpit rather than the second story balcony. What this meant to those crowded around the crossing and the hotel was that they were now one block to the west in the wrong place. Making the situation worse was that Lincoln began speaking before most spectators realized that a change had been made. Some people on the outer fringes of the crowd were able to spin around and rush over to the depot, but most were unable to extricate themselves from the pack. This turnabout meant that late-comers, who initially had undesirable positions in terms of the first site, now had the best ones, while those who had come early to stake out choice locations were relegated to the worst ones. From afar, the mayor and the president were visible but not audible. Clearly the mayor was speaking. For those who were close enough, he was in the process of introducing the man of the hour:

> Mr. President—I am charged with the pleasing duty, on behalf of my fellow citizens, of bidding you a most cordial and hearty welcome to the city of Rochester. Fellow Citizens—It is with the greatest pleasure that I now present to you the Hon. Abraham Lincoln, President-elect of the United States of America.[12]

Fifteen seconds later, Abraham Lincoln stepped forward. After a hearty round of cheers and applause had subsided, he addressed his audience:

> I confess myself, after having seen large audiences since leaving home, overwhelmed with this vast number of faces at this hour of the morning, I am not vain enough to believe that you are here from any wish to see me as an individual, but because I am, for the time being, the representative of the American people. I could not, if I would, address you at any length. I have not the strength, even if I had the time, for a speech at these many interviews that are afforded me on my way to Washington. I appear mainly to see you, and let you see me, and to bid you farewell. I hope it will be understood that it is from no disposition to disoblige anybody, that I do not address you at greater length.[13]

Just as Frederick Douglass later lamented, Lincoln's brief remarks lacked substance. But, from his perspective, Lincoln had once again accomplished his objectives, those of being seen and heard. Evidenced that he had achieved these goals was confirmed by *The Brockport Republic*, which shared with its readers the following observation: "Nearly all who saw him concur in the opinion that he is much better looking than he has been represented to be. He looks to be as though he split rails, and give force and effect to Republican principles."[14] While his ego did not require the positive strokes about his appearance, a newspaper piece like this allowed him to check off in his mind: "mission accomplished!"

In its post-mortem on the eight-minute visit, particularly its revised format, the *Rochester Democrat* attributed the decision to officials of the New York Central Railroad. Their rational for the change of venue was two-pronged. First was concern for Lincoln's safety. Just as the unexpected crowd surge in Buffalo was potentially harmful to the president-elect, the proposed walk to the Waverly Hotel held the same potential for disaster. The second factor favoring a change was the assessment that the original program would take too long. By the time Lincoln successfully navigated through the sea of people to and from the hotel, the train would be seriously late for its scheduled afternoon arrival in Albany. No self-respecting railroader would knowingly be an enabler of such a procedural blemish.

However, the revised plan was intended only to move the train forward halfway between State and Mill Streets, thereby eliminating the walk to the Waverly. The perceived need to run the train inside the shed also had safety as its root consideration, only more so about the welfare of the spectators than that of the president. This anxiety arose from the need to switch engines before the next leg of the journey began. The *Dean Richmond* had completed its service and was to be replaced by Engine # 84. With Lincoln speaking from the back platform, railroad crewmen could change engines at the opposite end without having to worry about crowd interference.

While some argued that railroad officials should not have unilaterally make decisions that altered agreed upon arrangements for the president-elect, the editor of the *Rochester Union and Advertiser* sided with the New York Central. The position of the press was that "the railroad folks had the President-elect for a passenger, and ran him across the state to suit their own convenience, which they had a right to do, we suppose, inasmuch as he was a 'deadhead.'"[15] Referencing Mr. Lincoln by this term was not as irreverent as it might seem, for it was railroad nomenclature for any passenger riding for free.

This allusion opens up to the larger question of just how the long journey was financed. A family of five, traveling from Springfield to Washington as directly as possible, would have been a pricey enough, but a meandering trip of thirteen days—with all the requisite transportation, overnight stops, and meal costs for not only the Lincolns but also the members of the official party—would have been astronomical.

This observation in the Rochester paper, though more of an offhand comment than a critical reflection, nevertheless represents one of the very few quotable sources on the subject. Even John Starr in his detailed study *Lincoln and the Railroads* could find no hard evidence regarding how the cost of the trip was covered, commenting that "at this late day it is seemingly impossible to get at the facts regarding these expenses."[16] The likelihood is that railroads absorbed the fares, and the cities that invited the president to extend his visit in their towns covered those expenses. Given the passage of 150 years, this topic offers fertile ground for an interesting comparison between eras. In 1861, public officials receiving support from private companies and governmental entities entertaining with the public dollar drew virtually no attention or inquiry. Not like today, when an investigative reporter would relish producing an exposé focused on just exactly how Lincoln's inaugural trip was underwritten.

All-in-all, for most residents of the Rochester area who had made the pilgrimage to see their country's new leader, his visit was rather disappointing. For, in addition to the aggravating change in the speaking venue, the *Rochester Democrat* pointed out that "the train started again after a stop of only five minutes, so that it left at the hour originally designated for its arrival and ten minutes before the hour appointed for its departure."[17]

One individual, however, did manage to salvage the memory of a lifetime, even if he went about it in a rather risky manner. As the train began to inch out of the station, Lincoln was standing on the rear platform. He could see the crowd pressing close around the car. What he did not immediately notice was the young boy who had scrambled up the steps and onto the platform beside him. Once the tyke's presence was revealed, President Lincoln shook the boy's hand and bade him to take care in hopping down from the train. Soon the special was heading full-throttle for the small community of Clyde, fifty-four miles to the southeast and ultimately Syracuse, which lay another thirty-three miles beyond.

Scheduled to arrive in Clyde at 8:44 a.m., the president-elect would stay only five minutes. The halt was one borne out of the necessity to fill the engine's insatiable need for "wooding and watering," as a local reporter termed the process.[18] Since Lincoln's train was a high-profile express, it did not follow one of the customary practices of railroading right through the 1860s, when "vast quantities of wood were purchased from farmers along the railroad—a trade which accounted for the clearing of many acres in Upstate New York."[19] For those able-bodied individuals riding the train, a temporary refueling stop was not their only imposition. Once "the train was halted along the way to pick up fuel ... it was the common practice of passengers—aware a quicker loading would mean a quicker take-off—piled out to help conductors and brakemen load up the tender."[20]

But, regardless of the motive, presidents did not stop in Clyde with any degree of regularity. Therefore, if one happened to do so, the prevailing thought was that everyone ought to seize the opportunity for a viewing. The resulting desire to see Mr. Lincoln manifested itself the next morning, when "the roads in every direction were filled with teams and loads of human beings coming to see the President-elect."[21] The streets of the small community soon thronged with people, eventually coalescing at the railroad station. Arriving on schedule, the roar of cannon and cheers from the assembled mass greeted the train.

Once the locomotive halted, the president stepped out of his coach and spoke a few words. However, before he went back inside, he lingered on the platform at the request of several local boys. They represented an amateur gun crew, manning a cannon in a nearby field, and they wished to fire a salute. Willing to accommodate them, he waited patiently until they had performed their tribute. A few minutes later, he reappeared and said: "I bid you all farewell."[22] At some point in the few moments in which the President was visible, "a daguerrean artist had made preparations to daguerreotype Mr. Lincoln and asked that he might stand still upon the platform of the car long enough to afford the opportunity."[23] This little incident was reported in the local paper, but unfortunately neither a copy of the photograph nor its negative has ever surfaced in the intervening years to corroborate the story.

Brief though the stopover was, the editor for *The Clyde Weekly Times*—Samuel Paine—had the experience of a lifetime in those fleeting seconds. Once the train stopped, the enterprising journalist bounded up the steps of the rear car and presented his card to William Wood. When the president first appeared, Paine stepped aside, though he retained a ringside seat on the steps and resumed his conversation with Superintendent Wood after Lincoln went inside. Then, as the train was about leave, the president reappeared, whereupon Wood introduced him to the newsman. As they shook hands, Mr. Paine promised that "he would disperse the shake to our readers in the next edition."[24] Also in those few moments which he had in the great man's presence, the correspondent was able to make an assessment of the president's height which he also shared: "We stood by Mr. Lincoln's side when he was bidding the crowd farewell, and to give some idea of his height, our head reached about halfway between his elbow and his shoulder, and though not tall, we are not among the smallest race of bipeds."[25]

With the train picking up speed, Paine hopped off, and Lincoln bid the crowd his customary bending adieu ... and then he was gone. The people returned to their homes, buoyed by the satisfaction that they had been in the presence of the president-elect. In time, they would realize that they had been blessed to see and hear not only their country's newly anointed chief executive, but also a truly great man.

As the last puffs of smoke from the train dissipated into the eastern sky, the good people of Clyde were left with an indelible memory. Up ahead, the citizens of Syracuse eagerly awaited the Lincoln Special, bringing them their own remembrances of the day the president came to town.

With additional spectators arriving on trains from the hinterlands, the waiting crowd swelled to over 10,000 people. Like so many places across the Empire State, Syracuse too owed its prosperity to "Clinton's Ditch." In a declining mode by 1865, the Erie Canal was still a prominent feature of the city's urban landscape, passing through the center of town as it did. Had he the luxury of time to explore the area where the train stopped, Lincoln, possessing the innate curiosity of the patented inventor that he was, would likely have marveled at the nearby Weighlock Building. Housed inside the structure only three blocks away was the unique apparatus from whence its name was derived. This contrivance allowed a boat's cargo to be assessed a toll, based upon the tonnage of its cargo. The boat entered the lock, the water was drained out, and the vessel came to rest on a cradle that was suspended from a balance beam. Subtracting the weight of the boat from the total pounds registered by the scales produced the taxable cargo.

While the Erie Canal with its system of locks, lift bridges, and aqueducts offered an interesting buffet of engineering marvels, central New York may have also been known to Lincoln due to politically charged issues, for the stretch from Rochester east to Utica was a hotbed for the abolitionist movement. From Frederick Douglass in Rochester east to Gerrit Smith in Peterboro, some of the giants of the movement resided in the region. Harriet Tubman and William Seward both owned homes in Auburn, twenty-eight miles southwest of Syracuse.

In 1850, a forum known as the Cazenovia Convention—organized by Smith and Douglass to protest the Fugitive Slave Law—was held twenty-one miles southeast of Syracuse. Within this geographic area of perhaps 5000 square miles, the city was the epicenter of the movement. Due to its central location, safe houses on the Underground proliferated in the city. Even the Erie Canal played a part, as its towpath was a very identifiable, easy-to-follow pathway to multiple objectives, any of which could mean freedom. Buffalo, Rochester, and Oswego were particularly desirable destinations, because from them passage to Canada could be secured.

Of all the abolitionist activities in and around Syracuse, the most celebrated event occurred on October 1, 1851. Known as the Jerry Rescue, the incident was ignited when a local cooper named William "Jerry" Henry was taken into custody by U.S. marshals, allegedly for theft. Granted he was a runaway, but Mr. Henry had been living and working in Syracuse since 1843. As fate would have it, the Liberty Party was holding its state convention only a few doors away from where the prisoner was being held. Angered because the new law was used to arrest Mr. Henry, a group of conventioneers stormed the building to free him. However, he was quickly recaptured and taken to jail. Soon a much larger mob descended upon this facility, battered its way inside, and spirited the captive away. Shots were fired by the police, but they did not stem the tide. This time Henry was secreted out of town by way of the Underground Railroad, eventually making his way north to Oswego, located on Lake Ontario. Ultimately safe passage was arranged to reach sanctuary in Canada. Like the weighlock, the Jerry Rescue site was only a stone's throw from Vanderbilt Square. But the tightness of Lincoln's schedule precluded any chance of seeing local sights of interest.

Along with the Erie Canal, the New York Central offered its own unique presence in Syracuse. Most places, when blessed with the benefits accrued from having immediate railroad access, tending to grow and spread away from the focal point of the station. Trains passed along the edge of the community, often through what was the industrial/commercial end of town. Syracuse, however, was different. As the canal passed initially through the heart of the city from east-to-west, the railroad did the same one block away. Over the years in large urban areas like New Orleans and San Francisco, the sight of trolleys and cable cars plying city streets was common and became part of that locale's charm. But large places—such as Syracuse—where full-blown, long-distance trains rolled through downtown streets at a mandated fifteen mph were not that common, particularly as time went by and the trains grew longer and more powerful, while the streets became increasingly clogged with both pedestrian and vehicular traffic.

In time, the hazards of having such a dangerous juxtaposition of man and machine made the relocation of the latter to a different location advisable. But in Lincoln's era, the train station was situated in the center of Syracuse at Vanderbilt Square. This placed the structure on East Washington Street, between South Salina and South Warren Streets, with two sets of tracks running down the center half of the street. From the western end of the station, trains exited perpendicular to and immediately across South Salina Street. Eventually, "hotels, restaurants, and other houses flourished in the area, as passengers from faraway points stopped over [in] the city for a quick lunch or for overnight."[26]

"The Syracusans were out in force," reported a duly impressed correspondent in the *Albany Evening Journal*, "and the spectacle was a most striking one as the cars came to a halt in the spot crowded for squares distant, with every balcony and window filled."[27] In keeping with the festive welcomes accorded him all along his route, the president's arrival was announced by a salute from local military units. In this instance, the first was the Washington Artillery which unleashed a thunderous, thirty-four round barrage from a nearby field, followed shortly thereafter by a regimental band offering a stirring rendition of "The Star-Spangled Banner."

The train continued to the station, which was one of somewhat unusual construction in that it was "294 feet long, 50 feet wide, and 26 feet high."[28] Designed in a Grecian style of architecture, it boasted triangular pediments at each end, reminiscent of the temples built by the ancients. On top was a small tower housing a bell that was rung to announce the arrival of a train.

To say that incoming and outbound trains ran right through the depot was true, for it had tall, wide portals at both ends. With its doors closed, the facility served a useful but different function. For not only was the existence of an easily accessible station a benefit to travelers, its presence was also a boon to the community in general, since "when not in use as a depot the building was the scene of many political and public meetings and addresses."[29] However, as the town grew larger and downtown became more bustling, there were disadvantages to having tracks cutting across the heart of the city. In addition to safety concerns, which eventually led to the main line's being relocated, the fact that buildings lined the right of way on both sides, creating a canyon-like effect, caused them to be repeatedly blackened with an unsightly soot from the smoke of passing locomotives. Though the

Syracuse's ride-through station with its Grecian-style pediments, as seen in this Civil War era photograph, was downtown on East Washington Street. From Maturin Murray Ballou, *Ballou's Pictorial Drawing Room Companion* **(Boston: Ballou Publishing, 1855) (courtesy Onondaga County Historical Society).**

attempt was made to impart a semblance of style, the fact remained that the original depot was not much more than a large shed—very utilitarian but not all that pleasing to see. Eventually, in 1869, the aging station was razed in dramatic fashion and in a sense by its tenants. An engine was attached to each end, and they jointly pulled the building apart.

Once the train halted at 9:52 a.m., officials harbored no expectations that the president would avail himself of a specially-constructed platform located south of the station. This hope was dashed in a telegram from Buffalo the previous day, informing them that there would be no use for the platform, as Mr. Lincoln objected to leaving he train. The back platform of the rear coach would again suffice as his podium. On the ground, the crowd closed in around the last car and the station, spilling back down East Washington Street. Over this unfolding scene, "Old" Glory hung on wires strung between buildings on each side of the street and above the tracks. Additional flags and numerous banners were also displayed from various hotels and stores in the vicinity.

Along with the reception committee and mayor, Lincoln had to share the limelight with another special guest—a bald eagle. Someone had decided that having this symbol of our country perched on the platform's railing would add an appropriate touch of living Americana to the proceedings. Apparently, the bird was none too animated, for he was described as being "among the decorations on the platform" by one paper.[30] However, the poor creature could hardly be blamed for not being caught up in the spirit of the day. For, instead of soaring free and unfettered through the open skies, the once-mighty hunter sat tethered amidst a loud mob of an alien species.

Nevertheless, the appropriate moment had arrived to present Mr. Lincoln. Mayor Amos Westcott moved forward to the coach's railing and made a rather longwinded introduction. For eating up valuable time in such an effusive manner, the mayor was not castigated by angry citizens, anxious to hear the main speaker and not the warm-up act. Whether he was mesmerizing, respected, or beloved, Mr. Westcott was afforded a degree of deference by the spectators that some of his counterparts in other towns were not allotted.

In those places, when the introduction got too lengthy and the time grew short, the spectators clamored for what in Vaudevillian terms was "the hook." But in actuality, not only was the local bureaucrat uninterrupted in Syracuse, but he wound up speaking longer than the president. His constituency's patience with his loquaciousness may have stemmed in part from the knowledge that a time crunch did not exist, as was the case in other stops. Since most of the visits were of the four-to-eight-minute variety, the thirteen minutes allocated to Syracuse may have somewhat eliminated the sense of urgency in getting Lincoln quickly before the people of the "Salt City."

When the mayor finally got around to introducing the famous guest, he said:

> Mr. Lincoln—I have the honor to welcome you to our city and to tender to you the cordial sympathy of our citizens in the trying position which you have been called to fill as the chief magistrate of the United States. Never in the history of our country has there been a time when there was such a demand for the exercise of sagacity and wisdom on the part of the chief executive of the nation as at the present moment. Sir, I am happy in the belief that you will, under Divine Providence, and aided by wise and honest counsels, be enabled to restore the integrity of the Union—to execute faithfully and fully the federal laws and to secure the enforcement of all the provisions of the Constitution established by our forefathers. We feel assured that you will conduct the Government generally, that when you retire from the high office which has been bestowed upon you by the free and unsolicited suffrage of this great nation, you will be enabled to transmit to your successor our national flag, not merely with its stars

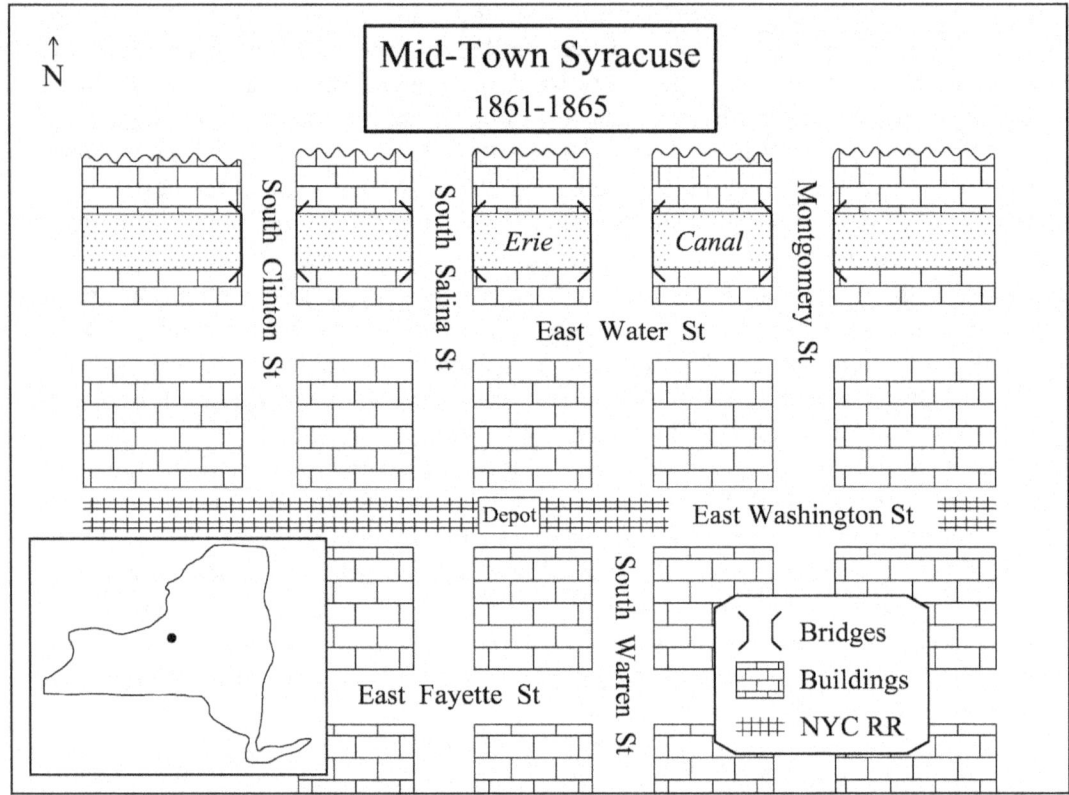

Drawn by Bob Collea.

undiminished in number, but with each star shining more brightly in the glorious constellation of Freedom and Liberty. I have now, fellow citizens, the honor of introducing to you Abraham Lincoln—the president-elect of the United States of America.[31]

The president was ready. Stepping forward to the center of the small platform, he addressed the crowd:

> Ladies and gentlemen: I see you have erected a very fine and handsome platform for me, and I presume you expected me to speak from it. If I should go upon it, you would imagine that I was about to deliver to you a much longer speech than I am. I wish you to understand that I mean no discourtesy to you by thus declining. But I wish you to understand that though I am unwilling to go upon this platform, you are not at liberty to draw any inferences concerning any other platform to which my name has been or is connected. [Laughter and applause.] I wish you a long life and prosperity individually, and pray that with the perpetuity of those institutions under which we have so long lived and prospered, our happiness may be secured, our future made brilliant, and the glorious destiny of our country established forever. I bid you a kind farewell.[32]

Then with approving cheers and applause ringing in his ears, Lincoln was introduced by the mayor to the Rev. Daniel Waldo. Clearly from his infirm appearance, the man was well-advanced in years which gave visible substance to his claims that he not only fought in the Revolutionary War, but that he had also voted for George Washington, just as he done for Lincoln. The president warmly shook the old soldier's hand and thanked him for coming down to the depot.

3. The Longest Day Begins

For those who had traveled miles and waited hours for this opportunity, Lincoln's remarks seemed to some a bit disappointing in their brevity, yet the president-elect was standing before them, and for these few moments they were grateful. Little did they know, however, that some of his best comments would not appear until the next day's paper, garnered by an enterprising local reporter who had hopped onto the train when it began to slow down entering town and remained aboard until booted off by an irate conductor. During the interim, the newsman heard some off-the-cuff gems that he shared with his readers. One involved Lincoln's response to a question posed to him: what did he think of the alarming presence of inebriated people in the audience? "After stroking his beard contemplatively for a moment, he replied: "Tis the salt, you see—they're *pickled*.'"[33]

As the train chugged out of the station, the president began his bowing routine, first to the left and then to the right. In this genteel manner, he acknowledged and thanked another segment of his constituency for coming out to greet him. While for the president this dignified gesture became his standard method of bidding adieu to his well-wishers in each town through which he passed, making the salute repetitious to him, this gesture was new to those observing him each time he gave it. With a 10:05 a.m. departure time, the train was leaving on schedule. Having already traversed 150 miles that morning, the halfway point to the state capital was almost achieved. For the next leg of the trip—Syracuse to Utica—the presidential consist would be hauled by the engine *Major Priest*. Ahead lay many more miles along with four brief stops before the day's long journey ended in Albany.

4

Next Stop, Utica
Gateway to the Mohawk Valley

The dash from Syracuse to Utica was notable for two reasons. First, the famished passengers were finally fed. While many had breakfasted in Buffalo, that meal was six hours ago. Travel in these early days of railroading meant many comforts that later became standard benefits—such as dining cars featuring white tablecloths, china dishes, and polite service—were not yet standard amenities. So, the entourage riding the Lincoln Special had to content itself with food taken aboard at Buffalo, which made a lunch of poultry, breads, and cakes as tasty and filling to the hungry riders as a seven-course meal at a five-star restaurant.

Another noteworthy aspect on this leg of the journey was the speed at which the train progressed. Moving across the last miles of the Great Lakes Plain, the right-of-way was laid relatively straight on level ground. With no scheduled stops in the fifty-four miles between Syracuse and Utica, portions of the run were made at close to full-throttle. Given the various hazards inherent in nineteenth century rail travel, such "high-balling" does seem needlessly foolhardy, especially considering the importance of at least one passenger. While no ill came of the rapid run, the *New York Herald* did express concern, commenting that "it may be a dangerous passage for the Presidential party, it is feared."[1] Railroad officials, demonstrating their cognizance that even in the best of circumstances the unforeseen can happen, had no less than five locomotives positioned along the route in the event of a breakdown to the *Major Priest*.

But danger notwithstanding, speed was a way that a railroad could demonstrate superiority. With respect to the New York Central, it was not a well-guarded secret that intra-divisional gamesmanship was also present, with each section trying to outdo the others in bettering the previous speed record for a given point-to-point run. Bets were allegedly placed on times for the Syracuse-to-Utica run. As an example of the breakneck speed which Lincoln's achieved, the six miles between Canastota and Chittenango were covered in five minutes and fifteen seconds—which amounted to an astounding rate of sixty-six miles per hour, even moving against a headwind during a raging snowstorm.

Though no stops were made between Syracuse and Utica, the train was slowed in passing through the communities of Chittenango, Oneida, and Rome. At each station "were clustered crowds of people peering anxiously into the car windows to obtain a sight of the President's face."[2] The views which the onlookers caught were those of a man in rare moments of repose. During this one-hour-and-fifteen-minute jaunt, Lincoln was afforded an opportunity to engage in pleasant conversations with his companions. For once, not a word of a political nature was uttered. A participant in the repartee noted that "there was no stiffness or formality exhibited, nor did the dignity of the President's office suffer by the familiarity and ease with which he conducted himself toward all who approached him."[3] When passing through one of these stations, the people gathered there "manifested their respect for the President in the only way available—by waving hats and handkerchiefs, cheers and cannon."[4]

Of all the small towns that the train passed on its way to Utica, one that would have especially interested Mr. Lincoln was Rome. As a stubbornly held bastion that helped save New York from being overrun during the British Army's Three-Point Plan of 1777, Fort Stanwix occupied the site upon which the present-day village was founded. Then, in 1817, the first shovelfuls of dirt were turned near Rome to commence construction of the Erie Canal. Now in the eighty-fifth year of the nation's existence, Rome owned the proud distinction of being a frontier outpost during the Revolution and then, forty years later, the starting point for an ambitious transportation improvement. As if Rome's honored place in American heritage was not sufficiently secured by these events, in 1860 the town became home to five-year-old Francis Bellamy, who as a youngster could have been present when Lincoln's train went past. Twenty-four years later, the now Reverend Bellamy would pen the Pledge of Allegiance to the flag. Rome could unabashedly boast of having hit a patriotic trifecta, the likes of which few places its size could match.

Long before Lincoln's train reached Utica—situated at the western end of the historic Mohawk Valley—residents from all parts of central New York's Oneida County had begun to gather in the city, eventually concentrating around the depot. It was noted that "the jam in the street was most oppressive, [while] the roofs and windows, and all other available seeing spaces, were occupied by ladies and gentlemen."[5] Illustrative of the newspaper's recognition that folks had come from "every nook and corner of the county" to witness this singular event was the presence of the senior class from Hamilton College, young men who had arisen early to make the ten-mile trek northeast from Clinton to Utica.[6]

Also included among the ardent supporters, general well-wishers, and curiosity seekers who had descended upon the city were delegations from the neighboring counties of Lewis, Madison, and Herkimer, all intent upon extending good tidings from their respective constituencies to the country's imminent leader. "Hours before the time of his arrival," observed a journalist for the *Utica Gazette*, "the streets were thronged with people."[7] Even the freezing temperature, blustery wind, and falling snow did nothing to dampen the ardor of the crowd, for winter weather had held the area in its frosty grip for some time. With a decidedly puckish attitude, the *Utica Telegraph* reported that "the people of that city had enjoyed 11 weeks of uninterrupted sleighing, and there is the prospect of its continuation longer. Utica is the paradise of people who think it is fun to catch cold on runners."[8] With inclement weather taken in stride, the scene had a festive air, for the mood of the assembled mass was very lighthearted. Acknowledging the import of the day, national flags were prominently displayed, with the steady breeze keeping the colors majestically unfurled. "The stars and stripes," for those gazing about the downtown area, "floated above our various hotels, the Railroad Depot, the *Morning Herald*, and other printing offices"[9]

* * *

While the special headed east and bound for Albany, 325 miles to the northeast another less-heralded train had that same morning departed from Bangor, Maine. Also destined by evening to arrive in a state capital—this one being Boston, Massachusetts—its passengers were traveling via the Boston and Maine Railroad. Onboard was a distinguished individual in his own right, the Hon. Hannibal Hamlin and his wife, Ellen. A former congressman and later senator, this highly regarded politician from the Pine Tree State had also briefly filled the office of governor before returning to the Senate. Now he was once again on his way to Washington, D.C., destined to serve in yet another high governmental capacity. Heading for the same March 4, 1861, inaugural ceremony as Abraham Lincoln, Mr. Hamlin was slated to become the sixteenth vice president of the United States.

Even though Hamlin himself was not enthralled at holding what he viewed as a valueless job, one in which he referenced himself as being like "a fifth wheel on a coach," his fellow Mainers were nevertheless justifiably proud of their favorite son.[10] Admitted to the Union only forty-one years ago, Maine had not had seen many opportunities for its citizens to shine on the national stage. Despite Hamlin's personal misgivings, being part of a presidential ticket was considered no small achievement by most Americans.

Though Hamlin hailed from a far more prosperous background than his running mate, the two men did share much common ground. They were of the same age, considered physically fit in their younger years, had practiced law, and served in both their respective state legislatures and the United States House of Representatives.

Each had experienced a difficult personal tragedy—Lincoln losing a son and Hamlin his first wife. The two shared the inherent ability to relate to the common man. A revealing anecdote about Hamlin held that when "Bangor once held a giant parade in his honor and offered him a carriage, he turned it down, saying 'I'll walk with the boys.'"[11] But the die that determined the future of the vice president's career, bringing him directly into the orbit of Abraham Lincoln, was cast in 1860 when he switched his political affiliation from the Democratic to the Republican Party. At the root of his defection was the issue of extension of slavery into the territories. While Hamlin was an abolitionist at heart, Lincoln and the Republicans seemed to offer the best chance of making any immediate inroads into controlling the despised institution.

Hannibal Hamlin, shown in this early 1860s Mathew Brady photograph, made a pre-inaugural train trip of his own to meet the president-elect in New York City (Library of Congress).

As far as the machinations that led to his nomination at the Republican Convention in Chicago that summer of '60, Hamlin was not even present at the conclave's hub of activity, known as the Wigwam. Opting to remain in Washington, he responded to all inquiries that he harbored no desire to fill the second spot on the ticket. While the chances of his nomination seemed remote, the political climate of that era was still a time when balloting at political conventions was very much a fluid process—emotion, timing, momentum, and connections—were just a few of the factors that could start a bandwagon and swing the nomination from one candidate to another or turn a dark horse into a front-runner.

In the case of Maine's favorite son, Governor John A. Andrew of Massachusetts gave a good accounting of how Hannibal Hamlin—a known poker player—wound up with the winning hand: "Mr. Hamlin's nomination … was not only the exact complement of the ticket headed by Mr. Lincoln in respect to locality, political antecedents, and manifest fitness for the office, but was the most natural result conceivable.… Mr. Hamlin was preeminently the first choice of the friends of both Mr. Seward and Mr. Lincoln, nominated in a national convention under more favorable auspices. Not one Republican can be found from Maine to Oregon who would desire any other result."[12] Upon receiving the news, Hamlin was shocked. Though in his heart of hearts he did not desire the nomination, he was a man in his words "faithful to the cause," so he would run.[13]

When the time came to leave his home in Hampden, Maine for the six-mile trek north to the depot in Bangor, the vice president-elect was accompanied by a bevy of friends intent upon giving him a proper send-off. In quaintly New England fashion, a procession of sleighs escorted him to the Bangor city line. Arriving at this transfer point, the Hamlin party was met by another welcoming throng which included the city's incumbent mayor. From here, the Hamlins were escorted to the station by another convoy, everyone riding in single or double sleighs. However, as the honorees, the esteemed couple was bundled into the limousine of nineteenth century winter conveyances—a sixteen-passenger sleigh. Accompanying them in this wintry conga line was "a procession of sleighs over a mile long, decorated with flags."[14] The presence of these well-wishers was ample evidence that they were immensely proud of their neighbor's accomplishment. Whatever zeal Hamlin lacked for his upcoming office, the homefolks more than compensated for it.

"Notwithstanding the early hour of this morning," an eye-witness reported, "Mr. Hamlin was received with enthusiastic cheers and the warm greetings and affectionate farewell

In an oversized, communal sleigh such as the one pictured, Hannibal Hamlin was conveyed by friends and neighbors to Bangor, where he began his trip to Washington for the March 4, 1861, inaugural ceremonies (19th century print, author's collection).

of thousands of his fellow-citizens."[15] Clambering atop a baggage table at the depot as spryly as his fifty-two years would allow, he then spoke briefly about how the increasing national discord might be weathered:

> I go to discharge the official duties which have been conferred upon me by a generous people, and relying upon Divine Providence, I trust, that confidence shall never be betrayed. I know full well that dark clouds are lowering around the political horizon, and that madness rules the hour, but I am hopeful still that our people are not only loyal to the government, but that they are fraternal to all its citizens. And when in practice it shall be demonstrated that the Constitutional rights of all the states will be respected and maintained by following the paths illuminated by Washington, Jefferson, and Madison, may we not reasonably hope and expect that quiet will be restored, and the whole country will still advance in a career which will elevate man in a social, moral and intellectual condition.[16]

With his words still hanging in the frosty air, Mr. Hamlin and his party boarded the train. The locomotive commenced to move, slowly gaining momentum. In an instant, he was gone. Under the stewardship of veteran conductor Elbridge Towle—a railroader of almost fifty years' experience and friend of the vice president-elect—Hamlin's train traveled 250 miles that day, arriving at its destination around 7:30 p.m. However, the enthusiastic send-off from Bangor was not matched by a comparable welcome in Boston. In fact, the presence of the distinguished party in Massachusetts caused barely a ripple. Since advanced notice of his coming had been low-keyed, no one was even sure at which of two Boston depots he would be arriving—the Eastern or the Maine Station.

When Hamlin's small party alighted, perhaps all of twenty people greeted them. Even more glaring than the paltry size of the reception committee, not a single Republican Party official was present to extend a formal welcome. In fact, so blasé was the greeting that when "one individual was enthusiastic enough to call for 'three cheers for Hon. Hannibal Hamlin of Hampton, Maine,' there was no response except a smile, and no enthusiasm beyond accommodating Mr. Hamlin in his efforts to find a Revere House coach."[17] Without a ceremonial welcome, much less any reporters seeking an interview, the Hamlins quickly took leave of the station and were whisked off to one of the city's best-known establishments. Upon arrival at the inn, the vice president was recognized by a few of the guests who made their own introductions, but, once again, no official acknowledgment of his presence materialized. At this point, the party retired to their rooms, for the vice president-elect's itinerary called for them to arise early on the morning of February 19.

* * *

While Hamlin was heading to Boston, the same half-past eight found Lincoln between Rochester and Syracuse. Even though he was not scheduled to leave the bustling Salt City on the shores of Onondaga Lake until 10:05 a.m., excitement was already building at the next stop down the line where the anticipated event was funneling people to the Utica depot. Not surprisingly, the occasion was viewed as a unique opportunity, representing a red-letter day for the city and its citizens.

For it was but rarely that a public figure of such prominence found his way into this neck of the woods. The last one who did in recent memory came in 1824. On that occasion, as a part of his triumphal return to the United States, the Marquis de Lafayette passed through the region.

However, of the previous fifteen presidents, only Martin Van Buren from Kinderhook in the Hudson Valley and Millard Fillmore of Summerhill in the Finger Lakes region had hailed from New York State. Yet neither had made an appearance in Utica while on his way to be sworn in, much less while in office.

Otherwise, there were only two individuals of presidential timber who had been to the vicinity. One was in 1783, when General George Washington conducted a post-war tour. He passed by what had been the location of old Fort Schuyler, upon which site Utica eventually grew. The point at which he forded the Mohawk River was within hailing distance of the eventual site of the depot at which Lincoln would soon be arriving. It could thus be said—albeit given a hiatus of seventy-eight years—that the paths of these two giants of the Republic once crossed in Utica.

The other instance of a decidedly pre-presidential nature was in 1784, when James Madison visited central New York to help negotiate a post-war treaty with the Iroquois. But those brief visits to the frontier were all a part of history now, well beyond the memory of most folks who stood waiting for the train's arrival on that brisk February day in 1861. Though no one could have foreseen the development then, forty-eight years hence Utica would serve not as stop on a politician's way to his Washington inaugural ceremony, but rather instead his starting point. For in 1909, John Schoolcraft Sherman—a hometown lawyer and former mayor—would be sworn in as the vice president of the United States under William Howard Taft. A boy of five in 1861, it is problematical as to whether the youngster's dad, a loyal Democrat, would have braved the elements and the crowd to see an opposing party's victorious candidate; however, at the very least, young Sherman was likely to have been aware of the extraordinary hubbub that invested the town that day.

Not that Utica on days without the presence of a celebrity was dull place, for in actuality it was a flourishing community on its way to prominence. Had he time to spare, the locale was a place that Lincoln undoubtedly would have liked and identified with quite readily. First and foremost, the town's growth had been predicated on transportation developments, a subject near and dear to Lincoln's entrepreneurial heart. By 1860, several railroads served Utica; here the east-west alignment of the Erie Canal and the northern terminus of the Chenango Canal built from Binghamton converged; and the Seneca Turnpike passed through the city. Collectively, they provided connections to places from Albany to Buffalo and beyond.

The farm boy in the president-elect would have felt very much at home amidst the rural setting of Utica, with the city being a transshipment point for agricultural products destined for distant markets. Lincoln the inventor would have enjoyed touring the textile mills of Utica, some having pioneered the use of steam to power machinery. Visible in the distance to the northwest on a prominent hill was a substantial building that would have piqued Lincoln's curiosity. Known as the New York State Lunatic Asylum, this massive stone structure, designed in Greek Revival style, was built in 1843 and would remain service until 1978. The first such publicly funded institution in the state, this facility became widely known for its progressive treatment procedures for the mentally ill.

Finally, the attorney in Mr. Lincoln would have taken a barrister's interest in the McGuiness Murder Trial that was to begin on the morrow. Involving the rape and murder of a young girl, who was "assaulted at a piece of woods near the city, strangled with a handkerchief tied about her neck, and thrown into the canal."[18] Allegedly the dastardly deed was perpetrated by two young men whose accusation was supported only by circumstantial evidence. Nevertheless, the sensational case caught the public's attention. Fraught with mystery, pathos, titillation, and sordidness, the editor of the *Oneida Weekly Herald* was moved to reference the proceedings as being "one of the most remarkable in the history of human crime."[19]

In many ways, Lincoln would have been attracted to the city of the Utica circa 1861 because it was a microcosm of Lincoln's vision for his beloved Illinois, with growth and prosperity tied to transportation and grounded in agricultural bedrock. But, unfortunately, Lincoln's visit would prove altogether too brief for him to take in any of the community's glories, beyond those he could see from the windows of his coach or hear from proud local boosters.

With the train nearing Utica, a singular moment occurred that featured the expression of a well-intentioned but eerie sentiment, one heightened in hindsight due to the tragic event that ended the Lincoln presidency. It seems that state senator Richard Connelly had been introduced to Mary Lincoln and engaged her in a brief conversation. Rising to leave, he casually commented that he "hoped that she would be as happy four years from this time as she had reason to be now."[20] For causes known but to her then, Mary's eyes welled up with tears, just as they would with reason four years later.

Then, at 11:35 a.m. on February 18, 1861, the *Major Priest* finally hove into view, its glowing headlight intermittently visible as its beam fought to pierce the steadily falling snow. The train's arrival was announced with the booming of cannon, a symbolic salute of thirty-four guns eventually being fired. This bodacious welcome was followed by a round of hearty cheers from the waiting crowd. With bell clanging, steam hissing, and whistle screeching, the iron horse and its abbreviated trio of yellow-hued coaches glided to a halt. Anticipation amongst the crowd rose to its highest level. Onlookers craned their necks and stood on tip-toes, hoping to catch sight of the man of the hour. Though the Lincoln Special made its appearance eighteen minutes ahead of schedule, an immense crowd—created by an influx of residents from the outlying rural areas to compliment the inhabitants of the nation's thirty-ninth largest city—had assembled.

Trumpeting a "Great Reception in Utica!" as its headline the next day, a local paper estimated that "the number present at the depot was not less than six to seven thousand."[21] While not a rowdy crowd, it was nevertheless densely packed. This mass of humanity was described as one that "writhed and twisted like a huge Pythonic monster full of joints, backwards and forwards, to the right and left as the spirit of patriotism (or curiosity) moved it."[22] In keeping with the prim Victorian perspective that ruled the etiquette of the day, concern was demonstrated for the unusually large number of women in the crowd. If met individually on the street or in a parlor, these females would have been extended all sorts of social graces by the same gentlemen currently crushing against them in the assembled horde.

But such large congregations tend to function impersonally and reflexively, such that each spasmodic reshuffling rippling through the pack caused people to be jammed unexpectedly together. Some of the fairer sex were literally swept off their feet and subjected to close encounters, which in many instances were unwanted. "It is barely possible that some enjoyed it," one gauche reporter surmised, "although on several countenances, male and female, there were at times expressions of disapprobation and disgust."[23]

As if being at the mercy of a restless mob's undulations was not discomforting enough,

The bustling city of Utica greeted the president-elect with open arms and much to see, such as Bagg's Square in the foreground, the Erie Canal heading east down the Mohawk Valley in the upper left, and the new lunatic asylum perched prominently against the skyline on the right. From Maturin Murray Ballou, *Ballou's Pictorial Drawing Room Companion* (Boston: Ballou Publishing, 1855).

its defenseless members were occasionally struck by snowballs, for several young rapscallions located outside the throng took great delight in randomly hurling icy orbs into the crowd. Helpless targets of opportunity abounded. Thrown hither and yon into a sea of potential victims, the missiles struck unsuspecting bodies with impunity.

However, once the train arrived, proceedings moved rapidly along. With the spectators watching intently, a flat-bedded freight car was switched onto the same track and then rolled up to the rear of the Lincoln Special. An elevated platform had been constructed upon its surface, so that a space was provided from whence a seated group of state dignitaries could be introduced to Mr. Lincoln. But that amenity was displaced to a later occasion with an admonition by William Wood, who rebuffed the waiting legislative VIPs with his pronouncement that the good citizens of Utica should not have their limited time with Mr. Lincoln taken up by state business.

Then, with neither fanfare nor announcement, the door of the rear car opened, and Abraham Lincoln stepped before them. All the discomfort accompanying the long wait quickly dissipated for the crowd. For those who had only seen campaign drawings of Lincoln in the papers, a mild surprise occurred when they beheld him in all his newly bearded grandeur. While Civil War generals were soon to be resplendent with their hirsute facial appearances, no president prior to Lincoln had ever sported a beard. Shocked or not by his unexpected appearance, the crowd still greeted him with round after round of enthusiastic applause. As it subsided, he moved from the train to the makeshift platform, where he was introduced to the reception committee by the Hon. Albert Hubbell and subsequently welcomed by the equally honorable Ward Hunt who said: "Mr. President—On behalf of the citizens of Utica, I welcome your arrival among us. Democrats and Republican unite in wishes for your happiness, in reliance upon the wisdom of your Administration, and the hope that our country will be speedily relieved from the perils that encompass it."[24] To the last of the dignitaries preceding Mr. Lincoln to speak, Utica's mayor DeWitt C. Grove, went the distinct pleasure of presenting the president-elect to the waiting audience.

Taking a position on the north side of the platform, which allowed him to address the largest portion of the assemblage, Lincoln gazed out upon "a crowd augmented continually, until as far as the eye could reach could be seen a pushing, restless tide of humanity, with thousands of faces turned upward toward the future ruler of the nation."[25] With snowflakes gently landing on his hat and coat and his breath crystallizing in the air, he addressed the people. But even in the brevity of his statement, Mr. Lincoln nevertheless provided evidence of his well-known traits of humility and humor:

> Ladies and Gentlemen—I do not come before you to make a speech. I have no speech to make. I have no time before the starting of the train to make one if I had. I have simply come to greet you and bid you farewell. I have come out to see you and enable you to see me. [*Laughter.*] And particularly since the ladies are here, I have the best of the bargain in the sight. [*Laughter.*] I repeat, I have no speech to make, and I bid you farewell, but I will reappear before you again before the train moves off. [*Cheers.*][26]

With no CNN or Fox News to point out later what would not be obvious to the assembled mass, Mr. Lincoln's folksy homily was in essence the same basic speech that he delivered at each of his quick stops across the state.

When he had concluded his remarks, a harmless—though somewhat foreboding—disruption occurred when "a crazy man, with long moustache and beard, with a shepherd's crook for a cane, and whose legs were incased in red flannel coverings, attempted to address the crowd who hooted and yelled at his singular behavior."[27] While the incident was but a temporary interruption, it spoke volumes about the ease of accessibility to past presidents and their vulnerability to injury. Given that the incident passed quickly, Ward Hill Lamon never had a chance to spring into action. In the present age when the chief executive is guarded by Secret Service agents, Lincoln's exposure to potential harm from an unexpected interloper was clearly evidenced. While a harbinger of a tragedy to come, the danger signal was not acted upon in any meaningful way.

Once the fracas subsided, Lincoln graciously moved to the south side of the platform. Here he offered some comments for the benefit of those who might not have heard his initial presentation: "I come around to say to you what I did to those on the other side, which was but a few words, and little more than a good morning, as it were, and farewell. I can't however say here, exactly what I did on the other side, as there are no ladies on this side. I said that there were so many ladies present that I had the best part of the sight, but bear in mind I don't make any such admission now. Farewell!"[28] Then he re-entered the car, but not before again promising the people that he would reappear to bid them adieu before departing.

Though the Lincolns most likely had yet to make his acquaintance, a new passenger was scheduled for departure from the Utica rail yards with them. Bound for Washington, this lone traveler was destined to partake in the inaugural celebration too. Eventually the travelers' paths together would take them to New York City and then finally the nation's capital. But rather than riding in the plush coach that bore the Lincolns and taking part in the ceremonial stops along the way, his trek to the nation's capital was in the baggage car. Who was this mystery rider? According to a short blurb in the *Rochester Daily Union and Advertiser*, a generous resident from the village of Wampsville, one E.W. Avery, was sending to Washington "the great inauguration gobbler which he has raised for, and is to present as a free will offering to the Republican President."[29] Two-years old and weighing in at thirty pounds, this particular bird closely matched the one that the same farmer had given to James Buchanan to help celebrate his inauguration four years earlier. At the behest of his son Tad, President Lincoln was known to have granted a presidential pardon to a turkey prior to Thanksgiving in 1863; however, the presumption is that farmer Avery's present wound up fulfilling his destiny, that of being roasted and gracing the White House table as an honored guest at the Inauguration Day dinner.

Though on its eighth day out from Springfield the train had arrived in Utica early in spite of battling the elements, a slight delay in its departure was necessitated by an overheated journal box on one the cars. Much to the chagrin of railroad officials, this was the same difficulty that had already delayed the train on its run between Batavia and Rochester. Though not uncommon and largely unavoidable, for safety's sake this problem was not one with which to trifle. The axles attached to the wheels of the cars were set in journal boxes, one on each end of the axle and suspended beneath the coach. Keeping these housings adequately lubricated—usually with oil-soaked rags known as packing—allowed for smooth functioning of the mechanism. However, a lack of or loss of grease usually caused what railroaders called a "hot box," which was the result of too much friction between the axle and the bearings surrounding it. Failure to address the problem quickly invariably caused a fire that could spread from the box to the car or the collapse of the car onto the axle, ending in a derailment with potentially dreadful results.

Among the train's crewmen, the task of keeping an eye peeled for just such an anomaly belonged to a brakeman. He was expected to periodically lean out a window, checking wheels on both sides of the train for telltale smoke, sparks, or flames. If deemed serious enough, he had the authority to signal for an immediate halt to the train's progress. Had the attention of the eager spectators not been so earnestly focused on Mr. Lincoln, they would have noticed several railroad workers gathered by the side of one of the cars and attending to the problem.

In time, after the journal box cooled, additional packing added, and a new inspection conducted, the malfunction was deemed addressed. While these repairs were being made, a fresh engine was backed up and attached to the cars for the run to Albany, with the *Chauncey Vibbard* replacing the *Major Priest*. Henry Harvey was the engineer assigned to the run. Then, in a matter of minutes following Lincoln's little orations, the shrill screech of the engine's whistle sounded over the snow-covered scene, its blast of hot steam rising upward through the cold falling flakes. Conductor Frank Clock checked his watch and then signaled the engineer. It was 11:40 a.m., and time for the Lincoln Special to go. Starting slowly, the train gradually picked up speed and altogether too soon bore the president-elect away.

Intent upon hanging on as long as possible to their last look at this man from whom so much was expected, several men and boys ran after the last car until the train's speed outstripped their ability to keep pace. In departing the station, Lincoln could be seen standing alone on the rear car's back platform, bowing humbly to the crowd. As folks waved goodbye, their parting image of America's new leader, eternally etched in their minds, was that of the quintessential Lincoln: polite, tall, gaunt, bearded, and clad in a top hat and coat. Looking back at the still waving crowd, Lincoln could easily have felt a sense of satisfaction at the welcome which he had just received. Henry Villard was certainly impressed, noting that "the Utica reception was very fine."[30] In his subtle campaign to win the hearts and minds of his people, the president-elect was making progress ... one town at a time.

5

East Through the Valley
The Historic Route to the West in Reverse

Once under way, the future president took his seat. With no stops for twenty-one miles, he could sit back, warm his chilled bones, and enjoy the ride. The truth was Lincoln needed the rest. Not surprisingly he had caught a cold, abetted by giving speeches while exposed to icy winds and pelted with wet snow. Though he was content to sit and chat with his companions, little did Mr. Lincoln know that his spouse had a sartorial surprise in store. Like many of us, his comfort level with his existing wardrobe far outweighed the somewhat slovenly appearance that these well-worn pieces projected. *The New York Times* described his ensemble as "a shocking bad hat and very thin old overcoat."[1]

Leave it to Mary, a fashion hound who spared no expense where her own attire was involved, to make perhaps one of the earliest executive decisions of any first lady-in-waiting. She decided unilaterally that the cherished duds, which her husband seemed content to wear until they fell apart, would no longer suffice. Propriety dictated that a head of state had to dress the part. The child of a proper Southern family, Mary Todd was accustomed to the finer things in life, stylish clothes being among them. Her husband, on the other hand came from far less privileged origins, one wherein apparel was viewed more as a necessary bodily covering and not so much an opportunity for personal adornment. During their White House years, Mary's extravagant spending on fashionable clothing became the source of reoccurring financial headaches for her husband.

But this time, she was thinking not of herself. Many of the politicians whom they had met along the journey thus far were men whose taste in clothes had made for impeccable appearances. Being a proud wife, she wanted her husband to display as much tailored splendor as a gaunt, six-foot, four-inch man could. Since he was indifferent to such considerations, the task was hers to make him presentable. Having prepared for this moment, she dispatched Mr. Lincoln's trusted valet, William Johnson, off on an errand to the baggage car.

In short order, Johnson returned with a new broadcloth overcoat upon his arm and a box containing an equally mint stovepipe hat. Mary had chosen well, for she had purchased the distinctive style of headgear which her husband preferred. Mr. Lincoln's favorite chapeau was one with a cylindrical core of black felt seven inches in height, a two-inch wide brim around its base, and a diameter of seven-and-seven-eighth's inches. Given his excessive stature, the hat accentuated his height, making his proportions appear even more imposing. When fully dressed, he exceeded seven feet. In the estimation of at least one reporter, the new garments successfully accomplished the transformation for which Mary was striving.

"Since then Mr. Lincoln has looked fifty percent better," a *Times* correspondent commented favorably, "and, if Mrs. Lincoln's advice is always as near right as it was in this instance, the country may congratulate itself upon the fact its president–elect is a man who does not reject, even in important matters, the advice and counsel of his wife."[2] In a sad postscript to this pleasant vignette, William Johnson would not survive the war, perishing of smallpox in early 1864, which the faithful servant contracted while nursing Lincoln back to health from the same disease.

For most of the next eighty-two miles of the trip, the Lincoln Special would be traversing a historic corridor known as the Mohawk Valley. Eighty-five years ago, this region represented America's frontier, at the forefront of settlement where civilization progressively thinned out west of Albany and the wilderness took over. Only the bravest of souls ventured forth to settle homesteads on lands just recently vacated by the Iroquois Nation. The magnet drawing settlers was fertile farmland. The price many families paid was with their lives. Commencing with the French and Indian War and continuing through the Revolution, desperate battles were waged here on many occasions between colonial forces and raiding parties of first the French and their Native American allies and later the Tories and with their Indian cohorts. This furious attention was largely due to the valley's importance in providing sustenance to American troops, earning the region the nickname "Breadbasket of the Colonies." The folks who would turn out to greet Mr. Lincoln were descendants of

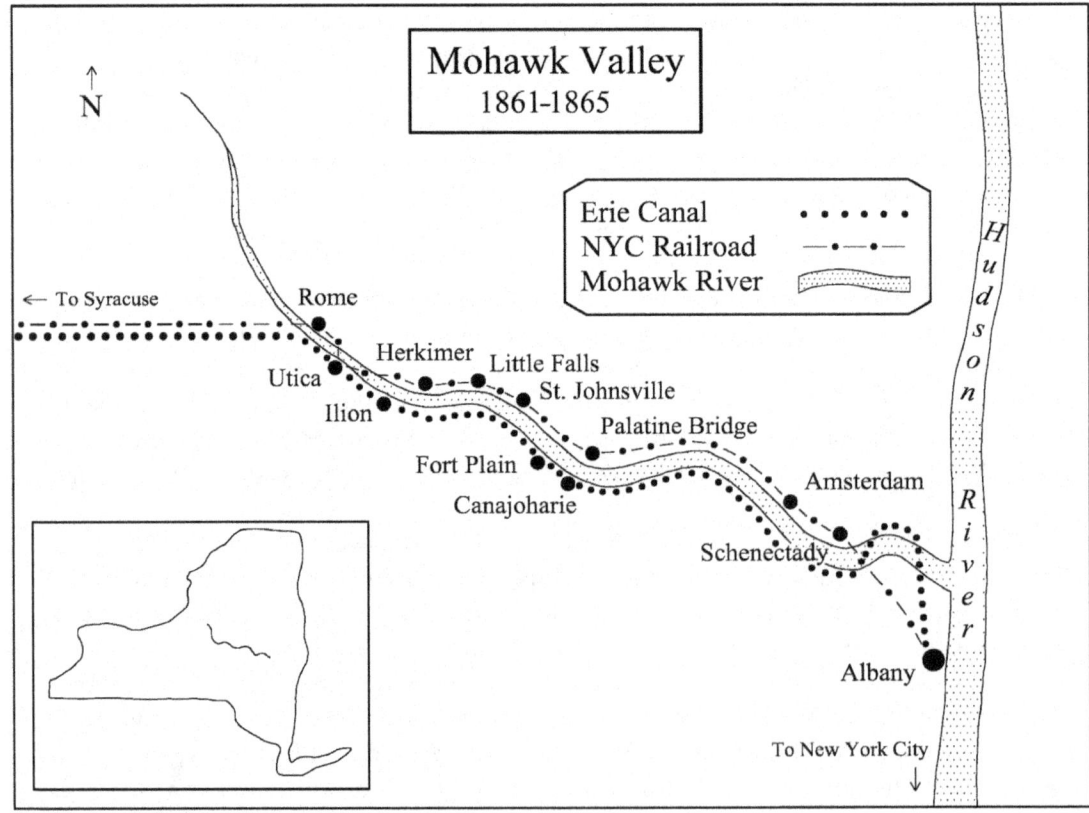

Drawn by Bob Collea.

these staunch patriots, a proud people who had given as much as anyone to the cause of independence. Little did he know that many of the upturned faces in the crowds he would see along the way would soon be answering another call to arms, fighting this time to preserve the continued existence of the same country to which their ancestors had given birth.

Following the War for Independence, the Mohawk Valley experienced rapidly increasing settlement. With the fear of hostile incursions removed, the frontier pushed steadily westward. In 1825, the opening of the Erie Canal spurred the development of not only the western portion of the Empire State, but also the lands from whence Lincoln hailed. After the canal boom, the rapid advance of railroads proved a further boost to areas into which their tracks were extended. Over the ensuing years, communities throughout the Mohawk Valley would become manufacturing centers for products that enjoyed access to a worldwide market. From the coach windows, he could have seen the first signs of this industrial might, as the train passed by Frankfort, Mohawk, and Ilion on the opposite side of the Mohawk River and then through Herkimer on its way to a brief stop in Little Falls.

As he moved eastward into the more highly settled parts of the state, the president could marvel at what hard work and perseverance could accomplish and, in the process, create man-made wonders, but the region was also truly one of impressive natural beauty. Slicing between the majestic Adirondack Mountains to the north and rolling Catskills to the south, the Mohawk Valley offered a narrow passageway connecting the Hudson Valley with the Great Lakes Plain. By the luck of nature, this narrow sluice was the only sea level route through the Appalachians from Maine to Georgia. Though there was a gradual uphill

As they traveled through the Mohawk Valley to Albany, the lowland corridor between the Adirondack and Catskill mountains offered many pastoral vistas to the Lincolns (A.C. Warren, "View of the Mohawk Valley," 1881).

climb of several hundred feet from Albany to Utica, the passage west that the gap afforded made this the path of choice for a boundless tide of settlers.

Once western New York had gained a sizable population, pioneers moved on into the Ohio Territory, an area that came to include Lincoln's own stomping grounds. Undoubtedly, he knew folks in Springfield who had either endured the trek themselves or were descended from those who had made their way west via the Mohawk Valley. In most places, the valley's walls were rarely imposing, being neither particularly high nor steep. A man could easily climb from the valley floor to its upper reaches without undue effort. Much longer than wide and narrower in some places than others, the Mohawk Valley nevertheless contained enough flat land for communities to grow and farmers to till. Villages like Ilion, Herkimer, and Little Falls, for example, had parts of their respective communities spread out on both lowlands by the river and hilly areas comprising the valley walls, giving them rather unique street grids, varied living patterns, and literal uptown/downtown dichotomies in their geopolitical layouts.

In many ways, the train's passengers were afforded a distinctive panorama, a one-of-a-kind vista rarely replicated elsewhere in the country. Traveling along, the initial feeling was that of being slowly enveloped by its walls. To the eye, the valley's defining borders on the north and south often appeared as an eighty-mile stretch of contiguous rolling hills. The top or rim was softly rounded rather than peaked, while the slope frequently took the form of a gently undulating, slowly rising upslope from the river, some places appearing as natural terracing. Though a late winter blizzard currently reduced visibility, the layer of pristine snow which blanketed the land only served to enhance the innate beauty that the Mohawk Valley already possessed.

Furthermore, passengers could also see where the industriousness of man had boldly introduced his own imprint. Perhaps the most immediately visible of these innovations were the differing forms of land, water, and rail travel that had been developed over the years. To their left or the north was the first of the man-made improvements—starting as an unnamed Indian trail, increased use in colonial times widened the narrow path into the King's Highway, and finally by the 1860s the thoroughfare became known as the Mohawk Turnpike. Under the Lincoln party's feet, rails of iron carried the New York Central Railroad from Albany to Buffalo, while to the south the engineering marvel of its time lay the Erie Canal, easily discernable winding its way along its east-west axis. Along with the primordial Mohawk River, all three modes vied for space on the valley floor.

Contesting for turf of their own alongside the transportation network were numerous villages that had grown—from tiny hamlets to sizable enclaves—in some instances with appreciable speed. More often than not, these burgs gratefully owed their rapid development to the multiple choices afforded its citizenry to cheaply ship produce and products to distant markets. Despite the falling snow and stands of trees that intervened, three of these enclaves could be observed in quick succession as the train rolled east from Utica: the rising communities of Frankfort, Ilion, and Mohawk were located along the southern banks of the Mohawk River. Here the valley from north-to-south was at one of its widest points throughout its entire length, perhaps a mile across the flats. Thus, ample room existed for communities to flourish without devouring all existing farmland. Though the Erie Canal ran through all three, the New York Central did not, though the day would come when these towns too would enjoy direct service provided by the West Shore Railroad.

Also taking up precious space were a variety of factories. In time, the Mohawk Valley from Utica to Schenectady would evolve into one of the premier concentrations of manufacturing in the world, a status it would enjoy for almost a hundred years. Even in its infancy, the existence of industry was sufficiently evidenced to impress the president-elect. For a son of the Midwest, nurtured in an agricultural environment, the progress that he was viewing contrasted sharply with that to which he was accustomed. In passing Frankfort, a community just six miles east of Utica, Lincoln would have his introduction to what would become a steady parade of industrial facilities. Here the initiative of William Grates was visible in the walls of his factory, behind which were workers producing the first practical sulfur matches. At Ilion, had he been watching out the right-hand side of his car, Lincoln could easily have seen some of the more prominent features of a manufacturing complex that would serve as a significant contributor to the Union cause in the Civil War. The company was known as Remington Arms. Fashioned by the hands of its workers would come not only contracted Springfield rifles, but also under the company's own name 125,000 of what some argued were the best revolvers available to federal troops. Relocated to the banks of the Erie Canal by Eliphalet Remington II, the business expanded from a small forge serving local patrons to a factory complex with an international clientele. Standing the test of time, shifting public attitudes about firearms, changes in ownership, and stiff competition, the company still occupies the same grounds where Lincoln would have viewed it.

But even if he had not been thinking ahead and projecting how a gun-maker in this upstate New York community might soon be called upon to serve its country's martial needs, his mind could just as easily have been focusing on the men whom he would need to fill administrative posts. Whether he had made any decision by then or not, the small town just east of Ilion—named Mohawk after one of the member tribes in the powerful Iroquois Confederacy—was going to provide him with a key appointee. The man's name was Francis Elias Spinner, but in time more recognizable as F. E. Spinner, which was the signature he chose to affix to the government documents that he would sign for the next fourteen years in the office of treasurer of the United States. Since it regularly appeared on currency during the Civil War—the well-known greenbacks—people were more familiar with his autograph than any of his contemporaries. That the presidential candidate knew of Francis Spinner prior to the election is evidenced by a letter from Lincoln, dated September 24, 1860, in which he thanked Spinner for some books, past correspondence, and shared with him his confidence in the reliability of Republican supporters in Pennsylvania to hold off the opposition.[3]

Moving deeper down the valley, the train rumbled through the village of Herkimer, the county seat named in honor of Nicholas Herkimer. An officer in the Tryon County Militia, General Herkimer had led his command in the bloody Battle of Oriskany on August 4, 1777.[4] Though his troops suffered heavy losses, including the general, the British attempt to reach Albany through the Mohawk Valley was thwarted. Nor had the passage of eighty-four years dissipated the martial spirit or patriotic fervor passed down to the progeny of that Revolutionary generation. For one year hence, when President Lincoln issued his second call for troops, men from the villages and farms that he saw on his way through Herkimer County would muster in the county seat through which he was passing, board trains at the village depot where he had just observed people waving at his train, and go off to war as the 121st New York State Infantry on the same tracks that he now rode.

The men of this unit would prove to be no garrison soldiers, but rather instead a workhorse regiment that would see action in such fiercely contested engagements as Gettysburg and Spotsylvania Court House. Yet, through all the hellacious combat they experienced, the soldiers of the 121st remained devoted Lincoln men. An example of one soldier's unshakeable faith in his commander in chief was revealed in a letter from Private George Collins who hailed from Russia, New York, to a cousin Emma Earle of Clinton, New York: "I think you wish that the war will end before Old Abes [sic] time is out will be gratified, for since it was decided that soldiers can vote I have an idea his time will not be out until the 4th of March 1869."[5]

With the train picking up speed as it passed through the lowlands along the river east of the town, an observant traveler would have noticed a narrowing of the valley. By the time the train gone the six miles to Little Falls, the valley walls were at one of their closest points along the entire corridor. Here in post-glacial times, a huge cataract rivaling that at Niagara, cascaded in a thunderous drop of several hundred feet. Over thousands of years, the swiftly flowing waters of the Mohawk River wore the bedrock away. By the arrival of the first settlers to the area in the early 1700s, the great falls had been seriously reduced by erosion. The once impressive plummet had been whittled down to a more graduated forty-five-foot drop. Ultimately, it was this diminished appearance that inspired the naming of the town. Yet the narrowed gorge and remaining change in elevation still held promise for future, since the rapids and falls that remained meant water power that could be harnessed for industrial purposes. By 1860, numerous mills had sprung up along the Mohawk's banks to take advantage of this perpetual force of nature.

Approaching the village from the west, Lincoln would have seen another of the interesting man-made adaptations to the constriction of the valley. This was a stone aqueduct built to transfer the Erie Canal across the river. In effect, aqueducts such as these served as bridges to get the artificial waterway over a naturally occurring one. Eighteen such structures existed along the Erie's 363-mile route. Aside from the fact that these aqueducts had to be perfectly level, the engineering techniques used to construct them were highly reminiscent of those applied by Romans centuries earlier in erecting conduits like France's famous Pont du Gard. Considering that neither the Roman Empire nor New York State had trained engineers, these stone constructions clearly classified as marvels of their respective times.

Given that that canal froze over in the winter, the Lincolns might have detected movement on the aqueduct that snowy February day. For, with its walls serving as a windbreak, the icy ribbon provided an excellent surface for skating. It was said that an ambitious person could actually skate from Albany to Buffalo on the canal. However, as enjoyable as that past-time might have been, the chance to see the president-elect would in all likelihood have caused a cessation in the sporting activity, temporarily eschewing a daily opportunity for a once-in-a-lifetime experience.

As the train had pulled into the Little Falls station at twelve-ten amidst this picturesque setting, yet another immense crowd awaited Mr. Lincoln's arrival. Accentuating the good vibrations emitted by the excited throng, the alternating sounds of booming cannon and pealing church bells served ample notice that this was indeed a special occasion. Adding to the celebratory mood, a brass band offered appropriate selections to further enliven the atmosphere. One number, "Hail, Columbia," inspired several hundred ladies gathered on the piazza of the hotel to "wave their handkerchiefs in unison, and the crowd hurrahed and cheered with lusty vigor."[6] While organizers pleaded with him to mount a specially constructed stage, he declined, as much in the interests of time as the fact that it would take him longer to detrain, climb upon the platform, and get back than he intended to speak. When the moment arrived for Mr. Lincoln's remarks, he was introduced to the assembled mass by the Hon. Seth Richmond, president of the Village of Little Falls.

By now, the future president had perfected a brief homily, one that he had begun to deliver on earlier stops. As far as he was concerned, this was not a political rally, but simply an opportunity for both parties—the leader and the led—to meet. The substance of what he uttered was nowhere near as important as was the peoples' chance to see him in the flesh and hear his voice, both of which for virtually everyone in the audience amounted to a truly singular experience:

> Ladies and Gentlemen: I appear here before you, solely for the purpose of greeting you, saying a few words, and then bidding you farewell. I can only say, as I have often said before, that I have no speech to make and no time to make one if had. Neither have I the strength to repeat a speech at all of the places at which I stop, even though other circumstances were favorable. I am thankful for this opportunity to see you, and of allowing you to see me. [*Applause.*] And in this, so far as regard the ladies, I think I have the best of the bargain. [*Laughter.*] I don't make that acknowledgement, however, to the gentlemen. [*Increased Laughter.*] And now I believe I have really made my speech and am ready to bid you farewell when the train moves off.[7]

Upon completing his remarks, Lincoln was rewarded with a prolonged round of robust applause. In a highly favorable reflection on the scene that he had just witnessed, a reporter for the *Little Falls Journal & Courier* effusively wrote that "those who saw the smile upon his countenance wondered that his face could be called homely, and all who heard his manly voice felt intuitively that it was the voice of an honest man."[8]

Another imbedded correspondent provided his equally optimistic impression of what transpired when he shared with Albany readers the following account: "At Little Falls took place what was pronounced the prettiest brief reception that President Lincoln has received since he left Springfield, and that pleasantly attested that the go ahead citizens of Little Falls were ready and prompt to do all they could in five minutes to attest to their loyalty to the President-elect, their love of the man, and undying zeal on behalf of the institution he is called by the voice of the people to protect and defend."[9]

Once the locomotive had pulled its distinguished passengers out of town, the valley began to open again. Here choice bottomland was readily available for farming, while the gentle slopes offered several upland plateaus which made suitable sites for further cultivation possible. While the covering of winter snow gave no hint of the rich soil that lay beneath its frozen crystals, the reality was that some of the most fertile land in all of New York State was visible from the windows of the Lincoln Special.

A half-dozen miles east of Little Falls, the train passed first through the village of St. Johnsville. With a population approaching a thousand residents, its basis for existence and prosperity was like that of many valley towns: available water power to operate mills. However, the town's biggest claim-to-fame was its railroad restaurant, one that had made the locale a popular stop for hungry passengers.

Next up for the eastbound travelers was Palatine Bridge, where a span across the river and the heritage of its first inhabitants combined to give the village its name. Even though no stop was scheduled, well-wishers and curiosity seekers alike nevertheless turned out, not only on the oft-chance of catching site of the president but also seeing an inaugural train, which represented its own novelty. Consisting of an engine, tender, and baggage, passenger, and sleeping cars, the express was a modest in length but one that still did "full justice to the superb rolling stock of the New York Central."[10] The rear car was especially worthy of scrutiny due to its uniqueness for the times, as it was a dedicated sleeping space for the Lincolns. In one of those rich twists of fate that history sometimes fashions, one of the occupants of this new-fangled notion of a railroad car—twenty-two-year-old Robert Lincoln—would eventually gain considerable wealth and prestige as the president of the Pullman Company of Chicago, a thriving business that specialized in the manufacture of railroad sleeping cars.

As the train passed Canajoharie and then Fonda, it approached an isolated whistle-stop known as Yosts. Members of the presidential party looking out of a coach window would have noted that the valley was beginning to narrow again. Observers would also have seen that there was much less tillable soil along the river banks than had previously been the case. In fact, it appeared that up ahead there was barely enough level land to squeeze the tracks between the river and the bluff that reached down from the looming heights above toward the water's edge. Furthermore, this phenomenon appeared to exist on both sides of the Mohawk River, causing the Erie Canal along the opposite shore to deal with the same tight fit confronting the railroad.

What the travelers were experiencing was a ride "through the noses." At a bend in the river, large outcroppings of rock—Big Nose and Little Nose—came down to the river's edge on opposite sides. At one time, the two geological formations had been connected, but, over thousands of years, water had eroded a passageway. From a distance, they easily presented the appearance of two high, wooded hills that were rounded in such a way as to conjure up a vision of two facing human noses. The larger of the two proboscis approached one thousand feet in height, while the lesser of the pairing topped off at a little over four hundred, making the contrast between them sharp and distinctive. Many travelers had long rated this stretch of the Mohawk Valley as one of its most beautiful vistas. Had someone pointed these landmarks out to Mr. Lincoln, the president's well-known funny bone might easily have been tickled by these striking creations of nature so colorfully named.

With the late winter's storm still raging, the express plowed on through the swirling snow until reaching Fonda, thirty miles east of Utica and not quite halfway to Albany. Along the tracks and across the station platform, it appeared to one observer as if "Fonda had turned out en masse to welcome the President."[11] Though the schedule did not call for a stop, another of the ubiquitous platforms had been constructed in the hopes of enticing Mr. Lincoln into stopping for a few impromptu words. Much to their surprise and elation, the train did coast to halt before them. However, the president-elect once more forsook the makeshift speaker's stand, telling the crowd that "though he would not get upon it, he wished it to be distinctly understood that he would never shrink from a platform on which he properly belonged."[12] He opted instead for the sake of expediency and informality to use the back of the car in which he had been riding. Here again, he continued his practice of making a light-hearted talk, the substance of which *The New York Times* pointed out contained "no allusion in any of them to national topics."[13]

After his short oration, the train began to move, sent off to a crescendo of approving cheers and applause. Even though these abbreviated chats served Lincoln's purposes, not everyone felt that he was using the national spotlight to its full advantage. Among those who were disappointed in the president-elect's lack of substance in his whistle-stop forums was Frederick Douglas, who wrote in his publication the *Douglass' Monthly*: "His speeches along the route are all the same purport ... [and] his short speech here [Rochester] did not touch on the great question of the day."[14] Yet for all the critics and naysayers, Lincoln knew exactly what he was doing. As explained by his good friend and protector Ward Hill Lamon, though "the people everywhere were eager to hear a forecast of his policy ... he was as determined to keep silence on the subject until it was made manifest in his Inaugural Address."[15]

In addition to the opportunity afforded the incoming president to connect with another segment of his enormous constituency, the short interlude presented a moment for an important dispatch to be dashed off to Albany's mayor George Thacher. Thanks to the then modern-miracle of the telegraph, his honor was duly informed that local authorities would be expected to "please provide two carriages for the Legislative Committee, four carriages for Mr. Lincoln and suite, and let them move in this order—other carriages following."[16] So much for advance planning ... the Lincoln Special was due to arrive in Albany in approximately ninety minutes, and arrangements were just now being made to provide needed transportation. Whether this late request was an afterthought or an oversight, this demand at the eleventh hour does offer telling insight into general lack of concerted collaboration on the part of those engaged in making administrative arrangements for the president's movements.

Contrasting with the clockwork precision and painstaking detail with which railroad executives approached their responsibilities in transporting and protecting the Lincoln entourage, the civil authorities' efforts came in a poor second. Certainly, in terms of distance, the Lincolns could not have walked from their disembarkation point to the Capitol, particularly since the second half of the promenade would have been seriously uphill. Furthermore, the tight schedule of planned appearances would have been severely thrown off had the Lincolns traveled by foot to their first engagement.

Unspoken, but not out of mind, was the overaccessibility that the president as a pedestrian not only offered to the excited crowds, but also to those who might want to do him harm. The carriage arrangements at Albany, even if made at the last minute, afforded much-needed convenience and protection.

The last two stops before reaching the state capital were Amsterdam and Schenectady, approximately eighteen miles apart and respectively thirty-five and seventeen miles northwest of Albany. Amsterdam, a community which by its name evoked the Dutch heritage of the capital region, represented another center of the flourishing industrial might contributing to New York's status as the Empire State. Like so many other villages along the valley's lowlands, power created by tributaries flowing off the highlands and into the Mohawk River provided the impetus for the establishment of mills and later factories. On the eve of the Civil War, Amsterdam's population had reached 2000 souls. The special stimulus fueling growth was the founding of the carpet industry. Arriving at 1:10 p.m., Lincoln first treated the waiting spectators to yet another rendition of his by now well-honed little talk and then saluted them in parting with his polite bows from the back platform of the last coach.

* * *

With the eyes of New Yorkers riveted on the progress of their future leader as he headed toward their capital, in the southern part of the country the focus was not on Abraham Lincoln's journey, but rather on the similar sojourn of another future president: Mississippi's Jefferson Davis. In a striking parallel to his northern counterpart, Davis too was traveling by rail from his home to a national capital. Also like Lincoln, his passage by train was used as an opportunity to appear before his constituents along the way. Toward this end, "he made twenty-five speeches on the route, returning thanks and complimentary greetings to the ladies and gentlemen and military at the various depots."[17] But in the eyes of many Northerners, the similarities ended there. The editor of *The Evening Post* in New York City pulled no punches in pointing out to his readers what he perceived as the most significant and telling difference: "Mr. Lincoln is the constitutionally elected President of twenty-five millions of free people, and represents not only the principle of order in general, but the noblest constitution of government that ever the wisdom of man devised. Mr. Davis, on the other hand, is the chosen officer of a packed convention of disaffected traitors and schemers who can allege nothing against the government from which they revolt and whose leading motives are a restless ambition and malignant prejudices against their fellow man."[18] Undoubtedly the paper had numerous readers who concurred with the editor's conclusion that "the conduct of these seceding states is, then, one of treason, folly, and infamy, and overshadows, by its enormity of crime, any other similar act recorded in the annals of time."[19]

As the crow flies, the distance from Vicksburg, Mississippi, to Montgomery, Alabama, is about 290 miles, but, after a week of roundabout travel, Davis arrived in Montgomery at 10:00 pm on February 17—having logged over 800 grueling miles north from Mississippi to western Tennessee, east across the Volunteer State, and then south into Georgia before turning southwest into Alabama. Despite the late hour, a substantial crowd was at the Montgomery station to greet him and hear the bellicose words that he spoke. In his brief but passionate speech, Davis "said that time for compromise is past, and we are now determined to maintain our position and make all who oppose us smell Southern powder and feel Southern steel."[20] Forty-five minutes later in response to calls from yet another enthusiastic crowd, Davis addressed aroused supporters from the balcony of Montgomery's Exchange Hotel: "we have nothing to fear at home, because at home we have homogeneity; we will have nothing to fear abroad, for if war should come, if we must baptize in blood the principles for which our forefathers bled in the Revolution."[21]

Compared to the insipid, non-committal utterances which Lincoln proffered at his stops, Davis delivered the equivalent of fiery stem-winders. The reason that Davis had traveled to Montgomery—with this city at the time serving the dual role as the designated capital not only of a sovereign state but also the newly constituted Confederate States of America—was to be sworn as the president of that same recently created country. On February 18, thirteen hundred miles away from where Lincoln was traveling via a train in New York, Jefferson Davis was riding in a carriage pulled by six white horses in Alabama. His destination was the statehouse, where he would soon be inaugurated. At precisely one o'clock, he was destined to take the oath as the provisional president of the fledgling Confederate States of America.

Shortly thereafter, just as Abraham Lincoln was giving one of his folksy homilies in Amsterdam, President Davis was delivering his impassioned inaugural address in Montgomery. Consistent with the speeches which he made in the days leading up to this important occasion, Davis concluded with more of the same oppositional rhetoric that epitomized his philosophy in the spring of 1861: "If a just perception of mutual interest shall permit us peaceably to pursue our separate political career, my most earnest desire will have been fulfilled, But if this is denied us, and the integrity of our territory and jurisdiction be assailed, it will but remain for us with firm resolve to appeal to arms, and invoke the blessing of Providence on a just cause."[22]

* * *

As routine as the Amsterdam stop was for Lincoln, his visit to Schenectady proved different, hallmarked as it was by fireworks both in the air and in print. The first blast occurred as the train approached the station, when a ceremonial cannon was recklessly discharged near the second coach, the one following the baggage car. Worse still, not only was the artillery piece too close to the train, but it was aimed directly at the tracks. While no shell was fired, significant concussive pressure was produced. The air burst hit the coach with frightening, though not fatal results. One of its doors was blown from its hinges, the lock broken, and three windows shattered. Those riders positioned nearby were showered with broken glass; however, other than being startled by the unexpected event, no one was seriously injured.

But for all of hullabaloo that preceded his appearance, Lincoln eventually stood before the assembled mass without a hint of discomfort or displeasure. As had come to be his proclivity, he declined what had now become the almost expected pro-offering of a stage. Introduced by a local dignitary—the Hon. Platt Potter, who at the time was a justice on the bench of the state supreme court—Lincoln gave what had become his patented message all along his route. Unfortunately, for those who wanted to hear what he had to say, the loud and boisterous crowd drowned out much of his discourse.

At this stop, as had been the president-elect's experience at others along the line, Henry Villard observed that "impertinent individuals addressed Mr. Lincoln in a very familiar manner and offered to back him against the world."[23] In return, "he very good-naturedly submitted to the courtesies of the crowd."[24] The likelihood here is that the breezy, amusing nature of the president's remarks may have encouraged the crowd to be more demonstrative, not out of any intended measure of disrespect, but rather in reaction to his informality with them.

The New York Times viewed the president's reception in Schenectady as especially gratifying, noting that "a larger and more good-humored crowd than the one which was there convened, we have rarely seen away from the large cities."[25] Upon the conclusion of his commentary, the train departed. Lincoln remained on the back platform, bowing once more to the waves and cheers until the well-wishers faded into the distance. In a curious decision, while the engine was switched—with the *Erastus C. Corning*, named for the founder of the railroad taking over the duty of hauling the Lincoln Special—the damaged passenger car, now most likely devoid of riders given the freezing temperature, remained in its place.

With one explosion having greeted Lincoln's arrival, the second detonation came in the pages of the local press the next day. *The Schenectady Daily News* was especially vituperative in assessing the president-elect's visit, dissing what "seems to be a strained effort at ostentation, gaudy display, and pageantry—a sort of royal progress in the movement of

A string of simple wooden buildings, ending in a covered waiting platform, served as the Schenectady depot that greeted the Lincoln Special on its way to Albany in February 1861 (courtesy Schenectady County Historical Society).

Mr. Lincoln to the national capital."[26] The paper, whose editors were clearly not backers of the president-elect, had previously spoken out against the existence of a "special train, a civic and military staff, heraldic announcements, obsequious puffs and holiday displays, and above all, a flood of flattering speech making."[27] In the days leading up to Lincoln's visit, the periodical's brain trust had engaged in a tongue-in-cheek, but still acerbic, campaign built around the suggestion that reception committee try to procure a fence rail. But not just any piece of hewn wood would do; no, the paper's suggestion was for the committeemen to obtain a rail from Illinois, a Lincoln—or "Honest Old Abe" as the president was irreverently referenced—original if you will. The point was to see if the renowned rail-splitter could identify his handiwork. "No doubt," the paper irreverently speculated, "the presentation would call up pleasant recollections of early days, and H.O.A. might indulge in telling a good story instead of making a speech."[28] It should come as no surprise that this publication had supported Stephan Douglas for president.

At 1:55 p.m., the time had come to leave. In hindsight, the greeting at Schenectady with its errant cannon blast may have served as a harbinger of the difference in receptions that Lincoln might henceforth anticipate receiving. In moving from the friendly prairies of the Midwest through the supporting plains of western New York, he had been traveling through lands filled with people whose roots were rural and their thinking akin to his.

Schenectady, however, was the gateway to an urban corridor stretching three hundred sixty-four miles from Albany to Washington and encompassing a string of the largest cities in the country, places whose urban inhabitants marched to different drums than their countrymen in more rustic settings. Unlike the places he had visited prior to Schenectady, the upcoming stops would present far-greater political challenges. To skeptics living there, he was not one of them. His rural roots held no sway among these urbanites. The proof of his competency could only come in the performance. In dealing with these individuals, tact and diplomacy would now become his greatest assets. Patience, tolerance, kindness, and humor his most useful traits. Over time, there would be a multitude of converts. Many doubters would eventually become supporters. But for the present, to open this new phase of his tour, president-elect Lincoln was headed for the capital of New York State, where its contentious intra-governmental squabbles and pro–Democratic base awaited him.

6

Arrival in Albany
Political Considerations Rule the Day

Next on the itinerary was the busy capital of the Empire State and the sovereignty's fourth largest city. Albany had begun humbly, first as a small trading outpost in 1617 called Fort Nassau and then expanded to a larger facility in 1624 christened Fort Orange. As growth continued, its name became Beverwyck. This appellation reflected not only the town's Dutch heritage, but also its primary source of its wealth via the fur trade, conducted with indigenous tribes living to the west.

When the British took control in 1664, name changes followed. New Netherlands became New York, while New Amsterdam was reconstituted as New York City and Beverwyck as Albany. By Lincoln's arrival almost two hundred years later, the state for the most part had been culturally Anglicized. Yet the Dutch imprint left upon the vicinity of Albany and the Hudson Valley was still in evidence. In place-names like Watervliet and Kinderhook, cozy homes with stair-stepped gables and tulip gardens, and family lineages like Van Buren and Ten Eyck, the heritage of the region's first European settlers remained indelibly etched.

While the raging storm subjected the president to some uncomfortable moments when he had to leave his warm coach, brave the wintry elements, and address the chilled but energized masses gathered before him, the weather awaiting him in Albany actually represented an improvement over the meteorological conditions in the vicinity of the capital earlier in the week. Only five days before Lincoln's arrival, a spring thaw wrought havoc amongst the wharves, streets, shops, and warehouses of lower Albany where the quay and nearby streets abutted the Hudson River. "In fact," reports confirmed, "there was scarcely a building east of Broadway but was inundated, and there were very many on that line of streets in the same condition."[1]

Even west of Broadway—which was a main north-south thoroughfare traversing Albany between its river boundary on the east and the uplands to the west, many businesses and residences did not escape the flooding. In many cases, the damage amounted to several feet of water in basements. "Our streets in the lower sections of the city," observed a local reporter, "are filled with flour, provisions, cotton, and other articles."[2] The destruction was attributable to forces of nature—ice and water being the villains delivering a costly one-two punch. According to reports, "steamers, barges, and canal boats were driven on the docks and into the streets by the immense bodies of ice."[3] Several bridges over the river suffered damage to the extent of being completely destroyed, partially wrecked, or at least structurally compromised. Stores and piers along the waterfront were stove in by the huge blocks of ice. Equipment, buildings, and boats of all shapes and sizes were borne downriver by floodwaters.

At eight o'clock in the morning of February 13, the ice sheet opposite the city broke up with a thunderous crash, precipitating a rapid buildup of flood waters in the streets along the river's banks. "Within twenty minutes after the start," it was observed that "the water rose four feet, and it has been rising ever since, until at present the rise is about seven to eight feet."[4] An ice dam in the river below the city proved the cause of the local flooding. With respect to the New York Central's properties, "a heavy towboat and other boats were driven through the first story of the frame freight depot of the Central Road, the whole front being knocked out, and the building, which is very large and two stories high, is much damaged."[5] As for the main station, "the Central Railroad passenger depot could not be reached by means of trains."[6] However, given the import of the dignitary about to arrive, any impairments to tracks, ties, ballast, or switches were causes for concern. The upshot was that the normal connection between Albany and East Albany, between the New York Central terminating on the Hudson's western shore and the Hudson River Railroad heading south on the eastern side to New York City, was temporarily interrupted.

This situation existed because "at that time there was no railroad bridge crossing the Hudson River at Albany, so the usual mode of interconnecting travel was for passengers to disembark from western trains at the depot in lower Albany and cross the waterway by ferry to the town of East Albany."[7] There they climbed aboard a southbound train belonging to the Hudson River Railroad "following the lordly stream down to the metropolis."[8] In the wake of the flooding, horse-drawn carriages were pressed into service, hauling passengers northeast eight miles to Troy on the opposite bank of the river. Since in 1865 the Hudson River Railroad terminated at East Albany, the short trek from Troy to East Albany was made via the tracks of the Troy & Greenbush line, with the right-of-way leased by the larger carrier for the sake of convenience to its passengers. This allowed travelers to continue their trip to New York City with one less train change.

Five days later, when the time came for the Lincolns to leave Albany, these same natural obstructions still presented a problem. As a result, a makeshift means was contrived to get the president's entourage across the river, one that would utilize the tracks of several regional railroads.

But by the afternoon of Friday, February 15, the natural disasters of the previous Monday had mostly abated, though the cleanup and repairs would take weeks to complete. Serving to deflect the peoples' attention from their troubles and lift their spirits was the impending arrival of Abraham Lincoln. Amidst a building national crisis, local flooding paled in importance, making expectations for what the new chief executive might say were eagerly awaited. Finally, at 2:20 p.m., twenty-one booming cannon blasts sounded—from artillery posted on the heights above the city—announcing the approach of the presidential express. The manner in which the arrival of the train was proclaimed and the corresponding signal to fire were triggered by a novel method. "As the train passed the West Albany shops, an electrical switch was turned off at the nearby Dudley Observatory, causing an electromagnet mounted on the roof of the capitol in downtown Albany to release a metal ball that slid down a pole," signaling military officials to begin firing their artillery in Capitol Park.[9] With a precision that could easily have coaxed a satisfied smile across the wizened face of the train's engineer—one William Freeman—the Lincoln Special rolled to a stop in downtown Albany at 2:30 p.m.—right on schedule despite the wintry mix in the air, moisture slickened rails, and the unplanned stops along the way.

With the locomotive patriotically adorned with flapping flags and colorful trailing streamers, the already eye-catching appearance of the gleaming engine, *Erastus Corning, Jr.*, was further enhanced by these decorative flourishes. Adding additional color to the scene were three large flags suspended across Broadway at the spot where the street intersected the tracks. Combined with the excited shouts of the animated crowd, a holiday atmosphere existed in anticipation of the Mr. Lincoln's emergence from his coach.

Once again, he would be greeted with another of the inevitable speaker's platforms, this one downtown where Broadway was traversed by the railroad. The presidential party disembarked at this point—which the *New York Herald* labeled the "extempore depot"—because the Central's main station was located in the most severely flood-damaged part of town to the south.[10] There an animated crowd stood ready.

Oddly, for a local constituency that was heavily Democratic in its political persuasion and had overwhelmingly cast its ballots for a candidate other than Lincoln—he had lost Albany County by 1500 popular votes—the exhilaration generated in anticipation of seeing and hearing the victorious Republican candidate was palpable.[11] Though the site for the welcoming amenities was of necessity altered, the reception was nevertheless as warm as its predecessors had been all across the state that day. One veteran denizen of the Albany area commented that "the city has seldom presented such a scene of excitement and enthusiasm as it has today."[12]

In fact, the crowd was so charged that the decision was made to temporarily hold off on any attempt by the president to address it, waiting until a proper security cordon was established. Unfortunately, a delay in the arrival of a military guard only provided additional time for the well-wishers to become even more boisterous. They began clamoring for Lincoln to appear. Eyewitnesses reported that "the crowd vented their impatience in cries of 'Come out on the platform,' 'Show us the Rail-splitter,' 'Trot out Old Abe,' and similar requests'!"[13] But Lincoln prudently remained sequestered.

Eventually, a contingent of 100 policemen arrived, intent upon providing protection for the president. While the crowd was more excited than a riotous, they nonetheless exhibited an irresistible surge toward the train which the lawmen strained mightily to contain. But their resistance was an exercise in futility. A battle of wills ensued, as "little boys and big men climbed under and over the train, only to be kicked and thrown back."[14] Individual policemen battled with some of the more aggressive members of the crowd. The group donnybrook visible from inside the coach certainly made its inhabitants all the more leery about leaving the safety of its confines. For the populace of a more culturally refined eastern city to behave in such an undisciplined, rowdy manner may have caused the Lincolns to wonder just exactly how far from the frontier they had traveled.

Along with the growing impatience of the spectators, another adverse effect of the delay was the extended opportunity to work the tightly packed throng afforded pickpockets. As the *Troy Daily Times* reported, "these infamous scoundrels, who always follow in the wake of every public personage, are unusually thick in the path of Mr. Lincoln."[15] Like a swarm of mosquitoes, these criminals hovered in and about the large crowds, preying on a distracted public and tarnishing for many what had otherwise been a memorable day. Numerous unsuspecting people, already being jostled about by the active crowd, rarely took heed of one more bump, let alone a stranger's hand slipping into their pockets and purses.

An example of one who experienced this random victimization was a James Ketchum, an elderly gentleman from White Plains. While he would remember the day that he saw Abraham Lincoln, he would also never forget having had his wallet pilfered.

Amid the confusion, Albany's mayor, George Hornell Thacher gamely braved the crowd. Just elected to his first two-year term in 1860—the Albany businessman would go on to serve four terms, unusual in that three were non-consecutive—he was not yet the most familiar of faces to the general public. Even if some recognized the persistent man trying to force his way to the train, the eminence of his office did him no good, as he was buffeted about by the lively multitude with the same indignity tendered any other citizen. For Thacher, bittersweet irony existed in his coming to Lincoln's aid, for in the campaign of 1860 the Albany mayor had been a Douglas Democrat. However, the obligations of his office necessitated that he welcome guests to his city, regardless of political differences. Eventually he fought his way to Lincoln's besieged coach. Gaining the steps of the rear platform, he parlayed with Superintendent Wood, suggesting that perhaps they should get on with the proceedings. But, in the face of the disquieting scene, Wood demurred. Better off waiting for the military to impose order.

Finally, reinforcements materialized in the form of Company B, 25th New York Militia, led Colonel Michael K. Bryan. With a band, a barouche, and several carriages in tow, the troops arrived over thirty minutes late. Two months later, these men, reconstituted and mustered into federal service as the 25th New York Volunteer Infantry, would again come to the president's aid, answering his first call for troops in the wake of Fort Sumter's fall.

Though they had expected to function merely as an honor guard, upon reaching the chaotic scene their duty quickly shifted to a far more earnest purpose: restoring order and security so that the president could emerge and stand safely before the assembled mass. From inside the last car, imbedded reporter Henry Villard watched as this force weighed into the crowd with gusto and, by using "clubbed muskets, soon cleared a way to the carriages and made a space upon the platform large enough [for the president] to stand up."[16]

Unlike Utica, where the staging was constructed upon a flatcar, the speaker's platform in Albany was on the ground between the rails at the Broadway crossing. By the time it was needed, the stage's surface was covered with mud, snow, and water, making the wet wood slick and somewhat hazardous. Since by being at ground level, the president would be more directly accessible to bold spectators, establishing a protective cordon was an extremely important task.

With the immediate area secured, President Lincoln made his long-awaited appearance. Though initially greeted with cheers and applause, many onlookers quickly became confused and then quieted appreciably, momentarily uncertain as to whose countenance they were now viewing. As the scene was described, "Lincoln, tired, sunburned, adorned with huge whiskers, looked so unlike the hale, smooth-shaven, red-cheeked individual who is represented upon the popular prints and dubbed the 'rail-splitter' that it is no wonder that the people did not recognize him until his extreme height distinguished him unmistakably."[17]

In what was surely one of the high points in his public life, Mayor Thacher stepped forward to welcome and introduce the honored guest to their common constituents:

> Mr. Lincoln—On behalf of the Common Council and the citizens of Albany, I have the honor to tender you a cordial welcome to the city. We trust you will accept the welcome we offer, not simply as a tribute

of respect to the high office you are called to fill, but as attribute of the good will of our citizens without distinction of party, and also an expression of their appreciation of your eminent personal worth and confidence in your patriotism. We are aware that your previous arrangements with the state authorities and the brevity of your stay will compel us to forego the pleasure of extending to you on the part of the city other and more befitting hospitalities, but we are happy to know that His Excellency, the governor and the senators and representatives in the legislature are about to receive you as the government of the Empire State and in so doing, they will represent the kind regards of the whole people, as well as the citizens of the capital. Permit me, therefore, to greet you in this union of the citizens and repeat the assurance of a most cordial welcome.[18]

Following the mayor's gracious introduction, the spotlight shifted to Mr. Lincoln. He appeared pale and worn. After having been on the road for eight days, the strain on his constitution was beginning to show. Still, he had to speak to these people, many of whom had been waiting hours:

I can hardly appropriate to myself the flattering terms to which you communicate the tender of this reception as personal to myself. I must gratefully accept the hospitality tendered to me, and I will not detain you or the audience with any extended remarks at this time. I presume that in the two or three courses through which I will have to go, I shall have to repeat somewhat, and I will therefore only repeat to you my thanks for this kind reception.[19]

Eighty-four words were all that he uttered. Certainly, he was capable of saying much with measured brevity, as the Gettysburg Address would so eloquently prove. But compared to the similarly short talks that he had been delivering along his inbound route, his introductory speech to the people of Albany was quite perfunctory, devoid even of any folksy observations or droll commentary with which he had entertained previous audiences. Perhaps his weariness was showing. Maybe he was saving his depleted strength for a more important oration which he was scheduled to make later that day before the state legislature. Regardless of the reasons, it was an underwhelming effort.

After Lincoln's remarks, the rest of the presidential party descended from the train, traversed a pathway through the crowd held open by the soldiers and policemen, and climbed aboard the carriages placed at their disposal. Participating in the abbreviated parade were the president and his family, the mayor, a legislative committee, and the Citizens' Committee. Also joining them for the short hop of about a mile to the Capitol was the Hon. L. Chandler Ball, who earned the spot in recognition of his work earned as chairman of the House Arrangements Committee. Mr. Lincoln rode in the open barouche, pulled by four bay-colored horses. Accompanying him was Mayor Thacher, State Senator William Ferry, and Assemblyman Ball. Luckily for the president, the parade moved at a leisurely pace, for he spent much of the ride standing and alternatively bowing left and right.

For reasons that suited him, the folksy, unassuming president-elect consistently offered the formal bending gesture to the crowd instead of casual waves. Following behind their bobbing leader, the remainder of Lincoln's retinue and local dignitaries followed in five elegant barouches. The procession—led by the 25th Infantry's regimental band and accompanied by the contingent of formidable-looking soldiers making a splendid appearance in their new overcoats—headed south along Broadway for nine blocks before turning right onto State Street. Among the airs offered by the band was the always-stirring "Hail to the Chief."[20]

The objective of this nineteenth century version of future motorcades was the state Capitol, located on a lofty perch at the head of State Street. As befitted the approach to the

6. Arrival in Albany 71

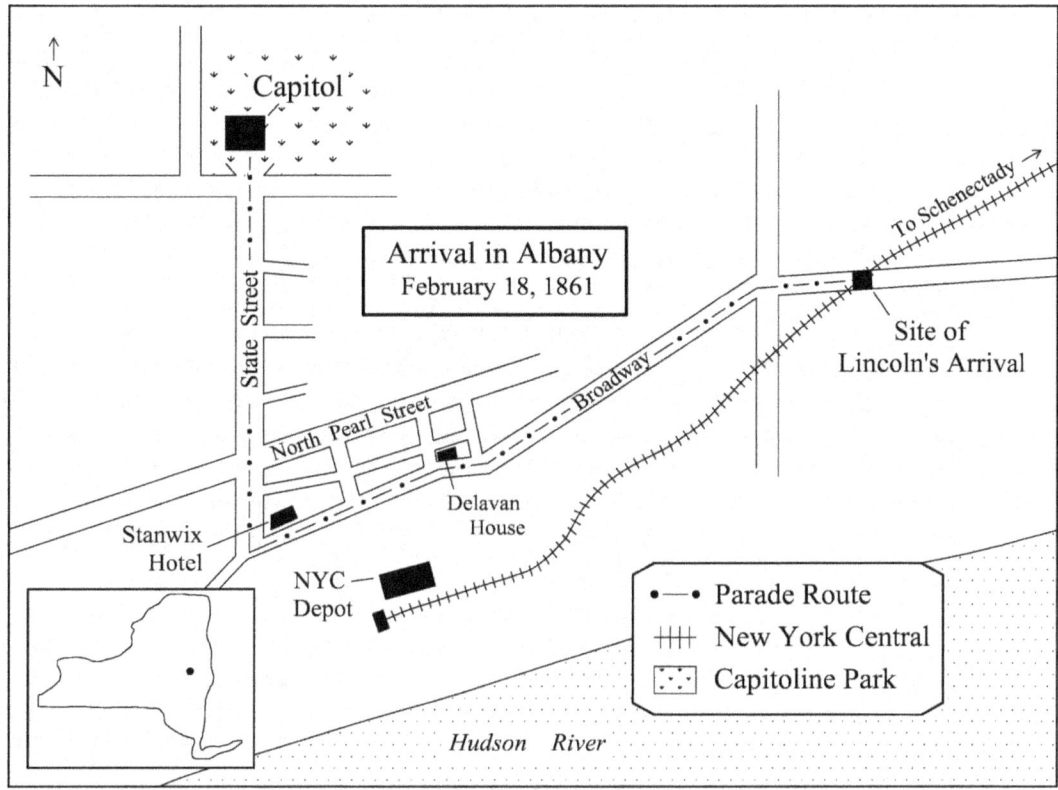

Drawn by Bob Collea.

Capitol, this thoroughfare was an especially broad avenue. Starting out fairly level, the roadway quickly rose in a steep ascent, which served to accentuate the prominence and majesty of the Capitol seated in a park near the crest of the incline.

Along the route, spectators packed both sides of the street, while additional onlookers peered from second story windows, lined rooftops, stood on balconies, sat on wagons, and even perched in trees. "Many residents displayed a profusion of flags," the press reported, "and across Broadway was hung a strip of canvas, bearing the inscription: 'Welcome to the capital of the Empire State. No more compromises.'"[21] All public buildings and hotels displayed American flags. Another banner, suspended from the windows of the Young Men's Association around the corner on State Street proclaimed: "We will pray for you—defender of the Constitution."[22]

For Abraham Lincoln, this supportive outpouring had to have been an especially gratifying and humbling experience. He had every reason to be impressed, for in the almost 250-year history of the city such an public expression of interest and excitement had been rarely witnessed. The uniqueness of this phenomenon was confirmed by the editor of the *Cohoes Cataract,* who commented that Lincoln's visit to Albany "was sufficient to call together one of the largest gatherings that ever assembled at the Capital to greet a public man. They came from all sections and classes, without distinction of party."[23]

As if Albany could not draw enough spectators from its own populace, residents from outlying areas also arrived. Citizens residing north of the city were assisted by the Albany

Division of the Rensselaer and Saratoga Railroad, which ran an extra train at seven o'clock that evening between the capital city and West Troy, "for the accommodation of those who desire to remain until after the departure of the last regular train to get a good look at the President."[24] The steady influx of people "caused the city to be thronged at an early part of the day, each railroad train ran double to quadruple its usual number of passengers, while vehicles from the surrounding country, swarmed into the city by every street."[25] Even the forbidding weather did not act as a deterrent, for "dull, gloomy, and somber as the morning was, ladies and men planted themselves in the mud along the streets, and waited there patiently for hours."[26]

In addition to the people lining route along Broadway and State Street, a large contingent trailed behind the carriages, all the way up the substantial State Street incline to Capitoline Park. Fortunately, no incidents occurred along the way to impede the cortege's progress or cast a negative pallor over what had been an exhilarating experience for everyone. One newspaper estimated that "twice the number were in the streets and windows as on the occasion of the welcome of the Prince of Wales."[27] The prince's visit and tour of America, which occurred the previous fall, were frequently used as a yardstick against which turnouts for Lincoln were compared.

Adoniram Judson Blakely, an Albany Law student, shared with his father an impression of what he had witnessed: "I have just come in from the throng of the thousands who had been greeting the arrival of Pres. Lincoln. I should judge that the crowd was quite large as that which was present on the visit of the prince [of Wales]. The streets and all the steps and windows of the buildings for more than a mile were densely crowded. And as for getting inside or within twenty rods of the Capitol building it was impossible after the throng had stationed themselves."[28]

"Here was gathered a vast assemblage, numbering at least ten thousand," estimated one observer, "all crowding forward toward the capitol steps, until the whole became a dense mass of human beings, from the midst of which it was hardly possible to extricate one's self."[29]

Henry Villard, traveling with the Lincoln party, made the same observation as young Blakely, commenting that "the Capitoline Park was crammed with people. The soldiery with some difficulty formed a line through the crowd, and Mr. Lincoln passed up the capitol steps the national salute being fired as he entered the building."[30] So tightly packed and unyielding was the sea of humanity at this location that "most of the governor's staff were unable to enter the building and the Veterans of 1812 and the Society of Cincinnatus, which had been invited to meet the President, were crowded out of sight."[31]

The edifice into which the president-elect was passing, now referenced as the "old Capitol building" in deference to a more lavish and ornate facility that opened 1887, had functioned as the focal point for New York State's governmental activities since 1809. For the first eight years, the facility did triple duty, serving as the hub of not only the state government but also county and local operations. Two-stories and rectangular-shaped, the structure featured a cupola crowned with a statue. Lincoln's approach was toward its east face, the one which looked down State Street to the Hudson River. The building was fashioned of stone, measuring one-hundred-and-fifteen feet in length and ninety feet in width.

After climbing seven long stairs that ran the across the middle third of the building, passing four thirty-foot tall marble pillars each surmounted with 3000-pound ornate capitals, and walking beneath the triangular pediment which the columns supported, the president entered the statehouse. Edwin Morgan was there to greet him. Shaking hands, the governor and his guest exchanged pleasantries: "I am glad to take you by the hand," to which Mr. Lincoln responded "And I am very glad to meet you, Governor."[32] The state's chief executive then solicitously inquired: "How have you withstood the fatigue of the journey?"[33] To which the president-elect replied: "Well, Governor, better than I expected."[34]

While the little delegation surrounding the president seemed all smiles and cordiality, the reality was that little camaraderie existed in the hearts and minds of the legislators toward their governor—reciprocated by his feelings towards them. In an ironic precursor to the national cataclysm destined to follow in the wake of Lincoln's inauguration, his impending visit to Albany had ignited a form of localized civil strife all its own. This "irrepressible conflict," as one paper called the Albany brouhaha, amounted to the disagreement between the executive and legislative branches of the state government.[35] While silly, bordering on the absurd in retrospect, this internecine squabble arose over which branch was going to determine how to fete the city's distinguished guest. Once the newspapers got wind of the discord, the intragovernmental dirty laundry became front page news. Under a column-heading "The Quarrel for the Custody of the President-elect," Albany's *Atlas & Argus* told of "the fight for the possession of Lincoln, which occupied the two Houses of the Legislature, their Committees, the Governor, the Press and the Lobby, all last week, continued up to the last moment; and, while the cannons were firing salutes of Welcome, the two Houses were discharging volleys of vituperation at each other, at the Governor, at the Committees, and at the arrangements."[36]

For the Lincolns, the whole episode proved mortifying. Since the governor thought that his was the only invitation to the president, he erroneously assumed the matter closed. But the reality was that the legislature had weighed in with its own proposal. The two offers arrived in Lincoln's hands simultaneously. Initially, the president-elect chose to accept the solons' invitation. A joint senate-assembly Committee of Eight was immediately constituted to work out a suitable plan for the president's reception. After several meetings, the determination was made that a formal, invitation-only dinner should be held at a local public house.

Still Governor Morgan persisted, holding out for his own private dinner. Though entertaining the president-elect held an allure, New York's chief executive had a less-than-savory motive. What really interested Edwin Morgan was the opportunity to probe Lincoln's mind, seeking to find out whether a compromise or a war was the most likely outcome in the offing. Possessing this knowledge would enable the governor to alert his brokerage partner to either hold onto or sell their company's holdings of Missouri bonds.

But to Morgan's unspoken dismay, ownership of the dinner was reclaimed, when the committee promulgated that their formal dinner would in fact be held. All that remained as of Thursday afternoon, February 15, was to draw up the guest list and select a suitable eating establishment. While disappointed, the governor graciously acquiesced. Then, later that evening—only days before the soiree was to occur—the legislative committee about-faced and agreed to let the governor entertain the Lincolns with a smaller, more intimate dinner. An attempt to overturn this reversal in the House was quashed the next morning by the speaker before it ever gained traction.

The Senate, however, was a different story For three hours, its members wrangled, engaging in a lively discourse. But in the end result, the august body settled on providing suitable quarters for the president and his family to repair to after his appearance before a joint session. The legislators also decided that they would sponsor a dinner for the retinue traveling with the president. When the existing situation was summed up by the local press, it revealed that there were actually three dinners proposed to tempt the presidential palate. "There was a sumptuous dinner for him [Lincoln] at Congress Hall [another Albany hotel], prepared by General Mitchell [ex-quartermaster general of the army who ran the hotel],—another at the Delavan, got up under the auspices of the Joint Committee, and a third 'in the Russian [family] style,' at the Executive Mansion, under the auspices of Governor Morgan."[37] The tongue-in-cheek suggestion was made by some that the president, for the unity of the party, should be required to partake in all three dinners. However, once the dust settled, the bottom line was that the governor's dinner was back on the agenda. With respect to the Lincolns, knowledge of this petty infighting was their second exposure that day to a display of ill-manner behavior among their hosts, the first being the hectic scene that greeted their arrival.

Though less of a direct concern to the Lincolns, the political in-fighting amongst the Albany law-makers had still yet another facet to it, one that had muddied the waters and sullied their reputations even further. Instead of food, this second bone of contention involved protocol. Specifically, to whom should go the honor of welcoming the president on behalf of the State? The Assembly felt that duty belonged to the Speaker of the House, the man who would preside over the Joint Legislative Conference which the president was scheduled to address. Contrarily, senators maintained that their provisionally presiding officer—filling in for the ill lieutenant-governor—Senator Nathan Lapham, President Pro-Tempore of their house, should chair the combined assembly of law-makers.

The stalemate was broken when a compromise was reached. This settlement allowed Senator Andrew Colvin to represent both houses of the state legislature in welcoming their distinguished visitor. But even this apparent resolution was fraught with overtones, for Senator Colvin was "not only the leading Democrat in the legislature, but the author of that eloquent invective against Gov. Morgan, which, virtually, impeaching him, has electrified the boldness and directness of its charges, and which has received the silent acquiescence of Republicans of both Houses! Nothing could mark the bitterness of the controversy more than the fact that the Republican majority, in both Houses, withdrew their presiding officers to make place for a Democrat fresh from the impeachment of Gov. Morgan! Indeed, it is acknowledged that neither the Senatorial question nor any other controversy, past or present, in the Republican Party, was ever carried to such an extreme of bitterness and hate, as this one, as to who should have custody of the President-elect."[38]

Having not eaten since consuming the boxed lunch earlier in the day, the presidential party was undoubtedly quite famished by this time; however, the much-debated dinners were still a few hours away. Escorted to the Executive Chamber in the Capitol, the noticeably tired and pale guest of honor was afforded but a few minutes of relaxation. Then President Lincoln and Governor Morgan reappeared on the Capitol steps, intending to address he assembled mass. However, given the festive mood of the crowd packing the park, the chances of any spoken words being audible were problematical beyond those standing nearest. After taking in the spectacle, Lincoln inquired of his host: "Do you think that we can make these people hear us?"[39] The governor conveyed his doubts with a shake of his head, though he made an effort to establish quiet by waving his hat. But "the hoarse roar of the people, and shouts of soldiers and police, made a din and confusion that rendered the speeches that followed a dumb show."[40]

Nevertheless, the two troupers stuck to the program. First up was the governor. In Edwin Morgan, though a staunch supporter of fellow New Yorker William Seward as a presidential candidate, Lincoln would nevertheless come to have a powerful ally when war came. Among the many offices that Morgan held—from ward alderman to United States Senator to national chairman of the Republican party—perhaps his most important contributions were rendered as the Empire State's "war governor," an appellation which he rightfully earned not only for his efforts in recruiting troops to support the Union cause, but also by virtue of his appointment as a major general of the volunteers and commander of the Department of New York.

But today, his mission was that of being charged to officially welcome his distinguished guest to the Empire State:

> Honored Sir: Chosen, as you have been, to the highest and most responsible office in the nation, or on the globe, and journeying, as you are, to the Federal Capital, to enter upon your public duties, you have kindly turned aside upon the invitation of the Legislature, for the purpose of a brief sojourn at the Capital of New York. On behalf of the people, irrespective of political opinions, it is a privilege to greet you, and extend a cordial welcome. If you have found your fellow-citizens in larger numbers elsewhere, you have not found, and I think you will not find warmer hearts, or people more faithful to the Union, Constitution, and the laws, than you will meet in the time-honored city, the Capital. The people thank you, Sir, for the opportunity you have afforded them of manifesting to you their great respect no less for yourself, personally, than for the high office you are destined to soon fill.[41]

Duly welcomed, Abraham Lincoln stepped forward. Just as he began to speak, a reporter for the *Cohoes Cataract* took note of a celestial event in which "the sun did not appear until President Lincoln took his place on the Capitol steps to address the multitude, but, as soon as he commenced speaking, Old Sol unveiled himself sufficiently to allow a single ray to rest approvingly upon the form of Honest Abe."[42] Highlighted by this good omen, Lincoln proceeded with his address:

> I was pleased to receive an invitation to visit the capital of the great Empire State of the nation on my way to the Federal Capital, and I now thank you, Mr. Governor, and the people of the State of New York, for the most hearty and magnificent welcome. If I am not at fault, the great Empire State contains a greater population than did the United States of America at the time she achieved her national independence. I am proud to be invited to pass through your capital and meet them, as I now have the honor to do. I am notified by your Governor that this reception is given without distinction of party.
>
> I accept it the more gladly because it is so. Almost all men in this country, and, in any country where freedom of thought is tolerated, attach themselves to political parties. It is but ordinary charity to attribute this to the fact that in so attaching himself to the party which his judgment prefers, the citizen believed he thereby promotes the best interests of the whole country; and when an election is passed, it is altogether befitting a free people, that until the next election, they should be one people. The reception you have extended to me today is not given to me personally. It should not be so, but as the representative for the time being of the majority of the nation.
>
> If the election had resulted in the selection of either of the other candidates, the same cordiality should have been extended him as extended to me this day, in the testimony of devotion of the whole people to the whole Constitution and the whole Union, and of their desire to perpetuate their institutions, and to hand them down in their perfection to succeeding generations. I have neither the voice nor the strength to address you at any greater length. I beg you will accept my most grateful thanks for this devotion—not to me but to this great and glorious free country.[43]

Similar to what had transpired when the president spoke upon his arrival, the extent that any appreciable number of people heard him was dubious. Lincoln nonetheless was duly rewarded by a hearty applause. As was his habit, he bowed in appreciation and then retired into the Capitol. Ushered immediately to the Assembly Chamber, he found a packed house waiting to hear his third speech in little more than an hour. Comprising this audience were not only state legislators, but also spectators who jammed the upper galleries and lower lobbies to capacity. With no fire codes to limit access, one observer commented that "the Assembly Chamber was crowded to suffocation."[44] Given that this was a momentous occasion, the ladies present were seen wearing "every variety of holiday costume, all in anxious expectation of the coming of the distinguished guest."[45]

At the scheduled hour of three p.m., Speaker of the House Littlejohn called for order, requesting all visitors to vacate the chamber floor and retire to the lobbies. However, unknown to those in building, Lincoln was still back on the train, waiting for the arrival of his transportation and escorts. Consequently, he would not reach the statehouse until well after three o'clock. Then there came the brief welcome with Governor Morgan on the Capitol's steps, so that the guest of honor did make his appearance in the Assembly Chamber until 4:40 p.m. When he first entered room, the president-elect was greeted by Senator Andrew Colvin, Speaker of the House DeWitt Clinton Littlejohn, and Senator William

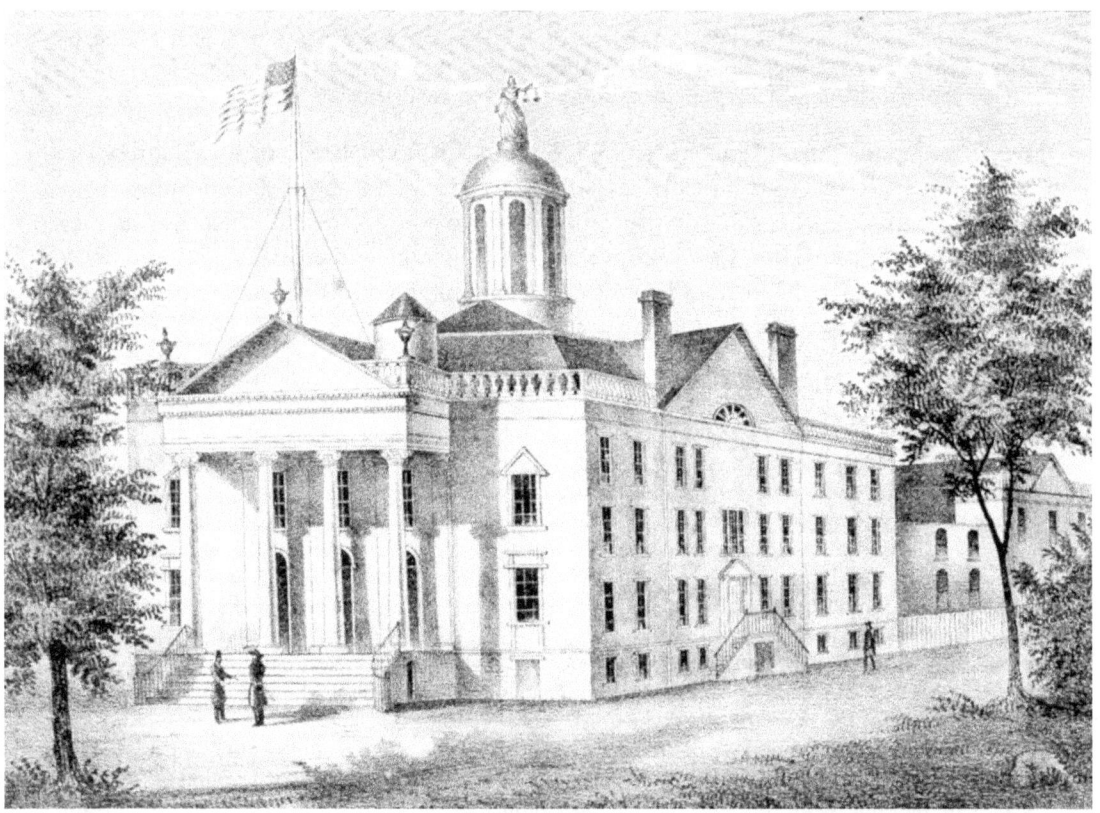

Inside the Capitol at Albany, President-Elect Lincoln addressed a joint session of the State Legislature after first speaking to the crowd outside from its front steps. From *Atlas of Schoharie County, New York* (Philadelphia: Stone and Stewart, 1866).

Ferry. Among the three men, Colvin and Ferry served but one term in the New York State Senate. Assemblyman Littlejohn, however, was of a different breed altogether. A political lifer—possessing a given name readily identifying him as having roots firmly planted in the Empire State—he was sent to the New York State Assembly for twelve terms. When the war broke out, he helped raise the 110th Infantry Regiment, of which was appointed colonel. While political appointees to military commands in the Civil War often experienced battlefield disasters, Colonel Littlejohn apparently acquitted himself acceptably, for he attained the rank of brevet brigadier general of volunteers in 1865.

Each of these three legislators had a designated role to play; however, before commencing with the presentation ritual, they had to wait for the thunderous applause and standing ovation to run their course. When quiet finally descended again, Senator Ferry stepped in front of the speaker's desk and said: "I have the honor to introduce to the Senate and the Assembly of the State of New York in joint convention assembled, the Hon. Abraham Lincoln, of Illinois, President of the United States."[46] Then Speaker Littlejohn came forward, greeted the president, and proceeded to lead him back to the desk, where Senator Colvin was introduced. After shaking hands with Mr. Lincoln, Senator Colvin moved to the clerk's table from which he formally welcomed the honored guest.

All eyes then shifted their gaze to Lincoln, who responded:

> Mr. President and gentlemen of the Legislature of the State of New York: It is with feelings of great diffidence, and I may say with feelings of awe, perhaps greater than I have recently experienced, that I meet you here in this place. The history of this great State, the renown of those great men who have stood here, and spoke here, and been heard here, all crowned my fancy, and incline me to shrink from any attempt to address you. Yet I have some confidence given me by the generous manner in which you have invited me, and by the still more generous manner in which you have received me to speak further. You have invited me and received me without distinction of party. I cannot for a moment suppose that this has been done in any considerable degree with reference to my personal services, but it is done in so far as I am regarded at this time as the representative of the majesty of this great nation. I doubt not this is the truth and the whole truth of the case, and this as it should be. It is much more gratifying to me that this reception has been given to me as the representative of a free people than it could possibly be if tendered merely as an evidence of devotion to me, or to any one man personally, and now I think it more fitting that I should close these hasty remarks. It is true that while I hold myself without mock modesty, the humblest of all individuals that have ever been elevated to the Presidency, I have a more difficult task to perform than any one of them.
>
> You have generously tendered me the united support of the great Empire State. For this, in behalf of the nation, in behalf of the present and future of the nation, in behalf of civil and religious liberty for all time to come, most gratefully do I thank you. I do not propose to enter into an explanation of any particular line of policy as to our present difficulties to be adopted by the incoming administration. I deem it just to you, to myself and to all that I should see everything, that I should hear everything, that I should have every light that can be brought within my reach, in order that when I do speak, I shall have enjoyed every opportunity to correct and true ground; and for this reason I don't propose to speak at this time of the policy of the government; but when the time comes I shall speak as well as I am able for the good of the present and future of this country—for the good both of the North and the South of this country. (*Rounds of applause*) In the meantime, if we have patience; if we restrain ourselves; if we allow ourselves not to off in a passion, I still have confidence that the Almighty, the Maker of the Universe, will, through the instrumentality of this great and intelligent people, bring us through as He has through all of the other difficulties of our country. Relying on this, I again thank you for this generous reception. (*Applause and cheers.*)[47]

Following the last of the president-elect's orations for the day, Speaker Littlejohn announced: "The joint committee of the two houses will now take a recess and give members of the

Senate and the Assembly an opportunity for introduction to Mr. Lincoln."[48] He may have been done speaking for the day, but the glad-handing was just beginning. Trailed by the two legislative bodies, Lincoln was led from the Assembly Hall to the Executive Chambers. Here he received the state officials, who subsequently returned to their seats and officially adjourned the special conclave. At the same time, the president-elect was being escorted to his carriage by the welcoming committee. Waiting for him to emerge were the members of the 25th Regiment's honor guard. While these troops had put in an arduous day too, they stood ready to perform one last ceremonial function. Standing at attention in two ranks, they presented their arms, as the Mr. Lincoln passed through their protective cordon from the Capitol to his barouche.

His next destination was the Delavan House. With a stellar reputation that reached from coast-to-coast, the Albany hostelry was locally recognized as a hub of political activity for over forty years, until the building was destroyed by a tragic fire in 1894. When word got out that Mr. and Mrs. Lincoln would be spending some downtime there, substantial public interest was generated in seeing what their lodging looked like. To appease the curious, a favored few were given a tour on February 18.

The two rooms set aside for the president consisted of a sleeping chamber and sitting room, furnished in very ordinary style. After describing the feeling generated by their

To formally greet the public, Mr. and Mrs. Lincoln each held receptions in the Delavan House, a well-known and oft-frequented Albany meeting place for state politicos (Delavan House stationary, author's collection).

appearance as possessing "anything but a cheerful and homelike air," the *New York Herald* offered its haughty cosmopolitan view that "New York hotel keepers would not have given a State Senator such accommodations."[49]

Heading back down State Street, the Lincolns were again thrust into the public eye, for the both sides of the street were still lined with people hoping to catch a glimpse of their future leader. The procession of carriages first went south and then north to a point in the vicinity of where the parade to the Capitol had originated several hours ago. The five-story Delavan House was conveniently located near both the river and the railroad, making it easily accessible to travelers. On this occasion, the Lincolns' visit to the hotel was of only a limited duration, affording them a brief respite before attending their much-celebrated gubernatorial dinner. During this pleasant interlude, several friends of the president were allowed to call on him.

While Lincoln was resting, others were hard at work behind the scenes. It may very well have been within the welcoming confines of the hotel setting that Lincoln's friend, advisor, and protector—Ward Hill Lamon—may have had an important meeting with Thurlow Weed, a powerful New York Republican, editor of the *Albany Evening Journal*, and lobbyist *par excellence* who carried much weight in governmental circles. Their discussion centered on a topic that at first blush seemed relatively inconsequential. Where was Lincoln to stay in Washington while waiting for his inauguration and in turn Buchanan to vacate the White House? Arrangements had already been made with a pair of wealthy backers to provide him with a rented house. Weed strongly advised against accepting this offer, stating that "it will never do him to allow him to go to a private house to be under the influence of State control. He is now public property, and ought to be where he can be reached by the people until he is inaugurated."[50]

With that determination made, the next decision involved selecting a suitable hotel. Among the prominent Washington inns under consideration was the National Hotel, though to some—including Mary Lincoln—the place was decidedly off-limits, due to a strange disease that had run rampant through the establishment several years ago. Hundreds of guests were afflicted, and several dozen deaths were attributed to the strange malady. Given Mrs. Lincoln's opposition, the two men decided that the new president should stay in Washington's Willard Hotel. Weed made the reservations, which amounted to a ten-day stay in rather pricey accommodations, which cost the unemployed president-elect the then princely sum of $773.75.

In the end, being quartered at Willard's worked quite well for Lincoln. Located in the heart of the city, only a few blocks from the White House, its accessibility to the movers and shakers of the times was easy. During his stay, Lincoln conducted a varied slate of conferences. He met with the men whom he defeated for office—John Bell, John Breckinridge, and Stephan Douglas. He successfully interviewed candidates for cabinet positions, and, though fruitless, he had discussions with members of the Peace Conference. Though his little visit cost him about 3 percent of his annual salary, the decision to hold court at Willard's proved most productive.

After resting for perhaps an hour and half at Delavan House, Abraham, Mary, and their boys found themselves on their way back to State Street, where the governor's residence was then located. The First Family's passage was once again cheered on by a large crowd which had maintained a vigil in front of the house. Six o'clock was the announced hour for the intimate dinner to begin.

Fifteen people constituted the attendees. It was reported that "at the gubernatorial dinner, no person was present save the immediate families of Gov. Morgan and Mr. Lincoln."[51] This proved true because the only individual outside of either family's circle who was invited, Thurlow Weed, elected not to attend. Another insider to Republican Party circles, newly elected Senator Ira Harris, while not an invitee, did call at the Governor's residence, but not until the supper was finished.

* * *

As the Lincolns dined in the warm glow of brightly lit lamps in the governor's abode, a few blocks away on Green Street another kind of illumination—stage-lighting—was shining on a twenty-three-old thespian named John Wilkes Booth. A rising star, he was a member of the cast presenting Shakespeare's *The Apostate* at the Gaiety Theater. Though their paths never knowingly crossed during Lincoln's stay, the young actor would have been hard-pressed not have known that the president-elect was in town. Booth was lodged at the Stanwix Hotel, an establishment which Lincoln's carriage had passed in its trips up and down State Street.

In the kind of tantalizing what-ifs that hindsight often affords, Booth it seems was almost done in twice during his appearance in Albany. The first near-fatality occurred by his own hand in a recent performance. Known as the "acrobatic actor," Booth liked to perform stunts as realistically as possible. One scene in the current play called for the brandishing of a dagger. Somehow the energetic actor took a tumble and accidentally stabbed himself in the chest with what should have been a harmless prop, but was instead at his assistance a genuine knife. Though painful, the wound was not life-threatening ... but for a matter of inches, the blade could have pierced his heart—and changed history.

The second near-fatal Albany incident involved Booth's paramour, Henrietta Irving. In a fit of despondency over having their affair ended by the actor, she tried unsuccessfully to stab him during an argument in the Stanwix Hotel's bar. While the episode proved only embarrassing, it illustrated a reoccurring flaw in Booth's character that he seemed unable to suppress. Certainly, the thespian in him did not shy away from publicity; however, the negative exposure which he sometimes achieved, through such incidents as the one with a jilted lover, was of questionable value in enhancing his career. Another example of Booth's poor decision-making occurred while in Buffalo the following year, where "he became enraged at seeing a lot of rebel trophies which were on exhibition in a certain store window, and one night shivered the window to atoms. He was arrested and paid the damage and a $50 fine, and the affair was kept out of the papers."[52] Booth would again appear onstage in Albany in 1865, making in March of that fateful year his final performance as an acclaimed actor before shortly assuming a new role as a despised assassin.

Fortunately for the president-elect and the nation in 1861, Booth's impetuosity and his hatred had not coalesced to the point of his engaging in any rash act on this occasion. However, the next time Lincoln, Booth, and a knife were in any proximity to each other would be four years later at Ford's Theater. Adding to the tragic irony on that occasion, the assassin would use a blade to stab and fend off Major Henry Rathbone, when the officer tried to come to the President's defense. Raised in Albany, Rathbone was the eventual son-in-law of Senator Ira Harris and, in the company of Harris' daughter Clara, the Lincolns' guest at the play that fateful April night four years later.

* * *

Following the dinner which afforded an enjoyable interlude, the Lincolns returned to the Delavan House, accompanied with full military honors this time by Company B of the 10th Regiment and its band. Once at the hotel, they were scheduled to appear in the fish bowl again. The antithesis of the private dining experience which they had just enjoyed, the next occasions were a pair of public levees. The schedule called for the concurrent events to run from eight through to nine-thirty; however, since the Lincolns did not leave the governor's residence until half-past eight, the start time for the receptions was pushed back. It would now be closer to eleven o'clock before the two functions ended. The lateness of the hour guaranteed that the day, which had started before 4:45 a.m. in Buffalo, was going to test the limits of Lincoln's stamina.

One gathering was intended as an opportunity for the general public to meet their new leader, while its opposite number was for ladies only, with the First Lady as hostess. Originally, the second reception had been planned for the following morning—Tuesday, February 19, 1861—however, due to the damage caused by the flooding, the president's departure had to follow a more circuitous route, necessitating an earlier starting time to maintain the day's schedule.

But that was tomorrow. For the present the Lincolns had to put on their game-faces and get ready for twin marathon sessions with the public. In Mr. Lincoln's case, the plan called for a receiving line set up in a first-floor banquet hall, appropriately decorated with flags, crepe in the national colors, and an engraved portrait of the president. Participation in this event would require the weary, fifty-two-year-old man to stand upon a rostrum the entire time. All those who wished to be presented were requested to access the Delavan House through the Broadway Street entrance and, after meeting His Excellency, exit the building by way of Steuben Street. Adding a touch of proper formality to the occasion, newly-elected Senator Ira Harris was located on the left, from which position he announced to Mr. Lincoln each individual coming through the line. Security was provided by a military guard, consisting of troops from Company B of the 10th Infantry Regiment, under the command of Captain Ira W. Ainsworth. Throughout the evening, the Albany Police Department also maintained a presence to assist with crowd control, helping direct well-wishers in and out the correct doors and through the receiving line.

Before the evening was over, more than a thousand well-wishers had met the guest of honor, while several hundred more his wife. Among those who took advantage of this opportunity to meet Mr. Lincoln was the renowned preacher, Henry Ward Beecher. This was a treat for both men, since Lincoln was accustomed to reading Beecher's sermons every Sunday. While the line seemed endless "with a great deal of crowding ... the two hours were passed very agreeably."[53]

While most of the well-wishers were everyday citizens, gratefully for the rare opportunity to meet their head of state, some of the visitors had come on specific missions greater than just obtaining a handshake. One such group of five had made the trek to Albany from New York City. Representing the city council, these emissaries were dispatched to invite Lincoln and his retinue to be the guests of the city, as they passed through on their way to Washington. As tangible evidence of the sincerity of their offer, the delegation presented the President "with a beautifully embossed copy of the preamble and resolutions introduced and adopted by the Common Council" which extended the offer of the city's hospitality.[54] Given that he would be arriving in New York City the next day, Mr. Lincoln orally acceptance the committee's offer, which included the understanding that his party would be put up at the Astor House. Since Mr. Lincoln was not yet a governmental employee, such generous offers to defray his expenses were gratefully accepted.

While her husband was engaged in meeting well-wishers downstairs, the evening's second affair was progressing well one floor above. Though most of guests were women, some men were included among the visitors received by Mrs. Lincoln. While the president was clearly the headliner of the evening's events, the first lady did not go unnoticed. In the perception of one attendee, "Mrs. Lincoln, although nearly forty [forty-two], was dressed like a girl of eighteen with little loops over her shoulders, her arms bare. She wore white kid gloves, and outside of her gloves she wore every ring she ever possessed."[55] Colonel Edwin Sumner of the United States Army had the honor of escorting her to the parlor, while the duty of introducing guests as they came to her through the receiving line was handled by John Dersheimer, the state treasurer of New York. Though impossible to have foreseen at the time, for Mary Lincoln the positive exposure which she received from such public outings along the journey represented some of her most satisfying post-election moments. The impression which she made led the *Home Journal* to reference her with the flattering sobriquet of the "Illinois Queen."[56]

When his levee ended, the president went upstairs, where he found over one hundred women waiting with Mrs. Lincoln. Tired but gallant, he shook hands with every one of them, tossing in a bonus kiss of the cheek to a little girl, remarking that as president "he had the right to do that."[57] Following the conclusion of their receptions, the Lincolns returned to the governor's residence to sleep. The weary was finally able to retire for the night at eleven o'clock, bringing closure to what had been a taxing eighteen-hour day before his head finally hit the pillow. His goal had been for the people to see and hear him, and thousands were afforded that opportunity. In the words of Lincoln's secretary, John Hay, who had been present through all of it, the day's history could be written in three words: "Crowds, cannons, and cheers."[58] His boss had weathered a long, arduous, but satisfying day. His reward would be to do it all over again on the morrow.

7

The Last Leg Begins
Via an Improvised Route

Tuesday, February 19, 1861, saw Abraham Lincoln arise at 6:00 a.m. However, given the fatiguing days which he had been experiencing of late, he was feeling under the weather. Still, too much was expected of him for any last-minute schedule alterations. He would have to put on his public face and persevere, for even at this early hour a crowd had already gathered around the Delavan House and the depot. As Lincoln's secretary recalled, "enthusiasm for the president had been spontaneous and universal, and, when we reached Albany, everybody present congratulated himself that he had been a witness of one of the most memorable triumphal processions which this or any country has ever witnessed."[1]

Although the Albany political scene left a bad taste in the Lincolns' mouths, the president had done well connecting with the people and positively impacting his image. Typical of how people had reacted to seeing him was the observation of one reporter who felt that "the impression made upon the masses here by the appearance and demeanor of the president-elect has been unexpectedly favorable. So much has been said in disparagement of the personal appearance of Mr. Lincoln that imagination had depicted him with ogre-like lineaments, but, his face having been much improved by the beard … he is found, on actual inspection to be a perfectly presentable man, and in his frank and open features and truthful the people read at once the sure indications of a kind, generous nature."[2]

No doubt the receptions which he just experienced would be difficult to replicate. Every mile down the Hudson Valley would bring the president-elect closer to the orbit of which New York City was the epicenter. Traveling across central New York provided him with a gentle transition from the rural nature of his Midwestern homeland to the more cosmopolitan milieu of the Atlantic Seaboard, where he would hang his hat for the next four years.

At 7:30 a.m., the mayor and various dignitaries arrived to escort the presidential entourage across the street to the Albany & Northern Railway Station, where what amounted to a shuttle service was waiting. Paused there was the engine *L. H. Tupper*, coupled to half-dozen cars—all belonging to the New York Central Railroad. Though the crowd at the depot numbered only a few hundred docile early risers, protection for Mr. Lincoln was present in the form of the Albany Burgesses Corps—a quasi-military outfit that frequently provided a touch of pomp and circumstance by marching in parades, escorting visiting dignitaries, and gracing civic functions. To accommodate the troops, the president's retinue and sixteen local guests, the train grew to a length of six cars. However, before the next edition of the Lincoln Special departed south from Troy, the number of cars was reduced back to three. As the train pulled out of the Albany station at 8:00 a.m., it did so to sounds that had become very familiar—loud, prolonged cheers and applause.

There were, however, two sounds that were not heard. One was a farewell cannonade, aborted after "several gunners made frantic attempts to explode a second-hand cannon by way of a salute."[3] The other was the Lincolns' personal appraisal of what they had experienced in Albany. Speaking from the vantage point of an onboard reporter with access to the first family, Henry Villard's assessment of their feelings about the last seventeen hours in the state capital painted a totally unflattering picture. "Having been leveed and recaptioned [sic] by remorseless ladies and gentlemen," Villard wrote, "too annoyed and angered to sleep, no wonder Mr. and Mrs. Lincoln departed Albany with feelings of gratitude for their safe deliverance, and with resolutions never to return thither again."[4]

In hindsight, there is little to wonder as to why February 18, 1861, was a day that the Lincolns would like to forget. Just its grueling length from arising at 4:40 in the morning till climbing into bed at 11:00 that night would have taxed people half their age. Add in the stress of repeatedly being in the public eye and then, upon reaching Albany, having to fulfill a continuous round of public obligations must have drawn upon every ounce of stamina Mr. and Mrs. Lincoln possessed. To complete this marathon day, particularly in light of all that they had been through just to get to Albany, was a truly amazing display of willpower, endurance, and commitment. When observers the next day commented on the president's woeful appearance, they failed to consider how exhausting the previous one had been. Not surprisingly, "Mr. Lincoln was so unwell and fatigued that he seemed to take very little interest in political conversations, [whereas] Mrs. Lincoln chit-chatted with her friends and seemed all life and enjoyment."[5]

That same morning, 30 minutes later and 175 miles east in Boston, vice president-elect Hamlin and his wife likewise boarded a train. Heading out on the second day of their journey, they would connect with the Lincolns two days later in New York City. But before that rendezvous, he too had stops to make, hands to shake, and speeches to give along the way. There were major substantive differences, however, between the two ceremonial processions: the vice president had an shorter distance to travel, his 650-mile trek from Bangor to Washington being about half that of Lincoln's journey; given the significant mileage differential, Hamlin made appreciably fewer stops, five to the president's fifteen just to get to New York City; and, although the vice president drew gratifyingly large crowds, they paled overall to the size of receptions that Lincoln was consistently accorded.

After leaving Boston at 8:00 a.m., Hamlin's train ran through to Worcester. Much to his surprise, 1500 people were amassed at the station, clamoring for the next vice president to address them. Coaxed to the rear platform, he was greeted by enthusiastic cheers and shouts of "Hamlin! Hamlin!" to which he responded with repeated bows. When the roar finally subsided, he returned their passionate welcome with a few well-chosen words:

> Men of Massachusetts: Your generous tones speak truly for the heart of this ancient Commonwealth. You men who are gathered here are the best representatives of the blessings of intelligent, productive, free labor, and the sentiments of your hearts are worthy of the ancient fame of the old Bay State. I know you are sometimes charged with being too fanatical, and I fear your complaint is chronic. [*Cheers and Laughter.*] It came from old '76, and I have no apology to offer you. [*Good.*] I sympathize with it too deeply. [*Enthusiastic cheers.*] Friends, maintain like men the principles of the Old Bay State, and all

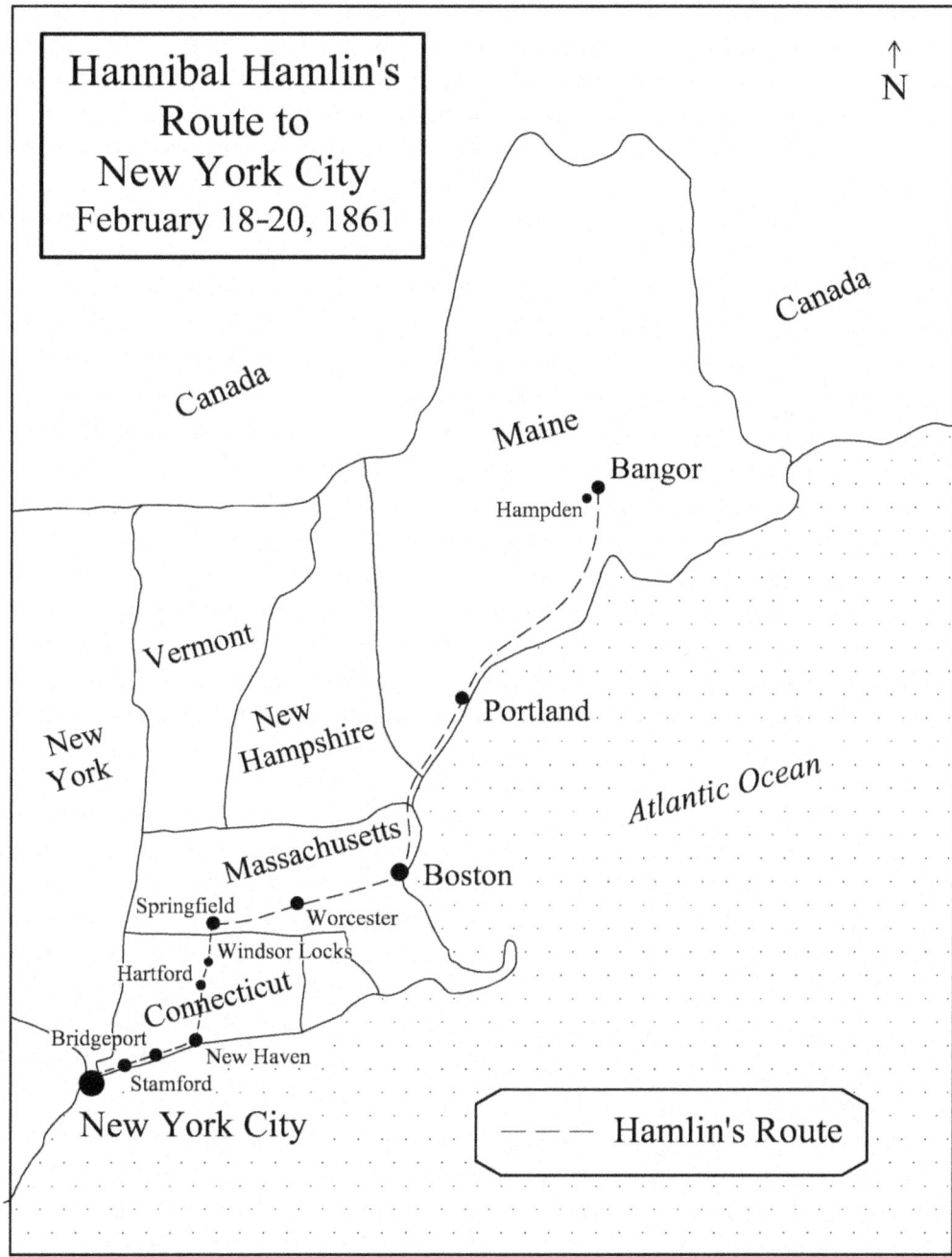

Drawn by Bob Collea.

will be well. Maintain the dignity of free labor [*We will*], and all will be well. Liberty was rocked in the cradle in Massachusetts [*Cheers*], and, my friends, stand by it in its old age, and see that it receives no blow, and it will—[6]

Being abruptly cut off in mid-sentence was not a customary experience for Hannibal Hamlin. But the railroad was bound by its schedule and not by a politician's need to complete his rhetoric. Too bad, for Hamlin connected with his audience and had them hanging on every word. His speech had been complimentary and flattering, exhorting and challenging—entirely different in substance from the low-key, humorous, but non-committal pronouncements by Lincoln. In all fairness, Hamlin knew his audience. He was a New Englander addressing like-minded neighbors. Furthermore, as the vice president, his words did not carry the weight of any impending governmental policy.

Lincoln's situation, however, was much different, since he was a Midwesterner. New Yorkers—especially the city dwellers—represented a population who did not relate to him as readily as Hamlin's did to him. Of course, the most significant disparity of all was his imminent inauguration as the leader of the Republic. Whatever statements he made carried the import of the high office that he was about to assume. His words needed to be calculated, and his ultimate message saved for the proper place and time.

From Worcester, Hamlin went to Springfield, another heavily industrialized city that would come to play its part in the war effort. From the factory of Samuel Colt came fine revolvers for Union cavalrymen, while the Federal Armory produced Springfield rifles which served as the staple weapon for blue-clad infantrymen. Here his journey turned south and passed into Connecticut. While the president-elect was scheduled to be in New York City that evening, as was Hamlin, the vice president took the liberty of spending another night in transit. Having friends in Windsor Locks, he decided to indulge in their hospitality. So, while President Lincoln endured a full day of public exposure, in sharp contrast his vice presidential cohort got to spend a quiet, comfortable afternoon and evening around a fireplace, enjoying the company of several prominent gentlemen and the visits of residents who came calling.

* * *

While Hamlin remained sedentary, Lincoln was on the move, though at a much slower pace than the previous afternoon when his express had traversed the seventeen miles from Schenectady to its Albany destination in twenty-two minutes—a rate of about fifty miles per hour. Traveling by rail, the distance between the capital and the train's next two immediate destinations, first an eight-mile trip to Troy northeast of Albany and then another nine south from Troy to Rensselaer—equaled the same distance as the last segment of the previous day, but, in taking sixty minutes, it required almost triple the time. This slower progress resulted from the roundabout route which was now required to cross the Hudson River, due to the previous week's flooding.

With no railroad bridge yet existing across the Hudson at Albany and the customary passenger ferry presently inoperable, a travelers' connection to the Hudson River Railroad had to follow an altered route. Since the president was the one involved, the decision was made not to inconvenience him by using a carriage to make the link up for his train to New York City. But to make this happen, the presidential express had to pass over the rights-of-way of three different railroad companies. In effect, Lincoln would be traveling north before he could go south.

As John Starr traced this circuitous route in *Lincoln and the Railroads*, "the train passed the west side of the [Hudson] river over the tracks of the Albany and Vermont Railroad, leased to and operated by the Rensselaer and Saratoga Railroad Company, to Waterford Junction. Thence to Green Island on the west bank of the river, the tracks of the Rensselaer

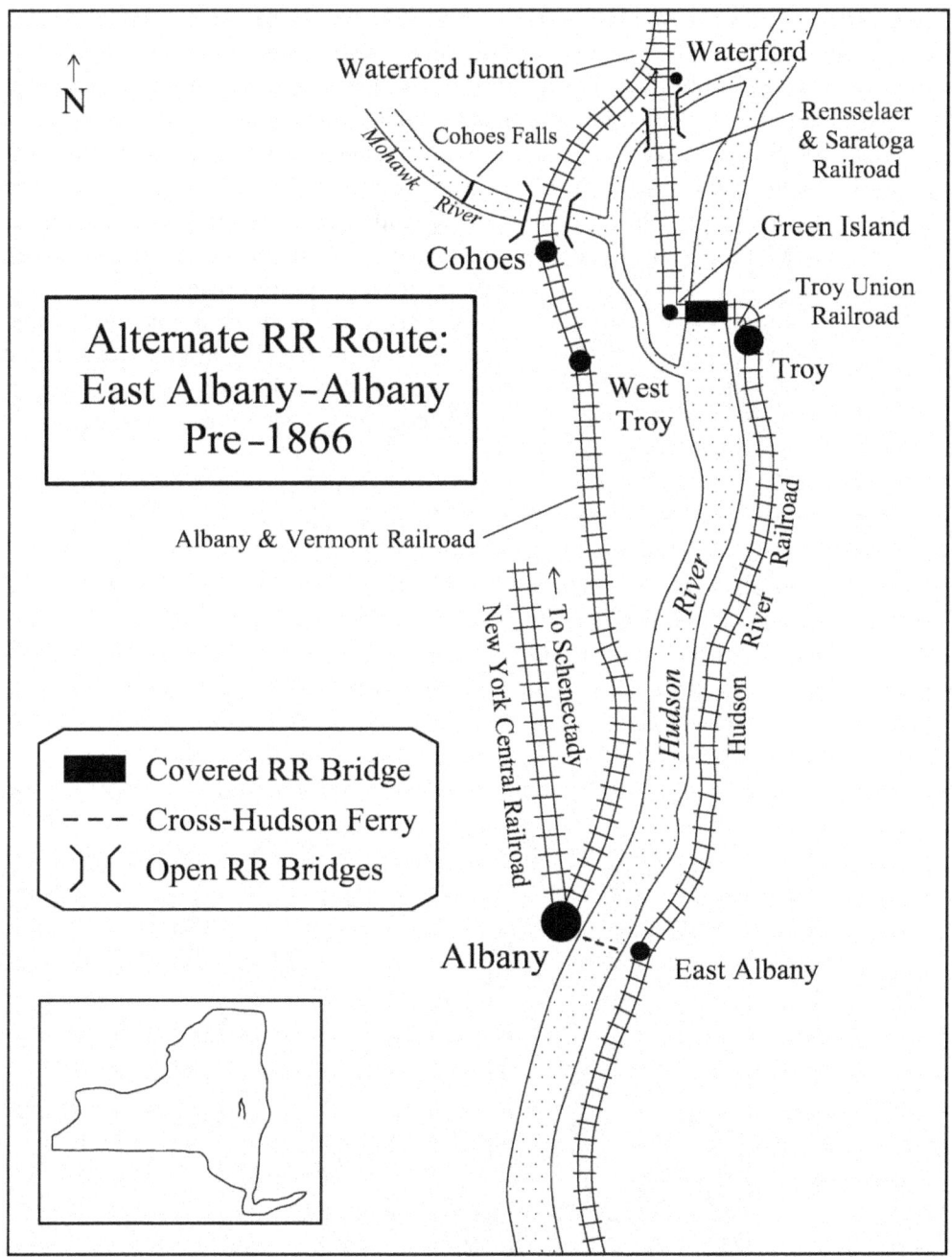

Drawn by Bob Collea.

and Saratoga proper were used. From Green Island to the east bank of the river a railroad bridge owned by the latter company over which the Troy Union Railroad Company had running rights was traversed, the Troy Union proper operating within the limits of the city of Troy only, and it was over this latter road that Abraham Lincoln and party arrived in the Union Station at Troy."[7]

Even though this improvised route increased traveling time, a beneficial by-product of this detour was that more people got to see the incoming president. In addition to the populace of Troy, places like West Troy (now Watervliet), Cohoes, Waterford, and Green Island were suddenly buzzing with excitement: Lincoln was coming! Were it not for the passage through the four small towns, a much higher rate of speed could easily have been maintained and the trip taken less time. But, aside from slowing down to afford the eager crowds a glimpse of Mr. Lincoln, there was another motive for the reduced speed. According to a published report, "the running time was purposely made longer in order to prevent too long a detention at Troy."[8] The departure from the birthplace of Uncle Sam—Troy native "Uncle Sam" Wilson is believed to have been the flesh and blood embodiment of Thomas Nast character which became the symbolic representation for the United States—was scheduled for 9:30 a.m. Lincoln's handlers apparently did not want him committed to staying any longer at the depot than necessary, possibly because of expectations for a longer speech than he customary gave at these whistle-stops.

Since West Troy amounted to only a pass-through, coupled with the early hour, meant that not many people were up and about to see the train; however, this may have been an instance when a watchful Lincoln could have seen a factory complex of particular interest. Passing on the west-side of his northbound coach were the grounds and buildings of the Watervliet Arsenal. Founded in 1813, this complex has served the nation well ever since. In time, its specialty became the production of large-caliber cannon. But when the Civil War erupted, the workers there began turning out accouterments, ammunition, and gun carriages for the Union cause.

Ironically, in the months following Lincoln's election, efforts had been made to upgrade the defensive capabilities of coastal fortifications, many of them in the South. As a result,

On its way from Albany to Troy, the Lincoln Special passed the Watervliet Arsenal, a bustling facility destined to make copious quantities of war materiel for the Union Army (*Frank Leslie's Illustrated Newspaper*).

it was reported that "thousands of tons of war material have been sent off from this station [Watervliet] to Fort Pickens, Jefferson, Tortugas and other fortifications."[9] Another article went on to itemized the nature of the shipments: "Shell, canister and grapeshot are being sent off to a fabulous extent, and heavy gun carriages to mount the forts have also been quite plentifully sent away."[10] Unfortunately, many of the destinations for this Northern-made war materiel were defensive positions eventually taken over by Southern troops, who often reaped a haul of artillery shells. This eventually lead to strange situations wherein Watervliet-made munitions were passing each other in flight, as federal artillery exchanged fire with their Confederate counterparts—the former using recently made shells, while the latter fired from its stock of captured projectiles.

At the time of Lincoln's passage through Watervliet, the peacetime arsenal employed approximately 150 workers; however, two months later, following the outbreak of hostilities, the labor force had quickly been doubled in size. At its peak of production during the war, "the number of employees at the arsenal ... [was] ... 1500."[11] In an interesting sidelight demonstrating that the war effort in the Albany area had contributors of both sexes and all ages, the *Albany Argus* noted with no hint of reprobation that during the war "there were employed some 500 boys and girls, some of whom made excellent wages. The girls were employed in making cartridge papers, and the boys in greasing and scraping bullets, and pinching cartridges."[12] While the time had not yet arrived for Lincoln to worry about war-related production capabilities, the capital district and its residents would eventually serve the cause well, not only on the battlefield but also on the home front. In addition to the outpouring of war-related materiel from the arsenal, other industries in the area contributed heavily. To wit, just across the river in Troy, an iron foundry owned by Henry Burden produced copious amounts of horseshoes.

In addition to being the host for the nation's oldest federal arsenal, West Troy might have also piqued the president-elect's interest due to a celebrated event that occurred there on April 27, 1860. On this occasion, the Nalle Rescue happened. Beginning in Troy and spilling across the Hudson to West Troy, the tale was one of high drama. The *Times* correspondent who filed the story did so in a thrilling description: "Troy has had an excitement, a sensation that stirred it from its ordinary tranquility—the arrest of a fugitive slave, his rescue, recapture, re-rescue, and final escape."[13] The runaway, Charles Nalle, was taken into custody after enjoying two years of freedom. Placed in chains, he awaited the arrival of a slave catcher, bent on returning him to the Virginia plantation from which he had absconded. While he was being detained in a downtown Troy office, word of Nalle's plight spread rapidly.

A crowd gathered, one that began to grow as more and more people joined its ranks. Initially, the mob remained restrained. That is until Nalle's aborted attempt to escape by climbing out of second story window, which left him half-in and half-out with his legs dangling in the air. "His friends urged him to drop," reported the *Times*, "but before he could do so—and if he had, he certainly would have been terribly hurt, as he was heavily ironed—some person in the room seized him and pulled him back again."[14] After observing Nalle's plight firsthand, the demeanor of the crowd rose to a fever pitch. The subsequent appearance of several policemen with the shackled prisoner in tow was all the provocation that the agitated mob needed. The throng surged forward, and Nalle became the centerpiece of a tug of war. Finally, the overwhelming number of rescuers managed to wrest Nalle away from his captors. They rushed him to the nearby waterfront and ferried him to West Troy. However, their bold efforts all went for naught, as authorities on the opposite bank were quickly alerted by telegraph of the prisoner's flight in their direction. No sooner had the fugitive landed and made his way to the main thoroughfare, than he was nabbed by a constable. For the second time in less than hour, Charles Nalle was in custody. His prospects for freedom looked dim.

But help was coming, and this assistance was notable for both its quantity and its quality. Per a published account, "a large number of rescuers from this side [Troy], apprehending [sic] what had occurred, crowded upon the steam ferry boat to the number of two hundred or more."[15] Comprised of members from the local Committee of Vigilance and a bevy of citizens who spontaneously felt the cause worthy, this impressive band was led by the most-heralded of all conductors on the Underground Railroad—Harriet Tubman. Upon landing, the liberators went off hurriedly in search of Nalle. "On finding that the fugitive was in the office of Mr. Stewart," the *Herald* reported, "the building was at once placed in a state of siege."[16]

Before long, the crowd rushed into the building and pushed its way up the stairs. Outnumbered, the West Troy police responded with deadly force. Shots were fired. Two rescuers wounded. However, even though twenty bullets rent the air, "that no one was killed is a fact attributable only to an astounding lack of accuracy in aim."[17] Finally, after overpowering the opposition, the crowd liberated Charles Nalle for a second time. He was quickly spirited out of town and safely hidden. In a feel-good ending to the story, not only was Nalle's freedom purchased for $625 by generous benefactors, but his wife and five children were also liberated and eventually joined him in Troy, where they lived until 1867 before moving to Washington, D.C.

Had he known of the event, Lincoln must have the viewed the story with mixed emotions. For certain, his stance on the institution of slavery is well-documented. However, regardless of how much he abhorred its existence, the lawyer in Lincoln realized that a society was reliant upon the duly enacted laws of the land to maintain civil order through obedience. With this philosophy firmly imbedded in his mind, he once uttered: "I do mean to say that although bad laws, if they exist, should be repealed as soon as possible, still they continue in force, for the sake of example they should be religiously observed."[18] If any conversation had come up about Charles Nalle among the passengers as the train, the president-elect would have undoubtedly spoken from his heart against slavery, but in his head held firm regarding the inviolate sanctity of legislated statutes.

Coming up next in the path of the presidential express was Cohoes, situated three miles to the north of West Troy. Cohoes was another town that owed its prosperity to abundant water power, which spawned the growth of industry. When the news was released that Lincoln's train would be crossing the Hudson to Troy by way of Cohoes, Waterford, and Green Island, great anticipation arose among the populace for miles around. For those unable to see Mr. Lincoln in Albany, the disclosure of this cobbled-together, side excursion by the president-elect offered folks a second chance. This knowledge resulted in onlookers descending upon the rail line. "On Tuesday morning, long before the hour announced for the arrival of the train, thousands had assembled at the depot anxiously awaiting its approach."[19]

At other points, factory workers had gathered along the route, so they too could see him. At 8:30 a.m., the engine came into view, its arrival announced with a screech from its whistle. The train was moving slowly. The crowd was set, eyes focused and necks craning. All were primed for a glimpse of the famous passenger. While no stoppage occurred, "the train passed slowly through, affording the crowds an opportunity to gratify their curiosity and give vent to their patriotic feelings."[20] That is, except for one small glitch, which the *Cohoes Cataract* sadly pointed out on behalf of a great many disappointed people: "But alas for human hopes! No 'Honest Abe'" made his appearance to recognize their spontaneous demonstrations and satisfy the curiosity of those assembled to greet him, until he had crossed Saratoga Street and was almost beyond reach of their vision."[21] For the few at the northern end of the village, who got to wave and cheer at the sight of their next president bowing to them, there was elation.

For the most part, however, the majority of the crowd returned home feeling less than fulfilled. Having neither seen much less heard Mr. Lincoln, it was poor consolation to them to say that they had viewed his luxurious coach or stood within a few feet of it as the train passed. "We venture to say," the local paper editorialized, "that the people of our village never suffered a keener disappointment."[22] Though Lincoln may have been leaving a slew of disenchanted citizens behind in Cohoes, at least the passengers onboard the train enjoyed a special treat and a pleasant memory. When the bridge over the Mohawk River was reached, the train was halted in mid-passage, so Lincoln could view the impressive Cohoes Falls—or the Great Falls of the Mohawk, as they were also called—located a mile or so upriver to the west. Even though most of his previous travels had been for business and political reasons, Lincoln had visited the falls at Niagara on a previous trip to New York. He could now make the tourist's boast that in his lifetime he had seen the two of the largest cataracts in the United States.

Proceeding on, the train entered Waterford. The scene there mirrored that of Cohoes: a crowd gathering at the depot; the train slowing down as it entered the village; anticipation building as the people waited; and everyone expecting to behold the president. But much to their chagrin, his visage was nowhere to be seen. While a reasonable explanation for his absence was later given, this belated revelation did not assuage the immense disappointment which had enveloped the well-wishers here too and turned their jubilant mood to stunned silence. Where was Mr. Lincoln?

From the vantage point of a railroad bridge over the Mohawk River, Lincoln got an unobstructed view of the Cohoes Falls in all the majesty of its seventy-foot drop. From William Cullen Bryant, *Picturesque America* (New York: D. Appelbaum & Co., 1872).

It seems that "he had laid down to rest a few minutes before, and so ignorant was he of the topography of the country which he was about to govern, that he probably did not know that he was passing a village which had turned out a thousand men, women, and children, more or less, to do him honor."[23] On this eighth day out of Springfield, having just put in a taxing seventeen-hour marathon on Monday, the wonder is not that Lincoln felt the need for a power nap, but rather why a member of his entourage did not wake him to acknowledge the well-wishers.

To make matters worse, "one gentleman attempted to play upon the crowd's credulity by appearing on the platform of the car and waving his handkerchief, and by sundry maneuvers and gyrations endeavoring to palm himself off for president; but his claims were not recognized except by hisses, for the people were not to be satisfied with anything less than 'six feet four.'"[24] The *Waterford Sentinel* espoused appropriate sentiments on behalf of the citizenry, offering that "our people will outlive the disappointment, bitter as it is."[25] Then the paper took a more optimistic approach to alleviate the public's angst. To wit, a well-intentioned flight of fancy was floated, but one that could not come to pass until Lincoln had completed his service as chief executive. "Then, if he has occasion to pass through our village again," the paper envisioned, "we can wish no greater honor to him than that our people may feel it in our hearts to give a greeting as warm, as disinterested, and as patriotic as that which was spoiled on Tuesday morning."[26] Regrettably, the editors of the local daily wrote a promissory note for Lincoln that John Wilkes Booth prevented the president from honoring. For, though Abraham Lincoln would return to the Capitol in little more than four years, the purpose this time was for him only to lie in state. The voice that once spoke before the legislature as president-elect would lay mute in the same chamber.

As the train rolled through Waterford, the eyes of one passenger could understandably have been excused for looking past the crowds and peering wistfully to the north, for only eight miles beyond was Mechanicville. Known as a manufacturing center, the village was also the hometown of twenty-four-year-old Colonel Elmer Ellsworth. While possessing no formal training, this enterprising young man nevertheless had developed an abiding interest in military affairs. This led him to study and then gain prominence as a proponent of what were called Zouave tactics, which amounted to a nontraditional approach to combat like attacking in less-densely aligned formations, reloading from a prone position, and exhibiting proficiency with the bayonet. Having relocated to Illinois, he formed a

A native of Mechanicville, New York, Colonel Elmer Ellsworth became not only one of Lincoln's trusted confidants, but also a deeply cherished friend of the president's family. From Frank Bramhall, *The Military Souvenir Portrait Gallery of Our Military and Naval Heroes* **(New York: J.C. Buttre, 1863).**

company known as the Chicago Zouaves, which he drilled to perfection. A year later, the summer of 1860 saw him take his unit on an exhibition tour of western and northeastern states. It was reported that "the novelty of their drill, their fantastic dress and the precision of their evolutions, attracted universal attention, not only from military men, but the general public."[27]

Young Ellsworth rapidly gained fame across the country as the originator of the Zouave drill, with his advocacy spawning companies in many major cities. This work cemented his reputation as a military thinker and earned him the honorary title of "colonel." But his subsequent study of the law under the tutelage of Abraham Lincoln was what got him on the train. By the spring of 1861, Ellsworth's star had risen to great heights. Not only was he a part of the president's trusted inner circle, but Lincoln viewed his protégé paternalistically, making the relationship more familial than professional. The *Albany Evening Journal* referred to this, noting that "President Lincoln entertained for him high personal regard."[28] Clearly Elmer Ellsworth was a man with a bright future.

But once the war came, the destinies of millions of Americans were inexorably altered—none more so than Colonel Ellsworth's. With the outbreak of hostilities, he went to New York City. There he raised another regiment of Zouaves. Eventually the unit was dispatched to Washington and shortly thereafter sent across the Potomac into Alexandria, Virginia. The evening before that deployment, Colonel Ellsworth wrote what was to be a last, prescient letter to his parents, one in which said:

> The regiment is ordered across the river tonight. We have no means of knowing what reception we are to meet with. I am inclined to the opinion that our entrance to the city will be hotly contested.... Should this happen, my dear parents, it may be my lot to be injured in some manner. Whatever may happen, cherish the consolation that I was engaged in the performance of a sacred duty; and tonight, thinking over the possibilities of the morrow and the occurrences of the past, I am perfectly content to accept whatever my fortune may be, confident that He who noteth even the fall of a sparrow will have some purpose even in the fate of one like me.[29]

Buoyed with an indomitable faith, Ellsworth led his men into Alexandria. There they came upon an inn known as the Marshall House, where from its rooftop a Confederate flag was prominently displayed. Ellsworth climbed to the roof of the building and removed the offending banner. But on his way back down, he was shot dead by hotel's proprietor. The news spread quickly across the nation. Making the sad story even more poignant, "the father of Col. E. happened to be in Mechanicville's telegraph office when the melancholy intelligence was received, and the first intimation he had of it was seeing the operative weeping. Mr. Ellsworth's grief was indescribable on learning the sad news."[30] In a heartbreaking experience that many parents across the country would come to share, the Ellsworths had lost their only remaining son, which in their case was magnified even more by the passing of his younger brother only one year ago. "The blow falls heavily upon the parents," commiserated one reporter, "[and] the heart of the people will beat in sympathy with the pangs of parental sorrow."[31]

Since he was a beloved figure in so many parts of the country, the young officer's untimely demise was deeply mourned by a shocked nation. "The death of Col. Ellsworth will mark an era in the history of this war," suggested the *Albany Evening Journal*, "and his name will hereafter stand by the side of Warren and others who fell among the first in the Revolution in defense of their country. The assassin who has deprived him of life has conferred upon him immortality."[32] Elmer Ellsworth was the first federal officer killed in the Civil War. The outpouring of grief over this single death was but a rivulet compared to the river of sorrow that was coming. If Ellsworth's family could take a solace from the circumstances surrounding their son's passing, it was that he was accorded a full array of honors: a funeral at the White House, a twenty-five-car trainload of mourners to his burial service, and a twenty-one-gun salute at his gravesite.

Perhaps, more than any of the tributes which the colonel received, the letter of condolence from the president to his stricken parents—Phoebe and Ephraim—was an indication of both the unique circumstances which existed early in the war as well as well as their boy's special standing in the White House. "On the untimely loss of your noble son," Lincoln wrote, "our affliction here is scarcely less than your own."[33] Eventually, the loss of life on far-flung battlefields would be so voluminous that for many of the fallen a quick internment in a shallow, unmarked grave was the best that could be accorded them, their families left to wonder about the exact nature of the fate which their departed relative met, along with the location of his final resting place. Letters of sympathy were not forthcoming from the president, but rather were penned by the hand of a company captain or friend, if they came at all. Given the exigencies of war, the closure which the Ellsworth's had quickly received became far more the exception rather than the norm. However, on this brisk February morning, national politics were still sufficiently fluid that the young officer had no inkling that he had but ninety-six days left to live.

Exiting the village, the train continued briefly to the north until it reached Waterford Junction. At that point, a committee from Troy climbed aboard, prepared to welcome Mr. Lincoln to their fair city which was his next scheduled stop. Then the train switched from the tracks of the Albany and Vermont Railroad to those of the Rensselaer and Saratoga. Reversing its direction, the presidential express was now headed southward toward Green Island, moving on a course roughly parallel to and a quarter-mile east of where it had traveled but minutes ago. The greeting in this waterfront village was on a par with those of the communities already negotiated that morning, with a another sizable crowd hoping to "gratify their curiosity and give vent to their patriotic feelings."[34]

Among those in the sea of upturned faces may well have been Methodist minister Truman Seymour. As much as anyone that day, this man of God was closely following current events, particularly as they were unfolding in the South. His interest stemmed from the fact that not only was his son, Captain Truman Seymour, a member of the 1st United States Artillery, but also because the West Pointer was stationed at Fort Moultrie in Charleston harbor. Lincoln would have been of interest to the elder Seymour, because the president-elect was about to become his offspring's commander in chief. Decisions made in the oval office would impact the lives of soldiers like Captain Seymour.

Later, by then under Lincoln's watch, Seymour and his comrades would abandon the less defensible Fort Moultrie and relocate to Sumter. There, on April 12, 1861, the 1st United States Artillery had the distinction of firing the bastion's opening salvo in response to the Confederacy's bombardment of their position. Undoubtedly, some fretful days followed for the father, knowing that his son had been one of the defenders of a fort that had surrendered. The Reverend Seymour's anxieties were finally put to rest on April 19, when the steamship *Baltic* docked in New York's harbor with the fort's paroled garrison. This was not be to be the last of the father's worries though, for his boy would take part in many of the war's major engagements, first with the artillery and later as an infantry commander. Eventually, young Seymour's dependable service led to promotions, until he ultimately attained the lofty rank of major-general. After having served his country well for thirty years, Truman Seymour left the service in 1876 and embarked on a second career, one that would garner him international recognition as an accomplished artist, concentrating in watercolors.

But as the Lincoln Special headed east out of Green Island, Captain Seymour's Civil War experiences were only possibilities, looming on the horizon for sure, but still in many minds an avoidable tragedy. Almost as a reminder of the war clouds gathering over the nation, as the train passed over the Rensselaer and Saratoga Railroad Bridge, the Troy City Artillery announced his impending arrival with a thirty-four-gun salute. Though a tiny community—currently its .07 of a square mile ranks it as the smallest town in New York State—Green Island in 1861 was a place of importance that belied its size.

One of its homegrown industries was a foundry owned in 1861 by Marcus Filley. In time, his iron mill achieved national recognition. Its signature product was an air-tight, wood-burning stove, with this item became a big seller in the South and far West where the wood was a readily available fuel. Little did anyone know—let alone Abraham Lincoln as he passed within yards of the foundry complex—that the Civil War would have a decided impact on Filley's major pool of stove customers. Over the four years of conflict which cut off trade between the North and South, owners of Filley's stove in the now Confederate States of America were unable to get any replacement parts nor were customers able to purchase new ones. With the limited state of rebel industry, what iron production there was in Dixie was focused on producing war materiel and not items like stoves for home use.

However, once peace was restored, Marcus Filley moved quickly. In what was most likely one of the earliest attempts at reaching out to the devastated South—as well as a fine example of both a humanitarian reconstruction effort and opportunistic American entrepreneurship—"Mr. Filley got in touch with his former customers, realizing that they would need help, so, in sending tools and materials, he was able to give them valuable assistance in re-establishing themselves. This, of course, had to be done on credit, Mr. Filley, taking his chances of being reimbursed. It is noteworthy that in a few years all of these debts were entirely paid."[35] While Abraham Lincoln did not live to see this, there is little doubt that the man who said that reconciliation in the war's aftermath should be approached "with malice toward none and charity toward all" would gladly have shaken the hand of Marcus Filley and thanked the Green Island stove-maker for embracing the spirit of reconstruction as the now deceased president had intended it to be.

But it was in terms of transportation that the village made its greatest mark, as the place was constantly humming with activity in-season. "One could look out over the river at any time of day," wrote Samuel Hutchinson, "and see either the *John H. Ide*, the *MacAllister*, or the *John Oliver* and the *Groux*, all little side-wheel tugboats moving up and down the river with canal boats in tow and numberless little tugboats running about and perchance a big side-wheel tugboat from New York City slowly making its way over to the side cut, where the tow would be broken up, some of the boats going through the Erie Canal, while others would be bound for the Champlain."[36] While all of this traffic on the waterway might have fascinated the former flatboat sailor in Lincoln, none of this nautical activity was observable during the winter months. However, what the president could see from the rear platform of the train was the terminal for the Rensselaer and Saratoga Railroad, along with yards containing locomotive and car shops.

In light of his long-standing association with railroads, these facilities would easily have caught his eye. The last example of transportation-related infrastructure of which Lincoln took note was the one which had brought him to Green Island in the first place. Completed in 1835, the Troy Bridge, or Long Bridge, was considered one of the engineering marvels of its time. Sixteen hundred feet in length, it required eight stone piers to carry it across the Hudson River. Except for a small opening at its mid-point, the entire structure appeared as an outlandishly elongated covered bridge, requiring the astounding amount of "1,700,000 feet of lumber" for its construction.[37]

So important was such a bridge to potential economic growth for the communities it connected, advocates in the city of Albany had long lobbied for another such span from the capital city to the opposite bank. The recent disruption of ferry service, caused by the ice jams and flooding, served to accentuate this need and gave impetus on February 20 to Assemblyman Charles Darey's "notice of a bill *for the speedy erection of a Bridge across the Hudson River at Albany.*"[38] Of course, regardless of the glaring need seen by some, others had special interests to protect, and they weighed in with all of the resources at their command, fighting hard to first delay and then ultimately kill the project. Those civic-minded Albanians, who had been politicking for a bridge since 1814, would have to wait until 1866 to see their dream come to fruition, for the process took several years "owing largely to the opposition from Troy, together with the ferry interests."[39]

As the Lincoln Special passed through the dark, tunnel-like confines of the Long Bridge, important preparatory activities were going on up ahead. Since the train that would carry the president's party to New York City could not be boarded at East Albany as per usual, it was brought eight miles north to the Troy depot, there to await the transfer of dignitaries who would become its passengers. Striving to put their best foot forward, the managers of the Hudson River Railroad provided the president with a lavishly appointed coach that had been specially fitted out for this occasion. The *New York Daily Tribune* exuberantly described the conveyance as being "unlike any other railroad vehicle before employed."[40] *The New York Times* lauded the car as "a very beautiful and unique specimen of coach architecture."[41] Affixed to its exterior were red, white, and blue silk streamers and the national flag at each end. But it was on the car's interior where no expense was spared, making the cost of construction to the railroad "about $3000."[42] An observer who looked inside noted how "the floor is covered with velvet carpet, and richly upholstered with sofas to take the place of seats. The sides are lined with royal purple velvet. The ceiling and drapery appear in the national tri-colors, with gilded stars scattered over the former."[43]

In the game of one-upmanship, the Hudson River Railroad pulled out all stops, first by constructing the posh coach for the family and then purchasing two new engines—dubbed the *Union* and the *Constitution*. Locomotive *#57*—aptly named the *Union*—was assigned to haul the three-car consist to Poughkeepsie. In keeping with the Victorian tendency toward overstatement in decoration, the engines were lavishly decked out with a red, white, and blue motif: "In front a flagpole at the head of the pilot and attached to the smoke-head of the engine has been put up, from which will float a streamer bearing the noble words in one case *Constitution* and in the other *Union*. This will fly between two 'jacks,' which are attached to the front corners of the engine. What are technically called 'whips,' studded with rosettes, will drape each side of the engine, and there will be six American flags waving from each iron horse."[44]

The second engine, entered as *#56* on the railroad's books, was called the *Constitution* and also appropriately festooned for the occasion. Adding a touch of pride to the presence of these two fine, cutting-edge specimens of motive power was the fact that both machines were locally produced, having just rolled out of the nearby Schenectady Locomotive Works only one month ago. They were as in about as pristine condition as they could be, having been subjected to only an obligatory test run before being turned over to their new owners and then trundled over the short hop from Schenectady to East Albany., and then in the case of the *Constitution* on down ahead to Poughkeepsie, from whence it would take over from the *Union* for the remainder of the run to New York City.

In addition to their shiny new exteriors, internally they were both representatives of the latest innovation in propulsion systems, one that could be fired by coal. Readily available in Pennsylvania, the two engines burned the bituminous variety, this source being a preferable fuel to wood because a tender-full lasted longer and burned hotter than a comparable load of split logs. It was estimated that each locomotive had taken on a ton-and-a-half of coal, which would suffice reporters were told "for the round trip to Albany and back, with some left over to meet any unforeseen contingency."[45] Victor Searcher, in his 1960 work titled *Lincoln's Journey to Greatness,* aptly defined the value of this technological development when he wrote that the "use of coal for locomotive fuel was as momentous a development then as atomic power is today. Coal marked a new era in railroading."[46]

As the Lincoln Special exited from the shadowy confines of the bridge and swung into a gentle curve leading south, the homes, businesses, and churches of Troy began to appear on both sides of the train as it rolled through the heart of town. Up ahead lay one of the largest crowds of well-wishers that had yet turned out to see the president-elect in the Empire State. The last-minute change in the route to New York City, coupled with the decision to make a lengthy stop here, would prove to be a fortuitous turn of events for both the visitor and the visited.

8

Troy Rejoices
An Unexpected Visitor Is Readily Embraced

As early as Saturday morning, February 16, those making the arrangements for the president-elect's itinerary knew that the flood damage in lower Albany was going to necessitate a change in plans, making Mr. Lincoln's connection with Hudson River Railroad different than was customary at that time. This information was telegraphed to Judge L. Chandler Ball, a member of the Legislative Planning Committee who was at that time in Utica, awaiting the train's arrival. The first revision, later adjusted, called for the Hudson River Railroad to send a locomotive and cars via Waterford Junction to the Albany depot of the Rensselaer and Saratoga Railroad to pick up the presidential party. Then, reversing its course, this would then become the train that would make the run to New York City. While the overseers of the trip really had no choice in accepting what amounted to Plan B—considering that Plan A, the ferry, was temporarily not an option and Plan C would have involved carriages to convey the Lincoln suite to Rensselaer—the only element left open for negotiation was whether they would consent to a stop in Troy.

Once Lincoln's revised itinerary was solidified, a hastily formed committee in Troy saw an opportunity to honor the president-elect and at the same shine a little of the traveling spotlight that accompanied his tour on their fair city. Hoping to make a pitch directly to Mr. Lincoln, sixteen members went to the Delavan House on the afternoon of Monday, February 18, to await the arrival of the train. Later that day, between his address to the state legislature and his dinner with the governor, Lincoln graciously agreed to receive the delegation. Serving as the committee's spokesperson, Martin I. Townsend formally tendered the invitation to the president-elect: "As a committee of citizens from Troy, we call upon you, Mr. Lincoln, and extend a cordial invitation to you to visit our city. Our citizens desire to pay you their respects, and it will rejoice them to have the opportunity to meet and greet the chief magistrate elect of the nation."[1] Much to the committee's elation, Lincoln responded in the affirmative.

With Lincoln's promise in hand, the delegation left Albany with approximately fifteen hours remaining to put together a program and then get the word out to the public. One of the committee's invitees—the paramilitary unit known as the Troy Citizens' Corps—burned its own midnight oil to prepare for its participation. A call also went out for the Troy-based Doring's Band to furnish music for the big event. On into the gathering late-winter darkness planning continued. By morning, Troy was abuzz with news of Lincoln's stopover. Not only was there jubilation that the president was going to pay a visit, but there was an extra measure of local pride in knowing that he would remain for "a longer time than he stopped in Rochester, Syracuse, or Utica."[2]

That one of the biggest moments in Troy's history should be brought to it, compliments of the railroad, was quite appropriate. For, even in the face of stiff opposition by maritime backers who wanted to preserve the ascendency of shipping interests, some foresighted members of Troy's commercial, financial, and industrial communities had pushed hard for the construction of a railroad. Finally, in 1832, their persistence resulted in the issuance of a charter that would culminate in the building of the twenty-six-mile-long Rensselaer and Saratoga Railroad. Three years later, its first train would rumble across a wooden span over the Hudson between Green Island and Troy. As if the bridge and rail line were not feathers enough in the city's cap, community self-esteem was further enhanced by the knowledge that the cars used on the Rensselaer and Saratoga route were locally produced, having been built in the Troy shops of the Gilbert, Veazie, and Eaton Company. The last piece to be added to the newest transportation system serving the town was a large depot, Union Station, completed in February of 1854. To celebrate the grand opening of this imposing structure, one which featured a massive shed several stories high that covered the boarding area over the tracks and platform, a lavish banquet was held on the premises.

Sadly, little more than a year after Lincoln's visit, sparks emanating from the smokestack of engine, which had just left Troy and was just starting across the Green Island Bridge, ignited shingles on the roof of this covered structure. Aided by brisk winds, burning pieces of the bridge became airborne and landed haphazardly about the town. With so many buildings being of wooden consistency, a firestorm spread quickly. The town was soon enveloped in a massive conflagration. By the time firefighters brought the blaze under control six hours later, downtown Troy ceased to exist. Close to seven hundred buildings, including the railroad station and over half the bridge, were destroyed. Miraculously, the death toll was limited to eight people. However, the morning light still revealed a scene of utter devastation. But to the credit of its resilient citizens, an undaunted lot who did not long wallow in their misery, the city's recovery from the disaster was rapid. Like a phoenix rising from its ashes, a new Troy took shape. By July of the same year, the vital bridge was reopened. November saw the burned-out district restored, this time with fire-resistant buildings of brick and steel. Included among these new structures was a spanking new depot.

At the time of Lincoln's visit in 1861, Troy was definitely a place on the move. Given all of the industries flourishing in the opportunistic, ante-bellum climate of the city, one modern-day writer appropriately referenced it as "the Silicon Valley of the 19th century due to its cutting-edge technology and wealth."[3] With a population of 39,235 souls according to the 1860 census, it ranked twenty-fourth nationally. Having to exist within the shadow of Albany consistently presented a challenge to the community's sense of worth, but Trojans would have a much deeper wellspring from which to draw municipal pride once hostilities began, for the Civil War would turn their city into a veritable boom town—effects of the fire notwithstanding. Considering itself as patriotic as any community when it came to answering the president's call for troops in the wake of Fort Sumter's surrender, the 2nd Infantry Regiment from Troy was one of the first to leave the state in response to the ninety-day call-up and had the distinction of participating in one of the war's first engagements, the Battle of Big Bethel on June 9, 1861.

The view from the western bank of the Hudson River clearly revealed the city of Troy as being the site of numerous factories, the importance of which would grow many-fold once the fighting began (*Gazette of New York State in 1860*).

However, above and beyond its manpower contributions to the Union war machine, Troy also stood out for its role as a source of military supplies and equipment. For example, six months later, Troy's industrial base would play a pivotal role in the construction of Union's the USS *Monitor*. "The majority of the iron plates, bolts, nuts, and rivets were manufactured in New York State. Holdane & Company, the Albany Iron Works, and the Rensselaer Iron Works provided tons of flat plates, and angle iron. The Niagara Steam Forge pounded out the eight-inch thick port stoppers. The turret and machinery were made at the Novelty Iron Works."[4] Often credited with being the cradle of America's industrial revolution, Troy's manufacturing might had made the city a key contributor to the Federal cause. In addition to supplying components for Union's first ironclad, Troy-based industries sent iron and steel across the Hudson to supply the Watervliet Arsenal with the raw materials needed to produce its martial products, while at the same time its own factories pitched in with the manufacture of rifled cannons, fuses, shot and shell, gun carriages, and transport wagons. In hindsight, it was well that Lincoln extended to the community the honor of his presence in the spring of 1861, for barely more than a year later the fruits of Troy's mills was afloat in Hampton Roads, parrying the bold thrust made by a Confederate ironclad. Similarly, on the battlefields of the conflict, Union soldiers were well-supplied with the necessary war materiel made in Troy to sustain them in combat.

8. Troy Rejoices

Having obtained the desired commitment that the presidential express would indeed stop, it would have been embarrassing for all concerned if the people did not turn out to welcome the honored guest. But the committeemen who stuck out their necks had no cause to worry. Their fellow Trojans did not disappoint them, for they responded enthusiastically to the windfall-visit which came their way. While the actual numbers became a matter of dispute, it was clear, regardless of which estimate was accepted as gospel, that a huge crowd was present, filling the spacious station to capacity. There was even a contingent of die-hard spectators who willingly paid fifty cents a head to stand in the depot's balcony, while the overflow outside of the building created an additional contingent of spectators estimated to equal in number those who were inside the train shed.

As reported in the *Albany Evening Journal*, Troy's Union Station was bursting at the seams: "That immense building was literally packed. At least 20,000 were inside the structure."[5] The *Troy Daily Times*, a homer as far as its sentiments were concerned, saw the *Journal's* 20,000 and raised it by half: "There could not have been less than *thirty thousand people* present in the depot to catch a glimpse of 'Honest old Abe.'"[6] Troy's *Daily Whig*, however, scoffed at what it believed to be vastly inflated numbers, opining that "ten thousand is a fair estimate of the numbers present."[7] The *Times* then accepted the challenge and rebutted the *Whig* with a rather lengthy and detailed justification for their original estimate:

The expansive Union Station in Troy provided ample room beneath its arched shed for both the horde of presidential well-wishers and two trains. From Maturin Murray Ballou, *Ballou's Pictorial Drawing-Room Companion* (Boston: Ballou Publishing, 1855).

"It is a matter of no practical consequence, and we do not care to have a controversy with the Whig about the number of people at the depot yesterday; but that paper having placed it at 10,000, and ridiculed us for calling it 30,000, we may state the facts. The clear space in the depot contains an area of 60,000 square feet. In the army, it is calculated that a men in a crowd occupy sixteen square inches each. Granting eighteen inches to each person, there would be room, if all was occupied for forty thousand, make a deduction for the room taken up by the cars, then add for persons on the balcony and outside of the depot building at each end—and how much will the figures fall short of the 30,000 which we stated as the probable number?"[8] Whoever was right was irrelevant. What really mattered was that the little duel with words over crowd size did nothing to take away from the pleasurable, once-in-a-lifetime experience that many folks had that February day, perhaps one of their last collectively good memories before the horrors of war turned everyone's lives upside down.

Regardless of the actual number of people compressed together, those in the traveling entourage who had seen the size of welcoming receptions along the way for the president felt that the outpouring of humanity "was probably greater here than at any place he has yet visited."[9] One paper went on to observe that "the crowd was so dense that crinolines stood little chance of retaining their natural rotundity."[10] In settings such as these, wherein the amorphous mass of humanity moved to and fro at will and rendered any individual resistance to withstand the jostling impossible, women in the mix were afforded no special considerations. Since the Victorian ethos of protecting the fairer sex was rendered impossible in such a fluid situation, women were alternately crushed, tossed, and swept away.

Surprisingly, given the unpredictable, spasmodic shifts in the crowd, no one was injured as the train slowly passed into the shed and stopped amidst the throng. The immediate efforts of the authorities to cordon off direct access to Lincoln's coach were as successful as they were appreciated. For those who looked for omens or signs that in some way these were special portents, it was at this moment as the train entering under the covering cathedral-like shed that "two beautiful white doves came sailing into the depot, perched themselves upon the centre of one of the arches, nearly over the platform, and for some moments gazed intently upon the glorious flag of the Union that hung suspended over the platform, and the sailed away."[11]

The presidential express entered the impressive 400-foot long station from its northern end, passing down the middle of the shed to the left or east of the waiting locomotive and three cars of the Hudson River Railroad. Once the incoming train came to rest, Lincoln stepped from its rear car's door. Overhead hung a large banner: "Lincoln and Hamlin! Honesty and Economy!"[12] His appearance triggered a deafening roar from the crowd. People yelled, clapped, and waved their hats.

The din was further embellished by the brassy strains produced by the band. Known down through the years as the Troy Arsenal Band, Troy Cornet Band, Doring's Kapelle, and ultimately just Doring's Band, its success was due largely to the all-encompassing commitment of its leader Charles Doring. So good was the quality of its performances that the ensemble gained a national reputation. When the war broke, the entire outfit was sent to the front with the 2nd Infantry regiment. After serving during General George McClellan's Peninsular Campaign, the musicians were sent home in June of 1862, when the war department tightened up on its tolerance for the proliferation of military bands.

Similar to the arrangement in Utica, a platform car was pushed up the track and brought to rest directly behind the president's coach. A wooden plank acted as temporary walkway for the honored guest to move onto the open car and into full view of the surrounding multitude, where he could take in "vast sea of upturned heads" and hear "noise and enthusiasm [which] were beyond description."[13] The Troy Citizens' Corps, working in concert with the police department, was arrayed on both sides of the car to keep the crowd a safe distance from the mat-covered, makeshift rostrum upon which the dignitaries stood. The Citizens' Corps, like its brethren the Burgesses Corps from Albany, was another local militia company that made itself available for ceremonial purposes, providing a uniformed martial look for parades and observances and, if need be, an element of security at official functions.

Since Lincoln was scheduled to remain only twenty minutes, there was no time to waste. Mayor Isaac McConihe immediately stepped forward to make the most important introduction of his life:

> Mr. Lincoln—On behalf of the citizens of Troy, who are assembled here in such large numbers, and whom I have the honor to present, I bid you a cordial welcome. We greet you, not as a politician or a partisan, nor as the representative of any platform or dogma, but as the President-elect of 30,000,000 of free and enlightened people. Aware as I am of the fatigue and anxiety which must weigh upon you, we expect from you no lengthy exposition of your policy or purpose.—Fellow Citizens—I have the pleasure to present to you Hon. Abraham Lincoln, President-elect of the United States.[14]

As had been the case on the Capitol steps the day before, the mayor's words were audible to only those directly in front of the platform, for the highly animated crowd generated such a continuous roar that drowned out his Honor's welcome. For the first few moments following his introduction, all the president could do was stand and bow to a joyous and sustained ovation.

When the noise level finally abated, Mr. Lincoln delivered his brief remarks:

> Mr. Mayor, and Fellow Citizens of Troy, N. Y.—I am here to thank you for this noble demonstration of the citizens of Troy, and I accept this flattering reception with feelings of profound gratefulness. Since having left home, I confess, sir, having seen large assemblies of people, but this immense gathering more than exceeds anything I have ever seen before. Still, Fellow Citizens, I am not vain enough to suppose that you have gathered to do me this honor as an individual, but rather as the representative for the fleeting time of the American people. I have appeared only that you might see me, and I you, and I am not sure but I have the best of the sight. Again thanking you, Fellow Citizens, I bid you farewell.[15]

Humble, self-deprecating, humorous ... the country lawyer had once again connected with a crowd. Once he had finished, the spectators showed their appreciation with resounding applause and hearty cheers. Lincoln next shook hands with the dignitaries present on-stage with him and then moved down off the platform and over to the last of two coaches comprising the abbreviated train waiting to make the run to New York City. All those who would be accompanying him, including his family, had already made the transfer. Lincoln had specifically requested that the train kept short, since he only want members of his party aboard. Standing on the back platform as was his custom, he bowed to the admiring crowd, whose members continued to shout, wave, and clap until the tall figure disappeared down the tracks.

The president-elect's visit represented a truly banner day in the history of Troy. "The

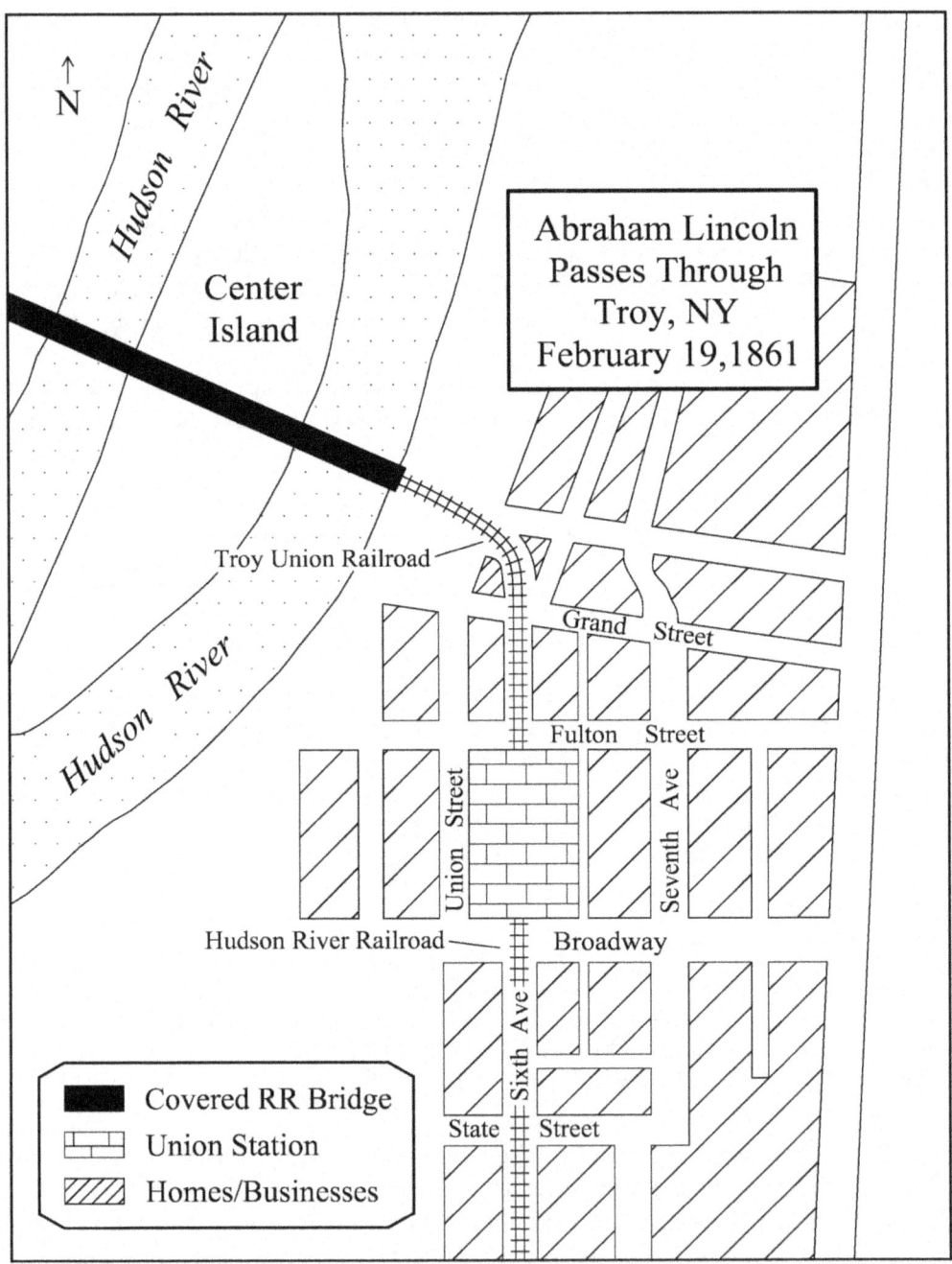

Drawn by Bob Collea.

whole arrangement for the reception was admirably carried out," was the approving assessment of the *Troy Times*. For those who managed to cram inside the station's shed, they would long remember as having been in the presence of Abraham Lincoln. The value of those few minutes, of course, increased many-fold with his death in 1865. Even though the featured event had concluded with the train's departure at 12:30 p.m., folks still basked in its afterglow, not yet ready to have the heady experience end. The festive aura was given an extended lease on life by the two paramilitary companies and local bands who had participated in the welcoming ceremonies.

Once Lincoln had departed, the Troy Citizens' Corps and the Albany Burgesses Corps—led respectively by Doring's band and Schreiber's band—marched through several of Troy's streets in the vicinity of Union Station. Much to the enjoyment of the residents of the various neighborhoods through which they passed, the two companies put on a well-received display of soldierly bearing and precision marching. Though from rival towns, the comradery that existed between the two units was palpable. When they had concluded their marching, the local company escorted its downriver guests to the Troy Armory, where their collective arms were stacked. Then the boys repaired to the Troy House for a generous breakfast spread. After an exhausting but pleasant morning's experience, the Albany Burgesses Corps left for home at noon. Given that communal relations between Troy and Albany had not always been cordial, the *Troy Times* was pleased to point out that "the flow of sentiment here and the good feeling displayed were happy to witness and pleasant to all concerned."[16]

Of all the travelers who were present for the glorious minutes that Lincoln spent with the hardworking populace of this important industrial town, one who took special note of the occasion was Colonel Edwin Vose Sumner, for he was once a resident of the city. In the army since 1825, he had amassed an impressive set of military credentials that any soldier would have been proud to call his own. Sumner experienced combat in the Black Hawk War and then the Mexican War. Along with his stint as the commander of the Carlisle Barracks followed by an assignment that brought him to "Bleeding Kansas," Sumner's solid performances had helped him gradually move up through the ranks, while being a participant in and observer of some of the major events in ante bellum American.

Once plans for the inaugural excursion were solidified, General Winfield Scott assigned Sumner to make the pilgrimage. With the advent of the war, colonel and later General Sumner held command positions, playing key though controversial roles in the Peninsular Campaign, the Battle of Antietam, and the Battle of Fredericksburg. Granted a leave in the spring of 1863 due to failing health, the man known as "Bull" passed away that June at his sister's house in Syracuse, New York.

Unfortunately, not all spectators left the depot that day with a good taste in their mouths. This bitterness was not due to any dissatisfaction with the proceedings or disappointment in Mr. Lincoln's performance. The disgruntled few were unhappy due to falling prey to the scourge *de jour*: pickpockets. In the estimation of the *Troy Daily Times*, the numbers of these "infamous scoundrels" were "unusually thick in the path of Mr. Lincoln."[17] While frequent arrests were made along the way by vigilant policemen, the clandestine efforts of every scalawag could not be thwarted. One victim, Barney Wendell of North Greenbush, was luckier than some. While enmeshed in the crowd at the depot, he did not feel the jostle that signaled the contents of his pocket being pilfered. But for all the risk that he took, all that the thief absconded with was a pair of mittens. In the same milieu, a man standing on the steps of the car, but a few feet from the president-elect, was boldly relieved of his wallet and twelve dollars.

Though he most likely would have expressed sincere empathy for the victims, Lincoln most likely never knew of these citizens' plights. He was now off on the last 150 miles of his excursion through the Empire State, destined in a few hours to arrive in New York City. He had to have departed Troy with a sense of satisfaction about his visit, for he had once again accomplished his goal of achieving public visibility. The *Troy Daily Whig* recognized this achievement when it commented "that 'I came—I saw—I conquered' was Julius Caesar's famous dispatch. Mr. Lincoln may say of yesterday's visit to Troy: 'I came—I saw—I was seen.'"[18]

9

Down the Hudson Valley
The Run to New York City

For the remainder of its passage through the Empire State, the Lincoln Special would travel south on the Hudson River Railroad. Over course of this run, Lincoln's party would cover 150 miles in five hours, which included six longer scheduled stops and several abbreviated, spontaneous halts. In all, the funeral train would pass through forty-five stations of varying sizes between Albany and New York City. The onboard accommodations were such that the lead coach was occupied by all those other than the president's family. These denizens would include a blend of reporters, politicians, soldiers, and friends. The convivial atmosphere abounded there, one where "fun, conversation, and the New York papers made the time pass very pleasantly in this car."[1] This left the rear coach to the Lincolns. In its comfortable confines, Mary "chit-chatted with her friends, and seemed all life and enjoyment."[2] But for her husband, feeling the after-effects of the previous day's taxing schedule, "was so unwell and fatigued that he seemed to take very little interest in political conversations."[3]

However, tending to the comfort of its passengers was only a part of the railroad's task. Leaving nothing to chance, management had given its responsibility to transport the president-elect considerable attention. In addressing a number of details, railroad officials—spearheaded by the company's President Samuel Sloan and its Vice President D. Thomas Vail—sought to insure both the safety and the efficiency of the run. For religiously tending to these matters, they were viewed as "indefatigable in their efforts to perfect their arrangements for the journey of the Presidential party."[4]

One of their first decisions was deploying the railroad's entire force of trackmen as sentinels along the entire right-of-way. Each individual was issued a signal flag and positioned so that he could see the men above and below him. As the train approached, the flagman was expected to walk along and carefully examine his assigned stretch of track.

Another protective measure saw a pilot engine sent down the line fifteen minutes ahead of the presidential express. Should an evildoer tamper with a track or a switch, he would derail only this first engine. However, should the saboteur succeed in loosening a rail, planting an explosive, or throwing a switch between the passage of the two engines, the back-up expectation was that the signalmen walking their assigned stretch of track would discover the miscreant's dastardly deed and flag the oncoming train safely to a halt.

As further insurance against a derailment, all switches were spiked in the open position once the pilot engine had passed. Additional support was afforded by assigning Edward Cadwell—the oldest and most experienced conductor in the employment of the company—

to oversee this high-profile run. As a final safeguard, a master mechanic, detailed from each division over which the train passed, was assigned to accompany the engineer.

Along the brief run between Troy and East Albany, Lincoln would have seen the everyday people who had placed their faith in him: "groups of men and women, all cheering; little girls in wide awake caps and cloaks … men solitarily firing guns as if for signals of distress, but more likely in tribute."[5] The train had barely time enough to gain a head of steam before reaching the first community along its southbound route. Here, eight miles below Troy, the express rolled into the tiny village of East Albany. But for the ice-choked river, the Lincoln party would have been ferried the half-mile directly across the Hudson to East Albany, caught the train on which it now rode, and by this time been well on its way to New York City. As for seeing the president-elect, folks got but a cursory glance. Once the train stopped, Lincoln stepped out onto the rear platform. He was greeted by rousing cheers from the 200 folks assembled there. A score of young women, who had the good fortune to be standing near the coach, were rewarded when he reached down and shook their hands.

Were more time available, President Lincoln might have enjoyed the fruits of a longer stop. Then he could have taken a short stroll and visited a historic site not far from the station, for near the river was a fine example of Dutch colonial architecture. Known as Fort Crailo, this fortified house served as protection in an era when raids by the French and Indians from Canada were an ever-present danger. However, though never attacked, the fortification's military affiliation was nevertheless contributed to its enduring fame. For it was on Fort Crailo's front stoop that a British Army surgeon sat in 1754, watching a passing contingent of colonial troops. The sight of what appeared to be an undisciplined band of ragamuffins inspired him to write a song intended to ridicule their unacceptable appearance, one which contrasted sharply with the spit-and-polish standards of the British military. Rather than be insulted by the doctor's little ditty, the American troops adopted "Yankee Doodle" as an unofficial anthem, with the air achieving great popularity during the Revolutionary War.

Adhering to its schedule, the presidential express departed at ten o'clock, bound for Castleton, Schodack Landing, Stuyvesant, and Hudson. Much of the roadway along this section lay near the river's western side. Spectacular views of the Hudson Valley abounded. Though proceeding at reduced speed, the train did not stop. In these places, Lincoln was treated to similar receptions: "crowds assembled and cannon were fired as the train passed along."[6] Due to the proximity of the waterway, most of the spectators had to position themselves on the eastern side of the track. But, regardless of where they stood, people caught a glimpse of the president-elect on the back platform, acknowledging those who made the effort to turn out. A prominent local who was not in the crowd at any of these locations, one whose presence might have caused Lincoln to respectfully order the train halted, could not make the trek due to infirmities. Residing twenty miles to the east at Lindenwald, his home in Kinderhook, was none other than New York's fabled "Red Fox"—former president Martin Van Buren. In failing health, he would pass away the following year. Had circumstances been more opportune, Lincoln surely would have enjoyed meeting another of his predecessors.

As the travelers progressed southward, various local vignettes were observed. "Imagine the train gliding along, this while, by the frozen Hudson across which women venture," one rider noted, "and standing upon the ice, wave handkerchiefs as the President flashes by."⁷ At other spots, skaters interrupted their races and figure eights to wave. Soon Hudson hove into view. Here Mr. Lincoln was heading into a town with an unusual heritage. Formerly known as Claverack Landing, this riverside settlement was for six decades following the Revolution a significant player in the nation's whaling industry. Seeking a less vulnerable location from which to ply their seaborne trades, for the British Navy had devastated their industries during the Revolutionary War, settlers from Rhode Island, Nantucket Island, and Martha's Vineland settled here in 1783.

Being a hundred miles from the ocean proved no handicap to Hudson's growth as one of the leading whaling centers in the country, rivaling even the heralded ports of New England for dominance in a highly competitive industry. At the time of the first census in 1790, the city ranked as the twenty-fourth largest in the country. But the same wave of industrial progress that placed Lincoln behind a coal-burning locomotive saw the decline in the public's use of whale blubber derivatives in favor of petroleum-based products. Eventually, whale men from Hudson no longer went down to the sea in ships.

Amidst this historic setting, the train stopped at 10:56 a.m. As the engine rolled slowly in, the track was clear of spectators. But their absence was only momentary, for "as it passed along the crowd closed in behind, and an irresistible pressure from the rear threatened to overwhelm the train itself."⁸ The impression that one witness had was how quickly "the crowd soon became a jam, and the jam a squeeze, until the whole assemblage might be taken for a collection of the *original rails* set up on one end."⁹ The train travelers were greeted with "another imposing sight," for "in the deep cut through which the track runs, on the arch over the tunnel, in windows and on roofs, were gathered several thousand people, and tremendous cheers arose upon every side in welcome to the President-elect."¹⁰

Since the station was located at the foot of hills to the east and the river a quarter mile to the west, spectators had plenty of room to spread out. Estimates placed the enthusiastic congregation at about 5000 people. Nor were they all necessarily locals, for it was noted that "hundreds of teams showed how far people had come to see the new President."¹¹ Thirty-four cannon blasts resounded from atop Promenade Hill at the west end of town— symbolically one for each state in a Union undivided. Adding an additional touch of gaiety was the Stockport Brass Band, which was prominently positioned on the awning of the depot, "where they performed several fine patriotic airs, saluting the train with 'Hail, Columbia' as it came in."¹² Once again a platform car was rolled out. mayor Samuel Bachman stood on it, beckoning the honored guest to step out onto the stage. However, as was often his penchant when previously offered a similar podium, Mr. Lincoln demurred and remained on the rear platform of the last coach.

The man that the spectators saw standing before them had a very distinctive appearance. While he would come to be one of the most recognizable figures in all of their country's history, in his day and age most Americans only knew his appearance from newspaper prints. A correspondent traveling in the press corps described the man upon whom the upturned faces intently stared: "He stands six feet four inches high; has a large head with a very high shelving forehead; thick, bushy, dark hair; a prominent, thin-nostrelled [sic] nose; a large well-bowed mouth; a sound pretty chin; a first crop of darkish whiskers; a clean well-built neck, more back than chest; a long lank trunk; limbs of good shape and extreme longitude; arms ditto with hands and feet symmetrical, but naturally long. He wore a black silk hat (plug), a dress coat, a turn over collar."¹³

While those arrayed before him intently studied his every mannerism, Mr. Lincoln delivered his brief message, one not much different in substance than the addresses he had been uttering across the Empire State. He excused himself from using the platform for lack of time, But assured them that he had no "intention to desert any platform I have a legitimate right to stand on. I do not appear before you for the purpose of making a speech."[14] He concluded his remarks with his customary his refrain about wanting to see and be seen, telling them that the presence of so many handsome women gave him the best of bargain ... and then he bid them farewell.

At its conclusion, the president-elect was rewarded with thunderous applause, capped by a rousing round of three cheers. That he had essentially delivered a canned speech would not be revealed until later. By then, he would have been whisked away, and, yet, in the final analysis, did what he had said really matter? Could he not have delivered Hamlet's soliloquy and been just as joyfully received? Was it not the mere gesture of stopping and being seen that counted the most? While the critics might later take him to task for being bland and repetitive, he had accomplished his twin goals once more: to be seen and heard by a segment of the American people, while preserving for his inaugural address any substantive commentary on the state of the nation.

Just before his departure, two incidents occurred that today would have galvanized the president's Secret Service detail into action. First, the inhabitants of the coach were the objects of "intense curiosity" from onlookers peering into the car and were perhaps even a bit startled when "a few ambitious individuals climbed up at the windows and secured a shake of the hand."[15] Next three young ladies approached a window of Lincoln's coach. Being of an accommodating nature, he leaned out and shook hands with each of them. This little gesture was followed by an unexpected concession, when Lincoln invited the ladies into the car for impromptu visit. Then he spontaneously engaged in a bevy of hugs and kisses with these winsome lasses, causing one reporter who observed the warm but platonic exchange to comment: "Suffice to say that all who saw the proximity of the President-elect's whiskers to the pouting lips of those sweet faces were fully persuaded that Presidents-elect, in one respect, at least, are not different than other men."[16] One can only wonder about Mary Lincoln's reaction to this whole episode, for the future first lady was notoriously jealous of her man when it came fending off those whom she saw as designing women. Fortunately, once her husband eventually got around to introducing his fan club to the missus, no volcanic eruption ensued. Since the admiring gaggle of charmers left the car shortly thereafter, the flirtatious little interlude concluded without an embarrassing dénouement.

Then, the sharp warning blast of the engine's whistle rent the morning air. "Promptly on the moment of time," an observer wrote, "the locomotive, *Union*, looking gay as a bride dashed promptly ahead, and whirled the train out of hearing of the cheers of the multitude."[17]

The next scheduled stop was Rhinebeck at high noon, five communities and thirty miles south. Here, as had come to be the custom at depots large and small across the Empire State, the area around the station was once more alive with a mass of humanity—all waiting for whatever peek at Lincoln's countenance or utterance of his voice with which they might be favored. While he made an appearance on the rear platform, Lincoln declined to speak. During the brief halt, the Honorable William Kelly joined the entourage on the train. The unsuccessful Douglas Democrats' candidate for governor of New York State in the 1860 election, his invitation to join the ride was a quite likely an attempt at political fence-mending by Lincoln, hoping to curry favor with locally prominent and powerful individual.

As the train rolled southward, the weather began to change. The sun had finally broken through the clouds, making the journey a much more pleasant experience and in the process lifting everyone's spirits. The little hamlets of Oakhill, Germantown, Tivoli, and Barrytown were all traversed at a reduced speed, but again no stops occurred. Each place offered its own reception, but the appearance amounted to "the same crowds, the same salutes, [and] the same cheering."[18] However, the feeling engendered among the people was of an entirely different sentiment. Most of these folks were in the exulted presence of their first and only living president. For rural residents and small-town dwellers, the sight which they were witnessing was a once-in-a-lifetime experience.

When the train arrived in Rhinebeck, the customary greeting awaited, though with a decidedly distinctive local flair. Standing at the ready, poised to fire a salute, was a six-man gun-crew. While cannon and cannoneers were frequently sighted along the journey, this battery's uniqueness came from the manner in which its piece fired. With no linstock for firing their vintage weapon, "the lieutenant in command gravely lighted the cannon with his cigar! The weapon boomed as the train stopped. Out came the president-elect. The artillerymen deserted their weapon posthaste and made for Mr. Lincoln, amid shouts of laughter in which he and they had heartily joined. A moment later, after he had excused himself from speaking, the soldiers made a rush for their cannon; "the lieutenant pulled at his cigar till his face was red as the cartridge flannel; boom! went the old gun."[19]

Off again, their destination was Poughkeepsie, approximately twenty minutes away. For railroad personnel, this stop marked the halfway point between Albany and New York City. There, just when it appeared all possible red carpets had already been rolled out, the welcoming "scene at Poughkeepsie was unsurpassed in effect by any on the road."[20] For certain the sight of another beckoning speaker's platform, this one being constructed trackside and thus stationary, did nothing to stir the president's heart. What did catch his eye, however, was the impressive manner that the people had arrayed themselves in hopes of seeing their leader-to-be.

That a crowd would have formed at the station was expected. But where Poughkeepsians had outdone their predecessors was by taking to the heights behind the depot. In appearance, the topography functioned as a natural amphitheater As one observer noted, "the hills on the east side of the road were covered with people, mostly ladies. Every height that could command a sight of the train, and every road winding up the hills, bore crowds of citizens."[21]

Adding to the festive occasion were "banners and flags and handkerchiefs waving in the sunshine and the exuberance of good feeling was manifested in almost deafening cheers, which were prolonged for some minutes."[22] As for the town, "the American colors were displayed throughout the city in honor of the event, and the Station buildings were gaily decorated, the stars and stripes being the principal feature."[23] Unlike some of the communities along the Hudson, Poughkeepsie was not built directly beside the river bank; instead, its locale was set back on an elevated position with the western side of the town sloping down toward the station and eventually the river.

With the preponderance of his audience located on the left side of the southbound train, Lincoln could be more easily seen and heard if he faced the people from an open position rather than standing on the rear coach's platform., so this time he would use a stage. While a concession certainly one appreciated by the spectators, a small glitch had to be first surmounted. Since the train had stopped slightly beyond the platform, Lincoln could not step directly to the stage. Rectifying the situation was confounded by the switchover of engines from the *Union* to the *Constitution* that was in progress, so motive power was unavailable. Therefore, to aid their new leader, a number of men sprang forward and muscled the cars into the proper position for Mr. Lincoln to achieve a safe crossover. The hearty cheers that followed were for them and the president-elect, who could now adequately address his well-wishers.

Meanwhile, amidst all of the excitement, some folks experienced a disheartening downside to being present in the crowd. These randomly chosen spectators, focused as they were on the train, their distinguished visitor, and the engine swap, became unwitting prey to thieves, once again present in the crowd's midst. These crooks had dogged the inaugural train all along its route. Though the vigilance of local police forces had significantly depleted their numbers, some of the more resourceful individuals among this light-fingered fraternity were still at large. For some unfortunate spectators, the high of seeing Abraham Lincoln was counterbalanced by the low that accompanied the loss of valuables.

But, as these personal tragedies were being perpetrated, the ceremonies continued. In keeping with the formalities of the times, the president-elect was welcomed and introduced to the waiting throng by a local dignitary. In this case he was the town's two-term mayor, the Hon. Charles W. Swift: "Mr. Lincoln: I beg leave, on behalf of our citizens, to bid you welcome to our city," he said, "and to give you assurance of our confidence in your patriotism and high purpose. I hope and pray that God in his goodness will give you wisdom to so administer this Government that the whole country may bless you."[24]

The president-elect then stepped forward. On this occasion, he was prepared to expand upon his usual canned speech and offer a more lengthy message. He first shared how affording mutual visibility was his primary goal and then complemented his audience on the fine reception tendered him. Then he moved into previously unchartered territory by referencing the election that brought him to office:

> If some are satisfied and some are dissatisfied, the defeated party are [sic] not in favor of sinking the ship, but are desirous of running it through the tempest in safety, and willing, if they think the people have committed an error in their verdict now, to wait in the hope of reversing it and setting it right next time. I do not say that in the recent election the people did the wisest thing they could have done; indeed I do not think they did; but, I do say, in accepting the great trust committed to me, which I do with a great determination to endeavor to prove worthy of it, I must rely upon you—upon the people of the whole country—for support; and with their sustaining aid, even I, humble as I am, cannot fail to carry the ship of State safely through the storm.[25]

By virtue of his altered approach, the remarks made at Poughkeepsie were deemed by some as "a manifest improvement on the earlier efforts on the route. Mr. Lincoln had found that there were things to talk about besides policy, and that it was better to yield himself up to the impulse of the moment than to be under the constant fear of saying some imprudent thing, concerning the character and the policy of the incoming administration."[26] When he had finished, the crowd cheered. But how many of the spectators had heard him? It is likely that more people read his comments in the next day's paper than listened to them in person.

With Lincoln's oratorical obligation completed, the railroad men could now prepare for departure at 12:40 p.m. Like some previous stops, the Poughkeepsie layover witnessed a change of engines and crew. As a salute to Lincoln's railroad heritage and acumen—in addition to taking advantage of the opportunity to parade its newest locomotives before a substantial crowd—the two locomotives were driven past the speaker's platform. The *Union* was relieved of its duties at the point, and the *Constitution*—with engineer William Buchanan at the throttle—switched over to the main line, backed up, and coupled to coaches. "Beautifully decorated with the American colors, and ... a lithograph portrait of 'Old Abe' on each side of the cab," the new engine was ready for the two-hour-and-twenty-minute run to New York City.[27]

So proud ... and perhaps equally as supercilious ... were railroad executives of these two fine, state-of-the-art locomotives that Samuel Sloan took hold of Lincoln's arm and, even though he had not quite wrapped up his speech, pulled him to the opposite side of the platform to watch the engines pass.

All in all, the president had made a good impression on the townsfolk. Overheard from the lips of various spectators were complementary comments, in particular about his looks. While in some ways it may seem cruel to be appraising him so superficially, Lincoln himself suffered no delusions about his homeliness. True to his self-deprecating humor, the unassuming country lawyer once responded to a challenge to his integrity, couched in a self-deprecating assessment of his appearance: "If I were two-faced, would I be wearing this one?"[28]

Fortunately, his countrymen were much less critical of his face than he was. Per those who took note of random remarks from spectators, one observer recalled hearing: "Why ... he is not such a bad looking man as the pictures represent him."[29] A reporter for the hometown newspaper went on to add that Lincoln did not "seem as 'old' as we might be excused for supposing him to be from all accounts. His countenance is not especially remarkable, but it has a strong expression of frankness and good nature. In short, we like 'Old Abe's' looks much better than expected."[30]

In the few moments before the whistle sounded, a touching tableau occurred spotlighting the Lincoln family. While generally avoiding the public eye, Mary Lincoln and the boys provided comfort for the president, helping to take his mind off the awesome responsibilities that he would soon assume. Not that Mary had been completely ignored, for she had already participated in several affairs of state along the way. Poughkeepsie's residents had welcomed the future first lady too, quietly presenting her with a nice bouquet of flowers. But, then, just before departure, members of the crowd added an even more human touch to the visit, creating in the process a memorable vignette by asking to see the boys.

In a day and age when recent presidents have tried to shield their offspring from public exposure, Mary Lincoln was quite obliging in response to the peoples' cries of "Where are the children? Show us the children!"[31] Seated by a coach window, she was recognized by the crowd. In response to their warm reception, she obligingly opened the portal. As she exchanged pleasantries with on-lookers, the query about her children was raised. In response, she summoned seventeen-year-old Robert over to meet the excited citizenry. Pleased but hardly sated, new shouts went up: "Have you any more on board?"[32] Mrs. Lincoln's response in the affirmative was far easier to make than fulfill. Her inability to accommodate the public's interest, however, was not due to the absence of another child, but rather because he was the wrong one. Willie, age nine, and Tad, age seven, were both in the car. But the bad luck of Mary's draw was finding Tad first. Had the option been sweet, obedient Willie, he would have complied with his mother's bidding. However, "Tad was tiring of the trip toward the end, and although he enjoyed watching the skaters on the Hudson, by the time they reached Poughkeepsie he lay down on the floor and said he would not make any more appearances."[33]

Clearly the youngest Lincoln sibling took exception to Mary's intent to put him on display, initiating an ill-timed tug-of-war between mother and son. "The more his mother endeavored to pull him up before the window," wrote a witness to the poor woman's plight, "the more stubbornly he persisted in throwing himself down on the floor of the car, laughing at the fun, but refusing to receive the proffered honor of a reception."[34]

Mercifully, the embarrassing episode ended when the time arrived for the train to leave. While the stopover in Poughkeepsie had lasted but fifteen minutes, a variety of interesting activities had been shoehorned into that brief quarter-hour. Once underway, thanks to the inventive genius of a Poughkeepsie resident Samuel F. B. Morse—whose home Locust Grove laid less than a mile east of the tracks—authorities in New York City were apprised. For "the telegraph had kept the people advised of the progress of the train, and it was known every half-hour that no accident or hindrance of any kind had delayed the Presidential procession that was steaming down the Hudson at the rate of forty miles an hour."[35]

Along with the communications from Lincoln's party, so also were telegrams transmitted to him at stations along the way. Among them were two wires from the Brooklyn Common Council, seeking a presidential visit on behalf of its constituents. Boasting its pedigree as the third largest city in the nation and laying only a bridge away from Lincoln's Manhattan destination, such a short side-trip seemed possible.

The accompanying exposure that such a stop would accrue made the opportunity seem at first blush like a win-win for both parties. But the immediate reply was that no decision would be made until the Lincoln Special had reached New York City. After patiently waiting, the mayor and several councilmen called at the Astor House in the evening of February 19. Unfortunately, when they left, the Brooklynites did so with bowed heads and disappointed spirits. The next day, the *Brooklyn Daily Eagle*, told why the air of chagrin: "He is not to Visit Brooklyn."[36] Regrettably, a packed schedule would not permit such a change in plans. Brooklyn—like Reading, Pennsylvania and Boston, Massachusetts which had also extended overtures—had to be left off Mr. Lincoln's itinerary.

After leaving Poughkeepsie at 12:40 p.m., the next station stop was Fishkill. Sixty miles north of New York City, the village lay in a picturesque setting surrounded by hills. Since its depot was the middle of the village, people could easily congregate at that site. At best, the train would slow to a crawl in approaching the waiting throng, so that most people would be lucky if they caught but a fleeting look of their future leader. Undeterred, a substantial crowd had assembled.

An array of sounds filled the air. Cannons boomed, music lilted, and cheers resounded. Although opportunity beckoned before an eager audience primed to hear him, the president-elect limited himself to a few cursory words. Characteristically, Lincoln found a way to excuse the parsimony of his remarks with a humorous slant on his need to stay on schedule. He explained to the upturned faces and pricked ears that "if he took the time to speak to all of the crowds that awaited him, he should not get to Washington until after the inauguration, 'which you know,' said he, 'wouldn't exactly fit.'"[37] Then, after a stop that was oh-so-brief, the cars began to slowly move. But the powerful *Union* gathered speed quickly and whisked the honored guest from the midst of crowd. One second he stood before them, the living embodiment of the country's hopes for the future. They had seen him. Some had heard him. They had been reassured by his easy bearing and unassuming appearance. Then in the next instant, he was gone ... forever in reality.

Bound for its next stop at Peekskill, the train passed through Cold Spring and Garrison. In the coming conflict, these little towns would make significant contributions to the war effort. Cold Spring's involvement was huge. Here, located one mile outside of town, was the Parrott Iron Foundry. Employing over 500 employees before the war, this facility was the largest of its kind anywhere in the United States. Prior to 1861, its workers made a variety of peacetime goods, but, with the opening of hostilities, its production capabilities shifted to a war-footing. Where once machinery for domestic consumption constituted its staple line, military implements now became its chief output. "During the Civil War, the foundry was credited with the production of "more than 1,700 guns [cannons] and 3,000,000 projectiles."[38]

Like Cold Spring, Garrison's importance was also tied to a martial affiliation. But unlike its neighbor, whose contribution was measured by its industrial output, Garrison served as a staging area. Located across the Hudson on a plateau one-hundred and-fifty feet above the river was the United States Military Academy. Many were the cadets who detrained at Garrison and then rode the Dock Street Ferry to begin their four-year transformation from private citizens into army officers at West Point. Had the Lincoln peered out a window on the right side of his coach, he would have seen several of the institution's gray stone buildings. Present on the campus at that time were many men whose names Americans came to know quite well. George Custer and Thomas Rosser were two in particular who would figure prominently in the looming war, roommates at "the Point" who would become opposing generals on numerous occasions.

Though the train did not stop this time, President Lincoln would return to Garrison on June 24, 1862. On that occasion, his presence was not a public relations outing. Unlike his high profile visit of 1861, this time he traveled to West Point in the dead of night, intending to see rather than be seen. He detrained at Garrison and took the ferry over to the Academy. The purpose of his unheralded trek was two-fold: one objective was to observe the test-firing at Storm King Mountain of Colonel Robert P. Parrott's newly designed cannon; and the other was to meet with the esteemed General Winfield Scott, from whom the President was seeking advice regarding some of the strategies of General George McClellan, then the commander of the Army of the Potomac.

The substance of Lincoln's visit was described by author Ralph Gary when he wrote: "The conference with Scott lasted about five hours, after which Lincoln inspected the apartments, barracks, and West Point foundry [i.e., Parrott's] opposite the academy."[39] After spending the night at the Cozzens Hotel, he left the next day. The trip back became a replay of the inaugural journey. Once word had spread of Lincoln's presence in the lower Hudson Valley, crowds materialized at stations along the line from Garrison to New York City. Conjuring up recollections of the triumphant inaugural tour, the enthusiastic citizenry hoped once again to catch a glimpse of their leader. As the train rolled by, they clamored for him to stop and speak. All would be disappointed, however, for Lincoln felt a sense of urgency to return to the nation's capital. He had been away for two days. Though telegraphic communications had kept him in touch with war-related developments, his steadying influence could not be imposed from afar. No, he needed to return immediately, and doing so in fits and starts caused by frequent stops would not do this time. Departing from Garrison on June 25 at 9:00 a.m., the president was back in the White House that same evening.

But that excursion was in the future. For today, he still had forty-two miles of New York soil to traverse. Next up on the schedule was Peekskill, its station located in a picturesque spot near the river, with the Catskills looming to the west on the opposite shore. Just above the town, the train passed a rock projection curving down from a thousand-foot elevation almost to the water's edge. Reminiscent of a pair of similar outcroppings on the Mohawk River, this protrusion was known locally as "Anthony's Nose." According to legend, the name derived from the formation's resemblance to the oversized proboscis of a ship's captain, a man whose vessel once plied the river in the vicinity of his namesake.

As the town came into view, its proximity to the banks of the Hudson was evident, for the village was situated at a bend in the river. On the opposite shore, Thunder Mountain presented an imposing sight, rising as it did to a height permitting a panoramic view of the surrounding country. Were a member of the traveling troupe sufficiently informed, someone might have pointed out for Lincoln the historical significance of the Peekskill area. Here, slightly to south, the British spy John Andre, attempting to aid and abet the treachery of Benedict Arnold, was apprehended and executed. To the north, the eastern terminus of the oversized iron links of a chain across the Hudson was affixed, intended to thwart British warships from sailing northward to Albany.

In the midst of this region steeped in American heritage, a stop had been scheduled, though the layover tallied a minuscule four minutes. As the train approached the depot, a twenty-one-gun salute commenced firing from a nearby hilltop. However, this tribute proved unique, for it did not consist of the traditional format of three-rounds of seven shots from a rifle squad. Instead, the Peekskill version amounted to twenty-one separate volleys, all fired from a pair of cannon by members of the Jefferson Guards, a local militia unit whose origin dated back to the War of 1812. With the artillery placed on South Street hill overlooking the station, the effect was impressive, with the measured blasts reverberating over the heads of the assembled mass.

As the echo of the last boom died away, the enthusiastic response from the waiting spectators became audible. They quieted only when the second part of the abbreviated program began, calling for the Hon. William Nelson to introduce his guest. The man who stepped forward was no stranger to Mr. Lincoln, for they had served together in the United States House of Representatives from 1847 to 1849, though their association amounted only to a passing acquaintanceship. While the two men had since gone their separate ways, their careers paralleled in that each had gained considerable regional prominence as an attorney. Given his lofty status and prior acquaintance with the president, William Nelson was a logical choice to request that the inaugural express make a ceremonial stop in Peekskill. When word was received that the train would in fact pause briefly, rewarding Nelson for his success seemed only fair.

So it came to pass that the eighty-year-old Peekskill barrister had the distinct honor of standing on the trackside platform and introducing the president-elect of the United States:

> I am requested, on behalf of the Corporation and the citizens of this village, to express to you their gratification in meeting you at this time, and welcoming you to our village as the President elect of this great Republic. This is not the time or the occasion for making a formal address to you. But permit me to observe that we, in common with your fellow citizens generally, appreciate the difficulties which probably will attend to you in the discharge of the important duties about to devolve upon you as the chief magistrate of this nation. We have, however, full confidence in the soundness of your head, and the purity of your heart, and with the aid of Divine Providence which you have invoked, you will be equal to every emergency which may arise in this critical condition of the nation. You have our hopes and prayers that your Administration will prove as prosperous and happy to our beloved country, and as honorable to yourself as the difficulties and dangers which now threaten you are great. Associated as we have been in the councils of the nation, I need not assure you of my own pleasure in thus meeting you again, and bearing to you this message from my neighbors and friends.[40]

Unfortunately for Mr. Nelson, his voice was none too strong and his audience impatient to get the warm-up act over. They had come to hear the president-elect, so every tick of the clock that the well-meaning attorney ate up cut into Lincoln's time. Poor Nelson was described as being "as long-winded as the crowd was ungracious."[41] The longer he spoke, the ruder the spectators became. At various points in his oration, shouts of "Time's up," "We want to hear Lincoln: we don't want you," and "Get down" were heard from the onlookers.[42] With Lincoln looking on, powerless to bail Nelson out, the old gentleman "blushed and stammered; the crowd hooted and yelled."[43] Then, according to Chauncey Depew's recollection, the situation took on an almost comedic turn: "The crowd was wild to hear Mr. Lincoln, but the judge continued speaking until the bell of the locomotive rang and the conductor said 'All Aboard!' Mr. Lincoln hastily jumped on the platform of the car, Nelson whose arms were gesticulating, and whose closing sentence was half-finished, while the audience cheered frantically and then roared with rage at the judge."[44]

Once his former colleague had mercifully relinquished center stage, Mr. Lincoln addressed the assembled mass. In what amounted to a rarity on this trip, he had moved from a detached location rather than remaining on the platform of the rear car. In retrospect, this may have simply been a willing concession in deference to Nelson, who had helped make the arrangements and yet had been treated so shabbily by his fellow townsmen. Identified as "quite a large assemblage, 1500 or thereabouts," those who were present that day later recalled that the demographics of the spectators constituted a cross-section of the town's residents.[45] The very young mingled with the elderly, and virtually every working class was represented. Villagers were joined by those from the surrounding countryside. Most businesses in town had temporarily closed. People had come from a fifteen-mile radius, even as far as the Connecticut border to the east. Some had even arrived the day before and took lodging in Peekskill for the night.

With great anticipation, folks had started gathering at the station around noon, in advance of the train's scheduled 1:41 p.m. arrival. To provide an element of crowd control, the Highland Cadet Corps from the Peekskill Academy and Boarding School for Boys marched in and formed a hollow square around the speakers' platform. "With shouldered muskets and fixed bayonets, preceded by martial music," these young lads made their combined commander and principal proud of their display of military bearing.[46] When the train rolled in, its presence had been welcomed with an appropriate explosion of cheers, hurrahs, and applause. The same potpourri of spontaneous recognition greeted the president-elect as he prepared to speak. In this instance, however, this ovation was cut short, the people being fully cognizant that his time with them was going to be brief and should not be consumed by too much applause, no matter how well-intended and deserving the ovation was.

With the audience silent, Lincoln spoke:

> Ladies and Gentlemen: I have but a moment to stand before you to listen to you and return your kind greeting. I thank you for this reception and for the pleasant manner in which it is tendered to me by our mutual friends. I will say in a single sentence, in regard to the difficulties that lie before me and our beloved country, that I can only be as generously and unanimously sustained as the demonstrations I have witnessed indicate I shall be, I shall not fail; but without your sustaining hands I am sure that neither I nor any other man can hope to surmount these difficulties. I trust that in the course I shall pursue, I shall be sustained not only by the party that elected me, but by the patriotic people of the whole country.[47]

While he uttered but a few hundred words, the message delivered was much more relevant to the tremendous task at hand than his folksy, pre–Albany discourses had been. Absent was any attempt at humor. Instead he voiced an earnest plea for support.

This noticeable change in the tenor of Lincoln's presentation may have been attributable to his understanding of the audience—that these listeners did not bring the same friendly pre-disposition toward him that rural upstate communities had possessed. Though after his short message the crowd did respond with applause and cheers, their positive reaction was one that was not necessarily the expected outcome. This uncertainty stemmed from the reality that the southern portion of Westchester County had not favored him in the recent election. Author Julie Morrisett pointed out the existence of this intrastate split when she wrote: "While the northern part of the county was pro–Lincoln, in keeping with the upstate New York counties, the southern part of Westchester, which included the bulk of the population, allied itself with New York City in its opposition to Lincoln."[48]

With three of the county's major newspapers—those of Yonkers, White Plains, and Peekskill—endorsing his opponents, Lincoln carried neither Peekskill nor Westchester County. But after the ballots were counted and combined nationwide, the 1860 election was settled with a 39 percent plurality for Lincoln in a four-way contest, "the crowd that ... [gathered] ... in Peekskill on the afternoon of February 19, 1861, to see and hear their new President reflected a mix of those who were strongly enthusiastic and those who were merely curious."[49] Chauncey Depew, a graduate of the local academy and a Lincoln supporter in the campaign, held misgivings about the reception which the newcomer would receive because "a large majority of our village was hostile to Mr. Lincoln, and fearful to the results of the election."[50]

The brief layover spent in Peekskill proved a busy one. It could indeed be said that every one of the two hundred and forty seconds was wrung for all they were worth. In addition to the high-visibility presentations which occupied the politicians and drew the public's attention, the railroad men unobtrusively went about their customary maintenance checks to insure tip-top performance by their equipment, and, in the process, guarantee the safety of their extremely important passengers.

Checking the drive wheels and journal boxes was basic procedure for railroaders. In spite of the companies deploying their best equipment for this highly publicized run, hot boxes were a frequent hazard for which vigilance was required. The fact that one had delayed the departure from Utica was proof that even quality rolling stock was subject to unavoidable breakdowns.

Along with the routine scrutiny of the engine and cars, the stop at Peekskill was also intended as an opportunity to take on both wood and water. Steam-driven locomotives were a thirsty lot, requiring gallons of water to go comparatively short distances, and, without adequate fuel, maintaining the conversion process of liquid to vapor was impossible to sustain for long. To facilitate the watering and refueling requirements, the engine was detached from the cars and run over to the location of the water towers and wood station.

Upon the conclusion of his message, Lincoln carefully stepped from the temporary stage back onto the train. From his favorite vantage point, he began his customary routine of acknowledging the warm plaudits of the crowd by bowing profusely. With the president-elect safely aboard, Conductor Joseph Hudson—a Peekskill resident and loyal Republican—signaled the engineer that all was ready for departure. Immediately the five-and-a-half-foot diameter drive wheels of the *Constitution* began to turn, slowly at first as the engineer gradually applied pressure to the throttle and then picking up speed once the locomotive was clear of the station and mass of humanity milling about there. Hat doffed, the president remained on the platform for all to see, until Peekskill had disappeared in the distance and only wisps of smoke hovering over the tracks marked the recent passage of the train.

The good news for the weary travelers, who had been riding for almost six hours in the confined quarters of only two coaches, was that they had little more than an hour left to go with no more speaking stops. The next town was Sing Sing, known today by the

Like virtually all stations along the route of the Lincoln Special, the depot at Sing Sing was also packed with spectators on February 19, 1861, eagerly waiting to see and hear the president-elect (courtesy Ossining Historical Society).

altered name of Ossining. The train was scheduled to roll through at 2:02 p.m. As with so many of the Hudson River communities, its location was in a beautiful setting. Situated along the river and on elevated terrain, beautiful views of the Hudson Valley, Tappan Bay, and the Catskills were afforded those who appreciated nature's vistas.

Taking in the man-made aspects of Sing Sing, the prevalence of structures fashioned from locally quarried marble was noticeable. The Mount Pleasant Academy was one such edifice. Another larger, more imposing use of locally quarried stone was in the construction of Sing Sing State Prison. Completed in 1829, the penitentiary was at the time only the second such state-owned facility of its kind, the city of Auburn hosting its predecessor. One of the oddities of the layout of the prison grounds was such that the railroad originally ran through its yard. This accessibility to the tracks enabled the prisoners, in a most unusual tribute, to line up in their striped garb and salute the Lincoln Special when it passed before them. In return, the engineer gave them a blast of recognition with the whistle.

After leaving the penitentiary grounds, the train's speed started to decrease in the vicinity of the Brandreth Pill Factory. Famous for its production of the Vegetable Universal Pill that was claimed to effectively treat blood impurities, the express passed the facility just prior to reaching the depot. With train slowed—accompanied by cannon blasts, a cheering crowd, and band music—the setting at the Sing Sing depot was highly reminiscent of previous welcoming scenes along the tour.

But events also occurred that were quite unique. One was in the moment, while the other needed time to reveal its importance. In the first scenario, "two 12-year-old boys, Franklin Brandreth, son of Benjamin Brandreth, the owner of the pill factory, and Franklin's friend Albert Tompkins, hopped on the back of the rear platform of the train where Lincoln was standing, and Lincoln shook their hands."[51] Even though the express was progressing at a veritable crawl, the boys' impetuous act was still dangerous. Fortunately, some members of the presidential party helped avert a possible tragedy by holding onto the urchins' hands until the train stopped and they could be gently lowered to ground, safe and sound with a story to tell.

A second distinguishing aspect of the visit, one which did not manifest itself until years later, involved the bell mounted on top of the *Constitution*. Steadily clanging, the cast iron fixture unmistakably signaled both the arrival and departure of the Lincoln Special. All along the way from Poughkeepsie to New York City, its distinctive, metallic sound was heard by thousands, alerting both man and beast to stay clear of the oncoming train. As the history of the *Constitution's* bell was traced by Norm MacDonald, curator of the Ossining Historical Society Museum, the so-called "Lincoln Bell" was a few years later removed from the engine, presented to the Ossining School Board in 1868, and retained in the local school system until 1972. At that time, ownership of the bell was transferred to the Ossining Historical Society Museum, "where it remains today on view to the delight of visiting school children. The children are fascinated when they hear the chimes of the VERY bell that Lincoln heard on his inaugural train in 1861."[52]

Above and beyond the special place this signaling device holds in the history of Ossining, it has an even greater significance when placed in the context of the entire inaugural journey. The honored niche reserved for this bell comes from the fact that it represents one of the very few pieces of tangible memorabilia from Lincoln's trip that exists today. In the absence of photographs, placards, and printed programs, the memories which most people took away from their visits to a depot were grounded in visual and auditory experiences. While some committed their recollections to diaries or letters, the task was left mostly to newspapers to preserve for posterity the passage of this one-of-a-kind event across the local landscape. While these accounts represent period pieces, they are still only about, but not of, the events described. Thus the bell's presence and its provenance stand out, connecting the past with the present by uniquely preserving not only an object but a sound as well that harkens back to special day over one hundred and fifty years ago.

At 2:30 pm, the *Constitution* began to inch out of the Sing Sing Station, taking with it the eventual heirloom bell, repeatedly ringing a loud but temporary goodbye. The ultimate goal of New York City was now just thirty miles away. For the remainder of the day's journey to the nation's largest city, the train passed through several small villages. The by-now established practice of slowing the train down, but not stopping, was the basic protocol used to offer some reward for the populace's having turned out to welcome the president-elect.

The first was Tarrytown, a place famous in fact and fiction alike. Historically, the Tarrytown Bridge figured prominently in Revolutionary lore, for it was there on the Albany Post Road that British spy John Andre was captured. While the young officer was later hung for his involvement in a plot to surrender West Point to the Crown's troops, the exposure of Benedict Arnold's duplicity in the affair was the most valued of the outcomes. The community's second claim to fame, even if fictional, was that it was the setting immortalized in the enduring Halloween favorite *The Legend of Sleepy Hollow*. Upon entering the town, the customary profusion of flags was on display everywhere, along with innumerable ladies waving their handkerchiefs.

Next up, two-and-a-half miles down the tracks was little Irvington, where for decades had resided the late, beloved American author Washington Irving for whom the town was named. The creator of characters the likes of Rip Van Winkle, Ichabod Crane, and the Headless Horseman, he lived in his home Sunnyside in sight of the Hudson River. The tracks of the railroad actually passed between his house and the water's edge.

Two miles beyond was Dobbs Ferry. Besides having been an important crossing point of the Hudson during the eighteenth century, the community also had a proud Revolutionary-era heritage. As the site of a 1783 meeting between George Washington and Sir Guy Carleton, the Van Brugh Livingston house in Dobbs Ferry witnessed the negotiation of the final terms recognizing American independence and calling for the evacuation of British troops. Here Lincoln observed a little girl standing beside the track, dressed in a get-up portraying the Genius of America. Found in period paintings and sculpted in bas relief on the triangular pediment over the east central entrance to the United States Capitol, this figure was an allegorical representation of America. Dressed in a flowing dress or robe, she was in essence a precursor in appearance and symbolism to Lady Liberty.

Before leaving the area, the paternalistic side of Abraham Lincoln came into play. The man who once said that "love is the chain whereby to bind a child to his parents" had a special place in his heart for young people. These feelings led him to request one last, brief stop, so that the children from the local female orphanage—patiently lined up along the track—might see him. Just another of his humanitarian gestures which, while garnering no votes, helped cement his legacy as a not only a man of the people but also one who truly cared about them. Next up was Yonkers, where the train was slowed for more booming cannon, waving flags, and another cheering crowd. Then, the engineer opened the throttle for the last dash to New York City, where the masses of the nation's largest city awaited the Lincolns' arrival.

10

New York City
The Last Stop in the Empire State

Winding its way along the lower Hudson, the Lincoln Special eventually crossed onto Manhattan Island. Traveling through the environs of the city, the greetings continued unabated. At the foot of 116th Street, the residents of the Institution for the Deaf and Dumb welcomed the president-elect, "and though voiceless to the external world, they yet through the beautiful pantomime, unfolded by Sicard, gave expression to their feelings called for by the event."[1] Soon an orphanage loomed into view, its youthful residents also lined up trackside and cheering. Lincoln again had the train slowed to acknowledge their greeting with his gentlemanly bows. In passing Manhattanville and then the uptown portions of the city, residents were visible in the windows of their homes and seated in carriages along the tracks.

For those onboard the express, their journey's end was fast-approaching. Passengers began gathering up their belongings—"packed their knick-knackeries together" was how the *Herald's* reporter quaintly described the ritual.[2] Preparing to reenter the fishbowl, Lincoln allowed the missus to give his appearance a quick lick and a promise. His clothes, hair, and beard all received some last-minute maintenance. When the primping was completed, Mary sent the private Lincoln off with a kiss, wishing him well as he morphed back into his public persona.

As he arrived at 3:00 p.m., the Thirtieth Street Station awaited in pristine condition. The president-elect and his retinue had the honor of being its first visitors. In anticipation of Lincoln passing through New York City, Samuel Sloan—president of the Hudson River Railroad—had ordered the depot's construction expedited. By the time the Lincolns alighted, the station lacked only furniture for the waiting area. Built of brick, this facility was over two hundred feet in length and twenty-five in width. For protection from inclement weather, the roof extended an extra fifteen feet over the rear platform. On the street-side, Victorian proprieties were observed with separate entrances for men and women. In addition to those unfurled on three poles atop the depot, the interior of the building was also decorated with flags for the special occasion.

Unlike the Albany fiasco, police were already on the scene. Stationed both inside and outside the building, New York's finest admitted no one without a ticket and kept those in the street confined to the sidewalks, allowing the thirty-five carriages carrying the presidential entourage to load without obstruction. Altogether, "thirteen hundred policemen ... were detailed to keep the streets clear for his triumphal march from Thirtieth Street to the Astor House, leaving the rest of the city to take care of itself as best it might."[3] That he took note of the Herculean efforts of his men to maintain order was personally conveyed to the superintendent of the New York City Police Department by Lincoln: "I am happy to express my thanks and acknowledgements to you, Sir, for the admirable arrangements for the preservation of order. I can assure you that they were very much appreciated."[4]

Along with the heavy police presence, New York's welcoming parade differed from that of Albany's in other ways, such as the weather. Unlike the cold, blustery day that chilled spectators for Lincoln's Albany appearance, New Yorkers' basked in bright sunshine under cloudless skies. While the weather undoubtedly contributed to the turnout, the sheer size of the metropolis virtually guaranteed a huge crowd. Considering that the city's political persuasion was predominantly Democratic, the numbers that lined the parade route were astounding, with several accounts estimating "that 250,000 people witnessed the arrival of the future President."[5] While some may have come purely to gawk and not to laud, their presence did not noticeably diminish the quality of the reception that Lincoln was accorded, for the observation was made that "there was continuous cheering from the depot to the hotel."[6] Even for a busy, bustling place like New York, a ribbon of animated spectators six miles long was an extraordinary occurrence, the likes of which no one could recall ever previously witnessing, and "the immense crowd was gathered together simply by their desire to see and do honor to a single man—their choice, their hope, their reliance."[7]

Another pronounced difference was the complete absence of any high-ranking New York City officials to welcome the new chief executive. Unlike other places where high-ranking representatives were on-hand to greet their distinguished guest, no such officials from New York City met the train. Viewed from the other end of the state, the opinion of some in Buffalo was that the absence of Mayor Fernando Wood was definitely beneficial: "The authorities of New York are making preparations to receive Mr. Lincoln. It is intimated that Mayor Wood will make the speech of welcome. We hope not. It would be an insult to the President to have such a dirty and seditious fellow even talk to him."[8]

Buffalonians need not have worried. Beyond the stellar police protection provided by the city government, Lincoln's arrival accorded no special recognition. The only governmental functionaries to greet him were a few members from the city's Common Council. On their own initiative, "delegations from the several Republican organizations of the city" were also present, as was a gaggle of enterprising reporters.[9] The future president could just as well have been any private citizen making his way from the station to a hotel. Though Lincoln never commented on what some viewed as an intended mayoral snub, the lack of any official pomp and circumstance to greet him was not necessarily surprising. Exactly what kind of reception he would receive, if any, might well have been in the mind of Lincoln's entourage. For, even though he had carried the state's popular and electoral votes, the president-elect was "crushed by Stephen Douglas in New York City, [where] … Lincoln had been deeply unpopular before his election."[10]

Yet, in its simplicity, Lincoln's introduction to the city and its people was as he would have wanted it. "There was no looking for a grand display," one reporter commented, "there was no promise, and no need of extraneous aids to address the throng—no drums, no uniforms, no speeches from loud-mouthed cannon or soft-mouthed politicians, were promised, expected, or desired."[11] It was further noted that the crowd "appeared to be of that peculiar extemporaneous character which is daily brought together, though on a smaller scale, by the constantly recurring events of life—poured out, as it were, from a thousand places of occupation on the spur of the moment, and then dispersed with as little ceremony on the termination of the excitement."[12] Being feted by what amounted to a spontaneous "peoples' reception" was certainly more suited to Lincoln's homespun tastes than a highly choreographed function ever would have been.

In one sense, given the efficiency exhibited by the police department, there was no need for officialdom to interfere with what proved to be an orderly procession. The police clearly understood their role—that of controlling the crowd—and all along the march they performed their duty most admirably. An esprit de corps was exhibited by the men, who had been urged by their commander to look spiffy to which they responded by wearing their best clothes, new belts, and gloves. Their day's work began at the depot, where 150 officers formed a hollow square on Thirtieth Street by joining hands and holding the immense crowd at bay, so the carriages could be loaded.

After all had been assigned their places in the cavalcade, Lincoln found himself facing forward and seated next to Judge David Davis with senator-elect Ira Harris and Alderman Charles G. Cornell sat opposite them. Pulled by six black horses, their carriage was given second-billing in the procession, behind that carrying the Reception Committee. The remaining twenty-four carriages were arranged evenly in two parallel lines. Of all the conveyances in the cavalcade, Lincoln's understandably received the most attention by the police. His barouche was fronted by a squad of mounted guards and flanked by a foot-contingent arrayed down both sides. Bringing up of the rear of the parade to ensure the integrity of the column from that end was another strong alignment of officers.

Noticeably absent in line-up were Mary, Tad, and Willie Lincoln, for they had been taken in two closed carriages directly to the Astor House. Robert Lincoln, meanwhile, had chosen to ride with the press corps. The parade route, covering about six miles of city roadway, went east on Thirtieth Street to Ninth Avenue; south down Ninth Avenue to Twenty-Third Street; east across Twenty-Third Street to Fifth Avenue, south down Fifth Avenue to Fourteenth Street, east over Fourteenth Street to Broadway, and then south down Broadway to the Astor House. Located in the lower portion of Manhattan, the hotel was only about twenty blocks north of The Battery near the island's southern tip.

As the parade started moving along Thirtieth Street, Lincoln remained seated; however, once the corner was turned onto Ninth Avenue, he stood. Doffing his hat with his left hand and holding onto Alderman Cornell with his right to maintain balance, he acknowledged the crowd with alternating bows to the left and then right. For five blocks, he remained bareheaded, standing, and gesticulating. Most noticeable, not only along the line of march but throughout the city, was the proliferation of the stars and stripes, with flags waving in the breeze from private homes, public buildings, and places of business. Off in the distance, to both the east and the west, an abundance of flags could be observed unfurled at Brooklyn and New Jersey sites, tendering their neighborly tributes to the festivities on Manhattan.

This colorful homage even extended out onto the surrounding waters, where in the harbor area not only American ships but also those foreign registry were gaily adorned with their national banners and varieties of multi-hued bunting woven through rigging. Indicative of the escalating national tensions, one glaring and telling omission from participation in this festive atmosphere was the snub by Southern shipping. "A number of these vessels were congregated in the neighborhood of the Roosevelt Street ferry," reported the *Herald*, "and their undecorated forest of masts formed the only break in the continuous

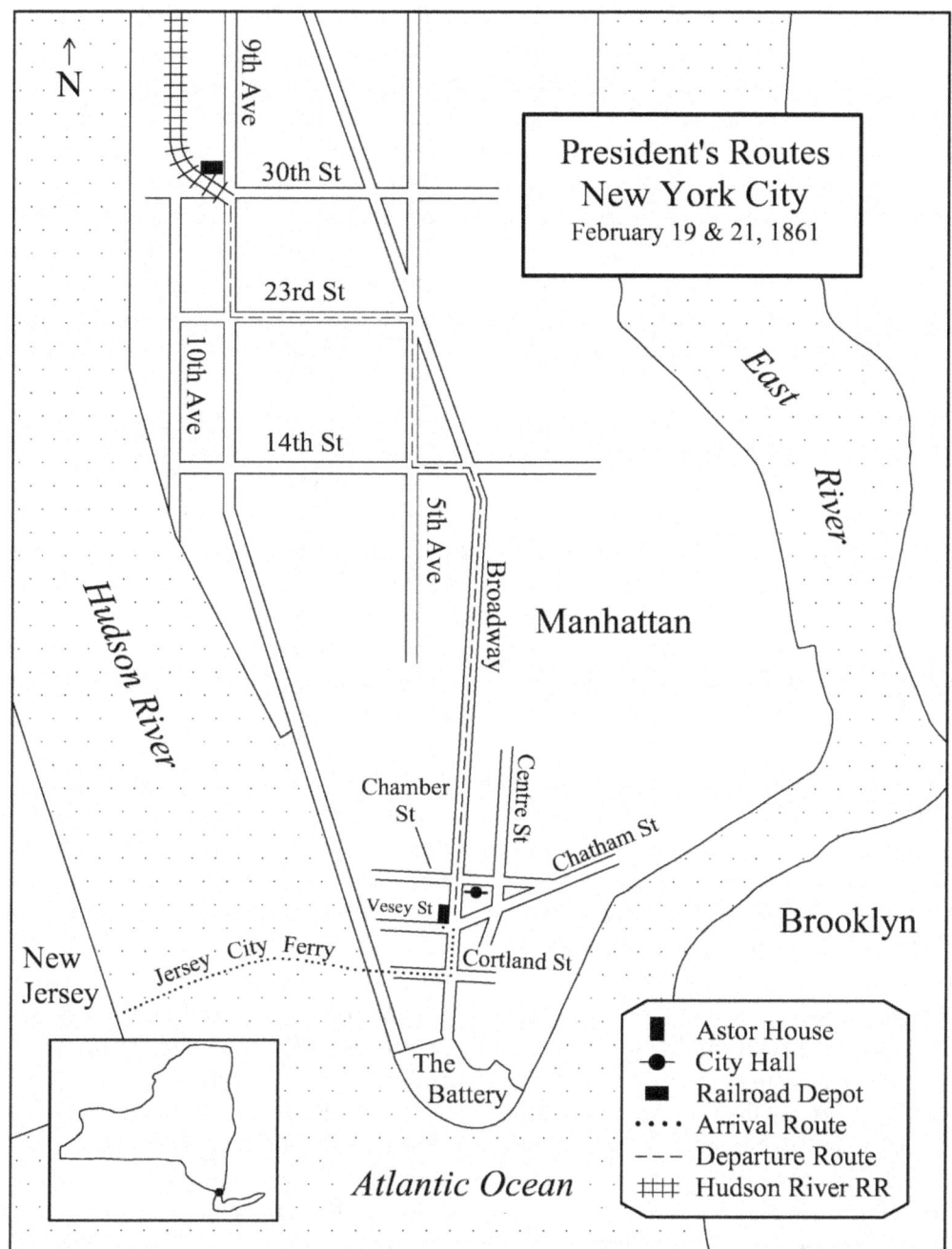

Drawn by Bob Collea.

panoramic display of bunting which ran the entire length of the river, from the Battery to the upper limits of the city."[13]

While the anti–Lincoln sentiments expressed by this lack of participation in the festivities were at least understandable, less obvious, but of far greater import, was what the presence of this Southern shipping in New York harbor represented—a strong, profitable relationship between Northern merchants and Southern traders. Just like Governor Morgan whose brokerage house had Missouri bond interests at stake, the outbreak of war would adversely affect this highly profitable commerce. Driven by motives grounded in personal profit, elements of New York's business community were highly in favor of a compromise to end the threat of conflict. To them, while Abraham Lincoln's lack of any public espousal about his intended course of action toward the South was unsettling, his very presence in office posed a serious threat to their interstate commercial interests.

As much as using flags to commemorate important occasions was a relatively common occurrence, another celebratory phenomenon was in evidence that day which proved as noticeable as it was unique. This was a predilection among significant numbers of onlookers to wave handkerchiefs as the presidential procession passed by them. "Through the whole route, from first to last, from Thirtieth Street to the Astor House, from the locomotive engine to the hotel parlor, the President progressed on the white breast of the most tremendous wave of handkerchiefs ever witnessed," rhapsodized an onlooker, "his coming was anticipated by a white ripple of rectangular linen; he moved forward on the white bosom of a huge linen billow of colossal dimension, and departing he left a wake of numberless handkerchiefs still gently tossing a multitudinous greeting—as if every hand of every arm outstretched to greet the honest had grasped a white flag of faith and trust—as if the city had been sown with some curious new seed, and endowed with a strange vitality, and every door and window and balcony of every house, along the whole route traveled by the guest of the city, had been planted with this wondrous crop, which had sprung up by magic, and blossomed into innumerable flags of peace, of welcome."[14]

The turnout of New York's citizenry was impressive. *Harper's Weekly* commented that "an enormous crowd lined the streets to gaze at him as he passed."[15] With approximately a quarter of a million people spread along almost sixty blocks of city streets, spectators were omnipresent with only the crowd's density varying, as some spots offered better vantage points than others. The street scenes awaiting the President's passage featured spectators spread across a variety of viewing posts. Some were standing along the sidewalks, desirous of getting as near to the passing dignitaries as possible. Depending upon the nature of the neighborhood through which the procession was passing, spectators could be observed perched on stoops, window sills, and balconies. Some of the younger, sprier individuals even climbed up trees and sat on branches, while others dangled from lampposts.

Overhead banners were occasionally displayed, touting such slogans as "WELCOME, May God preserve the Union, and give Abraham Lincoln wisdom and strength to rule over it" and "Fear not Abraham. I am thy shield and thy exceeding great reward—Genesis, 15, 1."[16] Store windows frequently held hand-printed placards, espousing the feelings of their proprietors such as "Welcome, welcome, none too soon!" and "Right makes might!"[17] Some people could be observed wearing special clothing, like the group of small boys, "with military caps and uniforms, waving little flags inscribed 'Lincoln and Hamlin.'"[18] Then there were the members of the Wide-Awakes dressed in their regalia consisting of capes and hats, with a solitary open-eye emblazoned on the front of each chapeau. Policemen along the way snapped to attention and saluted. At the Republican Party's headquarters, the front of the building "was covered by a large flag and a transparency which bore the inscription: 'Welcome to the President-elect. Prosperity to his administration and our Union.'"[19]

When the parade came to the home stretch, Lincoln sat down and put his hat back on his head. As John Nicolay later recalled, "Broadway had been kept clear, so the double line of carriages which made up the procession moved from the depot where the train arrived down the whole length of that magnificent street to the Astor House in perfect order and with plenty of room, giving to the people who crowded the side streets, doors, balconies, windows, and lined even the roofs of the buildings with a continuous fringe of humanity, a clear view of the President-elect."[20] Accompanying its progress southward, the cavalcade was paralleled by a stream of spectators who kept pace all the way to Canal Street. At that point, the sidewalks became more thickly thronged with spectators, negating the ability of parade shadowers to continue any farther. The closer the carriages came to the Astor House, the thicker the crowd grew. Unlike much of the route which had experienced more spontaneous accumulations of spectators, the immediate vicinity of the hotel was one that had witnessed an early influx of people. The build-up in front of the Astor House had started as early as two o'clock and grown steadily as the time of the president's anticipated arrival grew closer.

At 4:30 p.m., the cavalcade reached its destination. However, this was not before a gargantuan effort on the part of the police, who had to bring to bear all their collective patience, strength, and endurance to hold open a lane through an almost impenetrable

As one of New York City's elite hostelries in the middle of the 19th century, the Astor House had the dual honor of hosting both the Lincoln and Hamlin entourages during their two-night layover (Astor House stationary, author's collection).

mass of humanity. But persevere the gallant men in blue did, and President Lincoln was able to safely alight from his transportation. The great American poet Walt Whitman was situated amidst the onlookers that afternoon, seated providentially in a carriage stuck amidst the maelstrom of humanity. From his elevated vantage point, he took in the scene and later described seeing his country's new leader, a man who in the bard's estimation projected "perfect composure and coolness—his unusual and uncouth height, his dress of complete black, stovepipe hat pushed back on the head, dark-brown complexion, seem'd and wrinkled yet canny-looking face, black, bushy head of hair, disproportionately long neck, and his hands held behind as he stood observing the people."[21]

At the end of his account, Whitman had alluded to Lincoln's final act before disappearing into the shrouding depths of the Astor House. He described how Lincoln "looked with curiosity upon that immense sea of faces, and the sea of faces returned the look with similar curiosity… [Eventually] the tall figure gave another relieving stretch or two of arms and legs; then, with a moderate pace, and accompanied by a few unknown-looking persons, ascended the portico steps of the Astor House, [and] disappeared through its broad entrance."[22] After completing his brief perusal, Lincoln entered the hotel, made his way through the lobby, and gained the sanctuary of his third-floor suite. All totaled Lincoln and his entourage occupied eight rooms, four on each side of the hall and facing each other. The entire way was protected by a veritable gauntlet of uniformed officers, ensuring limited access to the presidential quarters.

Why was this particular hostel chosen to provide accommodations for such a distinguished guest? The building into which the president had disappeared, the venerable Astor House, was not much to look at on the outside. A six-story edifice, its heavy, block-like exterior shape was faced in granite. "Only a small temple front on the Broadway side, with two Doric columns and a precisely carved anthemion crest, distinguished Astor's 309-room project from a government storehouse" constituted one reporter's unflatteringly assessment.[23] But once inside, the real forte of the hotel manifested itself. The establishment boasted a staff of over 100 employees, nicely appointed rooms featuring black walnut furniture, spacious venues for large-group meetings, and a magnificent courtyard covered by a cast-iron and glass roof—all in an easily accessible downtown location.

William Bobo, a wealthy Southerner, who visited many hotels in his travels throughout the North and South, gave the Astor House what amounted to five-stars—if not six—in his 1852 book *Glimpses of New-York City*. He raved about the hotel's specialty—peerless service: "At most first-class hotels, the fare is about the same, but there are many little attentions to be had at the Astor that you cannot or rather *do not get anywhere else*. Call for *what* you want, *when* you please, and *where* you please, it seems, from the readiness to serve you that the waiter had anticipated your wish."[24] But, as lavish as this praise was, Mr. Bobo saved its most effusive encomium for last: "There's but one St. Peter's, one Niagara Falls, one Astor House."[25] Lincoln, too, was no stranger to its amenities, having stayed at Astor the previous year, when in town to make what became known as his Cooper Union Address.

Entering his suite, the president spent a few minutes alternately warming by a fireplace and glad-handing those dignitaries who had ridden in the parade. He was soon encouraged to go to the window and acknowledge calls for his appearance. He acceded, respectfully bowing to those below and was duly cheered in return. A few minutes later he repeated the gesture. Eventually, he was persuaded to make a few remarks.

To accomplish this, with what *Harper's Weekly* lauded as "his usual good nature," Lincoln had to unceremoniously climb out the window of his room.[26] With Alderman Cornell hovering attentively nearby, the president carefully positioned himself on the roof over the main entrance to the hotel. For all of the comparatively low trackside stages that the barnstorming president-elect had consistently spurned, he now curiously opted to access a precarious perch thirty feet in the air, one with no railing and never intended to accommodate a speaker. Still, with an estimated "5000 people" jammed within sight of his makeshift rostrum, the vantage point chosen was unquestionably as perfect as it was dangerous a spot from which to orate.[27]

Once the crowd had quieted, he began to speak:

Responding to the pleas of the huge crowd gathered in front of his hotel, the president-elect spoke briefly from the precarious position of a pediment over the building's main entrance (*Harper's Weekly*).

> Fellow-citizens: I have stepped before you merely in compliance with what appears to be your wish, and not with the purpose of making a speech this afternoon. I could not be heard by any but a small fraction of you at best, but, what is still worse than that, I just now have nothing to say that is worthy of your hearing. [*Applause.*] I beg you to believe that I do not now refuse to address you from any disposition to disoblige you, but, to the contrary. But, at the same time, I beg you to excuse me for the present. [*Applause.*][28]

Once again—in his final speaking appearance before the general public in the Empire State—Lincoln had continued his practice of saying few words and nothing of substance. The people had aspired to see and hear him, and they were rewarded on both counts. As if to confirm the lack of substance in his own bland offering, Lincoln was later quoted as saying that "there was not much harm in it at any rate."[29]

* * *

While Lincoln was accommodating New Yorkers, Hannibal Hamlin was about an hour from doing the same. Contrasting sharply with the Lincolns' early departure, the vice president did not leave Windsor Locks, Connecticut, until noontime. Before exiting, he and his wife spent the morning at the Connecticut Literary Institution in nearby Suffield. Seizing the moment as any good politician would with a captive audience in the school's chapel, Hamlin delivered a brief speech. A hearty round of applause greeted the conclusion of his remarks. He then returned to his carriage, passing between long lines of students respectfully drawn up on both sides of the walkway, and went back to his host's home for a luncheon reception before heading for the railroad station.

Upon reaching the depot, the vice president-elect found another large assemblage of well-wishers. After he imparted a few last words, he departed to ringing cheers. No sooner had the train begun to gather momentum than its forward progress slowed, for the express was stopping at Hartford. Arriving at 12:15 p.m., Hamlin "was greeted with tumultuous cheers from thousands of ladies and gentlemen who had assembled in and around the depot."[30] Constrained by the local police, the crowd clamored for Hamlin's appearance,. Finally the Pine Tree statesman stepped out onto the platform of the rear coach. Greeting him was Hartford's mayor, Henry Deming. A graduate of Yale University and Harvard Law School, Deming was an accomplished individual in his own right. Not only did he have the distinction of being a four-term member of the Connecticut House of Representatives and three-term mayor of Hartford, but later, as colonel of the 12th Connecticut Infantry, he would take part in the capture of New Orleans and subsequently be appointed mayor of New Orleans as a part of the occupation forces.

After introducing himself to Mr. Hamlin, his Honor then presented the vice-president to the eager throng packed before them: "I have the honor of introducing to you [turning to the crowd], Hon. Hannibal Hamlin of Maine, Vice-President of the United States. [*Three cheers for Hamlin.*] Long live the man, the office, the Constitution, and the Union! [*Great cheering.*]" Hamlin kept his words brief:

> Fellow Citizens: I am gratified to meet you here in such large numbers. But I cannot concur in all the kind words which my friend has uttered. It is not a mark of respect to myself personally, but as evidence of devotion to a common cause and a common Union. [*Cheers.*] Individuals are as unimportant in such a crisis, as the unreal atoms of dust driven by the wind. [*Cheers.*] But the principles inherited from our fathers will never perish. [*Cries of "good" and cheers.*]
>
> Let New England be just to all the broad land—let fraternal feelings be cherished toward all the Union—in the name of God let us administer the government in the principles upon which our fathers framed it. [*Cheers.*] With a heart that beats in union with the principles you have so patriotically espoused, I can heartily say, "The Union now and forever." [*Great cheering.*][31]

Closure came again as it had in Worcester, with the engineer crisply sounding the whistle and tugging vigorously on the bell chord. The guest of honor was still talking as the train pulled out, sent on its way to the accompaniment of applause and cheers. As her husband took his seat in the coach, basking in the afterglow of another warm reception, Mrs. Hamlin happily clutched a beautiful bouquet of flowers presented to her by a well-wisher.

From Hartford, the next station lay twenty-one miles south at Meriden, where Mr. Hamlin spoke from the baggage car. In keeping with the presentation style that had now become his established practice, Hamlin's oration was extemporaneous. Sharply contrasting with the Lincolns' highly-scripted itinerary and its pre-determined halts and layovers, only Hamlin's route through the four states appeared to be set in stone. Otherwise, his stops and particularly his overnight stay at Windsor Locks, like his speeches, all had an unplanned aspect to them. Even the impressive crowds that greeted him so warmly had materialized without much forewarning. This was confirmed by one of the imbedded reporters on the train, who commented that "the approach of Mr. Hamlin had been but a short time announced that at the various stations, so that mammoth gatherings were necessarily as spontaneous as the speeches of Mr. Hamlin; yet the receptions all along were characterized with a depth of feeling that must have warmed the heart and strengthened the resolution of the recipient."[32]

Indicative of this rather impulsive, open-ended approach was the fact that on Tuesday evening, as the vice president-elect was resting in Connecticut, a reception committee stood awaiting him at the depot in New York City. No one had apparently thought to pass on the change in his plans.

But such was the limited scope of the pre-planning that no prescribed timetable or security precautions dictated adherence to a rigid schedule. Besides, in the innocence of era before a sobering lesson was taught at Ford's Theater, what harm did a duly-elected, high-government official have to fear from his countrymen? At Hartford, drawing no overt response from the police, Hamlin was briefly harangued by a rude, vociferous heckler. At Meriden, the crowds pressed right up to the edge of the speaker's platform. Close enough so that "the bouquets which the ladies brought were tossed up to him and fell about his feet."[33] At his stop in New Haven, the crowd pressed in close as the incoming vice president spoke:

> We may disagree, somewhat, he said, in our political opinions, but we could have but one opinion of our duty to that country to which we owe allegiance—an allegiance which must be answered by every instinct an principle of manhood, and if necessary with our lives. [*Cheers.*] I think I know something of the New England head and the New England heart. [*Cheers and cries of "That's so!"*] I think I know that they are earnestly loyal to our Union as it is [*applause*], and I think I know also, that the head and heart are willing to concede to all Americans every constitutional right to which they themselves are entitled. [*Great cheering.*] We welcome the outcast and down trodden of all nations to our shores from the hovels of Ireland, from the mines of England, from the vassal states of France—only demanding in return, that when they have come, and joined us in this grand triumph of self-government, they shall be true and loyal American citizens! [*Vociferous cheers, many times repeated.*] We only ask, intend to ask, that all who are born beneath the benignant folds of our stars and stripes, and all who adopt the flag as the standard of their choice, shall be loyal to the idea typifies, and, in that loyalty, *discharge all of their obligations.* [*Rapturous cheers, in the midst of which the train started.*][34]

With the conclusion of his remarks at the Meriden station, New Haven loomed as the next place on his itinerary. At different spots along the tracks, the scenes mirrored those which Lincoln had been experiencing. People gathered at the smaller way stations, peered from the windows of their homes, stood on rooftops, and collected on hills and in fields—all "eager to catch a glimpse of the distinguished passenger and hurrahing in the most indescribable and unprecedented manner, as the train flew by, at the gratifying reflection that the President and Vice-President were en route for the Capital, and the eventful Fourth so near."[35]

On gaining the station at New Haven, Hamlin was met by another huge crowd overflowing the depot and its grounds. Gauged to be present in greater numbers than any of the previous crowds in the Nutmeg State, these folks also exuded an even more zealous demeanor than even the animated citizenry who had greeted Hamlin at the state capital. Aroused to a fever pitch, the crowd responded enthusiastically to Hamlin's well-chosen words. But no part of his oration elicited a greater roar of affirmation than when he invoked the name of the new president: "It was devotion to common principles that brought them together—the great principles of the Fathers of the Republic, now represented in the nation by that great and good man, whom the people had elevated to the highest office within the gift of any people on earthy—Abraham Lincoln of Illinois!"[36]

Would that such were even possible, the crowd's hearty response was ramped up to even higher decibels as the vice president's remarks fell upon their ears. The people spontaneously surged in as close as possible, as he obligingly leaned forward from the train in order to shake all the proffered hands that he could. Then the unexpected happened. Off-balance as he reached out, the sudden movement of the train caused Mr. Hamlin to pitch headlong into the crowd. The distinguished guest suddenly faced the prospect of remaining amongst his gleeful admirers, while his wife helplessly watched in surprise as her husband's visage faded into the distance. But the matter was soon rectified. The engineer applied the brakes, and locomotive screeched to a halt. Meanwhile Hamlin had managed to extricate himself from the grasp of his New Haven well-wishers. According to William Croffut, the *Herald's* reporter on the scene, "the train was pushed back to the platform, giving the orator time to round off his speech"—the only cost of this misadventure was a little lost time and his beaver hat, which fell from his head and was demolished by the sea of humanity.[37]

With New Haven behind them, Hamlin's party had approximately eighty miles to go. Only Bridgeport and Stamford remained in the Connecticut portion of their journey. Reaching Bridgeport, they found an impressive assemblage of spectators at this rapidly-growing city. They manifested their excitement when they "hurrahed for Hamlin, hurrahed for Lincoln and the Union, and clamored earnestly from some remarks from Mr. Hamlin."[38] Unfortunately, the vice president-elect was somewhat exhausted by his efforts to extricate himself from the New Haven crowd and perhaps just a bit reluctant to get mauled again—even if the intentions of the people had not been malevolent. After this abbreviated stop, the final appearance of the vice-president-elect in Connecticut was at Stamford, where once again he was able to briefly address the crowd. Then he was off to the Empire State and his rendezvous with Abraham Lincoln.

When the two newly-elected officials eventually united, mutual experiences about which they could converse were the train ride and speaking stops that each had made en route. Coincidentally, little less than one year before, presidential aspirant Abraham Lincoln had traversed the same New England route. He had initially occasioned to be in the vicinity due to a visit to Exeter, New Hampshire, where he had gone to visit his son Robert. In returning to New York, the candidate made some speeches on behalf of Republicans in Connecticut's gubernatorial election—support for them, exposure for him. Like Hamlin, he spoke in Hartford, Meriden, and New Haven. One significant difference was that on Lincoln's 1860 circuit, he was travelling as a private citizen, so the tab for his needs was generally covered by his own funds. However, expenses for room and board were occasionally defrayed by accommodating hosts along the way, such as in New Haven where lodging was provided by James F. Babcock, editor of the *New Haven Palladium*. Eight months later, when the Illinois rail-splitter was elected president, he did extremely well with the electorate in Connecticut, garnering 58 percent of the popular vote, a mark which easily surpassed the anemic 39 percent that he received from the entire country.

Not surprisingly, given the low-key nature of his passage up to this point, it was only fitting that the vice president-elect's entry into New York City would be equally unobtrusive. Desiring to avoid a grand entrance, Hamlin "had planned to come into the city as quietly as possible, and therefore did not apprise his friends here of his coming until along in the afternoon."[39] Arrangements were quickly made, so that the five o'clock arrival via the New Haven Railroad would be met by several carriages. While a small coterie of Republican dignitaries were present at the Fourth Avenue and Twenty-Seventh Street depot, a crowd did not materialize. In the *New York Herald's* estimation of the meager reception, "the whole number would not perhaps reach more than a hundred, the majority of these were boys and people of the immediate neighborhood."[40] With its progress unimpeded, Hamlin's party arrived at the Astor House by six p.m.

Hamlin entered through the front door, where he was cheered by a crowd of several hundred onlookers; however, once gaining the lobby, he went to his room comparatively unnoticed. Having traveled at his own pace to connect with Lincoln and, for the most part, kept the limelight to a minimum, Hamlin was henceforth going to exist in a different orbit, facing the scrutiny, expectations, and demands that accompanied ascension to a high governmental office. This new world into which he was ushered made its first intrusion immediately, for the Hamlins barely had time to get settled before Lincoln summoned his running-mate for a brief meet. For only the second time in their lives, the two members of the winning ticket conferred.

Immediately following their husbands' brief tête-à-tête, the gentlemen's wives were expected to partake in a formal dinner in a room that adjoined the Lincolns' suite. As the couples entered the dining area at 6 o'clock, Mr. Lincoln escorted Mrs. Hamlin and Mr. Hamlin escorted Mrs. Lincoln. From all observations, the two ladies presented an interesting contrast. Ellen Hamlin appeared as "a very neat-looking woman, with auburn hair, apparently about thirty-two years of age, and a lady of much simplicity of manners."[41] By comparison, Mary Lincoln was forty-two and 5'2" with blue eyes and reddish-brown hair. However, time and four children had added enough extra pounds to her torso that she could be considered stout. One peculiarity that she shared with Ellen Hamlin was that of being considerably younger than her husband. Ellen Hamlin at 26 was a half her husband's age, while Mary's 42 made her 11 years younger than the president. However, whatever shortcomings she may have had, one was not a lack of social graces. For, as the daughter of a wealthy Kentucky family, Mary Todd had experienced a genteel Southern upbringing, one which well-prepared her for dinner parties the likes of which she was about to attend and the various levees hosted along the pre-inaugural tour.

Once inside the chamber, the diners gazed at a most inviting room, for the hotel management provided an elegant setting. A substantial round table, capable of seating all ten guests, was at the center of the room. Fresh-cut flowers were placed in glasses at each setting, and a large arrangement commanded attention as a centerpiece. Buffet tables around the outer edges of the room were laden with all kinds of edibles. Under one of the tables, an array of decanters containing wine coolers was available. On another stand, a specially ordered silver tea set was awaiting its first use. Hung on the wall over the fireplace mantel was an oversized painting, set in a gilded frame, of *Washington Crossing the Delaware*. Ambiance and warmth was provided by a fire crackling on the hearth. The whole room was brilliantly lit by a crystal-glass chandelier.

Given that the Astor House may have ranked among the swankier establishments in which the Lincolns had been entertained, it came as no surprise that the bill of fare for this occasion was going to be outside the norm of what these simple prairie folk customary ate. Two menus were available: one was printed on "a scalloped edge sheet of note paper, in black with a gold border, on a white ground, oval in form, the outer part being in pink and 'other soft colors'"; and the second was offered on pea green paper and written in French.

Regardless of the version a diner selected, the menu featuring such items as "boiled salmon with anchovy sauce," "Tureen of goose liver," and "fillet of chicken with truffle sauce" may have exceeded the normal pale of the Lincolns' palates, but it was the president's observation regarding the "Shrewsbury oysters, baked in the shell" that elicited his most telling comment.[42] With a plate of these New England delicacies staring him in the face, Mr. Lincoln said: "Well, I don't know that I can manage these things, but I guess I can learn."[43]

Though the meal was sumptuous and the opportunity to relax appreciated, the dinner concluded when the president arose to attend the first of two political engagements. By then, the Lincolns had already put in twelve-hours filled with traveling, orating, touring, and socializing; yet, even on the heels of the long, grueling day just spent in Albany, the president was not yet quite free of his evening's obligations. At eight o'clock, he met in his reception room with Fernando Wood, several other city officials, some Republican committeemen, and a few prominent merchants. This brief introduction represented merely a courtesy call by the city's top administrative personnel, with the official welcome not coming until the next day at city hall. Then at about 8:20 p.m., Lincoln went downstairs to a dining area, referenced as the "gentlemen's ordinary," for it was reserved for males-only. Still on the night's agenda was a paying of dues—Lincoln had agreed to meet with a delegation representing the various Republican clubs of the city. Since their members had campaigned tirelessly on his behalf during the recent campaign, he owed them special thanks. Numbering 100 strong, they came to together at a local headquarters on Broadway and marched two by two to the Astor House.

By the time the president made his appearance, what was billed as a "private audience" for the party faithful had blossomed into a public reception, given the number of bogus guests who had connived their way into the gathering area. The scene which Lincoln beheld was chaotic. One reporter likened those present as "noisy as a lot of schoolboys on the playground and, not until repeated cries of 'order,' 'silence,' etc., had been vociferated could anyone have either a chance to speak or hear."[44] With great effort, the ever-alert police cleared a path through the crowd, so that Mr. Lincoln could reach a centralized location.

In the way of introductions, E. Delafield Smith—a prominent New York attorney and leading Republican functionary—did the honors. Smith began by highlighting the esteemed historical heritage of the room in which the president was about to speak: "It is a remarkable incident that there should have been but two receptions until tonight in this room. One was to Daniel Webster, the other to Henry Clay; and a third is to Abraham Lincoln."[45] This revelation elicited cheers from the packed room. Mr. Smith then concluded his brief comments with thoughts that were foremost in the minds of many Americans, not just those gathered before him: "Our country is in a condition that calls for the anxiety of all who love it. Our faith must be in the wise few and in faithful and honest many. We greet you earnestly and cordially, and ask that we may hear your voice for a few moments, in response to the welcome we offer you."[46]

Before he could begin, cries arose from the audience beseeching the president to stand upon a chair in order that all might see and hear him. Ever accommodating, Lincoln acceded to their wishes and mounted a table, making his accumulated height in the vicinity of an imposing nine feet. Self-effacing as was his want, he opened his address by sharing his feeling that "I am rather an old man to avail myself of such an excuse as I am now about to do. Yet the truth is so distinct, and presses itself so distinctly upon me that I cannot avoid it—and that is, I did not understand when I was brought into this room that I was brought in here to make a speech."[47] However, among as supportive an audience as he was apt to find east of Illinois, he did share with them the intent behind his reluctance to speak: "I have been occupying a position since the presidential election, of silence," he said, "of avoiding public speaking, of avoiding public writing. I have been doing so because I thought, upon full consideration that was the proper course for me to take." The expression of these sentiments was met with a great round of approving applause, to which he replied: "I have kept silence for the reason that I supposed that it was peculiarly proper that I should do so until the time came when, according to the custom of the country, I could speak out officially."[48]

For a speech that he claimed unprepared to give, this impromptu oration was undoubtedly one of the most revealing that he uttered in all of New York State. In his conclusion, he affirmed his position that he intended to act as the president of the whole country, not just one section: "I said several times upon this journey, and I shall now repeat it to you, that when the time does come I shall then take the ground that I think is right—the ground I think is right for the North, for the South, for the East, for the West, for the whole country. And in doing so I hope to feel no necessity pressing upon me to say anything in conflict with the constitution, in conflict with the continued union of these States in conflict with the perpetuation of liberties of these people or anything in conflict with anything whatever that I have ever given you reason to expect from me."[49] For a man who prefaced his remarks with the caveat that he was completely unprepared, the president-elect gave a highly credible account of himself, demonstrating that he possessed the valuable skill of extemporaneous speaking when the situation required such.

Having satisfied his supporters, he then had to comply with another expectation, which meant standing in a receiving line to greet well-wishers. Shifting to the opposite end of the room, the president was aided once again by the ever-present members of the NYPD. They positioned themselves in such a way that visitors were funneled toward the guest of honor, bringing order to the receiving line and in turn expediting the rapid passage of the public. In agreeing to this format, Lincoln knew the ordeal for which he was setting himself up. An aching, red, and swollen hand was often its painful after-effect. The handshaking ritual commenced about 8:30 p.m. Once Lincoln indicated that he was ready, "the rush commenced, and, after admonitions to please 'shake easy,' 'hurry along,' 'make quick work,' and sundry like suggestions, the crowd began to move out rapidly."[50] The speed of the line was enhanced by the technique that Lincoln adopted, "taking them hand-over-hand, with a hearty grasp and an earnest shake, saying to all 'How d'ye do?' 'God bless you,' 'Good to see you' ... as the moment suggested."[51]

Eventually the flow slackened considerably, and Lincoln seized the opportunity to conclude his commitment. He then retired under police escort to his suite. The reception in its entirety lasted until ten o'clock. After another lengthy day, Lincoln finally turned in for the night. As the weary man drifted off into a well-earned sleep, his mind may have replayed the events of a very busy but satisfying experience, one which caused the *New York Times* to first conjecture and then praise that "the reception in this City must have been particularly gratifying to him, and was also well worthy of the Metropolis."[52]

11

Final Hours in the Empire State
A Successful Stay Draws to an End

Arising in the morning of February 21, a travel-weary Abraham Lincoln did not have to worry about another taxing train ride until tomorrow. The trade-off, however, was to be whisked around metropolis by carriage ... and still subjected to the same public expectations and scrutiny, but with only city blocks rather than country miles between stops.

But, regardless of what the new day might bring, the president-elect had to be buoyed by the greeting which the city gave him. "If any doubt had previously existed of the steady loyalty and law-abiding temper of this City," the *New York Times* observed, "it is set at rest by the welcome which yesterday greeted Mr. Lincoln ... certainly no welcome could have been more cordial or respectful. The harmony of incessant cheers was unbroken by indecent language or gesture, or act of violence. Along the protracted route, the president was encountered everywhere by indications of the most earnest goodwill and respect for his person, and for his high and momentous vocation, and if there lurked anywhere those feelings of discontent and malignity, which a portion of the City Press has accustomed to debate upon, they had the courtesy to mask themselves perfectly for this occasion."[1]

The first appointment on the day's schedule was an eight-thirty breakfast, given in the president's honor by Moses Grinnell. A native New Englander, Grinnell was a successful merchant who liked to dispense behind-the-scenes advice to government officials. If in the process, he could land some sort of governmental appointment, then so much the better.

With his daughter helping host the early morning meal in his impressive mansion, Grinnell seized the occasion to invite a blue-ribbon group of twenty-nine local businessmen in for chance to meet the President. Such a gathering offered a splendid opportunity to establish connections. Being that Grinnell's friends represented various elements of the business community, some undoubtedly attended in anticipation of leaving with a foot in the federal government's door, one that could eventually prove profitable.

But most to a large degree came hoping to obtain a first-hand assessment of what the president-elect's intentions might be toward the South, for any actions that he took could have profound reverberations affecting New York City's economic life. Many in the room were already feeling a post-election impact in their wallets. Business in general had fallen off. The stock market was down. Among this stellar assemblage could be found a veritable who's who of New York City's business elite such as: financier and ex–governor Hamilton Fish; banker and railroad magnate David Hoadley; banker and shipper Thomas Tileston;

merchant, trader railroad mogul William Aspinwall; and manufacturer and philanthropist Robert L. Stuart;. Wealth and power abounded in profusion among this well-heeled assemblage. When one of the guests took note of the presence of so many millionaires, Lincoln—ever ready to put his own humorous slant on the gentleman's self-promoting observation—commented: "Well, that's quite right. I'm a millionaire myself. I got a minority of a million in votes in November."[2]

For financial reasons, these men held deep-rooted, personal interests in the impact that a civil war could have on their business enterprises. Since the attendees all had pressing obligations that did not allow them to tarry long, the get-together broke up relatively early. Lincoln was back at the Astor House by 10:30. But the prevailing feeling was that the breakfast had offered "very elegant entertainment and a free exchange of opinion on the present condition of public affairs."[3] For Lincoln, the event helped him to establish initial contacts with many influential men who backed him to the hilt when the conflict came. J. J. Astor, for example, helped raise millions to supply equipment to the troops, as well provide assistance to their families. William Aspinwall was one of the founders and first vice-president of the Union League Club, a group of loyal New Yorkers who led fund-raising drives to support the United States Sanitary Commission;. and Hamilton Fish served in several important diplomatic capacities over his career, one being on the presidential commission that set up the protocols for prisoner of war exchanges between the North and South. In addition to the many individual efforts, "a consortium of New York bankers … along with several Philadelphia and Boston financiers, collectively loaned the government 150 million dollars … [with] nearly one fifth of the amount coming from New York's 39 participating banks."[4] This was as prodigious as it was patriotic an effort, and the support spoke well of the confidence in Lincoln that city leaders had.

Upon his return to the hotel, Lincoln had a short break before making an important appearance at City Hall. Then, at 11:00 a.m., he was expected to be attend a formal welcome to New York by its mayor. Compared to his most recent travels across the state, this appointment would be easy to make, for the city's seat of government was just across the street from the Astor House. In the meantime, the president got to extend a courtesy that the people-person in him thoroughly enjoyed.

On this occasion, he was introduced by police superintendent James Kennedy to a ninety-four-year-old gentleman from Brooklyn named Joshua Dewey. A graduate of Yale and a former teacher, farmer, and legislator in upstate New York, Dewey's past record of exemplary patriotism was his golden ticket to a meeting with the President. For, as it turned out, the elderly nonagenarian, standing with an outstretched hand, was a veteran—not only of the War of 1812 but the Revolution as well, a war in which he served as a fifteen-year-old. Additionally, he had voted in every national election since George Washington had first run for office in 1789.

Even more germane to present company, Mr. Dewey shared that he had cast his most recent ballot on behalf of "Honest Old Abe."[5] As much as the opportunity to meet Mr. Lincoln must have meant to the old soldier, an observer also noted that "the President seemed quite happy at the circumstances, and received the congratulations of the venerable gentleman with evident pleasure."[6]

After a lengthy meeting, Dewey departed very pleased with both husband and wife. As a keepsake of the occasion, a friend of Dewey's gave the president an "elegant photograph" of the elderly warrior, "hoping that this simple memento may not be unacceptable to one who has been called to administer the government of so great, generous, and confiding a people."[7] Among the other dignitaries to whom brief introductions were granted was the famous preacher Lyman Beecher, known far and wide not only for his stance on temperance but also as the father of Harriet Beecher Stowe, the author of *Uncle Tom's Cabin*.

This pleasant interlude passed altogether too quickly, for the president-elect was soon ushered to a pair of waiting carriages and driven to meet the mayor. In keeping with any public appearance made by Mr. Lincoln on his inaugural tour, a sizable crowd and their interminable cheering greeted his progress toward the seat of municipal government. The *New York Times* affirmed that "the scene on the line of march was but a repetition of that which has characterized Mr. Lincoln's every appearance since the commencement of his present journey—only intensified up to the New York standard."[8] Again the indefatigable members of the NYPD provided crowd control, particularly noticeable at the end of the ride where officers had cleared a path for president from his carriage up the steps and into city hall. He was able to make the short walk "with as little obstruction as if he was in his own garden at Springfield."[9]

The building which was his destination could not be missed. Dating to 1830, it remains today the oldest structure of its kind still used in the United States. Designed in an ornate French Renaissance style, its main façade was of a rich Massachusetts marble, in effect putting its best face forward, for a much cheaper brownstone was used in the anterior portions. The municipality's headquarters was entered via a wide flight of steps leading to doors under a multi-columned portico framed by a balustrade, all of which ran the length of the stairs. In its general layout, the building resembled the U.S. Capitol in that its basic blueprint was a central core with attached wings on either side. Once inside, visitors found themselves standing under a great rotunda and facing an impressive marble stairway which led to the second floor. Of the several interior locations available, from the spacious chamber of the Board of Councilmen to the cramped press room, Lincoln was guided to one called the "Governor's Room." Here he was greeted by the city fathers, these being Fernando Wood and the City Council. The press was of course there too, out in force to report on this auspicious occasion.

When the Lincoln entered the room, he did so with hat in hand, displaying his customary humble, unassuming nature. Fernando Wood was waiting for him, standing behind a desk that had once been used by George Washington. Employing this hallowed piece of furniture as a barrier was likely a calculated strategy, keeping Lincoln at an arm's length and preventing an overly cordial welcome. The formal, stilted nature of the greeting was not lost on observers, for to some who witnessed the introduction the president "appeared more like a schoolboy, called up to recite his lessons, than the head of a great nation over which he was to exert great power and abiding control."[10]

Also readily apparent was the sharp contrast in appearance between the two men: where President Lincoln was "tall, gaunt, and rugged, with angular, rough-hewn features, but a kindly expression, unpolished in manner and ungraceful in speech, but evidently sincere and genuine," Wood came across "as erect and agile, with a perfectly smooth face, easy graceful manners and fine address, but with a countenance as devoid of any indication of his thoughts and as free from the least sign of impulse or genuineness of any kind."[11]

Escorted to a spot near the mayor, Lincoln stood attentively, arms folded, as his Honor addressed him:

> Mr. Lincoln: As Mayor of New York, it becomes my duty to extend to you an official welcome on behalf of the Corporation. In doing so, permit me to say, that this City has never offered hospitality to a man clothed with more exalted powers, or resting under graver responsibilities, than these which circumstances have devolved upon you. Coming into office with a dismembered Government to reconstruct, and a disconnected and hostile people to reconcile, it will require a high patriotism, and an elevated comprehension of the whole country and its varied interests, opinions and prejudices, to so conduct public affairs as to bring it back again to its former harmonious, consolidated and prosperous condition.
>
> If I refer to this topic, Sir, it is because New York is so deeply interested. The present political divisions have sorely afflicted her people. All of her material interests are paralyzed. Her commercial greatness is endangered. She is the child of the American Union. She has grown up under its maternal care, and been fostered by its paternal bounty, and we fear therefore, chosen under the forms of the Constitution as the head of the Confederacy, we look for a restoration of fraternal relations between the States— only to be accomplished by peaceful and conciliatory means—aided by the wisdom of Almighty God.[12]

While some felt that the he had been rude and disrespectful to the honored guest in his remarks—bordering on delivering a moralizing lecture—Wood's right wing philosophies were well-established by this time and came as no surprise. He had simply seized a high-profile moment to reiterate the radical ideology that he and many of his supporters had trumpeted long before Abraham Lincoln came to town. At the heart of their anxiety was the fear of severe financial loss if war came. Creditors' ledger books told one aspect of the story all too well—Southerners were heavily indebted to New York City merchants. Hundreds of millions of dollars were owed to Yankee businessmen. A civil war would conceivably abrogate any responsibility to make good these outstanding obligations. Depending upon the solvency of a given Northern enterprise, any defaults by Southerners could put the business owner's accounts in the red and force him to close his doors.

While these were individual tragedies, the city fathers were also collectively anxious about another unsettling prospect—a war could cost New York City its pre-eminent position as the port of entry for East Coast trade. The fear in this case was that a Southern port—such as New Orleans—buttressed by lower tariffs as a draw, could divert trade away from New York.

As if these thoughts were not enough to make the newly-elected president an object of suspicion, Wood had also been espousing a radical plan to create a "free city." If it came to pass that Union was dissolved, he then foresaw New York City seceding and establishing a Republic of New York. By maintaining a stance of neutrality, he envisioned the metropolis retaining its status as a trading center, for not only the North and South but the whole Western Hemisphere. Wood painted an attractive picture when he prophesized that "as a free city, with but nominal duty on imports, her local Government could be supported without taxation upon her people. Thus we could live free from taxes, and have cheap goods nearly duty free."[13] While the mayor had some support among the business community and one newspaper edited by his brother, the general consensus was pointedly voiced by Horace Greeley through the *New York Tribune*: "Fernando Wood evidently wants to be a traitor; it is a lack of courage only that makes him content with being a blackguard."[14] But to the peoples' credit, when the war finally came, fears of any sedition on the part of the citizenry proved groundless. For ultimately, patriotism trumped economics among the populace of New York City.

At the conclusion of the mayor's speech, applause followed by a murmur rippled through the crowd. Some approved of his message, while others were not necessarily in agreement. Most wondered with much anticipation how Lincoln would respond. They did not have long to wait, as he took the floor shortly after Wood had finished. With a calm look and broad smile gracing his face, he addressed those gathered before him:

> Mr. Mayor: It is with feelings of deep gratitude that I make my acknowledgements for the reception that has been given me in the great commercial City of New York. I cannot but remember that it is done by the people, who do not to a large majority, agree with me in political sentiment. It is the more grateful to me, because in this I see that for the great principles of our Government the people are pretty nearly or quite unanimous. In regard to the difficulties that confront us at this time, and of which you have seen fit to speak so becomingly, and so justly, as I suppose, I can only say that I agree with the sentiments expressed by the mayor. In my devotion to the Union, I hope am behind no man in the nation. As to my wisdom in conducting affairs so as to tend to the preservation of the Union, I fear too great confidence may have been placed in me. I am sure I bring a heart devoted to the work. There is nothing that could ever bring me to consent—willingly to consent—to the destruction of this Union, in which not only the great City of New York, but the whole country has acquired its greatness, unless it would be that thing for which the Union itself was made. I understand that the ship was made for carrying and preservation of its cargo, and so long as the ship is safe with the cargo, it shall not be abandoned. This Union shall never be abandoned unless the possibility of its existence shall cease to exist, without the necessity of throwing passengers and cargo overboard. So long, then, as it is possible that the prosperity and liberties of this people can be preserved within this Union, it shall be my purpose at all times to preserve it. And now, Mr. Mayor, renewing my thanks for this cordial reception, allow me to close. [*Applause.*][15]

Following his brief oration, Lincoln was expected to engage in one of the ceremonial duties that he found simultaneously enjoyable yet taxing—handshaking in a reception line. The first round was easy, calling for him to meet those remaining members of the common council to whom he had not yet been introduced. In the meantime, the waiting crowd had grown increasingly loud and unruly. Two guards strained mightily to keep the doors closed during the brief ceremony. Then at 11:15 the real challenge of the day began, for the first of over 5000 well-wishers were admitted. The immediate effect was as if a dam had burst, so rapidly did the mob surge forward that "a tremendous clamor and rush characterized the entry of the population."[16] The ensuing "jam was tremendous, and the scene inside the Governor's Room was ludicrous in the extreme" was how the *Brooklyn Daily Eagle's* correspondent assessed the situation.[17]

But the police were ready. To establish much-needed elements of control and order, officers had arrayed themselves in two lines, starting with the main entrance or center doors of the room and continuing across to and out through another set on the western or backside. After being ushered along the receiving line, at an estimated rate of "fifty per minute," the citizenry exited the room through an anti-chamber, then downstairs to the vestibule of the hall, and finally were disgorged from the building into the park in front.[18]

Lincoln's position in the line placed him in front of a bronze statue of George Washington by Houdon. Once again, he towered over all others, so that people entering the room easily spotted their objective. Mayor Wood had encouraged him to forego shaking hands, as much to spare him the agony that would eventually come as to speed up movement of the crowd. Lincoln, however, demurred. Like fellow politician Lyndon Johnson espoused one hundred years later, the old rail-splitter liked direct contact with his constituency—"pressing the flesh" was LBJ's earthy descriptor.

So Lincoln dove in with gusto. For each guest, he proffered a hearty grasp of the hand and a personal salutation. The progress of the line was unfortunately not as smooth as would have benefited the large numbers waiting outside the room, down the stairs, and on out in front. Given the impulses of various individuals, the line was prone to move in fits and starts, held up when someone wanted to hand the president a note, quote scripture to him, or whisper in his ear. As for whom these people were who turned out to endure inclement weather and brave large numbers, in an observer's assessment "a motley crowd they were, old and young, millionaires and mudlarks, some high in polish and social standing, and others proportionately low in both, respectable middle-aged gentlemen, with gold-rimmed spectacles and canes, and others, the neediest of the needy, and the toughest of the b'boys, all mingled together, and all eager to take the rail-splitter by the hand."[19] Most of these passers-by did so in anonymity, though occasionally a familiar face would appear and the mayor or one of the committeemen would make a proper introduction to the new president.

As their turn came before him, men respectfully doffed their hats. Virtually everyone offered a few words to Mr. Lincoln. "God bless you," "Stand firm," and "Glad to see you" were the favorite greetings.[20] While there was little time to engage in meaningful repartee, an occasional individual—such as ex-mayor James Harper—got a special introduction, as did former-governor Myron Clark.

Later, thirty gray-haired veterans of the War of 1812 passed before the president, presenting him with a series of complimentary resolutions. Many were proudly decked out in their old uniforms; other simply wore identifying badges. Their commander gushed that "I must offer to shake hands with you; we are Union men," which elicited an agreeable reply from the president-to-be: "Certainly, I must shake hands with all of the veterans."[21] At some point, an exceptionally tall man strode up to Mr. Lincoln, expecting that he might match if not exceed the chief executive's height. But he came up several inches short after the two men stood back-to-back. Lincoln's ready wit manifested itself at that moment. As the Vermonter walked away laughing, he said: "Well I will give in," to which Mr. Lincoln remarked, "I saw that he was stretching himself to make the question, so I thought I would try it."[22]

Another individual of unusual height soon made an appearance in the line. Bearing the name of Tom Hyer, he was but slightly shorter than the president at six-foot, two-and-half-inches. Famous in his own right, Hyer was known as America's first heavyweight boxing champion, gaining the title in 1841 and not relinquishing it until his retirement. Much to amusement of those within hearing distance, Lincoln put up his fists in a mock, pugilistic pose, while at the same time imploring "Don't strike me, Mr. Hyer!"[23]

As these vignettes bear witness, Lincoln was in his element exchanging snippets of repartee with the public. In these brief moments, his outgoing, jocular, unassuming, and courteous nature manifested itself in an easy, charming manner. Even the most fleeting exchanges had the power to etch indelible memories in the minds of their recipients, serving to further cement the impression of Abraham Lincoln as a man of the people.

As the flow of well-wishers continued unabated, the mayor suggested that perhaps his guest might let the doors be closed and the reception ended. Forty-five minutes of unabated handshaking led him to observe that "they will keep you here all day if you stay," but Lincoln assured him that he was game to continue until 1:00 o'clock.[24] His rationale for standing firm was straightforward and simple: "I will stay the two hours out, so as to keep up the bargain that I made."[25] But he was willing to concede that come 12:00 p.m., he would forego the handshaking for the second hour. However, one concession that he did immediately make was to let the mayor help him shed his overcoat, for the crowded room and vigorous pumping of hands—sometimes with both extended at one time to accommodate a pair of well-wishers simultaneously—had caused the Lincoln to be uncomfortably warm.

By the time the clock in the park struck noon, over 3000 people had already made their way through the receiving line. Given that he had been taking their hands at a steady, unrelenting pace, Lincoln now no longer balked at the mayor's previous suggestion that he discontinue this form of greeting. In the estimation of one who was present, "Uncle Abe couldn't shake any more ... in fact, he looked as if he required a rest."[26] From now on, he would be content to just bow, which meant that he was in for a lot of bobbing up and down as a non-stop flow of excited people swept through the room. In most instances, his bow was accompanied with a polite "How do you do, sir!"[27]

What passed before him was "one continuous heterogeneous outpouring of humanity, such as can be gathered together in no other place outside of New York. German, Irish, Italian, Frenchmen. Americans, republicans, democrats, people of no particular political opinions, old soldiers, young Yankees, all went to make up the picture."[28] Those who knew the composition of the crowd by its appearance recognized not only metropolitan New Yorkers from all parts of the city, but also country folk who had obviously made the trek in for a chance to see, their country's newly-elected chief executive. Unlike the orderly reception at the Delavan House in Albany, the receiving line in which he was currently participating bordered on a stampede. Part of the disparity was easily attributable to the sheer weight of numbers who turned out. The time of day only served to swell what would have proportionally been a bigger turnout anyway, as more people were apt to be out and about at noon than nine o'clock at night.

While the police strove mightily to bring order to the peoples' egress into the room, their efforts could only accomplish just so much. Channeling the procession of visitors in one door and out another amounted to the extent of their control. But the personal hygiene and manners of the crowd was not within the department's purview. This caused some to anguish that "the President-elect could not have formed a very agreeable impression of the first installment of New Yorkers who thus appeared before his vision."[29]

Concerns about propriety and appearance were certainly not unfounded. In waiting to gain entrance to the inner chamber, the crowd jamming the corridor and staircase was nothing short of boisterous—"rearing and surging like the waves of an angry sea" was one observer's impression.[30] Once inside the Governor's Room, the unwashed, unkempt, and disheveled look that many displayed was clearly noticeable.

If the appearance of the general public was of an uneven nature, so also did its passage before the president-elect lack decorum. Far from a leisurely promenade, individuals who had ventured forth with the intent of a pleasant introduction to Mr. Lincoln, instead found themselves caught up in absolute bedlam. Some were ushered in backwards, others at odd angles, and crawling on the floor. "Hats were smashed, shawls torn off, clothes rent, and the throng generally was put through a process of squeezing that they now doubtless think is much better to read about than repeat."[31]

Mercifully, one o'clock arrived. Having fulfilled his obligation, Lincoln was ready to conclude his public appearance. However, before departing, he agreed to say a few words, partly as a conciliatory gesture to assuage the disappointment of those turned away when the doors closed. Word quickly spread that the president would be speaking from the balcony. Stepping out onto the gallery above the entrance, Lincoln saw before him an estimated "eight to ten thousand persons."[32] Once a semblance of quiet had been established, he briefly addressed them:

> Friends and Fellow Citizens—I did not appear for the purpose of making a speech. I design to make no speech. I appear mainly to see you, and to allow you to see me. [*Cheers.*] And I have to say to you, as I have said to audiences frequently on the way from my home to this place, that I suppose I have the best of that bargain. [*Cheers and laughter.*] Assuming that you are all for the Constitution, the Union [*Cheers*], and the perpetual liberties of this people, I bid you farewell. [*Prolonged cheering.*][33]

Highly reminiscent of the succinct remarks which he made at the short station-stops upstate, this bone that he tossed nevertheless appeased the crowd. With cheers ringing in his ears, Lincoln made his way to a waiting carriage. Once again, the ever-present police did yeoman service in holding well-wishers at bay. In their effective, forceful but not belligerent way, the efforts of the blue-coated officers created a safe pathway for their honored guest from city hall to his waiting conveyance. Before departing, Lincoln graciously shook Wood's hand and thanked him for the kind reception and other pleasantries which were extended on behalf of the city. Then, in a matter of minutes, the president-elect was back at the Astor House, ready for the next round of obligatory functions.

Though he generally complied with the arrangements for him, Lincoln did exercise a bit of personal discretion in not joining his family members on their visits to Barnum's museum. Located just across the street from the hotel, the well-known attraction beckoned as an ideal place to take the Lincoln siblings. Known across the land for its unusual, amazing, and exotic exhibits, it was must-see entertainment for visitors to the city. During the war years, countless soldiers made reference in letters home to having paid the quarter admission to this one-of-a-kind tourist mecca. Before a spectacular fire burned the building to the ground in 1865, P. T. Barnum's American Museum was the place to go. Ever on the lookout for promotional boosts, Barnum recognized immediately what a bonanza in ticket sales a visit by the country's newly-elected chief executive would accrue. In effect, the great promoter envisioned Lincoln himself for a limited time as the featured attraction in his museum. No sooner had Lincoln arrived at the Astor House on Tuesday afternoon than the master showman sought to obtain his commitment for a visit. When Barnum was told that, yes, Lincoln would try to come the next day, the great showman responded: "You're Honest Old Abe; I shall rely upon you, and I'll advertise you."[34] Just as the Ford brothers would do four years later regarding an anticipated theater visit by the Mr. Lincoln, Barnum publicized that Lincoln would indeed be visiting his establishment the next day. The implication was for the curious to "come see the amazing Siamese twins, the unusual bearded lady ... and, of course, the one-of-a-kind former rail-splitter-turned-president." In the end result, "the advertisement appeared, but Mr. Lincoln didn't."[35] However, what Barnum did garner as a consolation prize was seventy-five percent of the remainder of the family. Mary, Robert, and Willie all made appearances at museum.

The second absent Lincoln, not surprisingly, was the often-contrary Tad. His interest could not be piqued, primarily because in the child's logic he need not see more bears, for he had the opportunity to do so aplenty back home. Robert went alone in the morning, as did Mary in afternoon. Willie also went after lunch, accompanied by a nurse and a policeman. He became a minor attraction in his right, with many giddy women appeasing themselves by giving him a kiss on the cheek—in lieu of being able to plant one on his father.

Another member of the entourage traveling with the Lincolns was also visible at the museum that day, though his presence was too was only as a temporary exhibit. This would be the tom turkey presented to the president at Utica. While not a guest at the Astor House, the bird was afforded satisfactory accommodations by P. T. Barnum—in return, of course, for his being on display to the paying public. The *Herald* noted that visitors "saw the great Lincoln turkey, however, and looked as though they enjoyed it."[36] "But," as the newspaper philosophized, "they didn't, though, for how can one enjoy the sight of a fine fowl fattened for another person to eat?"[37]

While his family was taking in the curiosities across the street, Lincoln had returned to his room to rest and recharge. Nevertheless, on two separate occasions that afternoon, his repose was interrupted when he was called upon to meet with visiting dignitaries gathered in the reception room. With the assistance of John Nicolay, his private secretary, Lincoln first greeted a collection of military, political, and business leaders. Among these distinguished callers were: the eminent lawyer and anti-slavery advocate John Jay, namesake and grandson of the former governor of New York and famous Supreme Court Justice; wealthy businessman and politician Robert McCurdy; and the highly respected co-owner/editor of the *New York Evening Post* John Bigelow.

After he had slept for two hours, a second reception was held for another group containing a similar cross-section of prominent well-wishers. Particularly eminent in this second contingent was Lyman Beecher and his wife, a couple with whom Lincoln interacted with great feeling—the Reverend Beecher was, of course, being the father of the Reverend Henry Ward Beecher, whom the president-elect had met the day before in Albany, and Harriet Beecher Stowe, whose acquaintance he would make the following year in Washington. In addition to the Beecher's, Lincoln also greeted many other notables, such as: the postmaster of New York, William Taylor; former mayor of New York City Amos Kingsland; and one-time state attorney-general and presidential offspring, John Van Buren.

While many more aspirants milled about the corridor outside the reception room than ever actually gained entrance, various ruses and connivances were employed in the hopes of gaining admission. Some tried to use connections to those inside, hoping to pull strings that would open the doors. One individual who had no difficulty gaining an unconnected entrance was Colonel John C. Frémont. Known as the "Pathfinder of the West" and in 1856 the Republican Party's nominee for president, this genuine American hero was accorded the special privilege of a private interview with Lincoln.

In addition to these sessions which occupied his attention that afternoon, a brief interlude occurred which could be described as that of the "dueling hatters." Knowing of Lincoln's predilection for a certain style of headwear, Charles Knox—a well-regarded local purveyor of such goods out of his nearby store at 212 Broadway—appeared at the door presidential suite, proffering the gift of an elegant silk "stovepipe" hat. Knox had certainly made his presentation to the right man, for as Lincoln scholar Harold Holzer pointed out: "Hats were important to Lincoln: They protected him against inclement weather, served as storage bins for important papers he stuck inside their lining, and further accentuated his great height advantage over other men."[38]

While Charles Knox was clearly an enterprising businessman, it was his son Edward, a bona fide Civil War hero, who would return from the conflict, assume management of the company, and take it to new heights, in the process building the world's largest hat factory in Brooklyn. In time, products that bore the Knox label would come to be recognized as being of the finest quality, eventually finding their way onto the heads of twenty-three American presidents. Not to be outdone by the challenge to hat supremacy that Knox's gift represented, a request for the president's cranial measurements was sent up from the hotel's resident hatter, James Leary. He maintained a store fronting the street at No. 4 Astor House from whence his company advertised that it "engaged to furnish, at a reduction of nearly fifty per cent, an article not inferior in quality and style to the most costly."[39] A short time later, a knock at the door revealed the delivery of yet another equally resplendent chapeau, wool headgear compliments of the hotel's shopkeeper. Lincoln graciously accepted both gifts. When later asked which of the two he preferred, he diplomatically responded that in comparative craftsmanship "they mutually surpassed each other."[40]

By the time he left New York City the next morning, the new president had acquired three new hats—the two he had received from New York's enterprising businessmen and the one his wife had given him on the train between Utica and Albany. While he no doubt appreciated the well-meaning gestures to upgrade his appearance, Abraham Lincoln was the antithesis of his wife when it came to harboring obsessions about his wardrobe. While Mary retained her own dressmaker and eagerly looked forward to shopping sprees for new clothes, "style was about last thing that Lincoln ever troubled himself with, but, while his general get-up was the reverse of fashionable, his headgear was simply too absurdly uncouth for common sense."[41] That President Lincoln, like so many of his countrymen then and now, preferred the choice of an old but comfortable article of clothing is borne out by his demonstrated attachment to one particularly well-worn hat.

As recently as February of 1860, while he was in New York City where he delivered his benchmark Cooper Union speech, the presidential aspirant purchased a new stovepipe, made by the Knox Hat Company—the same hatter who would present the successful candidate with a gift of a similar chapeau a little less than year later. Yet, when he was to eventually depart Springfield, Illinois, on his pre-inaugural journey to Washington, Lincoln was back to wearing an old black topper made by local hatter George Hall. Then came Mary's gift of a new hat just outside of Utica, but, by the time the train arrived in New York City, his old reliable headwear from Springfield was once again ensconced upon his head. Even though by the end of his second day in New York, Lincoln owned at least five different hats—with at least four being acquired with the past year—it was the battered old stovepipe that remained in favor, fending off the newcomers and retaining its lofty perch atop his six-foot, four-inch frame.

However, when the time came to leave New York, the treasured Springfield hat stayed behind. At some point, he had either given or swapped his old reliable stovepipe to Charles Knox. Over the years, the hat was held in veneration by several owners until it wound up in the possession of Charles F. Gunter and eventually passed from his estate to the care of the Chicago Historical Society. Other Lincoln headwear can be found in the possession of the National Historic Site at his Springfield home, which is the repository of a pre–1860 version, and in the Smithsonian Institution, which has the stovepipe that he wore on the fateful visit to Ford's Theater. It is well that these historical treasures have been preserved, for as Stephan Carter observed in *Smithsonian* magazine: "No other President is so firmly connected in our imaginations with an item of haberdashery."[42]

Then, with the supper hour approaching, the social amenities were concluded, along with the announcement that Lincoln would not receive any more guests. It was well that his immediate obligations were dialed back, so the he could enjoy a leisurely meal. For once he was done dining, Lincoln's schedule called for another obligatory public appearance that would last well into the night. This event found Mr. Lincoln headed off to attend an opera at the New York City Academy of Music. The performance which he would see was a new work by Verdi titled *Un Ballo in Maschera* or "The Masked Ball." With an irony that some found altogether too portentous, the plot revolved around the assassination of a head of state. Arriving after the performance had begun, the president's party quietly took seats in a large proscenium box on the right-hand side of the theater. Having entered discreetly, their presence was not noted until the end of the first act. Then the distinctive features of Abraham Lincoln caught the eyes of several discerning patrons. Before long, a spontaneous round of applause—accompanied by wild cheering and waving—burst forth from the excited audience. Lincoln stood to acknowledge the ovation.

Then the curtain rose, and to everyone's surprise and delight—especially the president-elect's—the two American cast members in the otherwise Italian troupe broke into a spirited rendition of "The Star-Spangled Banner." Eventually the audience, including the president, joined in the singing. At the anthem's conclusion, the spectators again applauded vigorously, while the highly pleased chief executive of the nation it saluted bowed in satisfaction. This touching tribute concluded spectacularly, with a huge American flag descending from the rigging above the stage. Lincoln was observed to have "pointed at it with obvious satisfaction."[43] The orchestra then concluded this patriotic tribute with a stirring rendition of "Hail, Columbia," while the audience and the president-elect enthusiastically contributed their voices in song. Departing before the end of the second act of three-act show, Lincoln and his party returned to the Astor House at 10:00 p.m.

While her husband was taking in the opera, Mary Lincoln had remained at the hotel, holding court at her third levee since coming to the Empire State. Situated in the hotel's Ladies Parlor, she greeted a combination of old acquaintances mixed in with several hundred strangers. Beginning at 8:30 pm, she entertained a continuous queue that kept the room filled until 10 o'clock. Assisted by her sister—Mrs. Elizabeth Todd Edwards of Illinois—the wife of the prairie lawyer acquitted herself admirably in the glare of the big city's spotlight. Attired in a tasteful dress of light-colored silk, Mrs. Lincoln received her guests with an aplomb that impressed a least one newsman covering the reception, who observed that she conducted herself "with an ease and grace, and at the same time cordiality, which augur well for the social qualities of the future mistress of the National Mansion, promising Miss Harriet Lane [bachelor James Buchanan's niece who served as his hostess and de facto First Lady] a worthy successor."[44]

Like her husband in his two brief afternoon receptions, Mary Lincoln was honored with salutations from many prominent individuals or their spouses. Among those whom she received in the latter category were: Mrs. Hannibal Hamlin, wife of the vice-president-elect; Mrs. August Belmont, whose husband was a financier and politician; and Mrs. Hiram Burnham, who was married a man who was a successful businessman, politician, and later war hero. A variety of gentlemen were also noticeable in her receiving line. In this group could be observed the likes of: Horace Greeley, editor of the *New York Tribune*; Erastus Benedict, a prominent New York City attorney and politician; and Robert Schneck, a lawyer, politician, and early supporter of Mr. Lincoln's presidential bid.

After paying their respects to Mary Lincoln, callers had the option to do the same with the Hamlins who were hosting a more scaled-down reception of her own. At their smaller affair, the couple received approximately two hundred well-wishers of both sexes. From eight-thirty until ten, Mr. Hamlin cordially received visitors with a firm handshake, a few pleasant words, and an introduction to his wife. The line was kept moving, so that everyone had a chance to meet the vice president's family. In the estimation of an observer, "the reception ... was calculated to create a lasting and favorable impression."[45]

Cognizant that the next day's departure was going to be early and its ensuing commitments taxing, the Lincolns returned to their suite shortly after 10 o'clock, intending to call it a night. However, only the exhausted president-elect immediately did so. The hope was that a good night's rest provide the rest would rejuvenate his system.

However, for Mrs. Lincoln, Mr. Hamlin, and other members of the presidential entourage, there were more well-intentioned tributes still coming their way. The first occurred in the hallway outside the door to the Lincolns' suite. Here the German Quartets Club of Hoboken, twenty-two voices strong, offered a late-night serenade consisting of several selections. The three pieces rendered were titled: "The Day of Our Lord," "Hymn on Music," and "Good Night."[46] Mary Lincoln provided the official presence, appropriately lauding the group at the completion of its last selection and making the excuse for his husband's absence on account of his excessive fatigue.

The next performance was a bit more grandiose. Sponsored by the Wide-Awake Central Committee, a serenade by a forty-eight-piece National Guard Band was on tap for a mid-night concert. Like so many of the events involving Mr. Lincoln, news of the impending concert led to a large gathering before the Astor House. With the first arrivals beginning to appear at nine o'clock, the build-up continued until an immense crowd had swelled to an estimated ten thousand onlookers by the time the band arrived. In addition to those congregating outside the hotel, the establishment's windows were occupied by guests on all floors, peering out in anticipation of the upcoming serenade. Scheduled to begin at 11:30, the musicians were not ready to play until midnight. Their arrival had been somewhat delayed by the impromptu parade which they led from the Wide-Awakes' headquarters. To the tune of "Dixie's Land," several hundred marchers, arrayed six abreast, made their way to the plaza in front of the Astor House.

With the foresight which its commanders had consistently shown throughout Lincoln's visit, a detachment of fifty policemen were already awaiting the processions arrival, dispatched to maintain order in front of the hotel. The officers proceeded to move the crowd back, forming a protective semi-circle inside of which the musicians could perform without interruption. Supporting the cordon of officers was a second, inner half-ring, manned by one hundred and fifty members of the Wide Awakes club. Secure from interference, the bandsmen played a variety of pieces. "First they gave selections from the opera *Nebuchadnezzar*, following with the 'Larien Quickstep,' and a finale from *La Trovature*."[47]

In between the different selections, the crowd had alternately chanted for "Lincoln" and "Hamlin," an expression of its never sated desire to see and hear the two men of the hour. However, as persistent as their appeal might have been, one object of their entreaties was just too exhausted to make an appearance. In fact, the truth be known, he was already asleep. Not wanting to completely disappoint the faithful who had turned out at such a late hour, Hannibal Hamlin was finally cajoled by his friends to appear at one of his suite's windows. Upon seeing him, the crowd erupted with enthusiastic cheers. The band struck up the ever-stirring "Hail, Columbia." All the future vice president could do was bid his time and soak up the scene, waiting for the music to end and applause to subside.

Eventually, he was presented to the sea of eager upturned faces by General J. J. Hobart Ward: "Fellow Citizens, allow me to have the honor of introducing to you Hon. Hannibal Hamlin, the Vice-President-elect." Standing in the open window, Hamlin proceeded to address the assembled mass:

> Fellow-Citizens: I am gratified to hear these generous tones that come from the honest hearts of the men who occupy the Empire City of the old state of New York. They speak as if devoted to a principle in which all have a common interest. [*Cheers.*] They give me evidence of the love they bear to a common country; they satisfy me here even in this great commercial mart, that the heads, the hearts, and the hands of our people are ready to vindicate the Government under which they live, and which they received from their fathers. [*Prolonged cheers.*] They show how truly a Government like ours may repose upon the popular will. They tell me how truly the great and good and honest men whom you have elevated to that first position that man can bestow will receive, in all times, that loyalty which the citizen owes his government. [*Applause.*] And that with your heads, your hearts, and your hands, you will rally to its support, in sunshine and in storm.[48]

After his remarks, Hamlin left the window with the sound of appreciative cheers ringing in his ears. While the night was far from young, the band got its second wind while the vice president-elect orated. With the floor theirs once again, the musicians struck up a pair of lively airs, first "Dixie" and then "Yankee Doodle." The evening's serenade came to a close with a rendition of the always heart-rending "Auld Lang Syne." With its final notes drifting off into the night air, the crowd began to disperse, as the lights the in hotel's rooms began to go out. The band and Wide-Awakes were invited into the hotel for refreshments, while Hannibal Hamlin—known for his convivial nature—continued to entertain guests on into the early morning hours. He and his wife could forego a lack of sleep at this point, since they were not leaving New York City until the day after the Lincoln caravan had departed for Washington.

But, for the already travel-weary Lincolns, their wake-up call would arrive altogether too soon. With the dawning of Thursday, February 21, 1861, their five-day excursion through the Empire State was ending. After having passed through New York State's alternating patchwork of large urban enclaves, small villages, and tiny hamlets, their journey would now take them down the Atlantic seaboard, along a corridor packed with many large cities until they arrived in the nation's capital. Due to some last-minute changes in the upcoming schedule, the new president's morning check-out from the Astor House was moved up an hour from his originally planned 9 o'clock departure. Even with the previously unannounced change, several bold politicians were on-hand, seeking to gain last-minute access to the president-elect. Though their self-serving requests were denied, one brief audience was granted to a patriotic Brooklynite, a lady who had hand-crafted a silken thirty-four-star flag which she was allowed to present to Willie.

Climbing into their waiting carriage, the Lincolns bid a warm thanks and fond farewell to hotel's proprietors. Then their traveling retinue headed off down Broadway in a four-carriage caravan, destined for the ferry terminal on Van Cortlandt Street. Compared to the masses who welcomed them to the city, their leave-taking was a much lower-keyed affair. While there were people along the streets who took notice, the cheering and applauding that had been the custom for the past two days was absent. The magnitude of Lincoln's send-off did not approach the level of his welcome. Certainly the early hour, altered schedule, and abbreviated distance were contributing factors. In the end, a quick, unimpeded departure was in Lincoln's best interests. He had already made a favorable impression on New Yorkers. Little could be gained by any further dalliance. With a full day's schedule ahead him, he needed to move on to the next state and its accompanying round of public appearances.

The party waited briefly at the terminal until its transportation arrived from New Jersey. Bedecked in a colorful profusion of flags and bunting, the *John P. Jackson*, a new side-wheeled steam ferry, soon docked, ready to provide the only nautical portion of Mr. Lincoln's journey from Springfield to Washington. On deck, a thirty-piece band played several stirring selections, among them being "Hail, Columbia" and "The Star-Spangled Banner." The gangway was lowered, and cheers went up as the carriages were driven onboard. Immediately the president-elect was greeted by a reception committee from New Jersey. Mooring lines were quickly cast aside, and the boat began its short trek across the Hudson to Jersey City. While in passage, a thirty-four-gun salute was fired from the ferry deck by the Hudson County Artillery. Other boats in the harbor joined in with salutes of their own. Eventually, Lincoln made his way to the railing and watched New York City fade into the horizon. Though the past few days in the Empire State had been a whirlwind tour, it was nonetheless highly successful experience.

In the end result, Abraham Lincoln would spend two nights, one full day, and parts of two others in New York City. From Tuesday through Thursday of February 19, 20, and 21, he had moved about in the spotlight of the largest city in the world. Entering an urban area that had previously demonstrated significant anti–Lincoln elements among its populace—particularly in the ranks of its political, financial, and business leaders—the welcome was expected to be underwhelming as compared to the warmth of the applause and accolades that upstate residents had showered upon him. As renowned biographer Carl Sandburg assessed Lincoln's experience in the metropolitan area, "the New York reception of the President-elect was the most elaborate, pretentious, detailed, expensive—and yet coldest—of all on the Lincoln journey toward inauguration."[49]

While this may have described Lincoln's visit at the official and short-term level, in the long run he did accomplish his personal goal of gaining public exposure, which generally bore the kind of fruit for which he had hoped, as by force of personality, strength of character, and sincerity of purpose he won over many doubters. Though there was an element of the upper crust—offended by his "awkward gestures and ambling walk ... his frontier pronunciation ... his offhand conversation and fund of homely anecdotes"—people who would never find him a suitable fit for the esteemed office of chief executive, a sufficient number of those with prominence and clout along with members of the rank-and-file took away a positive impression from their exposure to the president-elect and the buzz created by his visit.[50] Granted the city could not alter the outcome of its voting in the recent election, but its people could change their perceptions of the president-elect. When the war came, their support proved critical to the success of the Union cause and indicative of their faith in President Lincoln.

12

The Washington Years
When All the Joy Turned to Sorrow

By slipping through Baltimore at night, Abraham Lincoln avoided a potential confrontation with conspirators who wished to thwart his inauguration. Though he would survive to take the oath of office not once but twice, Lincoln's personal rendezvous with death was nevertheless already marked by fate on the calendar of his life, destined to arrive altogether too soon for a man who had so much work yet to complete. Perhaps more than any other president, the aura of death created a gloomy atmosphere that not only hung over the White House all four years, but also intensified as the days progressed.

Part of the veil of tears the Lincolns brought with them from Illinois was that they had left behind the remains of their beloved son Edward in the soil of Springfield's Hutchinson's Cemetery. Known as Eddie to his family, the poor boy had succumbed just shy of his fourth birthday to a consumptive disease. While the couple would be blessed with two more sons—for Mary was pregnant with Willie only three weeks after Eddie's passing and Tad followed two years later—the loss of their second child was a painful memory never completely assuaged.

Then the war came, bringing with it a time of grief for countless American families. Being the sensitive, caring man that he was, Abraham Lincoln felt the pain of sending the flower of his country's youth off to die in war. More often than not, his knowledge of these losses came in the form of statistics. Published in the newspapers and after-action reports, casualty figures were generally impersonal, as he rarely knew the individuals involved.

Sometimes, though, his distance from the men in the ranks became unavoidably shortened. With an increased familiarity to the facts in a given circumstance, there came an agony which he shared with the loved ones of a soldier. One such instance occurred when an elderly woman visited him. She explained that her husband and three sons had all enlisted to fight for the Union cause; however, her spouse had since perished in battle. His death motivated her visit to plead for the release of her eldest son from any further military obligation. Lincoln later explained his decision to grant her request by saying that "certainly, if her prop was taken away, she was entitled to one of her boys."[1] Filled with gratitude at the president's generosity, the happy woman made her way to the encampment of her son's regiment, but to her shock and horror she learned that he had just recently expired from a wound suffered in a recent engagement.

With a surgeon's note explaining the unfortunate turn-of-events written on the back of the president's order of release, the brokenhearted woman returned to the White House. Lincoln "was much affected by her appearance and story, and said: 'I know what you wish me to do now, and I shall do it without your asking: I shall release to you your second son."² While he wrote out the new order, the distraught woman stood by his side, tears running down her cheeks as she passed her hand softly over his head and stroked his hair. Handing her the paper, the president said: "Now you have one, and I one of the other two left, that is no more than right."³ Taking the precious document in one hand, she placed the other upon his head once more and said: "The Lord bless you Mr. President. May you live a thousand years, and may you always be the head of this great nation."⁴

Such cases of executive intervention were not everyday occurrences, but instances of citizens pleading their cases in letter or in person were quite common. Though he could not always provide the requested relief, Lincoln was nevertheless regularly exposed to the troubles of his constituents ... and his nature was such to share their burdens quite readily. While he did not know the individual stories of every soldier who served the cause of the Republic, through random interactions with their family members he was made painfully aware of individual plights and heart-rending tragedies. But from the cross-section of which he was painfully conscious, he could easily extrapolate the realization that further untold accounts of equal poignancy existed.

As if sharing the collective pain and suffering of his countrymen were not sufficient sorrows to stoop his shoulders, Lincoln had more than enough personal loss to bear. Only two and a half months into his presidency, he had to absorb the death of his young protégé Elmer Ellsworth. As much as anyone in those early months of the war, Lincoln was abruptly made aware that a terrible price was going to be paid by many before hostilities were concluded.

Willie Lincoln, right, pictured in 1861 with his cousin Lockwood Todd, left, and brother Tad. Willie Lincoln passed away unexpectedly in 1862 (Library of Congress).

Then on October 21, 1861, at the Battle of Ball's Bluff, he again lost a dear friend in the person of Senator Edward Baker. Commander of a volunteer regiment, then Colonel Baker was killed in the engagement. Lincoln's close personal association with Senator Baker was evidenced by his having named his second son—Edward Baker Lincoln—after the man whom he first knew as a law partner and later congressman from Illinois. When on March 4, 1861, Abraham Lincoln stepped forward to take his oath of office, he was proudly introduced to the people assembled before the Capitol by none other than Edward Baker.

Though the deaths of Ellsworth and Baker hit the president hard, for

Abraham Lincoln the most devastating loss of all during the war years came in February of 1862, when his youngest son succumbed to typhoid fever. Both Willie and Tad had contracted the disease from the fetid waters of the Potomac, the source from which the White House drew its drinking supply. Tad survived. Willie did not. Since the river's pollution originated in a large part from the army camps along its banks, the boy's passing was in a sense a war-related death. Ward Hill Lamon revealed just how shattering this tragedy was on the president, observing that "in the lonely grave of the little one lay buried Mr. Lincoln's fondest hopes, and, strong as he was in the matter of self-control, he gave way to overwhelming grief, which became at length a serious menace to his health."[5] First his friends, then his son—Lincoln was paying the same high price for the preservation of the Union that he had asked of his countrymen. The young boy was buried in Georgetown's Oak Hill Cemetery in vault space temporarily loaned by the William Carroll family, with the understanding that Willie would return to Springfield for reburial in the family plot, once his father's presidency had ended.

While the boy's passing was unexpected, the one death that was dreaded daily and would have surprised few had it occurred was that of the president himself. In a divided nation, where passions were inflamed to the point that Americans would kill each other, many people fixated their anger on the man who was perceived as the architect of all the misery visited on the country. By 1865, Lincoln-haters existed on both sides of the Mason-Dixon Line. The extent of Northerners' venom did not become fully evident until after his death, when a thick file—marked in his own hand "Assassination Letters"—was discovered in his desk.[6] The contents were chilling. According to one Washington source, "many of them threatened his life, [while] others warned him of plots to take it."[7]

One such diatribe was written on February 20, 1861—when the president-elect was in New York City—and excoriated him with the following vilification: "May the hand of the devil strike you down before long—You are destroying the country. Dam [sic] you—every breath you take. Hand of God against you."[8] That little changed as the war progressed is witnessed by a letter dated "January 4th 1864," one in which its author "Joseph" stated: "Your days are numbered, you have been weighed in the bal-

Among those traveling with the president was Ward Hill Lamon, an imposing mountain of a man who had dedicated himself to the role of Lincoln's bodyguard. Unfortunately, he had been sent on a mission to Richmond by the president just before the assassination (Library of Congress).

ance and found wanting. You shall be a dead man in six months from date Dec. 31st 1863. Thus saith the good spirit."[9]

At one time or another, Ward Hill Lamon, Edwin Stanton, and Ulysses Grant had each expressed fears for his safety. Of the three, Lamon was the only one who did not have other duties to perform, so he devoted himself to protecting his good friend. Wearing a brace of pistols and knives about his already formidable six-foot, five-inch frame, he was ready and willing to take on all comers. In the performance of his sacred duty, Lamon was even known to sleep on the floor outside of the president's bedroom at night. This faithful bodyguard would rue the day for the rest of his life that he had not been at Ford's Theater to thwart the machinations of John Wilkes Booth, but Lincoln had dispatched his trusted friend on a special mission to Richmond on April 13.

From his perspective, Lincoln knew the risks and did not dwell on the possibility of being assassinated. "If anyone wants to do so, he can do it any day or night," Lincoln said, "if he is ready to give his life for mine."[10] Fatalistic though he might have been at the prospects of his own violent death, relief from the continued anguish of reading of the daily battle deaths came for the president with the Army of Northern Virginia's surrender on April 9, 1865, marking an end to most of the significant fighting in the war. The nation, however, would not be so fortunate. While the bulk of the troops would soon be homeward bound, Lincoln's reelection would delay his return to Illinois until the spring of 1869. Little did anyone know that fate would soon intervene in the form of an assassin, plunging the victorious North into renewed paroxysms of grief and necessitating arrangements for a much earlier and far different train trip to Springfield than the Lincolns ever envisioned.

Prostrated by profound anguish, Mary Lincoln took to her bed. The widow's incapacitation destined her to take play no visible role in the elaborate obsequies for her husband, which followed over the next eighteen days. Confining herself to a second floor bedroom—a self-imposed isolation which she maintained for a period of five weeks—she was neither attended the funeral services held downstairs in the East Room nor accompanied the president's remains on the train. That solemn task was left up to eighteen-year-old Robert Lincoln, but then even he only rode the train as far as Baltimore. Poor Abraham and Willie were left to make the journey to their final resting places in the company of a few friends, a host of well-meaning strangers, and two of Mary's brothers-in-law. That her husband was to be buried in Illinois, conveyed there by an agreed-upon route, and accompanied by Willie's disinterred remains were the most significant of the few behind-the-scenes contributions which Mary Lincoln was able to make. Not surprisingly, save the decision to send the deceased child home with his father, making the choices of where the president's final resting place would be and by means of what itinerary they would get there did not come easily.

Very quickly, a tug-of-war had arisen, pitting the widow's desire to preserve as much privacy and dignity as possible for her husband's remains balanced against the need for the nation to say its own goodbyes. While Mary Lincoln abhorred the thought of her husband being showcased in a road show, she was persuaded to accept that he now belonged to the country as much as he did to her. Collectively the nation was grieving too. His fellow Americans deserved the opportunity to say farewell and bring a measure of closure to their own sorrow. In spite of her personal desire to vacate the city and get her husband home for internment as soon as possible, Mary in the end acceded to accommodate the feelings of the body politick.

Since all other plans hinged on the crucial determinations of destination and route, their resolutions became of paramount importance in the days immediately following the assassination. Of the two, site selection was of the utmost priority. Mary's initial choice was Chicago, followed by Washington, D.C. Some well-meaning folks were inclined to offer the confused widow still other possibilities. One proposed alternative was Mount Vernon, placing America's two foremost presidents together for all eternity. Other places suggested as possibilities were the Capitol Rotunda, the Congressional Cemetery, and New York City.

Finally, the city fathers of Springfield weighed in with their plan—in effect making the ill-considered, insensitive claim that Lincoln's stature as a public figure trumped the family's wishes and made the selection of a final resting place one that had civic implications which should be considered. Toward this end, the bureaucrats even invested in some pricey acreage in the downtown area. While she ultimately consented to Illinois as the destination for her husband's remains, the urban Springfield plot was eschewed in favor of the pastoral setting offered by the newly opened Oak Ridge Cemetery northwest of the town. This decision endeared her with few in Springfield, effectively estranging her from the city, but Mary Lincoln was driven by the desire to have sufficient plots for the entire family to be placed in eternal rest together, an outcome she was not confident the in-town location welcomed or assured. The poetic suitability that should cause the late president's burial to be in a serene, bucolic setting was noted by author Gary Wills when he observed: "So Lincoln, who delivered the most famous address at a rural cemetery, was laid to rest in the same kind of institution."[11]

Once the destination was finalized, the next consideration needing attention was that of the route which the funeral train would follow. Initially Mrs. Lincoln had her own wishes in this regard too. She was set on the cortège taking a direct path to Springfield. Stops would be kept to a minimum. However, friends and family interceded, trying to persuade her that her husband's elevated stature deeply altered the situation. Being a revered public figure, they argued that the people should be given a chance to pay their last respects. Reluctantly, Mary Lincoln acquiesced.

However, as late as the early morning of April 19, the final route had still not been determined. Four days of negotiations with Mary Lincoln had yet to yield any concession. Though hesitant to relinquish her desire for a more private mourning scenario, she finally acquiesced to the more extended route, with stops at state capitals and important cities along the way. From Washington to Cleveland, with but very limited deviation, the funeral train was scheduled to follow in reverse the passage which the inaugural tour took. Two differences of consequence from 1861 would be a stop in Baltimore, avoided the first time through ironically for fear of an assassination attempt, and Albany, where adverse weather had caused the need for an alternate passage across the Hudson River in 1861.

To satisfy the need for someone of authority to make the requisite preparations in Mrs. Lincoln's absence, secretary of war Edwin Stanton stepped forward. Possessing both the sufficient power and commanding presence necessary, he was just man to fill the void. However, having to already juggle the oversight of pursuing the assassins, bringing the war to a close on multiple fronts, and initiating the rudimentary steps in the reconstruction process, Stanton already had his hands full without taking on the delicate task of making funeral arrangements.

12. The Washington Years

When the war had begun to wind down, he had made it known to the President that he wished to leave his post at the War Department soon. The long hours which he had kept and the heavy burden shouldered had begun to take their toll after three years of service to the president and the country. Stanton was worn out. Lincoln, however, felt him too indispensable and made it clear that he would entertain no talk of his ablest cabinet member resigning. As a result, Stanton was still on the job when the assassination occurred. Having served Lincoln loyally and faithfully during the President's life, he committed to rendering the same service in the wake of his friend's death.

Since the secretary knew that he could not handle the added task of making all of the funeral arrangements alone, he sought the assistance of competent men to help him. The first individual to whom he reached out was General Daniel McCallum. An immigrant from Scotland, McCallum was a largely self-taught engineer/architect. Before the war, he had gained considerable acclaim as an innovative bridge builder. However, his real forte was managerial oversight, aided by his use of a well-regarded organization chart which he had designed.

With the outbreak of hostilities, Stanton brought him to Washington where McCallum was given the title of General Manager of the United States Military Railroads. Under his skillful leadership, the effectiveness and efficiency of the transportation network under his command made valuable contributions to the Union war effort. Now, in this time of great national import, Stanton gave McCallum the task of assembling the funeral train. To assist him with other aspects of the requisite arrangements—such as the exact route, determination of stops, and length of layovers—other tried and true railroad men were also summoned forth by Secretary Stanton.

Edwin Stanton, one of president's most-trusted allies during the war, was empowered by Mary Lincoln to oversee the arrangements for her husband's journey home to Springfield for burial (Library of Congress).

While many similarities would exist with the inaugural tour, the very nature of the mission presented to General McCallum dictated significant differences. For instance, in 1861, Superintendent William Wood strove to restrict the train to as few cars as possible. By parsing out the limited seating to only those who needed to be on the train, Wood buffered Lincoln from the noisome droves who sought access to the president in order to bend his ear on matters usually far more important to them than to him. To Wood, this meant a three-car consist. Furthermore, since the tab for the transportation to Washington was being picked up by the sponsoring railroad, being overly lavish with the generosity of others was probably not viewed as the best practice. Besides, Lincoln was not one for whom extravagance held any sway.

But four years and different circumstances put the matter of transportation in an altogether different light. No longer was Abraham Lincoln, private citizen on his way for his inauguration in Washington, being comped freebies by various railroads. On this occasion Abraham Lincoln, martyred president on his way for burial in Springfield, was being taken home under the aegis of the Federal government. Specifically, all preparations and oversight regarding the passage of his remains from the District of Columbia to Illinois were assigned to the U.S. Military Railroad officials. In effect, these men had temporary jurisdiction over the various lines over which the train passed. It was their fiat which subsequently dictated that the funeral train was to be made up of not less than nine cars.

Of all the preparations made, McCallum's task was certainly one of the most critical and visible. For years to come when many people recalled the day that they paid their last respects to the fallen president, the vision that came to mind was that of the long, slow-moving train. Due to all the people who required seating, the train would consist of eleven units—one engine, a tender, a baggage car, six coaches, the hearse car, and the officers' car. Only the last two were intended to be "through cars," that is converted coaches that would make the entire journey from start to finish. All of the other components of the train would change as the cortège passed from the territory of one host railroad to that of another.

In recognition of the important charge entrusted to them, the managers of all the roads involved in transporting the president's remains supplied their best equipment. The engines were configured in what railroad shorthand designated as having a 4-4-0 wheel arrangement: four large drivers to supply the motive power and two pairs of much smaller ones attached in front of the drivers on a flexible truck to help keep the locomotive on the tracks. At the very front of engine, positioned low to the rails was a metal grillwork known as the cowcatcher, intended to keep debris and animals from slipping underneath and causing a temporary stoppage, if not a dreaded derailment. Directly above, at the top front, was a large and powerful kerosene lantern serving as a headlight. Across the top of the boiler, which constituted the central power source of the great machine, were several prominent

Christened the *United States*, the specially constructed coach on the left—originally intended to transport a living president in comfort—became instead the bearer of his coffin, while the one on the right—known as the Officers' Car—carried various dignitaries on the journey to Springfield (courtesy Buffalo History Museum).

features: a balloon-style smokestack, a bell, a steam box, a sand dome, and a steam whistle. Encapsulating the back of the boiler was the cab. Containing all of the controls, this housing was open to the tender in its rear.

This compact little fiefdom was the domain of the engineer who operated the locomotive and shared the space with a fireman, the man tasked with keeping a roaring blaze stoked in the firebox, which in turn heated the water in the boiler. The steam produced was conveyed through a system of pipes and provided the force which drove pistons on each side. Their horizontal back-and-forth movement in turn propelled the four drive wheels. A link-and-pin system—a phrase sometimes run together and referenced as the "Lincoln pin"—was the mechanism by which the engine connected to its tender and likewise all of the trailing cars. A very durable and highly reliable piece of equipment, this style of locomotive was known as the "American." It was this model of iron horse which served the nation well during the Civil War and the settling of the West. Over twenty-five thousand were built, which makes it the single most-produced locomotive in American history.

While the engine was the most important unit in a train's composition, the tender was perhaps the most utilitarian. Functioning as a three-sided rolling bin filled with coal or wood, its open face fronted the rear of the engine. From the tender's stockpile, the fireman would shovel or toss fuel into the firebox of the engine. In order to keep up sufficient steam for propulsion over any significant distance, copious amounts of the chosen fuel were consumed, which meant arduous, back-breaking labor to keep the fire hot and periodic stops to replenish the energy source and water supply.

The baggage car was basically an empty storage van wherein the travelers could place their belongings. Under ordinary circumstances, this unit might also contain mail and packages. As for the wooden coaches, not a lot could be done to upgrade the fact that they were in essence little more than cars full of park benches. Certainly, the seats were cushioned and plush. Heat, if needed, was supplied unevenly by wood stoves at each end. Night lighting was produced by oil lamps affixed to the walls. While an attempt to provide comfort for the passengers, this combination of open flames and combustible materials often made for disastrous consequences should a derailment ever occur. Many were the nineteenth century train wrecks in which survivors of the initial crash perished in the conflagration that followed.

The last coach in the sequence was known as the Officers' Car. In this instance, the use of the term officers was not a reference to the coach's utilization by military personnel, but rather its function as a lounge for the directors of Philadelphia, Wilmington, and Baltimore Railroad, the ownership which loaned the car for the funeral train. Coincidentally, the Officers Car was very similar to the *United States* in both its interior and exterior design. One source of commonality was their subdivision into three chambers. The parlor and sleeping compartments corresponded to those in the presidential coach; however, the third area in the loaner car was a dining room, which represented a rarity on trains of the Civil War-like. In an interesting match-up, the outside panels of the private car were painted a vermillion, which came very close in hue to the color treatment used on the *United States*.

For all of those who came trackside to pay their respects, the focal point of their gazes was the next-to-the-last coach, the so-called hearse car. Built at government facilities in Alexandria between 1863 and 1865, this lavish coach was intended for the personal use of Mr. Lincoln. Since he often traveled by rail, the prevailing thought which gave birth to this particular car—named the *United States*—was to make his journeys not only as comfortable as possible, but also to reflect his exalted status as the nation's chief executive. But, anyone who truly knew the man would have understood immediately that such ostentatious accommodations were never going to be accepted. The senatorial candidate who once rode in boxcars to debates was not going to brook being borne about in a chariot fit for a pharaoh.

As fate would have it, only when he could protest no more would Abraham Lincoln ride amidst the luxury that he had intentionally forsaken. Commenting on this turn of events, the *Albany Evening Journal* observed: "How sad, how suggestive of the fleetness of all things earthly, is the fact."[12] Contrary to rumors that have persisted over the years, the car was not sheathed with armor. While this might have been a measure worth considering, the point was as moot as it was tardy by the time the coach was eventually pressed into service. It is worth noting, however, that the idea of such protection did in fact come into being for President Franklin D. Roosevelt. Since he too had a penchant for rail travel, his private car—named the *Ferdinand Magellan*—did in fact contain steel plating in its construction.

But, even in his disdain for opulence, Lincoln would have appreciated the craftsmanship that went into the coach's construction. With three finely appointed rooms—a parlor at one end, sitting room at the other, and between them a sleeping apartment and a narrow corridor connecting the two end compartments—its occupant could travel in style and comfort. Green-and-red upholstered furniture, mirrors, a glass chandelier, a marble-topped washstand, tapestry-style woven carpets, exquisite woodwork, velvet-lined births, and a metal stove at each end all combined to make for elegantly decorated spaces.

On the outside, the wooden paneling of the *United States* was painted a dark hue, at the time identified as "a rich chocolate color," which after recent research and analysis has been discovered to be more of a reddish-brown or deep maroon tint.[13] However, regardless of the exact shade of this paint, the one incontrovertible feature of the car's exterior appearance was a large oval containing the coat of arms of the United States. Inside this ellipse, centered under the coach's windows at the mid-point of the car, was depicted an American eagle. Accompanying this symbol of America were the Federal shield, stars, and clouds—all rendered in appropriate colors. While not intended for that purpose, the presence of the national emblem made the hearse car very easy to pick out, even from a distance, as the train rolled through small towns and across open farmlands.

However, once the car was appropriated for the funeral train, alterations were necessary to convert the interior to accommodate the two coffins. Since the car did not contain conventional bench seating attached to the floor, removing pieces of the free-standing furniture from the two end rooms was not difficult. In their place, "a plain stand, covered with black cloth, was placed in the south end of the car, on which the remains of the president were placed, and, on a like stand at the opposite end, the remains of Willie rested."[14]

Conductor William Henry Harrison Gould, who had charge of the Baltimore to Harrisburg leg of the journey, further elaborated on the unseen support system for the coffin, describing it as being "three trestles securely fastened to the floor of the car. Over these was crepe. Straps were fastened to the trestles and buckled around the coffin to hold it secure."[15] In keeping with the customs of the times, both the interior and exterior of the coach were treated with additional decorations themed in ebony. Black curtains, adorning the windows, were fringed with silver and festooned with heavy silver cord and tassels,

Typical of the style of engines that would pull both Lincoln Specials, the engines towing the funeral train were tastefully bedecked with various configurations of funereal cloth, floral arrangements, and the deceased's portrait (Library of Congress).

supported by silver eagles. The furniture that was not removed to create open spaces for the coffins was robed in black. Along the top outside edge of the coach, observers would note the presence of "a row of mourning gathered in black to white rosettes, and another similar row extending around the car below the windows."[16]

The adornment of the hearse car with various decorations predominantly black in hue, set off with minimal but complimentary accents in silver and white, was very much in keeping with the accepted practices of the time. As the train traveled along its route, the cities where the cortège stopped to permit viewing of the remains were all suitably festooned with similar ornamentation. Even the smaller towns and villages along the tracks found ways simple, touching, and original to pay homage to their fallen leader. The stature of the man, the distance between death and burial sites, and the use of a train—all subject to the overarching mourning rituals of the Victorian era—made for a series of somber yet unique farewells on a grandiose scale that had never occurred previously in American history and has not been approached since. Once Mrs. Lincoln had approved of the burial site, agreed to the route, and assented to public viewings, a checklist of both formal and informal protocols and procedures had to be addressed in order that all ceremonies were in line with the accepted tenets of the times.

13

Bringing the President Home
Funeral Arrangements Are Made

While not a common occurrence, still eight of America's forty-four presidents have died while in office. As leaders of their country, each was accorded funeral rites befitting the stature of the office. While some were more beloved than others during their administrations, in paying tribute to a deceased president their countrymen put politics aside and gave appropriate tributes to the memory of a man who had willingly taken on a difficult job. In these instances, the proceedings were usually conducted with all of the pomp and circumstance that should rightfully have attended the funeral of a high-ranking statesman. As Mary Lincoln eventually came to realize, a departed president belonged to the country first and his family second.

To varying degrees, railroads have played a role by assisting in the movement of their remains, with six presidents having to some extent been taken by rail to their final resting places. Only the second chief executive to die in office—Zachary Taylor—and the most recent—John Kennedy—did not have a train factored into their funeral arrangements. The railroad's absence in these two instances was due largely to their burials being in local graveyards. Taylor was interred in Washington's Congressional Cemetery and Kennedy at Arlington National. In addition, given that President Taylor expired right in the capital city, he was already at his funeral's location. By contrast, President Kennedy did die far from Washington; however, since he passed away in the modern era, an airplane represented the quickest means to bring his remains from the assassination locale in Dallas to the funeral site in the District of Columbia.

Due to the circumstances involving four other presidents—Garfield, McKinley, Harding, and Roosevelt—trains respectively transported the deceased to Washington from Elderon (New Jersey), Buffalo (New York), San Francisco (California), and Warm Springs (Georgia), these being the places where their final breaths were taken. However, in sharp disparity to the transfer of Lincoln's remains across over more than 1,600 miles, those of the other presidents traveled by uninterrupted routes. Contrasting markedly with the somber pageantry that accompanied and prolonged the sixteenth president's return to Springfield, none of the other deceased president's incurred any delays in route to or from the Washington funeral to a distant burial site.

Comparing Lincoln's obsequies with those of the other presidents who died in office, in terms of the lengthy timeframe from death to burial none rival that of the Great Emancipator. FDR did spend a considerable amount of time onboard a train, for his corpse had to be moved twice: first from Warm Springs to Washington; and then to Hyde Park, New

York. As a result, two separate passages via railroads were involved before he was finally interred. Yet only four days elapsed between the starting and ending points of those combined journeys. However, in the two legs of his journey, the transportation of the body by rail was simply a matter of expediency. No formal stoppages for ceremonies occurred along either segment of the route. For certain, as the trains in both instances wended their way north first to and then from the nation's capital, reverent citizens paid spontaneous, trackside homage, but only for fleeting seconds as the car bearing the deceased rolled past them. In terms of endearment to his countrymen for having led them out of a severe depression and through a hard-fought war, Roosevelt was due as much gratitude from his constituents as any president, including Lincoln. In upstate New York, the editor of the *Altamont Enterprise* addressed his acknowledgment of this reality when he observed that "the American people from Main Street to Riverside Drive mourned the death of Franklin Roosevelt."[1]

But no consideration was ever given to a series of wakes in major cities across the country, so that grateful countrymen could pay their condolences. President Roosevelt did not even lie in state in the Capitol rotunda. Had there not been strict directions to the contrary, President Roosevelt might have received much grander and more public obsequies than actually proved to be the case. But the fact of the matter was that FDR's funeral had been planned in considerable detail—in advance and by the president himself. It seems that in December of 1937 Franklin Roosevelt had drawn up a four-page document, one in which he succinctly spelled out how his funeral should be handled when his time came. The proceedings as he specified them were to unfold in a simple, quick, and private manner. Among his stipulations were orders that he would not lie in state, no public funeral should be held, and only family, friends, and neighbors could attend the services at St, James Church in Hyde Park. By his foresight, FDR had circumvented what could easily have been a much more prolonged and grandiose farewell.

Of more recent vintage, the arrangements accompanying the passing of John Kennedy were conducted in a manner that placed them on the spectrum somewhere between those of Lincoln and Roosevelt. They were similar to those of the World War II leader in their brevity. Once again, only four days elapsed from death to burial. But where the rites for President Kennedy differed markedly from those of President Roosevelt and aligned more closely with President Lincoln's was in the highly public nature of JFK's obsequies.

Where FDR's transition to the grave was as private as he could make, President Kennedy's allowed much greater access by the American people. While to some extent all of the exposure could not have occurred without the blessing and cooperation of the Kennedy family, the coverage by the television networks permitted the entire nation access to the proceedings. In retrospect, it was very fitting that the presidency of John Kennedy, born in part out of his success in televised debates, should have the same medium broadcast the final act of his highly visible administration. To the extent that modern videography has influenced our remembrances of 1963—offering images of a flag-covered coffin, the family and world leaders marching behind the caisson, and the eternal light at Arlington—so also did the embryonic art of photography frame how the Lincoln funeral rites have come down to us.

From the collection of artists' renderings and black-and-white stills which exist covering various aspects of the funereal trappings and proceedings, we are afforded a window into some of the complicated societal mores of that era, expectations that proscribed much of what transpired during a nineteenth century funereal observance. When Lincoln died, strict Victorian protocols had gained ascendancy over the bereavement process. While the deceased's station in life did not matter insofar as the expectation of adherence to basic rituals, the extent that the family's means allowed and its social standing dictated were mitigating factors in the final plans. However, there was no question that such a high-profile funeral as one for a president of the United States would be held to the highest standards and in turn scrutinized and critiqued for its observance of proper conventions. Just as television molded history's vision of John Kennedy's funeral, so also did another powerful force—Victorian mourning rites—shape the memories of Abraham Lincoln's obsequies handed down to posterity.

While England, led by Queen Victoria who began mourning the loss of her husband Albert in 1861, set the gold standard for what constituted proper bereavement rituals, Americans readily followed suit in embracing the recommended practices. The Civil War and its 720,000 deaths regrettably provided opportunities for far more funerals than would customarily have been the case in a normal four-year period. However, deaths on remote battlefields more often than not logistically precluded shipping bodies home for burial. In addition, problems in preserving the remains for long periods and the cost of their shipment over significant distances impinged upon adhering to what would have otherwise been the preferred mourning rituals.

Still, even as the war waged, those at home had to carry on with their lives as best they could. Just as they would have experienced in peacetime, relatives and friends passed away for a variety of reasons. The young and the elderly comprised the most susceptible groups, but those in-between these two extremes amongst a given family or community were not immune to being unexpectedly struck down in the prime of life. For these departed folks, the proper expectations for bereavement and burial could be followed.

On infrequent occasions, a soldier's remains made their way home for internment, so he too could be laid to rest according to the prevailing customs; however, military personnel, especially the rank-and-file, often wound up interred at or near the place where they perished. If the fallen were fortunate, a few appropriate words might be spoken by a chaplain, a letter of condolence sent home by his company captain, and a friend taking note of where the burial occurred. But for the grieving family, they were often left to mourn a memory, and, with no remains over which to place a tombstone, a cenotaph was sometimes erected to commemorate the deceased's existence and passing ... but alas not the burial site of the departed warrior.

Given the wartime shortages of materials and money, mourners did their best to adhere to the prevailing protocols, of which there were many covering all aspects of attending to the bereavement practices and burial processes for a deceased individual. For those who wanted to be as correct as possible, publications such as *Godey's Lady's Book* spelled out proper mourning etiquette. In the larger cities, department stores often had a section devoted to purveying the requisite attire, necessary cloth, and suitable decorations. To wit, Whitney & Myers located in New York's capital advertised its stock: "In Mourning Goods, We offer Black Bombazine, both English and French chemise Cloths, [and] Black Alapaca [sic] Cloths."[2] Specialty shops, known as mourning stores, also existed in which their entire line of goods catered to bereavement needs. Normally, the supply on-hand would be of sufficient quantity to meet requirements. However, the assassination of the president, like a one-hundred-year flood, could neither be predicted nor ignored. Lincoln's death touched so many people that it caused a run on establishments selling fabrics suitable for mourning purposes.

While the concept of purchasing new clothing and hanging distinctive ornamentation may today seem incongruous and even tasteless where the passing of a loved one is the base motivation, our forefathers' perception of this terminal event was different than ours. By virtue of these outward observances and displays, the deceased's life was honored and celebrated. "The ritual of mourning was done out of respect for a lost loved one," wrote Bernadette Loeffel-Atkins in *Widows Weeds and Weeping Veils*. "Paying tribute to the dead became a way of life in nineteenth century America."[3]

What makes Victorian mourning rituals so incongruous to us in the twenty-first century is due in part to a deep-rooted aversion that currently discourages any discussion of such a dark topic. In an odd juxtaposition of social mores, modern Americans can far more easily discourse on sex than on death, while for their Victorian ancestors the opposite was true.

Still, even the most open-minded of people today find many aspects of nineteenth bereavement customs somewhat unsettling, if not downright bizarre. One practice quite likely to arch modern eyebrows was the Victorians' penchant for not only having a photograph made of the deceased, but also one that possibly included living relatives in a group shot. In these instances, the dearly departed might appear propped lifelike alone in a chair, seated on couch between two relatives, or, if a small child, held in the arms of a parent. While sitting for such truly "last-minute" pictures may rub our sensitivities as being ghoulish, a fact of American life in that era was that most people did not have a mantle full of family pictures. For many, these death poses represented the only images ever taken of the deceased. When placed within the larger context of paying homage to the departed individual, this tradition does not seem so outrageous.

Nevertheless, as commonplace as taking these photographic mementoes was, Mary Lincoln decreed early on that she would not tolerate any such remembrances of the president. Daguerreotypes of her husband reposing in his casket were forbidden. Had she approved, prints would have sold like hotcakes, though the decency of such retailing could have been seen in poor taste. But then again, the times were different. In a comparable vein, Mathew Brady had a highly successful showing in his New York gallery of photographs taken on the Antietam battlefield, after the fighting was over. Though the subject of many of his shots was the bodies of soldiers, Americans lined up in droves to view Brady's work.

For those who did desire a keepsake of President Lincoln, a number of less objectionable options than a death picture were readily available. Mourning pins, badges, and rosettes were sold at affordable prices. The fifty-cent pins were fashioned of black satin in the style of military medals, with a black shield, a likeness of the president dangling beneath, and the inscription: "In memory of Abraham Lincoln, April 15, 1865."[4] Rosettes were a bit more elaborate in appearance, consisting of "crepe, steamers, a pin, and the likeness" that was presented in the shape of a rose.[5] The cheapest and most easily affordable to the masses were badges, costing only a quarter, with just the image of Mr. Lincoln and the inscription. For those who wanted a more formal and lasting remembrance, studios offered a variety of portraits, for Lincoln was the first chief executive to be photographed extensively. Cannon's Gallery of Art in Poughkeepsie, New York, was one such source, offering "the best and latest photographic takes of President Lincoln before the assassination."⁶ Mathew Brady's studio in New York City sold "imperial photographs of the funeral car and of the procession, taken from different points along the route."⁷ For those who with deeper pockets, Fowler & Wells of Broadway in New York City had "a bust of Mr. Lincoln, the size of life" for sale.⁸

Another common practice of Victorian mourners—one which manifested itself everywhere that people in the North grieved over the death of President Lincoln, but especially along the pathway of the funeral train—was their extensive display of exterior decorations. While a custom as foreign and incomprehensible to modern sensitivities as are pictures of the deceased, private residences, retail establishments, and civic buildings were festooned in a variety of creative ways as an outward demonstration of grief. Though the term "pageantry" seems inappropriate in describing such, all of the pomp and circumstance that greeted and enveloped the cortège's passage through cities where extended observances were held undeniably created definite spectacles.

Though once again the Victorians' outlook has a disconcerting effect on modern feelings, they actually perceived all of the attendant doings in a celebratory manner. The *Albany Morning Express* ran a headline heralding the late-evening procession which brought the remains from a Hudson River dock to the Capitol as a "A Midnight Pageant," and again in the next day's paper the funeral procession to the depot was described as "A Grand Pageant."⁹

Nevertheless, each one of these observances was conducted in a very somber and respectful manner. Spectators would be hard-pressed to mistake them for an event to the contrary. Black was the predominant color and featured on structural pillars wrapped in downward spirals of cloth, on borders sewn around the outside edge of flags, on wreaths hung on doors, and the lines separating columns in newspapers. In the realm of funeral-related etiquette, whole subsets of prescribed rituals governed how a home was to be arranged for the funeral, the type of apparel mourners should wear, and when to end the period of bereavement. Had Lincoln passed away as a private citizen, the total range of these rites would have been followed religiously. However, given the public and prolonged nature of his journey to the grave, featuring the extended thirteen-day, cross-country cortège, many of the traditional conventions never came into play.

Still, what Lincoln may have been denied, by not having the customary funeral services accorded him, was more than compensated for by the magnitude of the tributes offered. Each of the cities in which "Father Abraham" lay in state seized the opportunity to demonstrate its citizens' profound sorrow. The ceremonies in each city that accompanied a public viewing of his remains exhibited a solemn splendor. Far more simplistic but no less sincere, residents of the rural areas also paid homage to the president's memory. In the few moments available to them as the train rolled slowly past, a variety of moving vignettes were played out at small stations, rail crossings, and trackside farms and clearings. Though the extravagant ceremonies were the antithesis of what the humble man in Lincoln would have wanted had he his druthers, the send-off that he received is unmatched in American history. The twenty days of national mourning were alone singular, but, when the appearance of a traveling wake was factored into the process, the whole affair in hindsight was imbued with a Barnumesque aura. While Franklin Roosevelt managed to avoid becoming the centerpiece of such a public hoopla, Abraham Lincoln did not.

Certainly, the status quo which existed in Lincoln's era, one which had run its course by Roosevelt's and Kennedy's times, was that of the Victorian approach in dealing with death. These protocols were very real in 1865 and to ignore them was to risk social approbation. Whatever tributes were planned at the local level, it was incumbent that they be kept within the established milieu of mourning rituals, for it was against these contemporary standards that the obsequies for Abraham Lincoln would be weighed, measured, and judged. While the populace was familiar with what constituted proper bereavement procedures and protocols, their experiences had for the most part been on a comparatively small scale. Never before were funeral services conducted on a national level like that which was about to unfold. Covering over 1600 miles, crossing seven states, stopping in thirteen cities, and passing through over four hundred communities of all sizes, the coordination of movements of the president's remains by train represented a monumental undertaking and, given its extraordinarily high visibility, left little margin for error.

In light of the precision needed in all aspects of this endeavor, it is understandable why Stanton placed the oversight of the arrangements in the hands of army personnel. Immediately, he promulgated that "the railroads over which the remains will pass are declared military roads, subject to the order of the War Department, and the railroads, locomotives, cars, and engines engaged will be subject to the military control of Brigadier General McCollum. No person will be allowed to be transported on the cars constituting the funeral train save those who are specially authorized by the orders of the War Department. The funeral train will not exceed nine cars, including baggage and hearse cars, which will proceed over the entire route from Washington to Springfield."[10] While railroad officials would provide valuable expertise, Stanton had in effect nationalized the necessary railroads for the time it took the train to traverse their rights-of-way.

Having no manual to guide them, the military and railroad people jointly overseeing the entire operation were writing a one-of-a-kind book as they went; but, by virtue of their training and experience, they were solid planners who could also act swiftly and decisively when choices had to be made. For local officials in the Empire State's cities of New York, Albany, and Buffalo, the onus was thrust upon them to arrange for a municipally-sponsored wake on a grand scale with relatively short advanced notice. Those residents who populated the areas in-between the major stops—the lower Hudson Valley, the Mohawk Valley, and the Great Lakes Plain were left to their own devices to pay fitting tribute to their deceased leader, as his remains passed by on a moving train. It proved to be an epic event in American history, one that those who saw it would long remember.

14

The Return to New York
A City Pays Homage

The long, black-bedecked train that bearing President Lincoln's remains across New York did not enter the state ready to roll. Instead of arriving intact, it came piecemeal. That the funeral train started out in this manner occurred for two reasons. The first was due to the changeover in regional jurisdictions. In passing from one state to another, its hosts went from being the Garden State and the Jersey Central Railroad to the Empire State and the Hudson River Railroad. This transfer meant that the engine and all trailing cars—save the hearse and officers' car—would be now be supplied by a new rail carrier. The second intervening factor was the lack of any bridge connecting the two states, so that ferry service was required to shuttle the cars to New York City. Since only the two through coaches were being carried over from one railroad to the other, these cars became the only pieces of rolling stock taking boat rides.

Earlier that morning, Mayor C. Godfrey Gunther and the Common Council of New York City had come over and were now on board to accompany the remains across the harbor. As New Jersey's final tribute to the martyred president, a banner was hung over the ship's entryway bearing the heartfelt inscription: "Washington, the Father; Lincoln, the Savior of his country."[1] In keeping with its solemn assignment, the ferryboat was covered in mourning drapery. Folds of crepe were used to adorn the pilot house and cabins along the deck. Flags had been lowered to half-staff. When the vessel began to make its way across the harbor, its passengers noted the profusion of highly perceptible responses by their countrymen to President Lincoln's passing. "As far as the eye could reach," observed David Valentine, clerk for the Common Council, "in every direction, were to be seen the silent emblems of a nation's grief, in the mourning devices and half-mast flags which were everywhere visible."[2]

After an uneventful crossing, the *Jersey City* was guided expertly by its captain into his vessel's customary mooring slip. Waiting was a vast throng of New Yorkers, not only filling the immediate area of the dock but also spilling vertically back up Desbrosses Street and then expanding horizontally into several crossing side avenues. With their eyes riveted on the incoming boat, straining for a look at the hearse, the hushed crowd could hear the sound of a dirge emanating from the throats of the German choir aboard the ferry. At the same time, almost eleven o'clock by now, the mourners could also discern the sounds of minute guns firing in their emplacements on Governor's Island, church bells tolling from houses of worship across the city, and the distinctive chimes of Trinity Church.

With so many people jammed into a finite area, the potential for difficulty in moving

Top: Several trips were required by ferries to transport the casket, mourners, and the two railroad coaches that were making the entire trip from Washington to Springfield. *Bottom:* After offloading the casket at the ferry dock on DesBrosses Street, a procession brought the president's remains to New York's city hall for public viewing (*Lincoln Memorial: A Record of the Life, Assassination and Obsequies*, 1865).

the hearse to City Hall could have posed a problem. However, just as they had effectively maintained order for the president's visit in 1861, New York's finest proved once more up to the task of crowd-control. Working in concert, the city police and troops from the indomitable 7th Regiment of the New York National Guard kept the main thoroughfare clear for three blocks up to Hudson Street. That the 7th Regiment, clad in their original gray-colored uniforms, was present to receive the president's remains was most appropriate, for these troops had been the first unit to answer Lincoln's 1861 call and get to Washington in timely fashion to guard the vulnerable city. As an added measure to expedite movement of the hearse, elements of the military assumed the stance of a hollow square, a formation which moved in cadence with the hearse encapsulated in its center. From this point forward until the train left his jurisdiction, all matters involving the cortège's passage through the Empire State came under the oversight of General John Dix.

In retrospect, he would deserve a great deal of credit for orchestrating a challenging task in the full-glare of the public's scrutiny ... and doing so in a crisp, orderly, and controlled manner that went off without a hitch. While not mentioning his name but indirectly applauding his efforts, along with those of others involved in guiding the train along its way, a correspondent for *The New York Times* tipped his hat three days later in a complimentary assessment of the whole operation: "We are in Buffalo. Not the slightest accident has happened on the way from Washington, owing to the admirable arrangements and the faithful and experienced officers in charge of the train."[3]

Upon being off-loaded at one of the many piers ringing Manhattan Island on its southwesterly tip, the two through cars were coupled to a waiting locomotive and moved a short distance into temporary storage. Given that the president's remains were destined to city hall for a twenty-four-hour public wake via horse-drawn hearse, the two special coaches would not presently be needed. In the end result, five boat trips were required to shift even the limited aspects of the Lincoln Special that were moving forward: the coffin, the two cars, and all of the passengers. As for the casket, a hearse was waiting at the ferry wharf. Once the boat docked, the mahogany box was quickly transferred, for time was of the essence. The sooner the body could be placed in City Hall, the sooner the viewing could commence. While twenty-four hours seemed a generous allotment of time, the fact that the city boasted the largest population in the nation meant that long lines of mourners could be expected.

With the transfers completed by 11 o'clock, the first of two major water crossings for key elements of the cortège had been effected. The other comparable movement would be two days later and 150 miles northward, when only the casket and mourners from the train would be transported across the same Hudson River by a smaller ferry to Albany. These two water-borne transfers probably represented the two most critical moments in the entire journey. Understandably, when moving the president's remains, no one wanted a mishap to occur on his watch. But taking the body out on the water significantly raised the anxiety levels of those in charge. While a variety of precautions were taken with respect to the cortège's movement by train, putting the coffin onboard a boat, particularly in the wide and deep waters of New York harbor, did not leave any room for a Plan B—particularly if the vessel should suddenly start taking on water, as a burial at sea was decidedly not a preferred outcome. So it was with a sigh of relief when the president's remains were successfully resting on New York soil.

Then, with military precision, the participants in the procession lined up and headed out. Leading the way was a vanguard of policemen, then marched Generals John Dix and Charles Sanford, who despite their advanced ages, gamely kept pace in the company of various city officials. The 7th Infantry's regimental band playing appropriate dirges was next, followed by the front line of the hollow square, trailed by sergeants from the Invalid

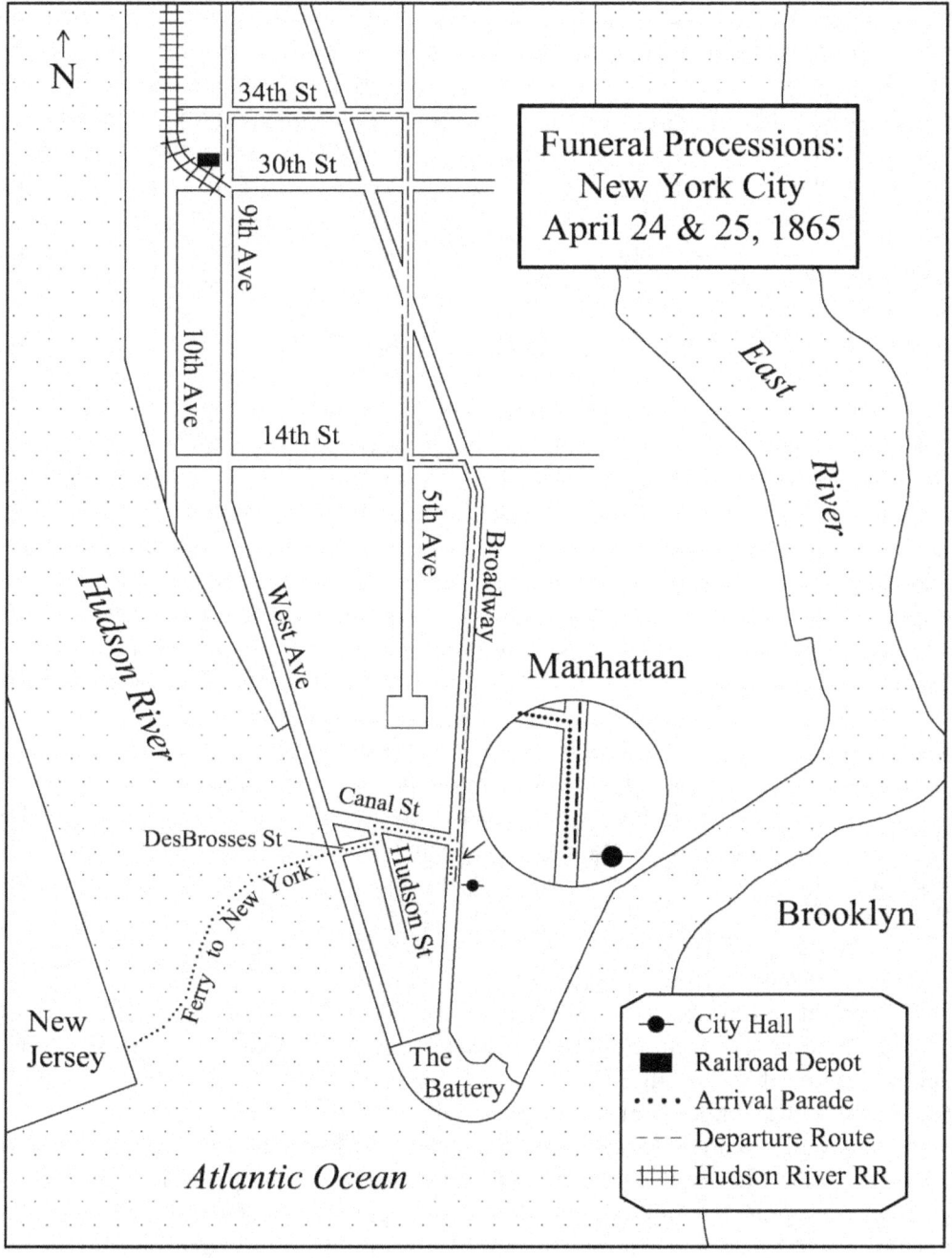

Drawn by Bob Collea.

Corps, and then the hearse itself surrounded by the remaining elements of the 7th Regiment which solemnly tread along with their rifles reversed, meaning barrels down and stocks up in a sign of respect for a fallen leader, this being a symbol of mourning commonly used in the British Army that was in vogue for time in America; however, it was a tradition that gradually lost traction after the Civil War.

Next in the procession were three rows of carriages carrying all the various dignitaries from the funeral train: relatives and family friends; the Guard of Honor; members of the Joint Congressional Committee; the substantial Illinois delegation; governors from several states; city officials; the German Singing Society; and bringing up the rear another cordon of police. As the cortège made its way through the city, the number of marchers began to increase appreciably, as "after them [the police] came the people by the thousands, in solemn and orderly demeanor, from DesBrosses and Hudson streets in a vast throng," wrote William Coggeshall, "following in the rear and reaching from curb to curb on Canal street. This column increased as it went, and, with uncovered heads and sad and steadily persistent steps, followed the remains of the lamented Chief Magistrate to Broadway, and in many cases to city hall."[4]

The focal point of onlookers' attention was, of course, the hearse (or hearse car, as the papers referenced it) not to be confused, however, with the railroad coach the *United States* which was also called a hearse car. Befitting both the elegance of the casket and the stature of the man inside, this conveyance certainly presented itself as a transport worthy of its esteemed passenger. The stylish look of the car, while appearing ostentatious to modern viewers, was very much in keeping with contemporary Victorian tastes. Its canopy rose fifteen feet. The platform of the car was fourteen feet long by eight feet wide. Raised five feet from the ground and containing a dais in the center, the coffin had sufficient elevation for people in the back of the crowd to see it, as it passed through the streets. The sides and back were covered by large plate glass windows, allowing for a clear view of its contents. Projecting from the top were eight large, full plumes comprised of black and white feathers. American flags were folded and attached along the top and bottom edges of the coach, accented with black and white festoons, and affixed with knots of black and white ribbon. Six gray horses, each covered in black drapery and led by a groom, provided motive power. As grandiose as this vehicle appeared, it was pressed into service from an existing stable. While it may have had a few extra adornments appropriately tailored in honor of its distinguished passenger—such as the flags, stars, and an eagle—Victorian hearses as a matter of course had showy looks to them.

The chosen route involved traversing four streets and almost twenty blocks, ending at the plaza where City Hall was located. The parade would travel northeast the three-block length of DesBrosses Street to Hudson Street, a quick left on Hudson for a short distance to Canal Street, then a right down Canal Street to Broadway, and eventually seven blocks south on this main thoroughfare to the Astor House, up Park-row to the eastern side of the Park at Printing-House Square, and finally into the open space before its destination in lower Manhattan. All along the route, the police had done a superb job in clearing the streets, which allowed the procession to move at an even, unimpeded pace. In contrast to the open roadway, "the sidewalks, windows, roofs, posts, trees, and all imaginable points for advantageous view, were crowded to their utmost capacity."[5] Though people would have turned out regardless, the fact that the spring morning dawned calm, cool, and clear made standing and waiting a much more tolerable experience than it could otherwise have been. Yet for many, the beauty of that glorious April morning—with spring flowers blooming, trees budding, and birds chirping—was a lost treasure on this particular day. With the profusion of mourning drapery all around, the reminders of the sad occasion that had brought so many people together were inescapable.

When the cortège passed a given point, the gentlemen gathered there respectfully removed their hats, and everyone stood in hushed silence. Save perhaps for those overcome by emotion. In an urban area the size of New York, a large turnout was not surprising. "The scene on the streets yesterday was one of an impressive character," observed *The New York Sun*, "both [sic] in relation to the funeral cortège, the gathering of the people, and the display of mourning emblems and mottoes."[6]

As the newspaper pointed out, where the residents of the city really went the extra mile was the impressive extent to which business proprietors and home owners alike decorated their respective properties. The all-encompassing nature of the community's response was described by David Valentine, who found that "scarcely a building in this city, public or private, from the Fifth Avenue mansion to the humblest tenement-house, could be seen, which had not some outward funeral decoration."[7] Prevalent among the thousands of displays adorning the front of structures both public and private, in addition to the various configurations utilizing crepe, festoons, rosettes, and flags, were banners with appropriate slogans. Among these verbal tributes were such adages as "Thou art gone, and friend and foe alike appreciate thee now" and "God moves in mysterious ways his wonders to perform."[8] On their persons, most people had affixed a mourning badge, with the established protocol being that these symbols were to be worn for thirty days.

In retrospect, the truly admirable quality that underpinned these tributes was that they originated from the hearts of the people. Not done per force as a dutiful response to any governmental fiat, but rather voluntarily representations of a grateful nation's thanks and farewell to its fallen leader. Without a doubt, New York could do processions and do them on a par with the best and generally better than most. But by their very nature, joyous occasions were entertaining and pleasing to pull off. In its handling of the Lincoln funeral, which involved two processions plus a wake of twenty-two hours, the city demonstrated that it could handle somber observances with equal aplomb and dignity.

As John Carroll Power shared in his contemporary impression, "New York paid a tribute of respect to the memory of Abraham Lincoln, the like of which was never approached in this country before, and has probably not been excelled in the obsequies of any ruler in the history of the world."[9] *The New York Herald* was just as admiring of the city's efforts, its civic pride gushing forth in sharing with its readers that "no one could behold the scene, in all its impressive solemnity, earnestness, and sincerity, without feeling satisfied that the funeral cortege of Abraham Lincoln was a triumphal procession greater, grander, and more genuine, than any living conqueror or hero ever enjoyed."[10]

Moving at a slow but measured pace, the procession covered the distance to the plaza in front of city hall in good time, with the head of the column entering the gate east of the park at precisely 11:30 a.m. While all along the route the crowds were densely packed, the numbers increased appreciably in front of its final destination, where estimates projecting upwards of 20,000 people were massed. Some had arrived as early as eight that morning in order to claim a prime viewing spot. In addition to those clustered tightly together at ground level, the windows, doorways, and rooftops of the surrounding buildings were also commandeered as viewing points.

What they observed was a one-of-a-kind display of pageantry. Somber yet inspiring, the ritual unfolding before their eyes was distinguished by its unrehearsed precision. With the crowd kept outside of the iron fence that defined the park's grounds, the hearse was brought in and stopped in front of the city's primary civic building. In anticipation of this solemn moment, the exterior of the stately edifice was done up in a tasteful mourning adornment: its eight tall columns wrapped in spirals of black crepe; both its first and second floor windows treated with ebony draping; and the national and state flags sewn with mourning borders waving on poles on the roof. In gigantic block letters, a huge banner was strung across the building's bolding proclaiming "A Nation Mourns."

With the clock already ticking toward the next day's departure, time was of the essence. To the accompaniment of a dirge offered by the combined talents of the army band and the German choirs, eight members of the Veteran Reserve Corps brought the coffin from the hearse and carried it up the front steps and into city hall. Six of the sturdy soldiers bore the brunt of the casket on their shoulders, while in front and back the other two members of the team helped to guide and stabilize the heavy mahogany box. After negotiating the wide but curving staircase to the second floor, they carefully placed their charge on a catafalque located in front of the Governor's Room.

Immediately, Dr. Brown, the Washington embalmer traveling on the train, came forward and removed the portion of the lid exposing the head and upper torso of the deceased. Before the public was admitted, he needed to be sure that the corpse was presentable, for this was the tenth day since the president had passed away. Even though Dr. Brown had guaranteed the preservation powers of his chemical treatments, all the traveling, jostling, unloading, and reloading of the casket that had occurred between Washington and New York was bound to adversely affect its mortal contents. What the doctor saw was to some extent anticipated and remediable. Those failings which he could address were limited to primarily cosmetic adjustments. Since a fair amount of dust had settled on the deceased's face, hair, and clothes, these particles were cleaned off with a handkerchief as delicately and thoroughly as possible. When he had finished prepping the body, the doctor addressed the outer surface and trappings of the casket which also showed the effects of prolonged travel and frequent handling.

However, the one aspect of Lincoln's appearance that was the most important from the standpoint of the mourners was his physiognomy, specifically the disturbing discoloration of the late President's face. "Mr. Brown, the embalmer, who skilled and competent as he is," warned *The New York Times*, "could not be expected to perform a miracle on short notice."[11] From the start, the damage inflicted by the impact of the assassin's bullet had caused dark circles to form in the eye sockets, a result of the fracturing of the orbital bones by the impact of the lead ball plowing through his brain. Then as time passed, the overall facial skin tone had begun to darken. The embalmer did what he could to render the appearance more natural, but still what remained was "a face dark to blackness, features sharp to a miracle, an expression almost horrible in its un-nature, a stiff starched countenance resembling none they knew of and expressive of nothing familiar."[12] Victor Searcher expressed it forthrightly when he wrote in *The Farewell to Lincoln*, "that in death his appearance was not the same as in life goes without saying; no one's is."[13] "To those who had not seen Mr. Lincoln in life," concurred *The New York Times*, "the view may be satisfactory; but to those who were familiar with his features, it is far from otherwise."[14]

Certainly, for those who knew the great man much more intimately, seeing the discolored, expressionless statue occupying the casket was the most painful and disheartening of experiences. Without the ready smile, the sad eyes, the furrowed brow, and most of all the compassion, the humor, and the humility, the lifeless form was no longer the man whom they had known, admired, and loved ... and nothing Dr. Brown could do was able to bring that back. For those whose familiarity with the deceased came only from prints and photographs, the frozen features appeared as they might have expected. But as *The New York Times* espoused, "those thousands who crowded zealously in the street, pushed vigorously on the stairs, strove earnestly in the corridor, glanced hastily at the face and passed hurriedly from the room, saw no Abraham Lincoln."[15]

Unfortunately, in their quest for what they perceived to be accurate reporting, newsmen created a contretemps with Dr. Brown. In the Fourth Estate's estimation, the corpse had deteriorated noticeably since leaving Washington. In its current state of decomposition, while during its prolonged exposure to the air in city hall, the body had experienced a marked decline in its appearance. From one reporter's perspective, "the color is leaden, almost brown; the forehead recedes sharp and clearly marked; the eyes deep sunk and close held upon the sockets; the cheek bones, always high are unusually prominent; the cheeks hollowed and deeply pitted; the unnaturally thin lips shut tight and firm as if glued together; and the small chin, covered with slight beard, seemed pointed and sharp."[16]

Since this was how the remains looked to some on only the fifth day of its journey—with eight more days and several viewings yet to go—concerns arose in many minds over what the president's body would look like in not only the more imminent stops of Albany and Buffalo, but particularly toward the end of long passage. By the time it got to the Midwestern cities of Chicago and Springfield, what kind of gut-wrenching, jarring encounter would viewing the corpse be for those mourners? Words like "ghastly," "decayed," and "shrunken" were being used to describe the current state of the deceased's appearance. Contrasting with all the doubt and criticism being sown by the vigilant press, Dr. Brown remained steadfast in his stance that the body would remain suitable for all of its scheduled public displays. But, with his professional reputation and future livelihood on the line, he had no room to waffle—staying the course was really his only option. Working in his favor were upstate journalists whose descriptions were much more flattering relative to the condition of the corpse. If the metropolitan press accomplished anything by its critical observations with respect to the body's appearance, it was to keep away many people who had seen President Lincoln on some previous occasion.

As if this controversy was not enough, another flap arose when two photographs of the body lying in state were taken. Unlike the debate as whether the corpse should still be considered sufficiently presentable for public viewing, the uproar over the pictures represented a vexation that never should have occurred in the first place. Given that photographs of the deceased were a common part of Victorian mourning rituals, the propriety of taking pictures under normal circumstances was completely acceptable. However, such remembrances were customarily produced at the behest of the grieving family. Since Mary Lincoln did not want them, Stanton promulgated that no reproductions were to be rendered. That should have ended the matter. But such proved not to be the case. General Townsend, who happened to be on the first watch over the body, granted a New York City photographer, Jeremiah Gurney, permission to take photographs from a higher level in the rotunda. In the thirty minutes which he was allotted, prior to the admittance of the public at 1:00 p.m., Mr. Gurney and his assistants were able to take two daguerreotypes.

Had the pictures been destined for a governmental collection, archiving for posterity a visual record of the Lincoln funeral, the tale might have ended there. However, a commercial photographer, having in his possession such a unique item, was still ultimately a businessman. In a milieu where people were already purchasing likenesses of the late President and even his assassin, a picture of Lincoln in death had the potential to be a lucrative piece. However, any visions of sugar plums that might have been dancing in Gurney's head were doomed never to materialize as the envisioned financial windfall. What General Townsend was thinking when he gave the okay for the pictures is uncertain, but there is no question that by doing so he was disobeying an order from his superior. However, Edwin Stanton's response when he learned of the unsanctioned photo op was neither cloudy, vague, nor delayed in coming. Once competitors began carping to the secretary about the apparent exclusivity that was granted to Gurney, a livid Stanton was galvanized into action. He immediately dispatched a directive to General Dix, ordering the plates and any existing pictures to be destroyed.

When cooler heads prevailed upon Stanton to check with the Lincoln family in the event they might have changed their minds, he issued a temporary hold on the previous order and asked that the materials be confiscated and sent to him. But General Dix had already commenced to do away with the offending pictures and thus able to send only one plate and a single photo to his boss.

In conferring with the Lincoln family, the secretary was told to continue with the elimination of the unauthorized photographs. But Stanton proved no better than his underlings at following orders. The plate was destroyed, but, instead of immediately tearing up the offending print, he stuck it in a file folder. Years later, the picture was found and sent to John Hay who, along with John Nicolay, was working on a multi-volume biography on the life of Lincoln. The thought of the sender, Stanton's son, was that Lincoln's war-time secretaries might want to include this one-of-a-kind picture in the appropriate volume of their work. Sensitivities caused them to demur on its use, so the wandering photograph wound up in still another file until discovered in 1952 by a fourteen-year-old student-scholar. While the shot is much more revealing of the general surroundings than the deceased, it nevertheless still represents the only post-mortem photographic image of President Lincoln in his coffin.

Interestingly, Gurney's daguerreotype was not the only image of the president in death's repose ... just the most celebrated. A second likeness was produced by a Frenchman named Pierre Morand. Though an amateur, he possessed a fair degree of artistic ability. At approximately two a.m., on April 25, Morand generated a drawing from his observation of the body. How much he was able to commit to paper while actually standing before his subject and how much was completed later is open to conjecture. Given the need to keep the line of mourners moving, it is not likely that this individual was accorded extended viewing time—unless of course one of the guards may have allowed Morand to linger because he knew him or the possibly had his palm greased.

Owing to the acquaintanceship that Mr. Morand had struck up with Lincoln in Washington during the war, he had some familiarity with the facial features of his subject. According to a recent story in *The New York Times*, after leaving city hall the artist "returned to his studio, made another copy and then a final ink and white gouache version."[17]

What he drew, while acknowledging that its true acclaim lies in the fact that it was the last likeness of the late president that ever produced, was lacking in detail and is more like an idyllic caricature rather than an attempt at rendering an accurate portrait. In Morand's interpretation, an unblemished face exhibits neither the after-effects of the bullet nor any of the deterioration noted in the newspapers. Lincoln looks as if he is serenely sleeping, not noticeably decomposing.

In the few minutes that were required to relocate the casket from the ground-level hearse to the second-floor catafalque, the crowd and the president's remains had switched positions. The people were transformed from stationary onlookers, rooted to a chosen spot and hoping to the catch a glimpse of the moving casket, and began to create a long line of mourners, waiting patiently to walk past the corpse which was now the entity that had assumed the fixed position.

With such a large portion of New York's citizenry already present for the procession, many simply decided that they might as well remain and pay their respects. By the time that the entrance doors to city hall were opened to the public, the column of mourners had grown considerably. As estimated by William Coggeshall, "thousands formed that line, which, like a river receiving many contributions nearing its debouchment, gradually lessened, till away up in the Bowery, three-quarters of a mile off, it narrowed as it were a source, till, however, receiving fresh supplies as an onward movement to the front gave a chance of nearing the object all so desired to look upon."[18]

Once entering the grounds, the mourners had to follow a serpentine pathway. Starting at the eastern basement door of the City Hall, visitors walked two abreast

President Lincoln lies in state on a second-floor landing as mourners passed up one flight of stairs and down another, though eventually others were permitted to view his remains by entering from behind through the Governor's Room (*Harper's Weekly*).

along several corridors leading to the foot of the right set of circular stairs in the rotunda, proceeded up those stairs to the landing, and continued past the casket. They continued forward, went down the opposite staircase, and finally exited through the rear door of the City Hall. Though one of the objectives in the original construction was not with an eye toward housing wakes, the architectural layout of city hall was quite conductive to hosting such functions—at least from the standpoint of crowd control.

Unfortunately, the location chosen to place the coffin proved not to be the most ideal for moving large numbers of mourners past the catafalque. Upon reaching the summit of the stairs, callers came upon the casket which was placed on the backside of a second-floor landing. The coffin's location was such that it was positioned feet-first, with the head facing those coming up the right-side flight of stairs. In addition, the head-end was raised up slightly, so that approaching mourners could see the body sooner. After viewing the deceased, the general public continued on down the opposite set of stairs, then out through a rear door, and eventually an east gate. For visitors who had come to the pre-inaugural reception to meet the president-elect, their passage through the building eerily followed some of the same route as it had in 1861, though on that occasion they came through the front door and not a subterranean passage.

In the initial stages of admitting mourners, special consideration was given to the families and friends of those in the hierarchy of the city's power structure. Bearing passes, these privileged folks gained admission by way of a different basement door from the one that general public was using. After climbing a private staircase, they reached the Governor's Room. Passing through from back-to-front, they were then able to approach the casket from its right side. At its onset, allowing this little perk caused no problem. That is until the flow of pedestrian traffic via this conduit increased to substantial proportions. Due to the liberal distribution of passes city councilmen, droves of people were showing up. The situation finally reached such proportions that all attempts to validate the origin and authenticity of the passes were abandoned.

In retrospect, opening a second line for everyone was a consideration which should have been instituted much sooner. When the viewing was terminated at noon the next day, a large number of mourners had to be turned away. While some would undoubtedly still have been disappointed anyway, having two separate lines entering the building from the start would certainly have made that number significantly smaller, for as it was half the viewing time was squandered on just one point of entry for the masses. Not surprisingly, New York's ever-vigilant newspapers did not let this oversight pass by unchallenged. *The New York Times* weighed in with a commentary that blasted the organizers of the proceedings. While not sure who to blame—be it the Common Council or some joint interaction that included the military—the press felt "bound to say that the arrangements, yesterday, for admitting the public to view the body of Abraham Lincoln were just as bad as human ingenuity could make them."[19]

Most of the paper's ire was directed at conditions outside of the building, where as the first day progressed into evening, the crowd became more and more unruly, challenging the best efforts of the police department to maintain order. This inability to successfully manage the streets was attributed primarily to a lack of sufficient numbers. This exterior instability contrasted sharply with the state of affairs inside city hall, where the 7th Regiment had more than sufficient strength to control the relatively small collection of people inside of the building at any one time. The condemnatory piece in the paper concluded by voicing the opinion that "the management of the whole affair was utterly discreditable to those had it in charge."[20]

For those visitors whose patience and stamina kept them in the slowly advancing line, their reward came when they finally gained the entrance hall. As they approached the staircase leading up to the landing where the catafalque lay, mourners had time to take in the temporary alterations in the facility's appearance, all of which were indicative of the solemn wake currently in progress. Clearly, extensive pains had been taken to appropriately drape the building's interior with suitable manifestations of bereavement. Looking up at the rotunda, they could see that black cloth had been used to mask the skylight around the dome, which served to create a soft, diffused illumination. Silver stars had been attached to the ceiling. Large national, state, and local flags were affixed to the walls. Across these banners at the level of Old Glory's field of stars was strung "a chain of black paramatio, which formed a deep hem as it were, bordering the partitions made by the flags."[21]

Facing the catafalque on the opposite wall of the room was a large portrait of President Lincoln, its frame bordered with black crepe and studded with silver stars. The framework of two large chandeliers suspended on long chains from the ceiling had been interwoven with an ebony fabric; likewise, the banisters on both of the sweeping staircases were black-draped in their entirety all the way up to and across the landing in front of the catafalque. Then, as the viewing line made its way forward, the centerpiece of the entire display and motivation for the peoples' presence was more completely revealed.

With each upward step, the catafalque, which was decorated in high-Victorian splendor, appeared with greater clarity to the mourners. What they ultimately beheld was a magnificently constructed housing under which the honored remains rested, described by one observer as appearing "at once impressive and mystic."[22] The catafalque was twenty-feet high at its center-peak and had a footprint that was ten-feet wide and twelve-feet deep.

Judging from the only known photograph and a few drawings which exist of the bier's appearance and location, the casket was placed on the second-floor landing at the confluence of the two staircases which curved up from its right and left. Ordinarily, a visitor who reached this point would turn and face the doors to the Governor's Room. Behind the visitors would be a balustrade overlooking the main entrance and open floor beneath the rotunda. The entrance doors to the Governor's Room appear to have been double-wide, creating the necessary space to accommodate the casket which was placed in the center of that opening, if not slightly inside of it. By virtue of this positioning, sufficient room existed for callers to pass in single file between the coffin and the railing with relative ease. Reasonable spaces also existed around the casket at both ends, allowing passage from the landing into the Governor's Room and vice-versa for those who needed such egress.

Eventually, when viewing was expanded to allow not just a privileged few, but also the general public to also enter from a back stairway into the Governor's Room, the ability to effect circumlocution of the casket was vital in expediting this one-way viewing stream out of the Governor's Room, past the opposite side of the casket from those entering by way of the rotunda, and then down one of the front staircases.

All through the night, the wave of humanity kept coming, though its forward progress at times seemed barely perceptible. While the Honor Guard changed every two hours, the poor people in the street could only stay in line and periodically shuffle forward toward their objective. Men and women of various age groups, social classes, and differing races comprised the throng which blended together in silent harmony. "Throughout the long early summer day, beneath the fervid rays of the sun, which shone almost uncomfortably warm," noted William Coggeshall, "into the cool hours of the evening, and away through the chilly hours of the night, till dawn was almost breaking, the seemingly ever unbroken line of people kept its ground persistently."[23] The procession of mourners reached its peak density "about midnight."[24]

While the queue never completely abated, the early morning hours saw the number of callers dwindle to its lowest rate, estimated to "not average above twenty a minute."[25] However, the final tally for visitations placed the average rate at approximately eighty persons per minute, while General Dix felt that the grand total was in the range of 110,000.[26] Yet, much to the credit of metropolitan New Yorkers, the deportment of the mourners was for the most part was highly commendable. In a city which contained residents highly capable of engaging in a riot, they proved in the obsequies for Abraham Lincoln that they were equally adept at turning their demeanor around and assuming a dignified posture. The local press was effusive in its praise when it noted that "it was generally remarked that a more well-behaved [sic], quiet or more orderly assemblage was never seen in the state of New York."[27]

Adding to the impressive numbers of indigenous New Yorkers who had turned out for the viewing all through the night, daybreak saw visitors coming by boat and train from Connecticut and the upper Hudson to pay their respects. In addition, ferries from Williamsburg, Brooklyn, Jersey City, and Hoboken disgorged full loads of passengers. "It was truly astonishing to see the immense numbers of people coming from the neighboring cities," observed a *Times* reporter, "who evidently had determined to merge themselves in the one great mass of New York citizens, and join with them in doing homage to the departed and heroic statesman."[28]

Most of those out-of-towners who arrived in the hours before noon quickly sized up the situation and realized that their prospects for viewing the remains were slim-to-none. Reluctantly but realistically, they redirected their focus to staking out a good spot from which to observe the upcoming procession. Even though for many this meant a standing for hours, they accepted this fate good-naturedly and remained orderly for the duration of their vigil.

As the morning passed, preparations for the funeral procession were stepped up. With businesses largely closed across the city, people were free to concentrate on the final stage of the municipality's farewell to their martyred leader. Inside city hall, calling hours were winding down. As the clock struck 11:00 a.m., the grand public wake entered its final minutes. Very soon the doors would be closed to the public. While the upshot of this curtailment of the viewing meant that thousands of everyday people had to be turned away, several contingents of prestigious mourners were permitted access for one last look.

First came the procession's Grand Marshal William Hall, accompanied by his half-dozen assistant-marshals; these gentlemen were followed by Brooklyn's acting-mayor David D, Whitney, along with his city council and other prominent officials from across the river; and, finally, several high-ranking army and navy officers were admitted, among them being Generals Dix, Townsend, Hunter, Ramsey, and Eaton and Admirals Farragut and Davis. At this point, the solemn scene was interrupted by the arrival of the Dr. Charles Brown, the embalmer, and Frederick Sands, the undertaker. Immediately they began to prepare the casket and body to resume their journey. As the scene unfolded, it consisted of "one more look—the dust was brushed away from the high forehead, the collar somewhat arranged, the lid was put on, the screws turned, the cold collapsed figure emboxed [sic], and the men whose commissions he had signed could see him no more forever."[29]

An unanticipated interruption occurred when a foreign delegation suddenly materialized. This mixed assemblage of dignitaries from Great Britain, Russia, and France had come to pay their respects, but unfortunately, they had arrived too late. When all was ready, six of eight non-commissioned officers comprising the pallbearers lifted the coffin on the shoulders, while the remaining two again provided stability at both ends against tipping. Down the staircase and across the entrance hall, they carefully negotiated their way, fully mindful with each step of the sacred mission to which they had been entrusted. They waited just inside the door for the appropriate transportation to be brought up to the front steps.

Upon the hearse's arrival at 12:50 a.m., General Dix waved the bearers forward. Out of the door and down the steps they went. All mourners in the vicinity doffed their hats, and more than a few tears were shed. The Seventh's regimental band struck up the mournful dirge "Rest, Spirit Rest," the tower bell tolled in city hall, the soldiers snapped to present arms, and the crowd of thousands looked on in silence. Opportunistic in commandeering every possible vantage point, "trees, houses, windows, tops of the windows, tops of the houses, and indeed, every place where a foothold could be obtained, were filled and covered with human beings."[30] Bordering on disrespectful in the eyes of many who saw them, a

An elaborate ceremony conveyed the casket from inside city hall to the waiting hearse, which then became the focal point of the procession up Broadway (*Harper's Weekly*).

number of the more nimble and brazen onlookers had the audacity to scale the nearby statue of George Washington and cling precariously from its head, neck, and arms.

Once the casket was placed inside the elaborate hearse, the centerpiece of the procession was ready to move forward. Getting all of the remaining parts of what would be a huge caravan assembled in the proper order would take some time. But for the covering of a few city blocks, New York City's tribute to the country's fallen leader was almost over. It would soon become the time for residents of upstate New York to bestow their own forms of homage. None, of course, would be able to match the grandeur and extravagance of the extensive obsequies which the nation's largest city had to offer, but the citizens of each bereaved community and rural setting, past which the Lincoln Special was scheduled to travel, would do their best to express appropriate sentiments in ways that local means and opportunity permitted.

Albany and Buffalo, like New York, would be allotted extended hours, allowing both to stage elaborate ceremonies. Other communities, such as Peekskill, Utica, Syracuse, and Rochester garnered a few minutes for trackside observances due to engine changes. But most locales would have to be satisfied with the handful of seconds that it took for a slow-moving train to pass by a small station or a country crossroads. But these tributes, memorable in their own ways, would occur over the course of the fifty-four hours once the Lincoln Special started rolling again. For the present, New York City still had one last part of its splendid multi-faceted tribute to present.

15

Leaving the City
A Grand Procession to the Depot

Though the hearse was ready at the appointed hour, other elements of the procession were not. Given the grandiose proportions of the parade, many components were still in the process of gaining their assigned positions. Much to the chagrin of the military and railroad authorities who valued punctuality, the pageant did not get underway until 1:40. The designated route of march was north on Broadway to Fourteenth Street, across Fourteenth to Fifth Avenue, north on Fifth Avenue to Thirty-Fourth Street, and finally through Thirty-Fourth Street to Ninth Avenue until reaching the railroad station. To make this route as aesthetically pleasing as possible, the streets were swept clean during the night.

While certainly disappointing to those who were devotees of timeliness, the unrehearsed nature of the march created some delay in getting organized. The number of participating units was unprecedented. First, in terms of sheer numbers was the military, comprising the parade's First Division. Gathered together were eighteen New York guard regiments and five more of United States and Brooklyn troops. These units, along with multiple artillery batteries, amounted to approximately fifteen thousand soldiers. Indicative of their mourning status, the troops would march with their arms reversed.

Immediately behind this formidable body came General Dix and his staff. Slotted next was the hearse. In size and splendor—save for being devoid of all color other than black, white, and silver—the hearse resembled one of the floats seen in latter-day parades on these same city streets. To keep mourners at a safe distance from the hearse, not only was there an honor guard marching along each of its sides, but both the guard and the hearse were once again shielded inside of a hollow square, formed by a double-ranked detachment from the Seventh Regiment.

In succeeding ranks came droves of amateur marchers. One reporter shared his personal estimation that following the soldiers "in the procession were also hundreds of different societies and organizations, the Masonic order alone turning out upwards of ten thousand members.[1] In all, including the military and the hearse, eight separate divisions constituted the lengthy column. The Second Division contained all of the national, state, and local officials, with a few foreign emissaries also included. The Third Division, led by the grand marshal and his assistants, consisted of "the professional, literary, political, and social associations of the city."[2] The remaining five contingents were respectively comprised of participants from fraternal orders, Irishmen, the mechanics and the caulkers associations, trades and societies, and civilians and societies from Brooklyn—with their placement at the end reflective of the rivalry between what were then the first and third largest cities in the United States.

But of all the subsections, the last group of marchers—one actually comprising an unrecognized ninth division—was the only segment that created controversy; however the hullabaloo was not caused by its members, but instead by those who would have preferred that this particular group not be included in the program. Assigned no official position in the column, black residents of the city waited patiently for the eight divisions to pass and then, 200 strong, they attached themselves as a de facto ninth division. Bearing a banner simply inscribed "Abraham Lincoln, our Emancipator," the presence of these mourners was as heartfelt, sincere, and legitimate as any of the other participants marching ahead of them.

Yet, astounding though it may seem in hindsight, this worthy element of the city's population was initially denied the right to be a part of the proceedings in any capacity. But following quickly on the heels of an ill-conceived order issued by the New York Common Council barring participation by "colored citizens," the city's police commissioner adamantly made it known that he opposed this action.[3] His stand was subsequently supported by an irate secretary of war Stanton, who informed General Dix that it was his desire "that no discrimination respecting color should be exercised in admitting persons to the funeral procession tomorrow. In this city [i.e., Washington], a black regiment formed part of the escort."[4] Wielding his virtually dictatorial powers over the funeral proceedings, Stanton pronounced in no uncertain terms that city's prohibition was henceforth countermanded.

The *New York Evening Post* registered its righteous indignation and moral outrage when it blared forth from its pages that "our late President was venerated by the whole colored population with a peculiar degree of feeling ... and [they] looked upon him as the liberator of their race. We have accepted the services of colored citizens in the war and it is disgraceful ingratitude to shut them out of our civil demonstration."[5]

If there was any aspect of the whole traveling wake that Lincoln would have supported, Stanton's decisive action in this instance would have had the late president's stamp of approval. Unfortunately, not wishing to be at the center of a storm, many of the city's blacks opted to forego their participation. Even though a phalanx of policemen marched in front and behind them, the turnout was far less than the 5,000 originally anticipated. But fears of retribution proved unfounded. Despite the prejudice manifested by the city's lawmakers, spectators along the parade route more than offset it, showing by their applause for the black marchers that they did not subscribe to the bigoted feelings of their elected representatives. In the big picture of the two-week journey to Springfield by the funeral train, this unfortunate incident represented one of the very few negative blips.

Shortly before one o'clock in the afternoon of Tuesday, April 24, 1865, the president's casket finally left the grounds of city hall. Though the next destination, the capital city of the Empire State, was situated only 150 miles away, that goal was not attained for almost eleven hours. The first three witnessed perhaps the slowest movement of the day, for only twenty city blocks were negotiated. That progress opened at such a snail's pace was due in part to the length of the funeral procession—estimated to be from "eight to ten miles" in length.[6] Its objective was the Thirtieth Street Station. The very same depot that Lincoln had opened on his visit in 1861 was now the departure point for his funeral train. For this next leg of the journey, the Hudson River Railroad had the honor of providing the host services and equipment.

Even though public access to city hall was not curtailed until shortly after eleven, elements participating in the march had already begun assembling. By the time everyone had lined up, the funeral procession was clearly going to be a vast undertaking, an extravaganza worthy of both the exceptional man whose life was being celebrated and the grand city sponsoring the tribute. Without a doubt, that which was about to occur in New York City would be unprecedented. In the unequivocal estimation of William Coggeshall, "the procession was the grandest—the most imposing ever organized in the United States."[7]

While many prominent people comprised the lengthy retinue of marchers, the focal point of the parade for spectators was still the casket. The hearse's impressive size and shape made it an unmistakable sight. A work of art and labor of love, Peter Relyea had thrown himself whole-heartedly into fashioning a masterpiece that would be the carriage bearing the remains of Abraham Lincoln. Given nine-thousand dollars for his efforts, Relyea spent the larger part of three days creating this special conveyance. Rising early and working late, he labored in full view of the public. Taking his commission seriously, he strove to fashion an outcome that was in keeping with the monumental event of which the hearse would assume the lead role. An undertaker by trade, he approached this assignment like his life up to this point had been preparing him for this moment. So invested in the project was the man that he slept beside it each night.

When he was finally finished, Relyea's artistic efforts disappointed no one. Held up against the exacting standards of Victorian taste, the fruits of his labor had resulted in his designing the Cadillac of nineteenth century hearses. One contemporary source praised his effort as an "elegant piece of workmanship."[8]

Fourteen feet long, seven feet wide, and fifteen feet high, his construction towered over every other aspect of the procession. Drawing from the same base materials that adorned buildings and homes across the city, Relyea's unique talents produced a one-of-a-kind carrier. Sitting five feet above the ground, the main platform of the hearse was entirely covered with black cloth, drawn tight around the platform's perimeter and overlapping its sides and reaching to within inches of the ground. Silver fringe on the bottom and silver stars all along the top edge provided decorative accents on four sides.

Centered five inches above the bed of the hearse was a rectangular dais which was intended as the resting place for the casket. Columns on each corner, topped with black plumes, supported a black canopy—lined with a contrasting white cloth on the inside—that rose to a peak in the center, where on the outside the covering was crowned with a small-scale rendition of the "Temple of Liberty," while on the interior side of the awning a soaring silver eagle dangled above the coffin. Three American flags on staffs were tilted outward from each column. As the finishing touch, the task of pulling this exceptional creation had to be equally outstanding, so that the three or four teams which could have effectively but as not flamboyantly handled the chore would not suffice. For this high-profile undertaking, Relyea pressed sixteen gray horses into service, with each attended by a groom to insure their tranquility. Draped in black coverings, this overabundance of equine participants was in reality a visually exciting introduction to the ostentation of the trailing hearse.

Once the coffin was placed on the hearse and the marchers queued up, the parade was ready to begin. Approximately forty-five minutes behind schedule, the lead elements finally stepped off. The spectators—whose numbers were estimated by General Dix "at over 500,000"—were massed along the entire route.[9] Many had staked out a desirable viewing spot earlier in the day and then steadfastly maintained a vigil lasting for hours. People were everywhere, just as they had been when the more abbreviated march had occurred conveying the coffin to city hall. However, on this occasion, they were packed much deeper and denser along the streets. As before, every elevated vantage point along the route was also occupied. Stoops, windows, rooftops, trees, and lampposts were laden with the bereaved. Some entrepreneurs, after having parked a dray arranged with benches in a key spot on a side street, proceeded to charge those willing to pay for a seat from which to watch the procession. In addition, temporary platforms were installed at intersections to accommodate spectators for a price.

Most noticeable in comparison with previous occasions when big turnouts had gathered in the city, "there was no cheering, no waving of flags, no clapping of hands, no lively martial music."[10] Though some individuals in large crowds often tend toward exhibitions of boisterous behavior, none was observed. Nor were any incidents of drunkenness, rowdiness, or fighting noted. With a degree of uniformity never before seen, solemnity was the universal order of the day. Though no official protocols or warnings were issued, the onlookers intuitively seemed to sense the demeanor appropriate for the occasion. With the first distant sighting of the hearse, all heads were turned in that direction. Necks were craned, and some people stood on tiptoes to catch a glimpse. The crowd experienced a

In an impressive farewell tribute, New York City honored the martyred president by means of a lengthy parade from city hall to the railroad station.

tightening, a surge as people tried to inch forward and thereby enhance their viewing position. Through no fault of their own, spectators in the front were pushed off the curb and into the street, which galvanized the nearest policemen into action that resulted in the innocent victim being forced back and off the street.

But no one had difficulty locking his eyes onto Peter Relyea's highly-visible funereal creation. When the president's remains passed before them, spectators removed their hats and bowed their heads in reverence. Tears flowed freely from the eyes of men as well as women. Parents held young children aloft, so they could witness an event unlikely to occur again in their lifetimes. As the cortège passed on by, heads pivoted once again, fixating on the historic sight passing before them until it was beyond their view. Many in the crowd began to disperse at this point. Having seen the focal point of the procession, they decided to call it a day.

For many, this decision was made more out of weariness than lack of interest. Some had already been standing for quite a spell, so by now they had reached the limits of their stamina. Having paid their respects, the time had come to bring closure to what for many had been a very emotional experience. Furthermore, the reality of the parade's alignment made excusing oneself quite easy. After viewing the hearse in the forefront of the procession,

Exacting craftsmanship and pride were invested by Frank Relyea in creating a hearse that was suitable in its richness and splendor for transporting the remains of Abraham Lincoln (*Harper's Weekly*).

the remainder of the mourners' time would be spent observing their counterparts in the line of march, essentially the bereaved watching the bereaved. For those spectators who chose to stay, they were in for a marathon session, considering that "the huge procession took four hours to pass a given point and was estimated to contain no less than fifty thousand persons."[11]

By virtue of sheer numbers alone, the marchers would require a long time to complete their passage from city hall to the station had they been in constant motion; however, in deference to the warm weather, the distance to be covered, and the inexperience of most participants, periodic halts were called to let people catch their breath and rest their feet.

Even though the spectators respectfully maintained a silent demeanor, the atmosphere surrounding the procession itself was far from devoid of sound. First the minute guns kept up their steady, metronomic beat once the march began, creating reverberations loud enough to rattle windows and startle horses along the parade route. Church and fire bells near and far joined in at the same instant, their rhythmic peals contributing to the overarching din. Emanating from the ground level, the tramp of soldiers' boots produced their own distinctly repetitive sound. Adding their own auditory contributions were the multitude of bands, numbering several score. "Band after band passed," observed a *Sun* correspondent, "playing mournful music, impregnating the very atmosphere with sounds of wailing and woe."[12]

In fact, the excessive length of the parade created one of the oddities of the whole day. For once the hearse reached the station, the casket was quickly loaded into the *United States*. Positioned directly behind the president's remains in the parade had been the mourners who would be continuing with the journey. Upon their arrival trackside, these dignitaries were also taken back aboard the Lincoln Special in short order. A few minutes later, the train departed. However, though the focal point of the parade was gone, the remaining divisions in the procession were still arriving, oblivious to the departure of the funeral train. By the time the last segments of the protracted pageant had reached the Thirtieth Street Station, Lincoln's remains were long gone up the Hudson River toward Albany. This meant that for the last several hours, mourners had been participating in somewhat of an altered tribute, one in which the object of the observance—present at the start—was by its conclusion far away from the proceedings which were still in progress.

For those discriminating mourners who had elected to stake out a viewing perch at the station, the prudence of their choice was duly rewarded, as there was much to be seen at this particular location. First, while they waited for the cortège to arrive, the train in its shining, steaming splendor sat before them. Given ample time to take in the entire consist, the crowd could carefully scrutinize the best that the Hudson River Railroad could supply and, in so doing, cast their gaze upon a very unique train, the likes of which they would never see again.

The two locomotives were sure to have caught their eyes first. One, the *Constitution*, was designated as the pilot engine, while its counterpart called the *Union* had the honor of pulling the Lincoln Special. Some among the onlookers—railroad buffs or those with a sense of history—may have recalled that these two iron horses had played an important role in then President-Elect Lincoln's inaugural tour, the former engine bringing him from Albany to Poughkeepsie and the latter delivering him from there to New York City. In 1861, both engines had been fresh from the Schenectady factories that had produced them.

Pulling the future 16th President of the United States on part of his journey to Washington had been a prestigious way to begin their careers. Now, four years later, the pair was pressed into the service for another high-profile assignment. Though not bright young ingénues of the rails anymore, they had been spruced up to look worthy of leading the ceremonial run up the river.

As would be the case with all locomotives selected to pull the express at some point beyond Albany, considerable attention was given to decorating them with the suitable adornments for hauling a funeral train. Since the situation was so novel, no standard existed to guide this task. Given the Victorian penchant for overstatement, not only the engines but all components of the train received some degree of mourning ornamentation. The rule of thumb followed seemed generally to be that of more embellishment being better than not enough. Of the two locomotives waiting at the Thirtieth Street Station, having been given a role more out of the limelight than its companion, the *Constitution* was decorated to a lesser degree. Still, with its combination of mourning badges, black ribbons and white rosettes, American flags bordered in crepe, and black cloth, the pilot engine was simply but neatly covered from its headlight to its cab.

But it was upon the *Union* that "the most elaborate and tasteful decoration" was lavished.[13] From the very tip of its cowcatcher in front, where a crepe-bordered flag identified the engine as the *Union*, to the engineer's cab in the rear, its hood festooned with black and white ribbons fastened with white rosettes and on each side below the windows was "placed a fine portrait of the departed statesman in black a frame and surmounted by a large spread eagle in silver," the engine was done up in fine style.[14]

Between these two extremes, a profusion of ornamentation had been affixed to various parts of the engine's superstructure: the front of the boiler was covered with black crepe, fastened on each side with white rosettes and streamers; the headlamp was encircled by a beautiful wreath comprised mainly of red and white roses, accented jasmine and azaleas—all surrounded by green laurel and, like the *Constitution* also, the glass was covered with black cloth; the bell, with a flag mounted on its top, was muffled and its framework was wound with ebony cloth; behind the bell, the steam chest and sand tower were also enveloped in crepe; and ten small American flags on short staffs and bordered in black graced the railings along the boiler.

Impressive as it looked standing in the station, once in motion the engine came alive, as it belched a plume of smoke and hissed clouds of steam. With flags unfurled and streamers flapping in the wind, its heavily-garnished appearance took on an enhanced three-dimensional quality that served to add greater emphasis to a special mission.

With respect to the remainder of the train, officials of the Hudson River Railroad made sure that the trailing cars were also appropriate treated, though to a decidedly more toned-down degree than the locomotive. Behind the engine came the tender, whose sides were draped in black broadcloth and highlighted by eleven silver spread eagles affixed across each side. The next seven units were all neatly but moderately draped with black crepe. The solitary baggage car was the only one featuring flags, fourteen in all in pairs, six down each side and two at its front end. The following six coaches had festoons of cloth draped above and below their windows, all attached at measured intervals by white rosettes. Noteworthy about the ninth or Officers' Car, was that it was "dressed in crepe draperies, edged with silver lace."[15]

The highly decorated funeral train left New York City from the 30th Street Station, the same facility that the president-elect had opened on his inaugural tour (*Lincoln Memorial: A Record of the Life, Assassination and Obsequies*, 1865).

Everyone's attention, however, was eventually drawn to one coach. Coupled eighth or next to the last in line, sat the main attraction—the *United States* ... the hearse car. Even without any of the telltale crepe, the eye-catching eagle motif, painted on each side of the coach beneath the rows of twelve-paneled windows, was an indication that this was indeed the special part of the train. Still the hearse car received an exterior treatment of mourning drapery. The edge of all four sides of the roof line was trimmed with delicate silver fringe. Similar to the other cars, crepe festooning was looped above the windows, attached and accented by silver stars and tassels. Draped between each of the dozen windows were long folds of black cloth, edged with additional silver fringe.

After the crowd at the station had taken in the train, they stood in relative silence, murmuring in low tones to one another while waiting for the cortege. Those who occupied the higher vantage points made visual sightings first, while, with a significant number of bands marching at various intervals in the parade, the reality was that the onlookers packed in at ground level were more likely to hear its impending arrival before actually seeing it. Throughout the vigil, the police—of whom over three-hundred were deployed in the immediate vicinity—performed yeoman service in keeping Twenty-Ninth Street open for the hearse to make its way unimpeded to the station.

Finally, patience was rewarded. At 3:20 p.m., a messenger came galloping down the open roadway, bringing word that the procession was approaching. This announcement galvanized the troops into action. Immediately they went from the status of "standing down" to that of long lines at "attention." Soon the mournful dirges emitted by the 7th Infantry's regimental band gradually became louder and louder, the long ranks of marching soldiers came into view, and slowly, ever so slowly, the black hearse edged nearer and nearer. Due to its bulk and shape, its oversized profile was unmistakable.

To the accompaniment of muffled drums beating a sad tattoo, the president's casket drew closer to the station. The soldiers already posted there snapped to present arms. Officers raised their swords in salute, and flag-bearers dipped the colors. Leading the procession were two more platoons of policemen, followed by the proud ranks of the 7th Regiment protecting the hearse. To help maintain an open pathway to the station, the officers of the law went forward to its entrance and formed lines on both sides of the door. In turn, the infantry troops, marching behind them, filed to left by company and formed a line along the sidewalk in front of the depot. Assuming these positions accomplished two goals: first, the street was cleared so that hearse could be brought close to the station's entrance; and secondly, the spectators were walled off from any possible interference with the process of unloading the casket.

Prior to the arrival of the cortège, several hundred people had managed to gain entrance to the station. They had milled about inside, for the most part trying to get a good look at the coach which was soon to receive the president's remains. However, once the procession's appearance became immanent, the order was given to clear the station and platform of all those not having passes. With that, the size of the crowd was quickly reduced from the two hundred who wanted to be present down to a score who needed to be. The time was three o'clock. At this point, all was now ready for the final act. Somewhat misleading to the spectators, the arrival of the very lead elements of the procession did not mean that the hearse was to be expected at any time soon. The reality was that another forty minutes would still have to elapse before the cortège itself actually arrived.

Once it did, however, events moved quickly. The crowd became silent. All eyes focused on the hearse. Hats were removed. Heads bowed. Using a specially constructed staircase with a top that rested on the side of the hearse and extended to the ground, the pallbearers went up and retrieved the honored remains from the hearse. They brought them through the depot and loaded them up into the *United States*. Those scheduled to continue on with the train were ushered into the waiting coaches. New to this contingent was New York's Governor Reuben Fenton and his staff, who would accompany the remains to Albany. While it had taken almost four hours for the procession to transport the president's casket to the depot, approximately fifteen minutes were all that were required to make the transfer from the street to the tracks.

Noticeable to many, the Thirtieth Street Station was totally devoid of any mourning decorations. This seemed odd, considering that from the moment Lincoln's remains were present in New York no stone had been left unturned to cover the city in mourning drapery. As to why was the depot was left unadorned, the property belonged to the railroad. Perhaps supplying a decorated train was thought to be a sufficient contribution. Possibly, since the station simply was serving as a transfer point of but a few minutes' duration, railroad officials felt that decorating the building was unnecessary. Placing flags at the entrance was deemed sufficient. While no one seemed to take umbrage, this glaring omission clearing stood out in a city that was awash in black.

At this juncture in the proceedings, a touching vignette occurred. Unexpectedly, a solitary figure appeared in front of the depot, just as the casket was being transferred to the waiting railroad car. Recognized immediately by the officers accompanying the remains, Lieutenant General Winfield Scott was warmly welcomed. "The gallant old general was simply attired in citizen's clothes," an observer noted, "wearing a deep crepe band on his hat, and was wrapped in a heavy regulation overcoat."[16] Even though aging and infirm, the old warrior had insisted upon making this farewell gesture to his most-recent commander-in-chief, the last of fourteen presidents under whom General Scott would serve. By coming to witness the his departure, the old officer was paying personal homage to a man whom he knew as a friend and advisee. A participant in the War of 1812 and the Mexican War, the general was still on active duty in 1861. But frail health precluded his actively taking the field against the Confederacy. Largely forgotten by his country as a new generation of generals rose to command positions, he was nevertheless remembered and valued by President Lincoln, who sought the aging war-horse's counsel on several occasions. As a difficult as it was for General Scott to get about, he felt that he owed Lincoln the gestures of respect and thanks that his visit to the station signified. Growing increasingly infirm, he would barely survive Lincoln, passing away in May of 1866.

Then, at 4:15 p.m., conductor James Toucey shouted "All aboard" and signaled the engineer, William Raymond, to open the *Union's* throttle. In rapid succession, the train's whistle blew, its bell rang, and the drive wheels turned. The next leg of the journey was underway. Several people had forgone watching the procession and instead opted to take positions outside of the gate which opened from the depot yard onto the main line. Standing alongside the tracks, they would be part of an immense crowd representing the last mourners in New York City to view the coffin through the windows of the hearse car. As the Lincoln Special proceeded northward on Manhattan Island, those who had been located along the parade route had long since begun dispersing. Within the hour after the procession had passed their chosen location, most city dwellers had returned to their homes, while those from outside the area sought out rail and steamboat terminals to provide transportation to destinations in Brooklyn, the lower Hudson Valley, and New Jersey.

For those mourners not yet ready for closure on tributes to their late leader, a ceremony was scheduled for 5:00 p.m. in Union Square. The program for this meeting was planned as an opportunity to offer "testimonials of respect and reverence for the character of the late President, and joining in appropriate religious exercises."[17] A combination of prayers, dirges, readings, and a speech, the proceedings were held on a specially constructed platform.

With the conclusion of the Union Square ceremony, the curtain was at last drawn on New York City's extensive obsequies for Abraham Lincoln. Mourning rituals dictated that people should continue wearing black armbands until thirty days had elapsed, and the decorations on buildings would be allowed to remain in place until the conclusion of the burial services in Springfield. However, one location that would see a more immediate dismantling of some of its mourning drapery was city hall, where the catafalque was being removed immediately. As for the area behind it—the Governor's Room—this space was "visited yesterday by hundreds who were unable to obtain permission previously."[18] Unfortunately, some of the curiosity-seekers wanted to not only look, but also to leave with memento; this proclivity manifested itself by their cutting of tassels and fringe that had hung from the canopy set up over the catafalque. These acts of well-intended vandalism necessitated posting a policeman in the room, charged to keep people moving through the area.

But for all practical purposes, the residents of the city had begun the transition back to their customary living patterns. While several weeks would pass before all financial and business enterprises were functioning on an even keel, stores and offices in both New York and Brooklyn reopened on Wednesday, April 27. Night life resumed in theaters and restaurants. Still to be seen about the streets were many of the out-of-towners, folks who had come into the city for the funeral proceedings and decided to stay on a few extra days to take in the sights of the metropolis. During this same interregnum, a proud Police Superintendent John Kennedy took the opportunity to praise his men for their yeoman service over past few days. He told them that "the best of order has been preserved, while but a few arrests were necessary, as well as from the good nature and right spirit of the people, as from the firm, yet conciliatory and gentle deportment of the members of the force."[19]

As New York City slowly regained its normal footing in the wake of the disruption that hosting the obsequies caused, the Lincoln Special slowly threaded its way northward along the Hudson Valley. But whether the locale was large or small, its mourners were deemed equally deserving of the chance to say goodbye. Would that a stop could have been made at every town; however, the reality was that such a consideration would have stretched an already prolonged journey to a point beyond the emotional endurance of everyone accompanying the remains, not to mention asking the immediate family of the late president endure a longer wait for its own closure.

16

Heading North
A Mournful Passage Up the Hudson Valley

The Hudson River Valley represented "old New York," for many communities dated back over 150 years through the Revolution to the original Dutch settlements. While not having any heavily populated towns like New York City and Albany, the eastern side of the Hudson Valley was nevertheless dotted with a string of small villages which kept the train from making any consistent headway. Even twenty miles per hour seemed at times like breakneck speed after the frequent reductions when passing through so many closely packed communities. Speed up, slow down, speed up ... progress often seemed measurable in feet rather than miles. But, then, no one was in any particular hurry to get to Springfield and part company with their beloved friend.

From the windows of the train, the scenes along the way to Albany would be similar. Gatherings of sad-faced people were observed standing along both sides of the tracks, and the larger the town, the bigger was the turnout. In the rural areas, solitary figures, frequently families, and sometimes groups of neighbors—all watched solemnly during the fleeting moments when the Lincoln Special passed their homesteads. "Groups of spectators were everywhere in the bright sunlight," observed one passenger on the train, "[with] boatmen on the stream [i.e., the Hudson River] lifting their hats, and here and there, several persons only are on the summit of a bluff or rock, with heads uncovered."[1] For those few seconds, all of these humble folks were participants in the long farewell to their fallen leader.

Once underway, the express did not travel far before the first of the local tributes began to manifest themselves. Only ten minutes out of the Thirtieth Street Station, the train passed a large crowd that had congregated at the Fort Washington station, where people of all ages were dressed in mourning clothes and holding aloft banners, as they stood in silent homage. At the Deaf and Dumb Asylum just outside of the city, its patients were assembled on the institution's grounds, which fronted the railroad, and stood there clad in appropriate mourning clothing. Manhattanville was next, where an estimated four thousand bereaved citizens had gathered at their depot to watch the express roll past. Fifteen miles north of the city lay the College of Mount Saint Vincent, noted for the school for women that was founded by the Sisters of Charity and became a liberal arts college in 1847. A crowd had gathered at the station there, so large that it clogged the roads leading down to the railroad. Distinctive among its decorations was a large black flag bearing white letters that shared the peoples' grief with the motto: "We mourn our Nation's loss."[2]

16. Heading North

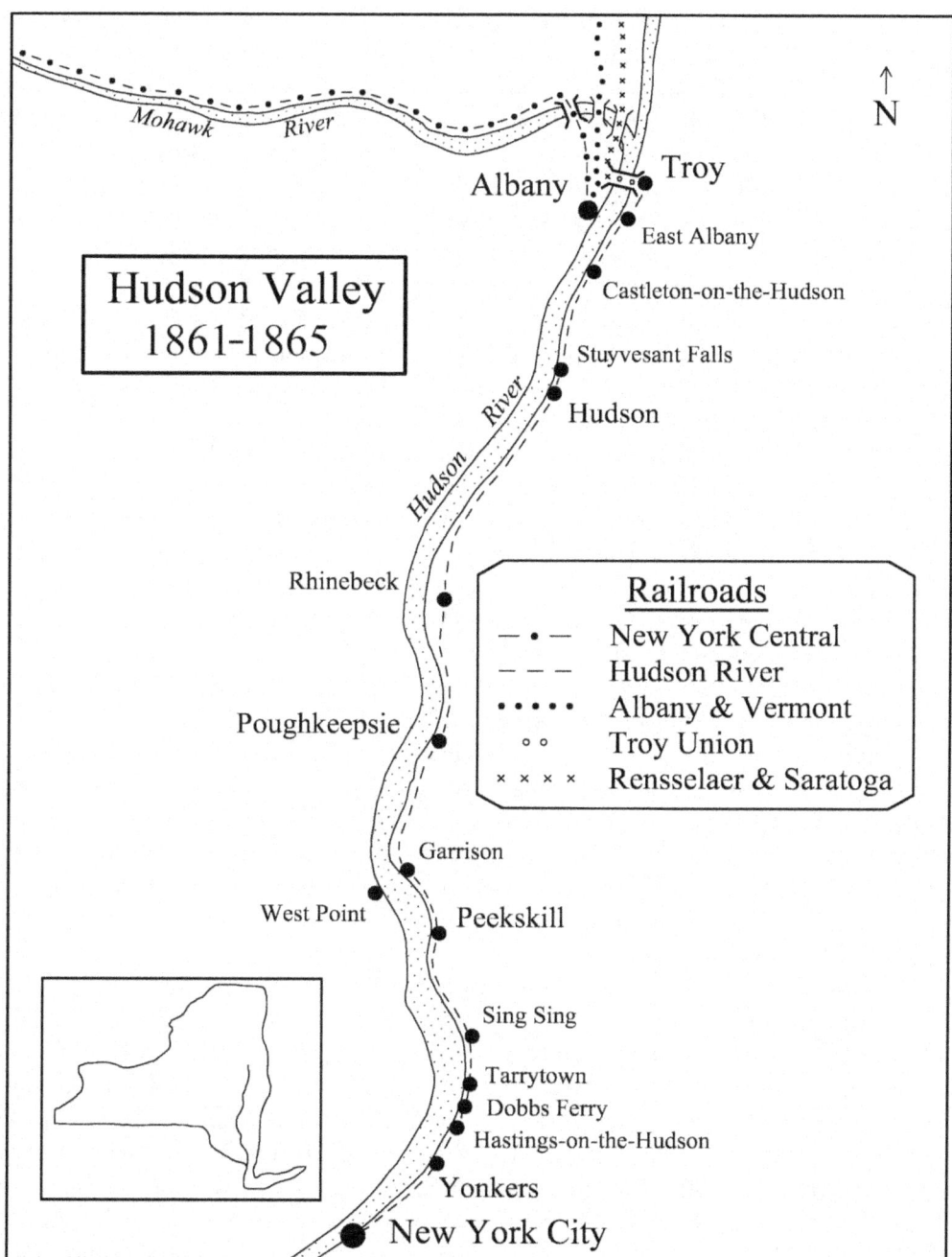

Drawn by Bob Collea.

    This particular aphorism seemed to strike an appropriate chord, as it would appear again among the tributes in other locations. At all of the stations, one unusual feature of the passing train which mourners noticed immediately was that "the usual hoarse clangor of the engine bell was deadened by the tongue being muffled, and as the train moved off it gave an indescribable air of mournfulness and woe to the scene."[3]

The next community on the itinerary was Yonkers, eighteen miles north of New York City and the first enclave encountered off Manhattan Island. During the war, the community had been a solid contributor to the Union cause. Townsmen not only worked in the Starr Arms Company's plant, where they made carbines and muskets, but also contributed almost four hundred recruits for military service. But on Tuesday, April 26, 1865, Yonkers had a different duty to perform. Having served President Lincoln faithfully for years, its citizens' final gesture of gratitude was to pay their respects, as his rolling wake passed through their town. A printed notice circulated that morning, one which encouraged people to congregate at the depot in time for the anticipated 4:55 arrival of the train.

At the appointed hour, not only had a crowd assembled, but all was also in place from a decorative standpoint. Flags were flying at half-staff. Homes and businesses were adorned with a profusion of appropriate mourning drapery, and, as the local paper observed, "a general feeling of solemnity prevailed among our citizens."[4]

Standing out as particularly eye-catching among the various tributes was a large mourning arch constructed near the depot and off to the side of the tracks. The two pillars of the arch were wrapped in black cloth and each topped off by a white urn containing laurel. Over the arch was a large stuffed eagle, its beak holding laurel, while underneath the curve was first hung a black-bordered flag and then below that a portrait of the late president also trimmed with black cloth. Finally, on the face of the arc were printed the words: "Yonkers Mourns With the Nation."[5]

In sentiment, similar to modern-day bouquets placed beside a casket with small banners stating "Dearest Friend" of "Beloved Father," but, in appearance, much more aligned with Victorian tendencies, the effect of which made the display public and grandiose.

About an hour before the anticipated arrival of the train, mourners started drifting toward the station. On a normal weekday, twenty regularly scheduled passenger trains and six mail runs passed through Yonkers, half going to Albany and the others bound for New York City ... and this accounting does not include the numerous loads of freight also plying the same routes. Rail travel in 1865 was very much a part of the fabric of everyday life, making the depot a very busy place.

But on this particular afternoon, the area around the station was going to brim with activity at a never before seen level, for an estimated 3000 people assumed positions along both sides of the track north and south of the station. Like other communities along the railroad, Yonkers' location was one that featured the tracks on level ground near the river, and the town east and upslope from the main line. In effect, the embankment created a natural viewing amphitheater facing the river and the depot. Here many people, electing for a more panoramic view of the impending proceedings, staked out spots on the grassy slope. Others congregated in the windows and on rooftops of houses built upon the terraced hillside of the village.

If one gauged the prevailing mood only by the weather on this comfortably warm, sun-drenched spring day, his assessment would have sadly erred. But the hushed demeanor of the people, the rhythmic tolling of church bells, the doleful strains of dirges, and the measured boom of minute guns gave ample evidence that solemn business was afoot. At 4:45, the pilot engine heralded the coming of the Lincoln Special. Then ten minutes later, the funeral train crawled into town, ever so slowly passed by the crowded depot, and remained visible until lost behind a curve north of the village. In but a few minutes' time, the *Union* had delivered and taken away the sacred remains. Any individuals standing along the tracks had less than sixty seconds to take in the eleven units moving south-to-north directly in front of them, with the hearse car being present at any one point for but about five of those ticks of the clock.

These few moments were all people had to bring closure to a presidency which they had seen about to begin in 1861 on his inaugural tour and then followed closely over the next four years. Now, as the local paper summed up the substance of their present experience: "Thus came and passed through Yonkers the body of Abraham Lincoln."[6]

As the people of Yonkers were making their way home, six miles farther north, the residents of Hastings-on-the-Hudson were preparing for their turn to receive the train. In a vein similar to that just expressed in Yonkers, another memorial archway was erected here too. Located over the roadway leading to the depot, this spectacular tribute consisted of not one but rather three portals, held aloft by four columns. With its pillars encircled appropriately with funereal drapery, the crowning touch was a large black-and-white shield with a gold star at its center placed above the middle arch. Hanging beneath was a wreath of laurel that encompassed a large letter L. As a final touch, large American flags were included in strategic spots to further enhance the overall appearance. Inscribed on the sweep of the arch were the words: "We will cherish the memory of Abraham Lincoln, by supporting the principles of Free Government for which he suffered martyrdom."[7] What made this unique structure all the more impressive was that its creation was funded by voluntary subscription. Apparently, a list was passed around town and those who wished to could sign their names and the amount which they were willing to contribute.

While the engineers piloting the Lincoln Special across the Empire State sometimes slowed the train from its speed of twenty miles per hour down as low as five when passing through small towns, a courtesy reduction for Hastings-on-the-Hudson was insured by a direct request to the war department from one of its leading citizens, Admiral David Farragut. That the old sailor was able to do this is borne out of his dual relationships with the deceased president. Not only was he Lincoln's most trusted naval advisor, but the admiral had also become a friend. As Author Gregory Smith pointed out in his article "Farragut and the Lincoln Funeral Train," the president held this officer in high esteem, noting that "Farragut and his wife had even been invited guests of Lincoln at his second inauguration in March of 1865."[8]

While none of the newsmen present that day reported such, the train is alleged to have stopped at Hastings for a brief interlude. Admiral Farragut certainly possessed sufficient clout to make it happen. According to James Hogan, who was among the elementary school children lined up along the tracks, Admiral Farragut stepped off the train during this interlude and "shook hands with Mr. Hogan and said a few remarks."[9] Nevertheless, like Yonkers before it and the many little villages yet to come, the passage still seemed altogether too brief.

Then, over the course of the next seven miles, three small communities would be passed in rapid succession: Dobbs Ferry, Irvington, and Tarrytown. In the first two places, people had gathered at their respective railroad stations and stood silently as the train rolled past. To those on board, mourning emblems were noted on buildings in the vicinity. At Dobbs Ferry, "the station house was almost buried in mourning drapery."[10] A display of eight large American flags, with the appropriate black crepe borders attached, completed the homage. As for Irvington, considerable funds were expended to erect another version of a memorial arch, a form of respect which seemed to have been favored in the lower Hudson Valley. Irvington's curving decoration was noted as being located on the east side of the tracks, highly festooned, and emblazoned with the motto "He still lives."[11]

At Tarrytown, several extra touches were offered: one consisted of a building with the entire side fronting the tracks completely covered by an American flag that was embellished with a trim of black and adorned with inspirational mottoes; another was an arch of red, white, and blue bunting that was erected over the tracks; and the last one featured a number of young ladies clad in white dresses and wearing sashes of black broadcloth, standing motionlessly with their hands clasped.

Among the impressionable spectators in the gathering twilight that day was Mary J. Madden. A girl of eight at the time, she remembered, in her interview for the local paper given sixty-nine years later, standing on the vantage point of a mound of dirt for a better view than her youthful legs afforded as the train passed through Tarrytown. Being at the station held another war-related memory for Mary, when four years before—in what she referenced as the "thrill of her life"—the young child had "linked arms with my brothers and marched down the street with them to the train where they embarked for the Civil War."[12] For this woman of now seventy-five years, the town depot, two trains, and the Civil War would forever be intertwined in her childhood memories, one a pleasant experience and the other somber. But she would by no means be alone in carrying the sight of the Lincoln Special imbedded in her mind throughout her life.

A bit farther up the tracks—thirty-seven miles north of New York City—lay the town known as Sing Sing, now Ossining. The 1861 inaugural express had stopped there very briefly. But this time, folks had to be content bearing witness to a rolling wake. The train would slow down, but was not scheduled to stop. Provided with sufficient foreknowledge of the date and time when the train would be passing through Sing Sing, a committee was formed to develop an appropriate observance for the town.

As its plan materialized in the late afternoon of April 26, a major part involved a procession, organized by Grand Marshall William Benjamin. Starting at Talcott Hall, the march went southeast through the city to the railroad station on the flatlands by the river. Preparatory to its start, all stores were closed. Among those participating in the parade were cadets from the nearby Mt. Pleasant Military Academy, several fire companies, a band, local dignitaries, various civic and fraternal organizations, and citizens. As historian Norm MacDonald described the proceedings, the whole spectacle "constituted a grand military and civil procession, such as seldom seen in a country town."[13]

Upon reaching the depot, the crowd dispersed evenly along the tracks, the intent being to allow everyone a reasonable opportunity to view the train. The cadets in their splendid gray uniforms stood in a sharp line, and several women dressed in white and black were also present. According to Mr. MacDonald, the crowd tallied somewhere between 5,000 and 10,000 onlookers, making this assemblage by far one surpassing any previous gathering in the community.[14] As was often the case with the train's passage, local numbers were bumped up by the influx of people who had come in from the surrounding countryside, as well as neighboring villages not situated along the main line. Also favorably comparable to locations large and small was the collective demeanor of the crowd, which displayed a solemn and respectful behavior that befit the somber occasion.

With the march commencing at five o'clock, the short walk to trackside viewing spots was completed by the time the pilot engine arrived twenty minutes later. To the sound of pealing bells and the thunder of minute guns, the Lincoln Special appeared and passed before the residents of Sing Sing. What had seemed like an interminable wait had suddenly morphed into a precious few seconds in which to bid farewell. Then the unexpected happened. Though no stop was planned, much to everyone's surprise the train halted. The cause of this temporary deviation from the tightly-constructed schedule was described in the *Poughkeepsie Daily Express* as being "a stupendous arch."[15]

The object that generated the reporter's awe had been erected just north of the station, spanning both sets of tracks on the right-of-way. What travelers saw was the second feature of Sing Sing's tribute to the late president. Built at a cost of several hundred dollars from public donations was a gigantic archway slightly over forty feet high and thirty feet wide. Much in the manner that Lincoln's top hat had added height to his appearance, the center of the arch was crowned with an urn—resting upon the initials "AL"—that added seven and a half feet to the verticality of the whole display.

The memorial arch at Sing Sing, an outstanding tribute marveled at by the bereaved on board, was funded by public subscription (courtesy Ossining Historical Society).

Silver stars, decorative cloth, and four flags near the two bases of the twin pillars on each side were all woven together to create an impressive tribute. One additional feature that jumped out immediately when viewing the arch was the huge motto that filled its lower half. One side read "We Mourn Our Nation's Loss," while the other was inscribed "With Charity for All."[16] Scrolled across the two support bases were the words: "We will cherish the memory of Abraham Lincoln by supporting the principles of free government, for which he suffered martyrdom."[17] *Harper's Weekly* tipped its journalistic hat to this heartfelt tribute, recognizing that "a magnificent memorial was erected by the citizens over the Hudson River Railroad."[18]

As it turned out, the reason for the sudden, unplanned stoppage was not a mechanical failure, but rather the archway. So impressive was its appearance that the train was momentarily halted so that those on board could get a better look. In that brief time, one of the embedded reporters left his coach and dashed off, seeking to find someone who could give him the structure's dimensions. Though he was unsuccessful in his quest, those on board were appreciative of the opportunity to take in the magnificent tribute, a display that many judged to be "finer than that at any other station along the route."[19]

Moving on from its brief hiatus at Sing Sing, the train headed for Peekskill. Though forty-one miles north of its starting point, over an hour-and-a-half had elapsed in progressing only one-quarter of the way to Albany.

Peekskill was one of several communities across the state which had fond memories of the then president-elect's visit on his way to Washington, for it had the special distinction of being his only stop in Westchester County. On this current occasion, too, Peekskill would be the beneficiary of a layover by the presidential express, primarily due to its need to take on supplies of fuel and water.

Making the most of this ten-minute opportunity, a select committee put together a simple program to serve as its community's tribute to the late president. Similar to that offered by Ossining, Peekskill's homage also consisted of a march through town to the railroad station. With places of business largely closed, a procession led by the president the village and its board of trustees started off at five o'clock. Wheeling into line behind them were members of the fire department, the Highland Grays from the Peekskill Academy, a band, and a large coterie of mourners. As centerpiece of the ceremony, "a large portrait of the President, encircled with roses and red, white, and blue tassels, was prominently displayed."[20]

Leaving behind another heartfelt display of black-bordered flags at half-staff, funereal drapery, and appropriate mottoes, the Lincoln Special departed the Peekskill Station at 5:59 p.m., leaving subdued mourners standing in its wake until the last car passed from view. A few miles up ahead, directly in the pathway of the train, lay Garrison and Cold Spring, while in between on the opposite shore was West Point. All three, while small in size, were part of what one reporter called a "historic neighborhood."[21]

Already steeped in events tied to the American Revolution, these places had made important contributions to the recent war effort and, for such, were known to President Lincoln: West Point for training military leaders; Cold Spring for producing armaments; and Garrison for supplying cross-channel transportation. However, on this particular evening, normal pursuits were set aside, as people congregated at this trio of sites. Separated by several miles and the river in the case of the military academy, they were nevertheless bonded by the common interest in bidding farewell to their nation's fallen leader.

First up was Garrison, with its little station adorned with flags that have been festooned with crepe. The Eastman College Band, which had boarded the train in New York City after participating in the obsequies there, played an appropriate dirge. Their musical tribute was complimented by the cadet band which performed a funeral march at the head of the train. Swelling the numbers of the local populace congregated about the premises was a company of West Point's cadets, lined up ramrod-straight in their gray uniforms, and the officers who accompanied them, standing off to the side with their hats removed. Simultaneously, from across the river rising from the academy's grounds, the repeated roll of half-minute gun salutes being fired was clearly audible In a simple, dignified manner, the military thus said goodbye to its former commander-in-chief.

At this time, as noted by an on-board member of the press, the whole scene was bathed with the mellow light of a setting sun that was dropping behind the Hudson Highlands to the west. This was soon followed by a "glorious sunset—appropriate and suggestive in view of the event which calls us to its exhibition."[22] All the efforts of mankind to provide homage came in second to the quiet beauty of nature, one which ended the day in a colorful, uplifting display that constituted a different kind of salute to the president's memory. Unlike the stark blacks and whites that clothed the land below, a panorama of red, yellow, gold, and orange painted the heavens above the blue-tinted Catskills—offering hope, as Lincoln had, that tomorrow would be a better day.

Cold Spring was ready to receive the train, when it arrived at 6:40 amidst the gathering twilight. Off to the side of the tracks near the station, residents had raised their memorial arch. The twist offered in this instance was the presence of a pedestal centered under the structure. On this limited platform were three individuals: a young lady clad in black crepe portraying "Liberty"; and two boys, one dressed as a soldier and the other a sailor. The girl knelt, in a posture of sorrow, while holding in one hand a national banner which was covered by a transparent veil of black, while her other rested a floral anchor. In addition to the people forming a circle around the arch, a large contingent of area residents covered the station's grounds and spread out along the tracks.

From Cold Spring, the express had twenty-one miles to cover before reaching the important, mid-trip destination of Poughkeepsie. Along the way, citizens were observed at Fishkill Station, New Hamburg, and Milton Ferry Station, where they had a chance to pay their respects when the train rolled past. From their seats in the coaches, each of these locales appeared in similar succession to the passengers—knots of bereaved people clustered around a depot draped in the trappings of mourning.

For the travelers aboard the train, their arrival Poughkeepsie loomed as a welcomed respite from the four hours of confining travel which they had just experienced. Here they were afforded the opportunity for a thirty-minute respite. Since most had not eaten since the procession had begun in New York City, most were famished by the time the *Union* ground to a halt. Lying eighty miles north of New York City, the halfway point in the journey to Albany had not been reached until 8:30 p.m. Waiting for those on-board was dinner in a trackside restaurant, thoughtfully furnished by members of the community. Following this generous repast, a few minutes remained for the riders to stretch their legs before climbing aboard to resume the trek to Albany.

The same generous layover that was appreciated by the entourage aboard the funeral train proved an equal blessing to mourners who wished to pay their last respects to their late president. Whereas most places had to be satisfied with a view of a moving train and a fortunate few communities garnered a brief halt, Poughkeepsians had the windfall of a half-hour. People had begun heading down toward the river as early as four o'clock that afternoon. Along the way, some would have passed Cannon's Gallery of Arts, a Main Street studio offering "the best and latest photograph taken of President Lincoln taken before the assassination."[23]

As the developing scene at the station was depicted in the *Poughkeepsie Daily Press*, "an immense crowd gathered and lined the tracks at every point where the funeral train was visible."[24] As had been the case in 1861, townspeople had the additional choice of locating themselves east of the tracks on the banks that swept down from the upper reaches of the village on the highlands above the river. Just as in Peekskill, a natural amphitheater existed on the hillside. Those who would rather have a panoramic view of the entire scene as the train came in, halted, and eventually moved on opted for a spot on this slope. Others, who desired instead to stand in close proximity to the hearse car, in turn positioned themselves trackside. Conspicuous among the mourners could be seen a large contingent comprised of the student body and faculty from the Eastman National Business College.

With onlookers estimated at six thousand to eight thousand in number, contingents of the provost guard and the 21st Infantry Regiment were at the ready to provide any crowd control required, both with a view toward keeping the tracks clear and the crowd away from the hearse car. However, these preventative measures proved unnecessary as the mourners assumed a posture akin to "death-like stillness" with the approach of the train.[25]

As soon as the incoming express was sighted, all the bells in town began tolling, accompanied by the thud of nearby minute guns. Soon the muffled sound of the engine's cloth-shrouded bell clapper was audible. Once the train had come to a halt and its passengers went to eat, a protective cordon of guards was established around the hearse car, allowing only a limited number of ladies to enter the *United States* and lay wreaths and flowers on the coffin. One of the floral tributes was particularly distinctive, taking the shape of a large white cross and reportedly catching the approving eye of many mourners. In fact, the display held its freshness all the way to Albany; there the Poughkeepsie tribute was placed near the casket, when it was opened for viewing in the state capitol building early the next morning. One who saw it there felt moved to pen a heartfelt message to the editor of the *Poughkeepsie Eagle*, one in which he wrote: "They will soon fade and die, but ever will there remain in the memories of the ladies who so kindly placed them there, a dear, unfading thought of him whom the nation so loved and honored."[26]

Along with the meal and the floral tributes, several other memorable occurrences during the layover are worthy of note. First, Poughkeepsie's own, the Eastman College Band, offered a dirge. Having lent its praiseworthy talents to the obsequies in New York City, this first-rate corps was invited to accompany Lincoln's remains all the way to Springfield, performing at various places along the way as the opportunity presented itself. Unlike modern college bands comprised of students, this ensemble drew its "twenty-six first-class performers" from the ranks "of gentlemen of means attached to the college, five of whom formerly have been leaders of bands."[27]

By contrast, where the music was an audio homage, a contrasting visual tribute was offered by a seven-year-old girl, held aloft by her mother, wearing a costume so as to appear as the "Genius of Liberty." Adorned in a flowing white garment, a black sash, and a cap, she held "in her hands a small American flag, and on the top of the staff a beautiful wreath composed of shells, she attracted much attention from the funeral suite."[28] Unfortunately, for all the positive aspects of Poughkeepsie's tribute, one local paper observed that "our own station through some oversight was not draped as it should have been," save that done by the proprietors of the railroad restaurant.[29]

Once the train was underway, the crowd slowly dispersed. One individual who had been among the spectators was Matthew Vassar, founder of the college that bore his name. On his way to meet the train, he had clipped several magnolias from a tree in front of his Poughkeepsie home and brought them to be placed on the president's coffin. Like Ossining which has the bell from the *Constitution*, the locomotive which pulled the inaugural train south from Poughkeepsie in 1861 and then served as the pilot engine for the funeral train in 1865, Poughkeepsie still has Vassar's cherished magnolia, a witness tree that indirectly participated in the town's mourning of Lincoln.

After the lengthy Poughkeepsie stop, the Lincoln Special was within three hours of its destination for the day. Little towns began to once again flow past the windows of the coaches in rapid succession. Up came Rhinebeck, where the prevalence of torches in the hands of men along the tracks was seen for the first time. Now that darkness had descended over the land, some of the tributes became more difficult to discern, though a black-bordered flag with the motto "We mourn our nation's loss" was visible. At Tivoli, Germantown, and Catskill Landing, the lateness of the hour did not deter crowds from gathering at their respective stations. The train coming out of the darkness added a surrealistic quality to their evening vigil, one that two weeks ago none of the mourners would have anticipated needing to keep.

Continuing into the night, the village of Hudson was gained at 9:45. With many people gathered at the station in the lower end of town, many portions of the village—which included homes and businesses—were empty. This situation left open a golden opportunity for thieves, who were known to be making the rounds and indiscriminately stealing mourning decorations. With righteous indignation, the *Poughkeepsie Daily Eagle* inveighed that "such wretches disgrace the earth."[30] Around the same time, West Troy was also experiencing similar depredations, prompting the *Albany Morning Express* to vent its anger too, unequivocally stating that "a man who would pilfer this drapery would despoil his mother' tomb."[31] Sad to say, no occasion seemed off-limits to those who made their living at the expense of others; in these instances, compounding the mourners' already somber state with the added misery and frustration that follows when personal property is stolen.

Then, with the train traveling at times precariously close to the river's edge, passages through Stockport, Styvesant, Schodack, and Castleton followed over the next forty-five minutes. At each station, the local tableau visible to the mourners on the train mirrored the one at the next—large crowds, somber, tear-stained faces, decorated buildings, and glowing torches. On bluffs along the river, bonfires were observed, lit in tribute by those who chose to watch the passage of the train from a distance. In a half-hour, the day's rail-borne odyssey would end when the Lincoln Special pulled into the depot at East Greenbush a half-hour north of Castleton. They would next experience a seventeen-hour layover in Albany, complete with a public viewing and two stirring processions. Their vigil would continue with a grueling trip to Buffalo, one that would require withstanding more than double the time and distance which the passengers just endured.

17

Second Arrival in Albany
The State Capital Offers Its Last Respects

For those few passengers aboard the funeral train who had made the 1861 trip, the view outside the window from New York City to Albany was radically different from that of four years ago, when winter was drawing to a close. But the Hudson Valley is one of those special settings that offer beautiful panoramas any time of the year. It was not by accident that Thomas Cole and other artists chose its vistas as subjects for their landscape paintings, forming the basis of a genre that became known as the Hudson River School of Art in mid-nineteenth century America. Weighed down by personal despair, the current travelers could be excused for missing the world outside of their coaches. But late April in New York was a special time. A vibrant mantle of green was returning to the land. Spring flowers bloomed. Trees began to bud.

In this season for uplifting spirits so long shut in by winter, the presence of a slow-moving, black-draped funeral train seemed incongruous. However, as much as the two images generated incompatible feelings, the arrival of spring was important to those on board the funeral train because of its implications in determining the route which they would take to arrive in Albany. Specifically germane to the task at hand, the snow and ice had melted back into their liquid state. Since the Hudson River was once again open to cross-channel navigation, the ferry connection between East Albany and Albany was operational. What the restitution of this service meant to the bereaved passengers was that the president's casket could be transferred to lie in state more quickly than would otherwise have been the case. Now, in death, Lincoln got the boat ride that he was denied in life, though the funeral train itself still had to make the land link by way of the same serpentine route used by the inaugural train. This was necessitated to get the two through-coaches—the hearse car and the Officers' Car—transferred from the Hudson River Railroad's tracks to those of the New York Central, where the new carrier would supply the engine, tender, and cars for the rest of the funeral train's trip.

While the ocean–going, interstate ferries connecting New Jersey with New York could accommodate railroad cars, this same capability was not true for the smaller Hudson River carriers. The distance across the Hudson from the ferry landing in East Albany to its counterpart in Albany was approximately a quarter-mile. The waterway has a slight current at this location, a bit more so in the spring when the winter's runoff adds to its volume. However, ferry operators used side-wheeled steamboats, vessels possessing more than sufficient power to overcome any currents when making their round-trip crossings several times a day.

17. Second Arrival in Albany

As the time for the train's arrival approached—10:55 p.m., on Tuesday, April 25, 1865—a crowd began assembling at the dock in lower Albany. Standing in silence, "eyes strained to see, and the ear was acute to hear," reported a witness, "all that could indicate the coming of the funeral train, as it was, by the measure of the time, nearly due at [East] Albany."[1] However, a train traveling on the opposite shore rarely revealed its presence visually during the day, much less in the dark of a moonless night, for a combination of the curving river, impediment of shade trees, and presence of channel islands blocked its progress from view.

Then, just before eleven o'clock, the suspense was broken when the sound of a train was heard emanating from the inky blackness to the east. All doubt was removed by "the whistle of the locomotive, as it announced the approach of all that was mortal of the martyred dead."[2] Further confirmation was added by the sound of artillery. By order of Albany Mayor Eli Perry, a minute gun was to commence a measured fire from the moment of the train's arrival until Lincoln's casket was placed in the Capitol. Commanded by Captain Harris Parr, the battery maintained a steady cadence, the cannons' fire adding to the surrealistic aura of a night like no other before in the city's history with a deep boom emanating every sixty seconds from an unseen iron throat.

Also hidden from sight to those on the capital city's side of the river were the people gathered around the black-draped East Albany Station. "The whole vicinity of the train was crowded with residents of the villages upon the opposite side," an observer recalled, "anxious to see the mournful line and to get a view of the coffin which enclosed the remains of the lamented chief."[3]

That brief look was about all folks who had turned out at such a late hour saw: a transfer of the casket from the railroad car to an intermediary hearse pulled by four gray horses and then to the waiting ferry. In keeping with the solemnity of the moment, the spectators maintained the proper order and decorum throughout the unloading and loading process.

In addition to the locals who were present, a delegation had previously traveled from Albany to provide a ceremonial escort for the remains across the river. Constituting this honor guard were members of the city's common council, the leaders of both houses of the state legislature, and its fire department. A ferry, commanded Captain Seth Green and aptly christened the *New York*, had transported them over and was now moored at the dock, waiting for the return trip. The number of officials going back on the ferry would be somewhat higher, for the new arrivals were joined by a second party of state representatives already on the train. Governor Morgan, state solons, and common councilmen had previously gone to New York City in order to accompany the body north.

For those who did catch sight of the finely-crafted wooden box encapsulating the president, what they saw was a lot closer to the splendor of an Egyptian ruler's sarcophagus than the enclosure in which most of them would someday spend eternity. In the words of one who saw the casket, "its splendor and magnificence could not well be surpassed."[4] From its stunning appearance, all evidence indicated that the hands of a craftsman had fashioned a coffin worthy of the great man who occupied it. Appropriately, the design and manufacture of this important piece of woodworking was carried in out Washington, at an establishment on 7th Street only a few blocks from the White House, by a team identified as "Messers. R.F. and G.W. Harvey, undertakers."[5]

Even though only its exterior was visible, a sense of the quality materials used was clearly evident. The wood was mahogany, covered with a rich black cloth and a multiplicity

The casket which would bear the president's remains home to Springfield was a tasteful but ornate example of the cabinetmaker's skills, a work of art very much in keeping with Victorian expectations (*Harper's Weekly*).

of silver adornments in the form of tacks, stars, fringe, tassels, and braid arranged to stylishly accent and offset the black. For example, all along the lid was a row of silver tacks, extending the whole length a few inches from the edge. The handles for the pallbearers were of silver also, set inside large silver medallions. Encircled by the outline of a silver shield and centered on the top surface was a plate of the same color inscribed: "Abraham Lincoln, Sixteenth President of the United States, Born February 12, 1809, Died April 15, 1865."[6] In the eyes of one beholder, the overall impression created was that of a coffin which was "really beautiful and finished with exceedingly good taste and fine workmanship."[7] In a sense, the casket in its ornamentation represented a microcosm of what was considered the high end of acceptable and pleasing Victorian funereal artistry. Evidence that expense was not a consideration was the estimate that the Harvey's bill was for a coffin "costing above $1000."[8]

Guided by blazing torches, the hearse was loaded onto the boat, and the short trip across the channel commenced. All was shrouded in respectful silence among those on board, with the only exceptions to the stillness being the pulsating sound of the steam engine below deck and the constant swishing of the paddlewheels churning through the Hudson's dark waters. In the distance, the minute guns and church bells could heard, their sounds becoming louder as the opposite shore grew closer. During the brief voyage, passengers had time for personal reflection. The scene left the impression on a member of the party as being one in which "civilians and chieftains, legislators and people, governors and governed, alike stood in mute awe around his cold remains. Sacred moments!"[9] From the Albany shore, the ferry's transit was seen as "a bright fragment on the river, amidst the gloom of night, deepening as the Hudson's course is northward to the dense shadows of the mountains, and as it hid in the foliage of the group of islands that act as sentries to the upper river."[10]

17. *Second Arrival in Albany* 205

The president's remains were ferried across the Hudson from East Albany to Albany from this site, while the train continued north to cross at the Troy bridge to deliver the two "through cars." From John Warner Barber, *Historical Collections of the State of New York* **(New York: S. Tuttle, Publisher, 1841).**

For those onlookers steeped in classical literature, the eerie sight of the torch-lit boat slowly gliding toward the near shore may have recalled a story from mythology. To the ancients, the dead were taken to the Underworld by a ferryman named Charon, borne across the rivers Styx and Acheron in his boat. On these voyages, the way through the darkened waters was lighted by a burning torch. This passage to the land beneath the earth gave rise to the common practice—still in vogue in Victorian America—of putting a coin in the mouth or over the eyes of the deceased. These tokens were intended to serve as payment for Charon's services. The alternative for not compensating the boatman—the first undertaker—was for the body to be left behind, doomed to wander the earth for eternity as a ghost.

In a similar phantasmagorical vein, but in a more updated twist in keeping with the beliefs of some at the time, the coins served to keep the eyelids closed, "because a corpse whose were not closed was thought to be a threat to its living relatives."[11] Upon his death in the Petersen House across from Ford's Theater, coins were placed over Lincoln's eyes; however, on the several occasions when public viewing of the corpse was in progress, the currency was removed, as they presented a rather startling appearance.

Once the *New York* had docked and the casket removed, the second and last of the coffin's waterborne transports was over. At the ferry landing, along the adjacent wharf, and onto the nearby streets, a sizable crowd had gathered. Mirroring the one that had greeted the train in East Albany in its subdued demeanor, it differed only in that its numbers were significantly greater. As would later prove to be the case on the journey from Albany to Buffalo, the lateness of the hour did nothing to deter the turnout. These people, like their neighbors across the river, also hoped to see the casket. Unlike the situation in 1861, a significant police presence was on hand to control the spectators, but on this somber occasion, no physical restraint was necessary.

Considering that there had been no rehearsal, the procession formed up quickly for the march to the state house, moving out at a little past midnight. In the lead was a contingent of policemen, followed by a drum corps, Schreiber's Cornet Band, and finally the Eastman College Band. Next were Companies A and F from the 10th Infantry Regiment of Albany and Troy's Company C of the 25th, marching with their rifles held in the reverse position. Behind them was the hearse, drawn by six white horses and flanked on either side by a Guard of Honor. Several carriages carrying the pallbearers, the governor, committee members, and councilmen brought up the rear. Along the column's outer edges marched one hundred firemen, holding torches aloft to light the way. Starting at the dock, the sad, slow-moving procession went up Ferry Street and turned right onto Broadway.

Even at such a late hour, many of the stores and public buildings along this thoroughfare were illuminated. This lighting, in addition to aiding the marchers, also allowed passersby to view the various window treatments created in tribute to the deceased president. One establishment identified as being among the most beautifully adorned was that of Singer Sewing Machines. In one of its two front windows "was a genuine white marble monument representing a cross, about four feet high. On it was a portrait of Abraham Lincoln, surrounded with a wreath of white flowers. Immediately over it was a placard, 'Let us resolve that the martyred dead shall not have died in vain.' On the base of the cross were the words, 'Be still and know that I am God.'"[12] Filling the adjacent glass panel was the representation of the Angel of Mercy, positioned as if to be looking at the cross with sorrowful eyes.

To onlookers, the sight was stirring and well-worth the wait. One observer was moved to comment that "no arena could be more impressive or solemn than the torchlight route of the dead President through the crowded streets."[13] For anyone present four years ago, this was the point where their memories of 1861 surely returned. Back then, on a cold February day, president-elect Lincoln stood tall in a barouche, bowing to the right and then to the left in acknowledgment of the cheers and applause showered on him by the excited crowds. A challenging destiny then awaited him in Washington, one which the people fervently hoped that he would capably fulfill and wished him Godspeed in so doing. He had not let them down.

In a well-worded assessment of the rise of Lincoln's stature between 1861 and 1865, a local journalist captured the prevailing sentiments of his fellow Albanians when he penned the following: "Then he was untried; now he has passed the severest test, and has not been found wanting. Then, he was honored here by comparatively few; now he is most sincerely and deeply mourned by all the vast multitude of citizens and strangers. Then, hurrahs rent the air, and handkerchiefs were gaily waved; now the hearts of the most stalwart are melted with anguish."[14]

But winning the war was only part of the task; more heavy lifting was still to come, if a successful reconstruction was to follow. His remarkable wisdom and guiding hand were needed yet. But instead of sleeping for the night in his White House bed and gaining strength to tackle the problems of another day, he lay before them instead at rest for eternity in a casket, forever free from his unfinished earthy labors.

Given the time of night, the expectation might have been for the mournful cavalcade to pass relatively unheralded to its destination, particularly since public viewing hours were not scheduled to commence until six a.m. However, such was not to be the case. From Pearl Street—one block above Broadway—up the incline of State Street north to the imposing iron fence surrounding the Capitol grounds was a sea of humanity. An observer commented that "the crowd of people ... was the greatest we have ever seen in that Avenue."[15]

Beyond the numbers, the most noticeable difference between this gathering and its predecessor in '61 was in its demeanor. This time there were no joyful expressions, waves, and applause at the sight of the marchers, for in their stead could be seen only distraught faces, as "tears trickled from the eyes of tender women, and the heads of stalwart men drooped as with an overwhelming sorrow."[16]

That whole sad drama was played out in the dark of night seemed most fitting to one reporter who saw the scene as an appropriate reflection of the peoples' feelings. "Darkness, lighted only by the gleam of a hundred torches overcast the spectacle," he wrote, "and darkness overcast every heart."[17]

As the procession gained the entrance to the Capitoline Park, the front gates were opened by the sentries, part of the larger contingent posted all around the perimeter. The exterior of the venerable old building was appropriately decorated with black cloth. Inside, mourning drapery had hung in the halls, with both the Senate and Assembly chambers equally adorned. An added touch in the lower house was the presence of a motto suspended over the spot where the speaker presided: "I have as an oath registered in Heaven to preserve, protect, and defend the Government.—A. Lincoln"[18]

The casket was carefully removed from the hearse and taken into the Assembly Chamber. This gigantic room, the very one in which president-elect Lincoln had humbly addressed a packed house, was now devoid of all furniture. Looking ahead to the public viewing, the legislators' desks and chairs were removed to open up the space and thereby expedite the flow of mourners past the coffin.

By using a desk, suitably festooned with crepe and affixed with silver mountings, a makeshift catafalque was created. In an impromptu gesture of personal grief, a silk American flag was wrapped around the casket by the daughter of Lincoln's old Republican confident, Thurlow Weed. At this point, the military companies left to assume positions around the perimeter of the building. The 3rd and 21st Regiments of the United States Reserve Corps were assigned to picket and patrol the state house grounds, while guards drawn from the state militia would be stationed throughout the interior of the building. These troops would man their posts until the President's remains were on their way to the train. For the remainder of the night and the next day, members of the Veteran Corps and the Guard of Honor—divided into three-hour rotations—would remain in the room to watch over the remains and assure smooth passage of the hundreds who would come to pay their respects.

At this point, after midnight by now, the doors to the chamber were closed. In a slight deviation from the orders of General John Dix, who had proclaimed that the coffin would not be opened for viewing until six a.m., the lid was removed and those present permitted to see the body. Among this select group were members of the state legislature and common councils from surrounding cities and towns. Then, at 12:30 a.m., the guests were ushered from the room and the building. The lid was closed. The only ones who remained in the room were the six members of the Honor Guard who had drawn the 12:00 a.m. to 3:00 a.m. duty—and the mortician.

Of those who rode the funeral train, two of its most important people were Dr. Charles Brown and Mr. Frank Sands. Although among the least-heralded members of the traveling entourage, as embalmer and undertaker they respectively had the Herculean task of keeping the president's mortal remains presentable for twenty days. The expertise of Dr. Brown was familiar to the Lincoln family, for it was he who had been called upon to embalm the beloved Willie in 1862. As a trusted practitioner by the family, Dr. Brown was asked to come to White House, embalm the president's body, and prepare it for its initial showing. These requests were fulfilled on the morning of April 15. After completing the introduction of a preservative into the deceased's veins, he added the finishing touch of trimming back the famous Lincoln beard, leaving but a tuft on his chin. According to William Henry Harrison Gould, conductor on the funeral train from Baltimore to Harrisburg, "the body was dressed in black with white shirt and black tie, [and] I was informed that the suit he had on was the suit he wore at his first inauguration."[19] Finally, "a few locks of hair were removed from the President's head for the family, previous to the remains being placed in the coffin."[20] Following his timely service, Dr. Brown was then asked to accompany the president's remains to Springfield and do what he could to maintain an acceptable appearance.

By the time of the scheduled Albany viewing on Wednesday morning, April 26, 1865, Abraham Lincoln had already been deceased for twelve days. Under normal circumstances, most corpses would have been long-since interred, much less still be in a condition presentable for viewing. The cool, rainy weather experienced along the way was not ideal for purposes of delaying decomposition. Adding to the good doctor's challenge was the continuous jostling of the casket while aboard a moving train, its uneven movement in several parades, and its subsequent hauling in and out of buildings by straining pallbearers. Regardless of how careful all handlers were of their sacred charge, an element of unavoidable bumping and manhandling had to have occurred—none of which was good for a body that was naturally undergoing a degree of incremental deterioration and discoloration with each passing day.

Had the assassination happened a decade earlier, three weeks of alternating travel and display would not have been possible. The corpse would never have held up. However, one of the few silver linings of the tragic war just concluded was the advances made in various fields, medicine being one. With so many ghastly wounds to tend, doctors had opportunities to develop life-saving procedures that might not yet have been attempted in peacetime operations. Borne of the same urgent need, breakthroughs were made in performing plastic surgery and creating artificial limbs. Regrettably, the deaths of hundreds of thousands of soldiers also spawned another need, one leading to improved techniques in the preservation of cadavers.

For those families who wanted the remains of a fallen soldier brought home, any means of slowing down the decomposition process was a welcomed procedure. The man and the method came together in the person of Dr. Thomas Holmes. Called the "Father of Modern Embalming," his research built upon the work of others in the field to produce a successful, affordable method of embalming. The procedure that he pioneered, known as "arterial embalming," involved replacing the deceased's blood with a chemical solution. Intending to use an arsenic-based fluid in the process, Holmes obtained a commission from the United States Army Medical Corps to prepare the bodies of Union officers for shipment home. The cost of the procedure was forty dollars; add in another twenty or so for the freight charge, depending upon the destination, and a family of fair means could conceivably retrieve the remains of a loved one for a sixty- to eighty-dollar outlay.

To the extent that Dr. Brown was a skilled practitioner of his trade, he was able to give assurances that the president's corpse would reach its destination in viewable condition. While no reason has come to light to cast dispersions upon his motives as being less than humanitarian, Dr. Brown's reputation and that of his profession had a lot riding on the challenge of keeping Lincoln's body presentable. While perhaps crass to think in these terms, the reality was that three weeks of viewing by thousands of mourners and the accompanying coverage by countless newspapers was tantamount to free advertising for a fledgling technique that had yet to gain widespread traction among the masses.

While in the early phase of its travels—the first five days from Washington to Baltimore, Harrisburg, Philadelphia, and then New York City—the casket was opened for viewing at each stop. But when the *Washington Evening Star* subsequently reported on April 25 that upon leaving New York City "the remains will not again be exposed to view until the arrival in Springfield," this piece of news caused a flap in the state capital.[21] However, regardless of whether a case of correcting misinformation or bowing to political pressure, a clarification occurred somewhere between New York City and Albany, when General John Dix telegraphed orders ahead of the train's arrival that the casket should indeed be opened in Albany.

Over the first five-day stretch, which was preceded by six days from the President's death until the funeral train departed the District of Columbia, the body held up well. When the casket's lid was opened in New York City, one reporter's take was that "the appearance of the dead President bears no evidence of pain, but the eyes are sunken, and the face is somewhat discolored and sallow about the lower part, and dark around the eyes and cheeks. The lips are very tightly compressed."[22]

Later, when the corpse was viewed by mourners in Albany on April 26, an observer said that "the features of the deceased were well-preserved and readily recognizable—the only changes being a slight discoloring about the eyes and mouth."[23] Another individual who may have seen the body later in the day commented that "the face of the President is evidently growing yet darker despite the chemicals used as preservatives."[24]

That being said, evidence would indicate that Dr. Brown had done his work well. For sure, from an embalmer's perspective, he could do no more. His chemical procedure was a one and done process. Unfortunately, an irrevocable trade-off came in employing the new technique of embalming. While Dr. Brown's method effectively delayed the body's decomposition—a consideration of no small import given the three-week window from death until final viewing—the process turned the deceased remains into a rigid, unbendable figure. What was once warm and pliable flesh and flexible joints now had the consistency of a cold, stone statue.

For the remainder of the journey, the only attendant touches that could be administered were cosmetic. Frequent references in newspaper accounts spoke of Brown's "removing dust" from the body, which most likely amounted to brushing off any dirt accumulated by the hearse traveling on earthen roads to and from places where the body lay in state, as well as shaken from the clothes of the mourners and kicked up by shuffling feet passing the catafalque. Undoubtedly the facial powders were touched up from time-to-time in an effort to offset the darkening of the features that was noticeably occurring. However, in the final analysis, without the use of embalming the long journey with its intermittent stops and frequent viewing would never have been possible. Following the funeral services in Washington, the remains of necessity would have gone to Springfield by a direct route. If the result was going to be some facial discoloration, the trade-off of millions getting to pay their respects was deemed worth the deceased's less-than-perfect appearance.

As the president's remains lay in state for its last moments in the crepe-adorned Capitol, a hearse waited outside to carry them through the streets of Albany to the railroad (MOLLUS, U.S. Army Heritage and Education Center, Carlisle, PA).

With the placement of the president's body in the middle of the assembly chamber, phase one of the three-part ceremony was concluded. During its seventeen hours in the capital of the Empire State, the casket would be moved but twice between three places—from an arriving train to the state house for the public viewing and then from there to a departing train. The second stage would begin later in the morning with the casket on display until 1:30 p.m., and the final leg of the tripartite pageant would occur with a parade from the capital to the New York Central Railroad station, from which the funeral train was slated to depart at four o'clock.

While the opening of the coffin in Albany was a departure from the originally advertised plan, another significant deviation occurred at 1:30 a.m. At some point after everyone but the guards had been ushered out at half-past twelve, the decision was made to not wait until 6:30 in the morning for the scheduled public viewing to begin. Albany was clearly jam-packed with people, which a simple visual reconnaissance easily verified. Even at the late hour, "thousands of people had congregated in this vicinity," reported an eye-witness, "and every one seemed anxious to gain admission, in the hopes that they might be permitted to few the remains."[25] Thus, opening the gates and admitting mourners made good sense.

In 1865, Albany boasted a population of slightly over 62,000 souls. A reasonable turnout by its inhabitants alone would have generated a sizable crowd, but a widespread desire to pay their respects to the country's fallen leader temporarily swelled the capital's population many-fold throughout the course of the day. Some prognosticators had foreseen this possibility, one predicting that "tens, nay hundreds of thousands of citizens of Massachusetts and Vermont, of Northern New York, and of the counties in reach of Albany, will pour into the city on Tuesday and Wednesday."[26] In addition to those individuals voluntarily making the trek, surrounding towns had been invited to send official delegations.

To accommodate all those seeking transportation from outlying areas, the various railroads serving the capital city did their best. Extra coaches were added to existing runs, and, when the local supply was exhausted, freight cars were pressed into service to haul passengers. In few instances, additional excursions were scheduled. Boats also brought in additional people from river towns along the Hudson. Though the tremendous influx of mourners constituted a fitting tribute to Lincoln, their presence placed a strain upon available services. To wit, more travelers sought hotel rooms than there were overnight accommodations available to shelter them. By ten o'clock in the evening of April 26, all inns were filled. A case in point was Albany's premier hostelry, where it was reported that "the corridors and offices of the Delavan are turned into dormitories, and many took their night's rest on the stairs and entries of the establishment."[27] Two-to-a-bed was rule, with many happy to sleep in chairs if such was the best they could be offered. Private residences helped by taking in some of the overflow. Even school houses were pressed into temporary service to put up travelers.

Once the front gate was opened at 1:30 a.m., the wisdom of the decision was immediately evident, as people streamed into the capitol building. Mourners entered in lines two-by-two. On reaching the assembly chamber, the pairings split, with one individual passing on the left and the other to the right of the catafalque. This arrangement allowed those who came to pay their respects to be accommodated more rapidly and in greater numbers.

At what seems like a rather rapid pace—but one necessitated by the huge turnout—mourners "passed by at a rate of 60 to 70 a minute."[28] In spite of all these people funneling through, the great room was enveloped in silence. The light shuffling of the mourners' feet and an occasional sob were the only discernable sounds. There were instances when choral groups came in, stood off to the side in the great chamber, and offered fitting renderings.

Given patience and time, visitors eventually got near enough to recognize the features of Abraham Lincoln. But altogether too quickly, mourners were ushered past the deceased. There was but time for a momentary gaze at the late martyr's face, accompanied maybe by an unspoken farewell, the shedding of tears, or the start of a short prayer. Another gesture was that the coffin was frequently "strewn by ladies with flowers, expressive of the feelings of those who have contributed these delicate and beautiful tokens of sorrow and affection."[29] These floral offerings took a variety of forms which included a bouquets, baskets, wreaths, and even a cross. Those who lingered a bit too long were gently shepherded forward by one of the guards.

Regardless of how fleeting the interlude, personal respects had been paid. Perhaps the bereaved had caught a glimpse of the president in 1861 or at best only recognized him from pictures; yet, despite the lack of a relationship that was cemented by frequent interactions, the genuine feeling existed in the hearts of those who came to say goodbye that they had lost a revered friend. As expressed by the sorrowful expressions on their faces, they were truly distraught, as if a member of their own immediate families had passed away. Continuing beyond the casket, one file exited the chamber through the north door and then the grounds by way of the north gate, while those in the opposite line did the same through corresponding apertures on the south side of the building.

The flow of mourners was steady throughout the remainder of the night and into the next day. "The crowd surging toward the entrance to the chamber was perpetual," was one man's take, "from midnight to the gray dawn of the morning at noonday the jam was the same."[30] Even though a significant number visitors had made their way to the city the previous day, new arrivals continued to pour in Thursday morning. Trains were once again running at capacity. Due to this constant infusion of new people, the lines to view the remains never abated. An observer looking to the east from the state house noted that "they reached from the Assembly Chamber at the Capital to the foot of State Street, in a prolonged and patient line four deep."[31]

At one point between nine and ten o'clock, the line bent in serpentine fashion around the corner of State Street and continued for several blocks north on Broadway up to the Delavan House. Another individual near the same vantage point commented, due to its densely packed nature, that the line never seemed to move.

Still, as anyone who has ever waited in a long queue knows, patience is a necessary virtue. For progress was made only in fits and starts by the mourners, when "every now and then a hitch occurred, however, which brought the anxious ones a few feet nearer the point descried."[32] Overall, people were extremely understanding and cooperative. But as always, every crowd has its outliers. One rather nimble man managed to scale a section of the arched iron fence, which was six feet above the ground at the mid-point of its curve. Upon landing, he was quickly accosted by a guard and responded by pulling a gun, causing the sentinel to then charge with fixed bayonet and run it through the trespasser's coat. Thanks to their jointly-demonstrated martial ineptitude, neither was injured. In another instance, a woman who tried to climb over the fence had her effort foiled when her clothing got caught on its pointed top.

In perhaps the only moments of discord during the entire stopover by the funeral train, a stir was triggered at 10:30 a.m., when guards unexpectedly closed the gates and caused mourners in front to be crushed against the metal barrier by the upset, surging mass behind them. The reason for this unannounced act was to allow the legislators to pay their respects. A week ago, the solons had met in the same building to offer their thoughts and reflections about Abraham Lincoln's life. State Senator Charles Cooke reacted in fervent disagreement to Booth's use of the word "tyrant," offering that "[if] there was one prominent trait in the character of the late President that stood in front of all others, it was the goodness of his heart, the kindness of spirit, toward the errors of humanity, that almost appeared to look upon crime as seen by other eyes as an offense which need simply be repented and to be forgiven."[33]

In comparing his country's fallen leader to noteworthy predecessors such as Jackson, Clay, and Webster, a colleague suggested that while Lincoln was "lacking somewhat of what they had, he had somewhat of what they all lacked. And it was by this, that he laid his hand upon the heart of the people, and it beat responsive to his touch."[34]

Once the hundred-plus elected officials had filed past the catafalque, the time was eleven o'clock. The gates were quickly reopened, and the public readmitted. By the end of the viewing hours at 1:30 p.m., a *New York Times'* estimated that "nearly fifty thousand men, women, and children" had paid their respects.[35]

Sadly, to comply with the scheduled departure of the funeral train, access to the Capitol had to be terminated at 1:30 p.m. While this literally meant slamming the doors in peoples' faces, no alternative existed. For those thousands who were still lined up in front of the state house and denied entrance, their only consolation came from being well-positioned to observe the forthcoming funeral procession.

For those who had already been able to pay their respects, Albany-in-mourning offered much for them to see while waiting for the grand procession to begin at two o'clock. Since the Victorian way of death was a celebration, visible demonstrations of feelings were everywhere, for Albany was bedecked in decorations in a way never before seen or repeated since. "There was a scarcely a house, from the home of the poorest widow to the mansion of the richest citizen, that did not exhibit some emblem of sadness ... [for] the whole city was dressed in mourning, from the center of trade on Broadway and State Street, to the lowest cottage on the outskirts of town."[36]

Rendered in good taste, the embellishments took on a variety of forms. Drapery-twined columns, curtains of black cloth, white rosettes, black festoons, and portraits of the president were the most frequently used features in the displays. Mottoes were also popular accents and could be seen in great profusion adorning store windows, proclaiming such thoughts as: "Washington, the Father of his Country. Lincoln, the Savior of his Country. The Martyr"; "The great heart of the Nation throbs heavily at the portals of his grave"; and "His deeds are known."[37]

Unlike modern holiday decorators who are sometimes as inspired to one-up their neighbors as they are in celebrating the spirit of the season, a "genuine, heartfelt exhibition of grief for the Nation's loss" was the reason identified for the city's being so thoroughly and completely dressed in mourning.[38] Even though armed with the knowledge that the funeral train would not arrive until Tuesday, townsfolk began as early as the previous Saturday to dress business establishments, public buildings, and private homes in the proper state of mourning. "Everything that stores contained that day that could be used for mourning was purchased. The merchants immediately took measures to replenish their exhausted stocks, and day by day since, as opportunity offered, our citizens have made additions to the then overwhelming demonstrations."[39]

Against this backdrop, the third phase of the pageant was about to begin. Since this stage was an outdoor event, cooperation on the part of nature was a vital element. Some might have preferred overcast skies, dark and ominous in their portent. Thunder, lightning, and rain would for them have seemed the most suitable backdrop to complement their own tears and sorrow, but such was not to be the case.

The morning of Wednesday, April 26, 1865, dawned bright and clear. "Heaven could not have granted a better day" was the *Albany Evening Journal's* thankful appraisal. Blue skies, bright sunshine, a warm temperature, low humidity, and a light breeze would combine to make for a pleasant day. From the standpoint of the procession, the best-case scenario existed. Foul weather would have soaked the unprotected mourners packed along the streets. Decorations would have become sodden and runny. The hearse and casket doused, and marchers drenched to the bone. Runoff would have cascaded down State Street hill and, in its rush to meld with the Hudson, turned the thoroughfare into a disagreeable muck.

As the clock ticked away the morning hours, anticipation began to build for what was sure to be a memorable, once-in-a-lifetime experience. Stores locked their doors at eleven and drew their blinds—only restaurants remained open to accommodate the out-of-towners. In private residences, curtains were closed. Church bells began to peal, while the cathedral's chimes added their own unique ring. Minute guns commenced their steady cadence. As for the human element, "at noon, State Street, which is nearly one hundred feet broad, was filled with a living mass, and Broadway, together with many of the side streets, were equally crowded."[40] Various parade participants had begun to form up along the south side of the Capitol.

In spite of the obvious solemnity of the occasion, not everyone present amongst the assembled throng waiting for the cortege to pass was there out of respect and bereavement. Like ants swarming to a picnic, some people were present in the tightly packed mass only to take advantage of the unsuspecting. As one paper characterized the wake they left behind, "yesterday was a harvesting season for burglars, thieves, and pickpockets."[41]

Just as been the case when Lincoln's inaugural tour stopped in Albany in 1861, pickpockets—known then by the quaint term "knucks"—once again found ample opportunities to display their dexterity. "Without exaggeration," one paper proclaimed, "we may say that we heard, during the day, of at least one hundred persons who had been subjected to the skillful manifestations of the 'mobs' from New York and Philadelphia."[42] With so many strangers from neighboring communities in town, standing next to an unfamiliar face was not the immediate cause for caution that it might have been on another day.

In addition to having to guard their person from depravation, a second element of thievery interjected itself in the form of burglars. Simple deduction would conclude that the presence of people in the crowd downtown meant a lot of empty homes elsewhere in the city. The various newspapers serving the area did their best to forewarn honest visitors and unsuspecting residents. "We would caution all to look well to their pocket books and watches," warned the editor of the *Albany Times and Courier*, "and also to our own citizens, to have cared how they desert their homes today." But despite such forewarnings, pickpockets working the crowd met with success. Pocket watches and cash were to the two most commonly pilfered items.

While the haul of the pickpockets was limited to only those items such as could be carried about a victim's body and filched in a split-second of contact, burglars on the other hand had more time and the run of a whole house to discover their treasures. An example of the plunder which was taken from one home was the discerning haul stolen from John L. Randall of 187 Hudson Street, a residence located only a few blocks south of State Street: "one gold watch, one gold chain, two large silver medals, one small silver medal, eleven silver spoons, one silver salt spoon, a set of pearl jewelry, a pair of gold cuff buttons, one silver knife, one silver fork, twelve plated forks, twelve plated tea spoons, six plated table spoons, three silver napkin rings, and $25 in bills."[43]

Though many returning folks found to their utter dismay that the privacy of their homes had been violated, the Albany police had by no means been shirking their responsibilities. If any appraisal were due them, the assessment would be that they did their best to handle double duty. First and foremost, overseeing the pageant by keeping the route open and the spectators under control were their paramount objectives.

As for the pickpockets, given that the police estimated that over 200 of these heartless scoundrels had descended upon Albany, riding herd on such a profusion of professional brigands would have been a difficult enough task all by itself. Nevertheless numerous arrests helped thin the population of pickpockets, gentlemen whom one Albany paper chortled "were furnished with quarters in the jail, and last night had a quiet time for reflection."[44]

While these individual vignettes of theft and arrest were playing out on a microcosmic level, the funeral pageant was rapidly moving toward its grand climax. The closing of the gates to the capital grounds signaled the end of the viewing. After twelve hours of access to an open casket, the second phase of the program was over. The final segment would now unfold. Inside the Assembly Hall, undertaker Frank Sands tidied up the appearance of the president's body, removing any dust accumulated over its half-day of exposure. He then closed the coffin's lid and screwed it down tight. With the crisp, measured movements of trained soldiers, members of the Veteran Reserve Guard aligned themselves on each side of the casket. Acting in unison, they hoisted the heavy chest to their shoulders and marched in perfect lockstep. Exiting from the hall, the building, and the grounds on the south side, they found the hearse waiting for them on State Street, facing west.

Beginning at noon, participants in the parade had begun to assemble along the same side of the Capitol, facing to the west. The lineup grew steadily into a long array of marchers. Among the most active individuals during this preparatory stage was Frank Townsend. As incongruous as the designation may appear today for a funeral procession, this eminent resident of Albany—a successful businessman, former mayor, and a battle-tested general—was accorded the honor of serving as the parade's "Grand Marshal." According to published accounts, he and his assistants were very active and competent in giving preparatory instructions to all of the various groups, so that "when ... the hour for commencing the march had arrived, all were in readiness and there was no delay."[45]

Once the procession got underway at 2 o'clock, thirty minutes would be required for all of its participants to pass a given point. The route, as laid out by planners, was not a direct one. Had that been the preferred approach, then out the front east-facing door, down State Street to its intersection with Broadway, and then left or north a few blocks to the waiting train would have been the most expedient pathway; however, a little prelude was added that sent the cortege initially in the opposite direction. This route was west on State Street to Dove Street, north on Dove to Washington Avenue, east down Washington to its intersection with State Street in front of Capitol Park, east on State Street to its intersection with Broadway, and then north on Broadway to Lumber Street.

Though slightly longer, this adjustment not only allowed more mourners an opportunity to observe what was after all a public display, but, more importantly, the modest extension provided what amounted to a staging area. By virtue of following this more circuitous route, participants were given a few shakedown blocks to get organized and comfortable before making the grand descent down State Street hill, which would be the most highly visible portion of the entire observance.

The wisdom of including an extra warm-up distance was further confirmed when the route was extended yet an extra block. Instead of marching west on State Street and turning north at Dove Street, the entire entourage was directed to proceed to the next street above Dove, which was Lark, and then make a right turn to cross over to Washington Avenue. The rationale given for this last-minute tweak was to help shake out the kinks in the line and have good order established before reaching the main part of the route.

While some of those partaking in the walk had gained experience in similar processions, most participants were not so acclimated. The amateur section of marchers fell into two categories: government officials and civic organizations. With the hearse placed in the center of the column, the pallbearers were aligned on either side. Positioned directly behind the hearse were several carriages, paired off to save space. For the most part, those less-polished in close-order marching skills were slotted in at this juncture. They were admonished to carry neither banners or placards nor adorn themselves with any badges or devices of political affiliation. Here could be found all of the state officials, starting with governor and his staff and followed by members of the judicial and legislative branches.

Next in line were representatives from the local governments of surrounding communities. Delegations were present from Troy, Lansingburgh, Cohoes, Watervliet, Waterford, West Troy, Schenectady, and Hudson. In addition to elected officials, a fair number of private citizens had made the trip too. Even Utica, eighty-five miles to the west, sent a group of marchers.

Following this contingent of elected officials were members of Albany's civic organizations, all of whose rosters turned out at or near full capacity. Among these were several church-affiliated societies, some union groups, three Young Men's Associations, and multiple ethnic clubs. Observers noted that for groups not accustomed to marching, they all gave a good accounting for themselves. Striding in compact files and rows from eight-to-fourteen abreast, they maintained perfect order. Slotted along with this section of the marchers was the Burgess Corps from Troy. In a later review of the pageant, this venerable military corps, sixty-four members strong, was praised for presenting "a very fine appearance yesterday in their red coats and bearskin caps."[46] Bringing up the rear were members of the fire departments of Albany, Cohoes, East Albany, East and West Troy.

As marchers moved out, the first sight that those lining the streets would have was of a phalanx of policemen leading the column. Beyond visually providing a stabilizing influence, these officers rightly earned a place of honor in the procession. Their presence had been very noticeable from the first arrival of the president's remains, and their performance in dealing with the huge influx of people over the entire time since had been highly commendable.

Positioned between these officers and the hearse were several military units, all of whom brought an element of professionalism to their participation in the cortege. In the front ranks were the 10th and 25th Infantry Regiments from Albany, led by General John Rathbone. Behind them, commanded by Colonel Isaac McConihe tramped 24th Regiment of the N.G.S.N.Y. out of Troy. With a combined strength of over 2000 troops, these battle-hardened veterans comprised the heart of the army's contribution to the proceedings and acquitted themselves exceedingly well, for they were rated by some who witnessed the pageant as "one of its most attractive features."[47] Marching with guns reversed in a slow, steady pace, they made a highly favorable impression.

Behind the foot-soldiers rumbled the Light Horse Battery of artillery. Comprised of four pieces, the ominous power they projected also caught the eye of the crowd. The remainder of this lead segment consisted of officers who were assigned to accompany the remains were either active or former naval and army personnel. The last buffer before the hearse was members of Congress and other delegates who had made the trip from Washington.

Then came the centerpiece of the procession, a sight that grabbed and held the attention of everyone—the catafalque and coffin. In keeping with the profusion of funereal decorations all over the city, the hearse represented an exquisite piece of craftsmanship that befitted the exulted status of the individual whose remains it bore. The car was pulled by six gray horses, each attractively caparisoned and attended by a groom. With a main platform measuring twelve feet long and six feet six inches wide, the appearance of the funeral carriage itself was that of an oversized, canopied four-poster bed on wheels. Black cloth, white satin, and silver tassels were combined to create a stunning visual effect, motivating the press to offer high praise for its being "so elegant and beautiful a piece of work the kind has never before been seen in our city."[48]

The base platform was covered with an ebony material that was draped over the sides and bordered with a looped silver cord hung at intervals with tassels of the same color. The mahogany casket rested on a slope-sided dais, also black-sheathed and accented with silver cord. Supporting the canopy above the deceased were four fluted columns, bound in black with strands of ivy blended with white flowers interwoven in spiral fashion down their length. Black plumes reached skyward from each corner. The canopy featured white satin on its inner surface, from which black wreaths dangled, and black cloth on its outer surface. A gilt eagle on top and a national flag at each end completed what was an elaborate work rendered with artistic skill and imbued with a taste commensurate with the times.

Not to be overlooked were the musicians interspersed in the procession: marching bands with each featuring a full drum corps. Altogether five units participated: Albany's own Schreiber's Cornet Band placed ahead of the 25th Regiment; Doring's Cornet Band from Troy led its hometown 24th Regiment; two of Dodworth's bands from New York City preceded the 10th Regiment and the Burgess Corps respectively; and Eastman's College Band from Poughkeepsie fronted the fire departments. The last of these performing groups, Eastman's, had already done yeoman service for President Lincoln, for they had played for him 1861 when he came to Poughkeepsie and then in New York City, Poughkeepsie, and now Albany as a part of obsequies in each of the three cities. When the procession progressed slowly down State Street hill, the marchers did so to the accompaniment of a variety of appropriate dirges, selections which included "Love Not," "Auld Lang Syne," and "Come and Let Us Worship."[49]

An observer noted that "throughout the entire length of the route, the sidewalks and streets were packed with a dense mass of human beings."[50] Another estimated that "such a mass of humanity, probably not less than sixty thousand, was never before seen in the streets of Albany."[51] Many had been there in 1861, sharing the triumph and hope that the newly elected president was taking with him to Washington. Then they had cheered and clapped as he rode past them. Now most were back again. Only on this occasion, bowed heads, solemn faces, aching hearts, and red-rimmed eyes replaced the gestures of unbounded joy displayed four years ago. Some held tissues in their hands again, only now they were used to absorb tears instead of offer salutes.

While mourners wedged in wherever they could, by far the best view of the cortege was afforded those standing at the foot of State Street hill. From this vantage point facing to the west and looking up, the sight line was such that the full length of the pageant could be taken in as it proceeded slowly down the incline. From this perspective, one onlooker shared his vision of the striking panorama: "the great width of the street and the extremely steep grade presented the whole body of the procession at a glance, surrounded by the vast numbers who crowded into this area."[52] So numerous and tightly packed were the spectators, jamming right into the street on both sides, that they almost impeded the parade's progress.

In an apt word-picture, the scene looked like "a sea of heads, and only the motion of the march indicated the line of division between people and procession."⁵³

As had been the case four years ago, people appropriated every possible means by which to obtain an unobstructed view—resulting in groups watching from windows and balconies and individuals perching in trees and dangling from lampposts along the line of march.

Upon attaining the corner of Broadway and State Street, the cortège did not turn right and head south for the New York Central depot. Instead, the procession went left. In keeping with the overall spirit of retracing the 1861 inaugural tour in reverse, the president's remains were being taken directly to the funeral train, which "was waiting at the place where the Central Railroad crossed Broadway."⁵⁴ For Albanians and their association with Abraham Lincoln, the wheel had turned full-circle. They would now be bidding a last adieu from the very spot where they once offered their first tumultuous welcome. In a fine display of military precision, the infantry regiments leading the procession turned left out of the column and lined up along the west side of Broadway, facing to toward the east and the Hudson River. In an impressive array, they stood solemnly at "present arms" as the catafalque passed.

To avoid a jam up in the boarding zone, most of the trailing portion of the cortège behind the hearse turned west off Broadway at Clinton Avenue, approximately four blocks before the train. They then took the next left onto Pearl Street, which led the marchers back to State Street. With the procession having reached its goal, the recently concluded event had now passed into the realm of history, but in the words of one observer "the magnificent pageant, the vast throngs that had congregated here, and the sadness of the people, all made a scene that will ever keep fresh in the memories of the many who witnessed it."⁵⁵

To the immediate left of the troops, the funeral train was waiting, steam up and ready to begin the long trek to Buffalo. The entire consist was comprised of ten units: an engine, tender, and eight cars. The casket was removed from the horse-drawn hearse and placed back aboard the *United States*. After dropping off Lincoln's remains at the East Albany station, the two through cars had been shunted over to Albany via the same circuitous route that the inaugural train had taken in 1861.

The *Chauncey Vibbard*, which had pulled the inaugural train east from Utica to Albany, was slotted to cover the same distance west with the funeral train in tow (courtesy Edward L. May Memorial collection).

At 3:50 p.m., the pilot engine, pulling its tender and a single coach, set off to insure the safety of the roadway. Named the *Chauncey Vibbard*, the engine was appropriately decorated by its engineer Henry Harvey with a picture of Lincoln, surrounded by mourning material affixed to its front. Also bedecked in appropriate fashion was the engine assigned to pull the funeral train on its first leg—the *Edward H. Jones*.

Promptly at 4:00 o'clock engineer Peter Arthur slowly opened the throttle. The train gathered speed, and soon it was gone, heading west through the Mohawk Valley corridor toward the setting sun. In its wake, a crowd of solemn mourners stood watching, most lost in their own thoughts. Many had only seen the great man twice. The first time he passed through their community, it was as an unknown commodity, heading for Washington and bearing their hopes for the preservation of the Union. Now he was departing as a martyr to the cause which he had so successfully defended. As one among them later described the scene, perhaps in his personnel eloquence sharing the feelings of his fellow townsfolk, "after a splendid tribute of our affection and reverence, he whose life was devoted to his country, and whose death was a sacrifice for us, whose virtues are enshrined in our hearts was borne from our midst."[56]

18

Into the Heartland
The Mohawk Valley Bids a Sad Farewell

The train that chugged from Albany would never have been mistaken for the one that had delivered the presidential party four years earlier, though one point of confusion existed: both were called the Lincoln Special. This was due primarily railroad nomenclature, for a train that was not regularly scheduled was called an "express" or "special." Perhaps interjecting an extra word, as in "Lincoln's Inaugural Special" or "Lincoln's Funeral Special" could have provided clarification. Of course, at the time of the first special, no one was anticipating a second one.

Obviously, observers in 1861 and 1865 knew which train they were viewing. But for purposes of historical clarification, noting that both runs were identified as Lincoln Specials is important. Besides heading in the opposite directions and one being clad in mourning ornamentation, other significant differences existed. The funeral special proceeded at a speed of twenty miles per hour, while the inaugural express averaged fifty miles per hour. Perhaps the most noticeable of all the alterations, the train bearing Lincoln home in 1865 was more than twice as long as the one that brought him east in 1861, with eleven component parts in the former but only five in the latter.

But the primary reason for the dissimilarity in the two trains stemmed from the divergence in purposes. In 1861, Superintendent of Arrangements William Wood, wielding virtually dictatorial powers over all matters involving the inaugural trip, strove to shield the president-elect from having to deal with too many people who wished to bend his ear. This goal was successfully accomplished in part by limiting the number of coaches to two or three cars. Ergo there was simply not enough room to fit all of the politicians and lobbyists who wished to get aboard.

By contrast, the circumstances surrounding funeral train required more rather than less space for passengers. The people aboard were there out of respect for their fallen leader. Most Northern states had at least one representative making the trip, with four governors along with twenty-three members of Congress aboard. Many friends of the deceased president also accompanied his remains. A few extended family members were present. A fair number of military personnel were included to provide a ceremonial guard at stops, and numerous railroad employees made the journey to insure a smooth run. Where the inaugural train transported less than one hundred passengers, its funeral counterpart accommodated double that number. Even with the understandable need for extra space, access to the train was still controlled. According to William Henry Harrison Gould, one of conductors for the Lincoln Special out of Albany, "each member of the train crew, and all of those who were entitled to ride on the train, wore a special badge. This badge was their ticket of transportation."[1]

A second major variation between the two passages across the Empire State was that the inaugural train traveled only by day. Since that tour sought public exposure for Mr. Lincoln, passing through communities in the evening would be counterproductive. However, the funeral train was a different consideration. Intermingling with the public was no longer paramount, so a balance had to be struck between letting people pay their respects and getting the remains to Springfield in timely fashion. The 150 miles between New York City and Albany, even at twenty miles per hour, were easily accomplished in part of a day. Traveling for six and a half hours meant an average speed of 23 miles per hour. By comparison the journey from Albany to Buffalo was almost twice the distance. By maintaining a speed of 20 miles per hour, the travel time from Albany to Buffalo was going to consume about fifteen hours.

Since two-thirds of the westward passage would occur at night, a time when the travelers would ordinarily be at rest, the standard coach accommodations that the Hudson River Railroad supplied for the New York City-to-Albany leg would no longer suffice. Conscious of making the long ride as comfortable as possible, the management of the New York Central provided several brand-new cars. Per one assessment, "no pains have been spared to fit up the seven passenger cars furnished by the Central."[2]

One of these upgrades was the baggage car and three were coaches outfitted with the typical fixtures, but it was easy to see that "the seats and panel, and the whole interior equipment, are first rate style."[3] The remaining three units were novelties in that era, for they were outfitted as "elegant sleeping cars."[4]

When the cortège reached the train at 3:45 p.m., the marchers could see that the entire consist was covered in mourning drapery. Starting with the engine, which had been "beautifully decorated" and "refitted, repaired, and burnished throughout," each car had been adorned both inside and out with arrangements made from "black alpaca and white bunting."[5]

Accompanied by the sounds of church bells, minute guns, and mournful dirges, the casket was loaded into the hearse car. Father and son were reunited once again. Simultaneously, all members of the official party boarded too. Because of an obligation to be present for the impending adjournment of the legislature, governor Reuben Fenton had to remain behind; however, the executive branch was duly represented by a legislative delegation which his Excellency had appointed to ride through to Dunkirk.

Also noticeable to those boarding the train was the armed guards. As noted by William S. Porter—a Civil War veteran and railroad brakeman on the Lincoln Special—"a crack New York City regiment of soldiers escorted the body and performed guard duty over the entire trip."[6]

Posted four to a car, a pair of these sentinels stood at each end on the moving train. When it stopped, they left their respective cars and stood at the bottom of the steps on each side of the train, both front and back. Their assignment at this point was to challenge anyone who wished to get onboard, requiring the individual to show a permit or badge. Once the engineer sounded the whistle for departure, the guards immediately climbed back aboard and stood at head of the steps until well underway. Then the four guards per car would return to their positions inside the coaches.

While passengers were boarding the funeral train, the pilot engine departed at 3:50. With the interests of safety paramount, railroad officials had decreed that "the Pilot Engine and the Train will have the right to the track over all other trains, and no train will run within thirty minutes of their time."[7] Though these precautions made perfect sense when a living president was being transported, some questioned the need for a funeral train to require such a safeguard. However, the reality was that the pilot engine served multiple purposes beyond the protection of passengers by ensuring the integrity of the railroad's infrastructure.

First, riding in the coach pulled by the advanced locomotive, was an Albany-based telegrapher named Adam Whipple. He had in his possession a portable machine. This piece of equipment was "a small apparatus, so that if at any time an accident or interruption should occur, he could detach the wires on the line, and command communication at any point."[8] Also present was a master mechanic, available to provide emergency repair services should a breakdown occur. Completing what was a triumvirate of personnel available to address a crisis was Major Zenas Priest, the assistant superintendent of the New York Central's division encompassing the road between Albany and Utica.

For conspiracy theorists who saw perpetrators of nefarious deeds abounding in the land, the idea of a corpse being stolen and held for ransom, especially an important one such as President Lincoln's, was not an unthinkable act. As ghoulish as the thought of body-snatching might be, almost fifty years later the remains of Abraham Lincoln were exhumed, identified, and then encased in cement to guard against just that rumored possibility.

Still, even though stealing a cadaver may have seemed a bit far-fetched, railroads of that era were known to suffer derailments due to equipment-related failures. Just ten days before, on April 16, a train bearing the body of Colonel Robert Janeway from Jersey City to Brunswick, New Jersey, experienced a derailment. As stated in a published report, "on approaching the Passaic Bridge, from some unexplained cause, but most probably owing ... to a misplaced switch, the engine ran off the track, dragging the tender with it, both being disabled, and the latter greatly damaged."[9]

Unfortunately, the officer's cortège did not rate a pilot engine. Though no one was injured and the sanctity of the colonel's rest remained undisturbed, an object lesson was there to be learned. How horrifying and embarrassing would it be to have had the president's hearse car destroyed in wreck, spilling the casket if not the body out onto the tracks? No, a pilot engine was the better safe than sorry measure to take.

Then, precisely at four o'clock, Conductor Honus Williams shouted "All Aboard!" Engine George Wrightson signaled two quick blasts of the whistle to clear the track, and, with its bell slowly clanging, the *Edward H. Jones* headed slowly westward. Ahead lay a patchwork of farms, hamlets, villages, and a few cities. Places populated by citizens who had solidly supported Lincoln's candidacy in 1860 and now passionately grieved his passing.

Nevertheless, even though the collective approval of its residents for Abraham Lincoln was four years in the making, little doubt could have existed on this warm spring day in April of 1865 that city of Albany had not done his memory justice. In the way of a civic pat on the back, the *Albany Evening Journal* reported that "a distinguished General, who came with the remains, remarked to one of our officers, that in no place had the preparations been so excellent and so well-prepared."[10] Even though possessing the prestige of being the state capital, Albany existed in the shadow of New York City—forever relegated to be second fiddle in the state to one of the world's greatest metropolitan complexes. Yet, even though the various ceremonies and tributes that occurred across the state as the funeral train made its way to Springfield—including those in New York and Albany—were not proffered in the spirit of intercity competition, the inhabitants of the capital could not be faulted for a feeling an immense sense of civic pride in how splendidly their farewell had turned out. Regardless of what part an individual played, "the magnificent pageantry, the vast throngs that had congregated, and the peoples' sadness, was a scene that will ever keep fresh in the memories of the many who witness it."[11]

As the train passed between Albany and Schenectady, residents of rural areas took the opportunity to pay their last respects too. Mourners were randomly located along the tracks. With the sun still shining, they watched for the telltale wisps of smoke signaling the approach of a train. Later, when darkness enveloped the land, they waited patiently for the sounds of a steam engine, which in the still of the night was unmistakable.

First, the pilot engine came past. Ten minutes later, their gaze beheld the funeral train. Bell ringing a measured cadence, the anomaly of a slow-moving express glided in before them. From the train could be seen men with hats in hand and women holding handkerchiefs. All had sad countenances on their faces, and tears were observed flowing freely

Add six more cars, pack in 2000 people, reverse the direction of the pictured train and one would create the scene at the Schenectady's depot as it would have appeared when the funeral train briefly stopped on April 26, 1865, before heading westward through the Mohawk Valley (courtesy Schenectady County Historical Society).

down the cheeks of both sexes. Adding another element to the crowd, one reporter noted of the many enterprising individuals who had found their own niches from which to take in the unfolding scene. Some were perched atop "railroad coaches, at the windows, on the porches, on house-tops, in the trees—every elevated position having an occupant."[12]

Even at a reduced speed, ground was being covered at a rate of one-third of a mile a minute, allotting mourners precious little time in which to take in the decorations ... pick out the hearse car ... bow their heads ... envision the man laid out there in ... say a mental prayer ... and then bid him farewell. For those who had seen him in 1861, that four years could have elapsed already seemed as implausible.

At 4:45 in the afternoon, the *Edward Jones* pulled into the station at Schenectady. Like the residences and stores in the community, the depot was appropriately bedecked in mourning finery. A company of infantry stood at attention along each side of the tracks. The train halted for five minutes, giving those who had made the effort to appear trackside the opportunity to pay their silent respects. In their own salute to the memory of Mr. Lincoln, the maintenance workers in the West Albany yards had positioned themselves in a line along the tracks. Signalmen, stationed at intervals beside the tracks, held in their hands white square flags, bordered with black.

Along the eighty-two-mile right-of-way between Albany and Utica, the funeral train passed fifteen stations. Mindful that no group of mourners was any less sincere in its grief than any other, the train could justifiable have stopped at every one; however, to do so would have made the existing long trek even more extended odyssey. The only concession that could reasonably be made was to maintain a slow speed. On a route that would ordinarily feature a conductor walking through the coaches, announcing as he went the next stop, only silence now reigned as the train approached a depot.

That which the mourners onboard had witnessed in Schenectady was only the first of what would be a succession of similar heartfelt homages. William Coggeshall—an Ohio journalist who served for a time as a bodyguard for President Lincoln—praised the local efforts in a post-journey reflection of the local observances in the Mohawk Valley: "In all the cities, towns, and villages along the thickly populated line of the Central railway, demonstrations were made as appropriate and suggestive as any which had been witnessed on the journey from Washington."[13]

Seventeen miles west of Schenectady lay Amsterdam, another of the prosperous industrial centers in central New York. Here the train "passed through an arch, decorated in red, white, and blue, and draped in morning."[14]

Then in rapid succession, the villages of Fonda, Palatine Bridge, and Fort Plain followed, as the train moved into the heart of the Mohawk Valley. In each of these locales, stations, businesses, and homes were done up in mourning drapery. The citizenry of these small towns, joined by residents from the surrounding countryside, turned out to pay a silent homage to the memory of their revered leader. Though the mourners were themselves hushed, the resonance of tolling bells and booming cannon sounded across the valley. During the war, the locale around Fonda had been no stranger to large gatherings of people, for the flatland northwest of town served as a training ground and staging area for federal troops. In 1862, the 115th Volunteer Infantry—comprised of recruits from the counties of Montgomery, Fulton, Hamilton, and Saratoga—had gone off to war from the same station now decked out in mourning drapery.

Continuing on, at the approach to the village of Palatine Bridge, "a white cross was erected on a grassy mound. This Christian symbol was robed in evergreens and mourning. On each side was a woman, apparently weeping. Inscribed on the cross were the words, 'We have prayed for you; now we can only weep.'"[15]

At the station, a military band played dirges. A bevy of women were lined up on the bridge, a structure that was adorned with American flags and black cloth. Spanning the tracks as well as the river, this lofty perch afforded the ladies an unimpeded view of the scene unfolding below. From there, they could see the town's little depot, which also "was elaborately draped in front with National flags, neatly associated with black cloth. The roof of the building was festooned with long pieces of black and white, the drapery elevated on the posts and gracefully drooping."[16]

For such a comparatively small town, an impressive gathering had turned out to see the passing of the cortège, boosted by residents from Canajoharie. These folks had walked across the bridge from their homes on the south side of the river. Along with the crowd on the bridge and those positioned along the tracks, "the roads and both sides of the hills … were lined with spectators of all ages and both sexes."[17] When the express reached Fort Plain, students and faculty of the hometown academy were lined up along the tracks, standing in silent tribute as the train passed through the station. Behind them, "a large National flag, edged with mourning, was displayed, held at the four corners by as many lads."[18]

Fifteen minutes and five miles later, the village of St. Johnsville came into view. Though its population of a thousand souls alone did not warrant the scheduling of a thirteen-minute stop, another consideration ramped up the town's importance. Since most passengers had not eaten for seven to ten hours, they were by now quite hungry. St. Johnsville offered them a chance to get some much-needed nourishment. Since railroads did not offer onboard dining facilities, strategic stops were pre-arranged at trackside restaurants such as the one at this location.

A former resident of the town, a woman named Emma Randall Taber, recalled that "during the Civil War traffic on the railroad was heavy and all trains stopped at our town, where the passengers patronized this restaurant, which was run by a man whom we all called 'Colonel Cook.' Some days three or four hundred would have dinner there."[19] Apparently the management of the eatery had been contacted by Captain John Penrose, designated the Commissary of Subsistence for the funeral train, to provide a "bounteous supper" at their trackside refractory."[20] Known as a "collation" in period vernacular, the meal was served family style.

Provided with sufficient advanced notice, the restaurateurs had geared up to serve the large group about to arrive. To complement its regular staff, the voluntary assistance of twenty-two local ingénues was recruited. In keeping with the solemn purpose that had brought everyone together on this day, the young ladies were as properly attired in mourning colors. Wearing white dresses, black sashes, and black scarves, each waitress was assigned to serve a group of five or six passengers. Given that the tight schedule allotted but a quarter-hour to get seated, served, and sated, table talk must have been kept to a minimum and a priority given to consuming supper.

With the meal completed, the serving-girls were accorded a special privilege. In appreciation for their fine service, the ladies were permitted to walk through the hearse car to pay their respects and lay a floral wreath upon the casket. One of the young women, who had served a table of five generals, was accorded a special remembrance of the occasion when an officer later presented her with a package as she was alighting from the train. "Upon opening it," she shared forty-nine years later, "I found one of the silver stars which had been among the decorations in the car."[21]

At the same time the mourners were eating, the *Edwin Jones* was also having its own voracious appetite met. For along with regularly providing meals for itinerant guests, St. Johnsville was also a refueling stop for locomotives. With the current location only sixty-five miles west of Albany, a sense is afforded of how quickly the onboard supplies of water and wood were depleted. A man named Anson Brown, who was familiar with the services available at this stop, offered his recollection of the extensive nature of the logistical support the town provided when he said: "I remember when the New York Central locomotives burned wood and part of the ground on which the present village of St. Johnsville is situated was covered with wood eight feet deep to refuel the wood burners."[22]

In what must have seemed but a heartbeat, the respite ended. As the train left the station, in its wake was a sad, familiar scene. For, "here as at other places along the route, an immense crowd had gathered to evince, by their presence, the deep sorrow which pervaded every heart."[23]

As twilight descended over the valley, the train maintained its slow but steady speed. For the rest of their passage to Buffalo, the travelers who remained awake had the opportunity to experience an unprecedented sight—the earnest and touching expressions of the peoples' grief. In what appeared as a continuous band of mourners, folks whose presence would have gone unobserved but for the surreal illumination from flickering flames had positioned themselves at random intervals along the tracks. "Bonfires and torchlights illuminated the [rail]road the entire distance," wrote John Carroll Power, "[and] minute guns were fired at so many points that it seemed almost continuous."[24]

Also rising in the cool night air were requiems offered by choral groups and dirges by brass bands, all adding to extraordinary nature of this unprecedented tribute. Not since the Revolution had so many flames and cannon shots disturbed the countryside. In describing the effect of the seemingly endless nature of these displays, Power surmised what passengers were thinking as they gazed at the passing vignettes: "Thus through the long hours of the night did the funeral cortège receive such honors that it seemed more like the march of a mighty conqueror, than respect to the remains of one of the most humble of the sons of earth."[25]

Ten miles farther west, the train reached Little Falls, a place that had wholeheartedly welcomed the president-elect in 1861. In what may have been due them for that warm reception, the villagers were accorded the honor of a brief, unscheduled five-minute stop. With the sound of bells, cannons, and drums reverberating off the narrowed valley walls, the grieving citizens maintained their silent vigil in front of the station and along the tracks. In a creative but unorthodox approach to providing some illumination, idle locomotives in the rail yard had been positioned to project beams from their headlights onto the ground by the depot. The few minutes that the funeral train remained stationary allowed for the placement of a striking wreath created by a group of local women. "These flowers were most neatly woven into the form of a shield, a cross, and a wreath," an admirer of their work commented, "and to say that they were most beautiful is to give but faint expression to the fine perfection these designs."[26]

Bearing their home-crafted floral design, eight ladies, accompanied by several gentle-

Inside the appropriately decorated *United States*, an honor guard accompanied Lincoln's remains throughout the entire journey (*Frank Leslie's Illustrated Newspaper*)

men, were allowed access to the hearse car, so they could place their tribute directly on the president's coffin. Included with the arrangement was an inscription that read: "The ladies of Little Falls, through their committee, present these flowers. The shield, as an emblem of protection which our beloved President has ever proved to the liberties of the American people. The cross, of his ever-faithful trust in God; and the wreath as a token that we might mingle our tears with those of our afflicted nation."[27]

Having accomplished their goal, the party was allowed a few moments of personal reflection. The silence pervading the car was broken only by the muffled sobs of the grieving women. The men, trying to maintain their masculine composure, could not hold back the tears that rolled down their cheeks.

Leaving Little Falls at 7:20 p.m., the train's passage through the Valley took it to Herkimer, a scant seven miles to the west. Once again, the schedule had called for a run straight through to Utica. But, like Little Falls, Herkimer too had its advocates. Some of these gentlemen used their political clout to wheedle a brief stop by the train. Handbills were posted around town publicizing the event, and an invitation was extended to residents in the nearby village of Mohawk.

On Tuesday afternoon, a two o'clock meeting was held with interested parties at the county courthouse, where plans were agreed upon for Herkimer's tribute. These arrangements consisted of two main features: "buildings in proximity to the depot should be appropriately draped in black; and that thirty-six ladies, representing the States of the Union and dressed in mourning, should present themselves at the depot while the remains were passing through the village."[28]

The design selected for their attire turned out to be quite striking in appearance. The ladies would be clothed in white dresses, crossed with black sashes affixed with a white rosette, and a breastpin made of a cedar sprig; the whole ensemble was topped off with a wreath of evergreens, trimmed with white roses, worn as headgear and a Union flag bordered in black carried in one hand. Alternating between the women were gentlemen, all clad in black suits and grasping American flags trimmed in mourning cloth.

When the neighboring contingent arrived with a band in tow, the musicians were assigned a prime location on the balcony of the Maine & Sanders Hotel, an establishment facing the tracks from a set-back location. Along with the unusual sound of nocturnal church bells and minute guns, the night was alive with sights not normally present on a spring evening. Firemen, for example, were lined up on the north side of the railroad's right of way, perpendicular to the hotel and creating a hollow square with another line on the opposite side. Once the train halted, crowds on both sides of the tracks tended to gravitate toward the hearse car, easily identifiable in the torch-lit night by the American eagle on each side.

To forestall a crush of spectators wishing a closer view of this singular coach, an announcement was made, informing everyone of what constituted their best chance of seeing the desired car. "The body of our departed friend is in the second car from the rear," Colonel Byron Laflin—former commander of the 34th New York Infantry—assured the crowd from the platform of one of the coaches, "and if the citizens will retain their present positions they will be able to see the car when the train again moves."[29] Then, at 7:05 p.m., the engine started slowly forward. The cars lurched slightly as each was taken under tow. Five minutes on the clock had elapsed quickly, but left an indelible memory vastly disproportionate in value to the time invested.

The train had barely achieved a head of steam when the Ilion depot loomed up, three miles ahead. Another small oasis of flickering light framed by the surrounding darkness was the telltale sign of mourners ahead. Another blaze of light off on the train's left across the Mohawk River, perhaps a half-mile to the south and on the near northeastern edge of the village, pinpointed the location of the Remington Arms Company. In its own tribute to President Lincoln, the factory complex was completely illuminated. Though he had never been any closer to the plant than these tracks in 1861, he would have been familiar with brand name if not the town too, for thousands of weapons were shipped from here to supply the army's needs. Stamped on every weapon was the distinctive label "E. Remington & Sons, Ilion, NY."

When the building craze began in New York State during the early to-mid 1800s, many railroad lines were constructed along the north side of the Mohawk River. By Lincoln's time, the smaller operations had been consolidated into the New York Central; however, due to its location, the main trunk was a half-mile from downtown Ilion. In time, a station was built in an area referenced by locals as North Ilion. Though a few houses were eventually built in proximity to the station, there was not a lot of room for growth. From the north bank of the river, which flowed west-to-east as a tributary of the Hudson, a narrow strip of land separated the waterway from the Mohawk Turnpike. A depot was built on this intervening piece of ground.

After crossing the tracks, a thin band of grass separated the New York Central from the highway. Once across this road, the terrain started upwards almost immediately to form the north wall of the Mohawk Valley. It was here that a few residences sprang up on the gentle upslope to the east and west.

What all this geography meant to the residents of Ilion was that they would have to leave town and make their way over the river to pay their respects. This was one of the a few such gaps that existed along the route from New York City to Buffalo, wherein the town was noticeably separated from the railroad and its local depot. In due time, communities on the river's south side would have the West Shore line built through them, but, for the present, being in a reasonable proximity to the New York Central was their only option for rail service.

To publicize the community's plan to pay respects, handbills went up around town. Residents were invited to meet at the Osgood Hotel at 7:00 in the evening of April 26. This announcement was the second one in a week's time that conveyed information related to the President's passing. The first document, issued by order of the village trustees April 18, informed the citizenry of the community that "whereas on Wednesday, the 19th day April instant, the funeral obsequies of our late lamented and beloved President, are to be celebrated with becoming ceremonies."[30] The circular went on to request that all businesses be closed, flags flown at half-staff, and homes and places of business be decorated with some type of mourning emblem.

At twelve noon the following day, a religious service would be held in the hall at Osgood's. This particular celebration was a part of nationwide observances in honor of the late president. Cities and towns across the North would be collectively, but separately, holding similar commemorations. On that same day, the official funeral service would be conducted at the White House in Washington. As of that moment, the route of the funeral train had still not yet been finalized, so Ilionites were not yet aware of the impending opportunity with which they and fellow New Yorkers would be afforded to pay their respects in a more direct way.

However, on the 26 of April they did know. Newspapers had been publishing the train's schedule for several days now. A second important handbill on April 25 had urged townspeople to take part in the trackside vigil. This was the impetus that brought them to the mid-town gathering point of Osgood's Hotel, from which mourners were to march the half-mile to the depot and await the passing of the funeral train. Since the hotel was at the corner of Main and Otsego Street, the mourners had to walk a half-block west on Main to its intersection with Railroad Street, turn right, cross a lift bridge over the Erie Canal, and head north down Railroad Street (now Central Avenue).

Eventually the impromptu parade crossed another bridge, a much larger one this time spanning the Mohawk River. From its northern portal, the Central's main line lay seventy-five feet ahead, while across the tracks to the right was the North Ilion depot.

Since night had fallen before the mourners had departed on their walk, a number of the marchers carried lanterns or held firebrands to light the way. Had he been able to witness this nocturnal procession—in effect a torchlight parade—the observation of this popular phenomenon of the times would have brought back warm memories to Abraham Lincoln. During his campaign, a popular strategy of his supporters was an evening march through the streets of a town. To light the way and garner attention, torches were carried— many being specially made and emblazoned with an appropriate campaign-related slogan such as "Hurrah for Lincoln" etched on the oil receptacle; sometimes the marchers sang patriotic songs and shouted out praise on behalf of the aspirant for office—all of which made for an impressive, eye-catching sound and light spectacle.

One of the most memorable of these nocturnal events occurred in Chicago, when in

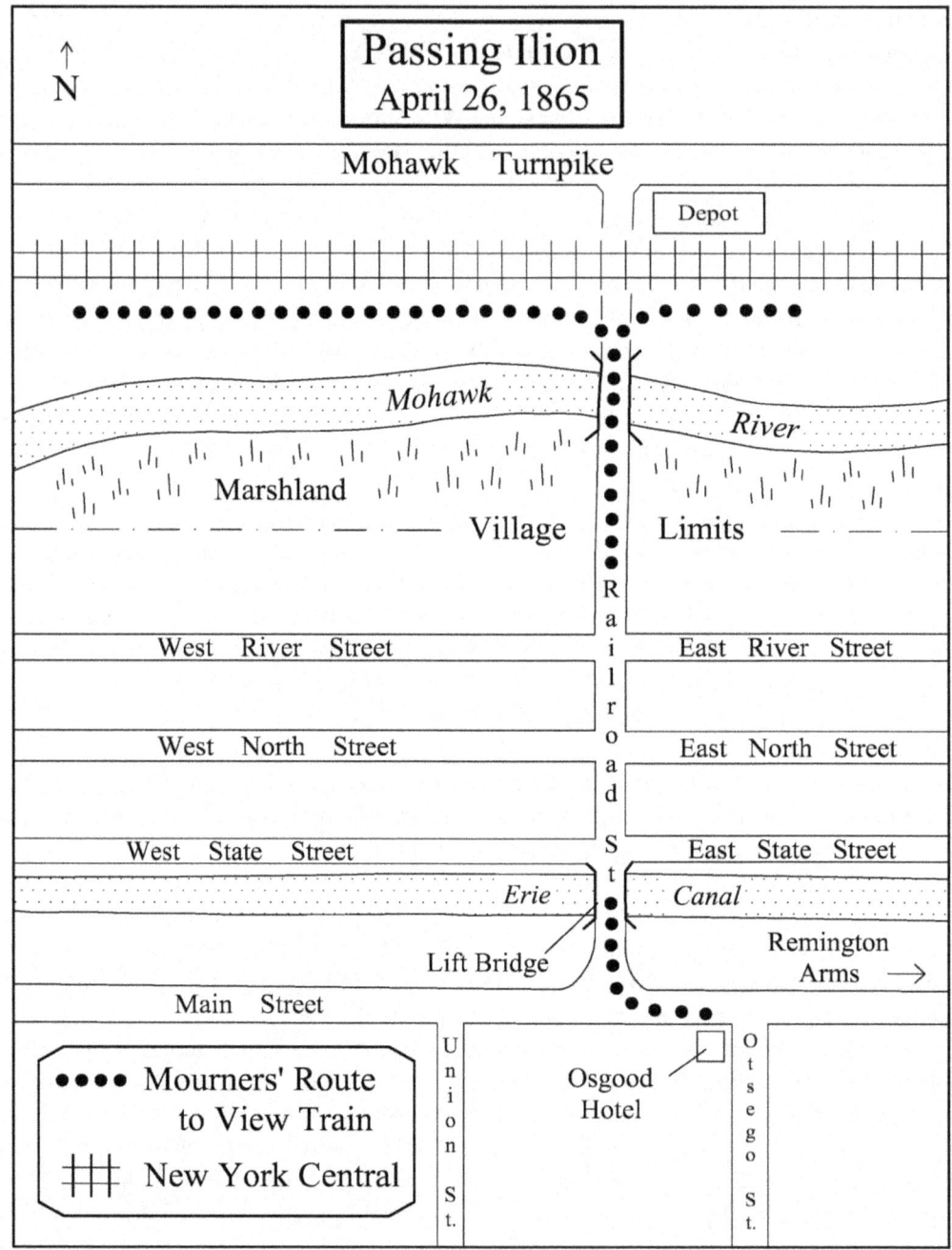

Drawn by Bob Collea.

October of 1860 over 10,000 of Lincoln's supporters lit up hundreds of torches for a spectacular evening rally through the city's streets. The whole experience was one of exuberance and joy, but those were different times. There would be no such revelry tonight.

  The mourners moved slowly down the slight incline of Railroad Street. After crossing the bridge, they fanned out along the tracks. The train was due at 7:56 p.m. After the pilot engine passed, hopeful glances were cast eastward. The dimmed headlight of the train, though shrouded in black cloth, would still cast a faint glow against the otherwise inky blackness. Since Herkimer lay a bit to the northeast behind a protruding hill, the oncoming express had to swing around a curve in a gentle southwesterly to westerly arc that kept it from view until it was about twenty-five hundred feet from the Ilion depot. Then the rails entered a straight stretch which took them past the Ilion depot.

Finally, the long-awaited moment came ... and, in reality, a few moments is all it was. The flickering glow from their torches and lanterns permitted the mourners to distinguish each unit of the passing express. The *Edwin Jones*, its tender, a baggage car, and six cars rolled slowly past. Then the onlookers were rewarded for their patience, for they finally beheld that which they had come to witness—the tenth one in line ... the coach with the distinctive eagle emblem. Their eyes followed the hearse car's passage until it was swallowed up first by darkness and then eternity.

Viewed from the train, hundreds of mourners were visible; their features were alternately shrouded in shadow one second and exposed by the dancing lights they carried in the next instant. The tears staining many cheeks glistened in the artificial lighting. Most folks were standing with bowed heads, while some knelt to pray. Men respectfully doffed their hats. Women folded their hands in supplication, occasionally dabbing their eyes with handkerchiefs. Here and there a sobbing individual was consoled by the understanding embrace of a friend or relative. A small contingent of boys, dressed in Zouave uniforms, stood at attention. Looking smart and cute, they called to mind for some—in the crowd and on the train—Lincoln's friend, the late Elmer Ellsworth. Four years in his grave by now, he was on the inaugural train when it passed this spot in 1861. Intended to honor President Lincoln, the presence of the colorfully uniformed children was actually a tribute to both men, one which each would have appreciated and approved of on behalf of the other.

Over in a matter of seconds, the scene at Ilion was not unique. If anything, it was a repetition. For those riding the train, it blended in seamlessly with those tributes that preceded it and those that would follow. When taken in the context of all the others, both large and small and official and unofficial, it fit into a mosaic of what was one of the greatest outpourings of public and personal grief that the nation would ever experience.

Chauncey Depew, secretary of state for New York and one of Governor Fenton's delegates on the train, took note of this trend in his summation of the incredible journey. "Wherever the highway crossed the railway track," he recalled, "the whole population of the neighborhood was assembled on the highway and in the fields…. As we would reach a crossing, there would sometimes be hundreds and at others thousands of men, women, and children on their knees, praying and singing hymns. This continuous service of prayer and song and supplication lasted over the three hundred miles between Albany and Buffalo."[31]

In passing Ilion's observance, the funeral train had only progressed seventy-two miles from Albany. Ten more and the Mohawk Valley would level out into the flatlands of western New York. The terrain would change, but the hearts of the people would still beat in unison with their eastern brethren. Though the tributes in the upcoming urban areas would reach grander scales, the same sincerity and sorrow underpinned their intentions. As his way of complimenting the valley residents on their many heartfelt demonstrations of sorrow, a reporter for the *New York Tribune* wrote that "a funeral in each house in central New York would have hardly added [greater] solemnity to the day."[32]

19

From Utica to Syracuse
Places Large and Small Pay Homage

The cortège reached Utica at 8:20 p.m. While by no means an ungodly hour, still not one that would normally find many people out and about on a Thursday evening. But, since this night was of extraordinary import, customary social dynamics were temporarily displaced.

Primarily intended as a refueling stop and engine change, a twenty-minute layover was scheduled for the train. Yet, regardless of its brevity, the break still provided a window of opportunity for Uticans to offer a farewell tribute. When president-elect Lincoln had previously visited Utica, snow had been falling. But even with the cold temperature and a north wind chilling the crowd that February day, the presence of dancing flakes and rosy cheeks added a merry touch to the already festive gathering. A cascade of pristine snow can do that, possessing an inherently magical way of uplifting spirits in young and old alike.

In contrast … and some would say appropriately so … a light rain had now begun falling as the Lincoln Special arrived. Umbrellas hovered over the heads of the mourners. People, who already had tears streaming down their cheeks, probably welcomed the gentle mist, for it seemed as if the heavens sympathized with their pain and shared their distress.

But, then, by 1865, a grieving family somewhere in the city was a common occurrence, for the reality of war had frequently touched Uticans. Passing someone dressed in mourning clothes on the street was not unusual. With a number of companies from the city off to war, the potential for local boys becoming casualties remained an ever-present thought, weighing on the minds of many on the home front as they went about their daily lives. By 1865, some of troops were home already, the results of honorable discharges due to a severe wound or the end of an enlistment term. The rest would be returning soon, now that the war was over. Yet, even amidst the joyful prospect of families once again reunited, many would forever carry an abiding sorrow in their hearts, since not all who had gone off to war would be homeward bound.

Thirty-seven-year-old George Bingham was an example of one such local man. A captain in the 117th Infantry, he had survived the vicissitudes of war until May 19, 1864, when he was shot in the hip at Drewey's Bluff in Virginia. His final moments were recounted in a local paper. The article told how, as his regiment was forced to retreat and leave him mortally wounded on the battlefield, the dying officer waved his hat and shouted: "Go on boys and give it to them! I am hit, but not conquered."[1] The paper then saluted the soldier's courage with its own brief epitaph: "Such souls are never conquered. They fight on, even if the body dies."² It further noted that "the death of Capt. George W. Bingham of the 117th New York Volunteers ... adds one more in a long list of names to be inscribed on our country's roll of honor ... [an officer who] was beloved by his men, trusted and respected by his superior officers, and particularly esteemed in his native town."³

In a letter to the editor, a soldier at the front addressed the implications of this officer's

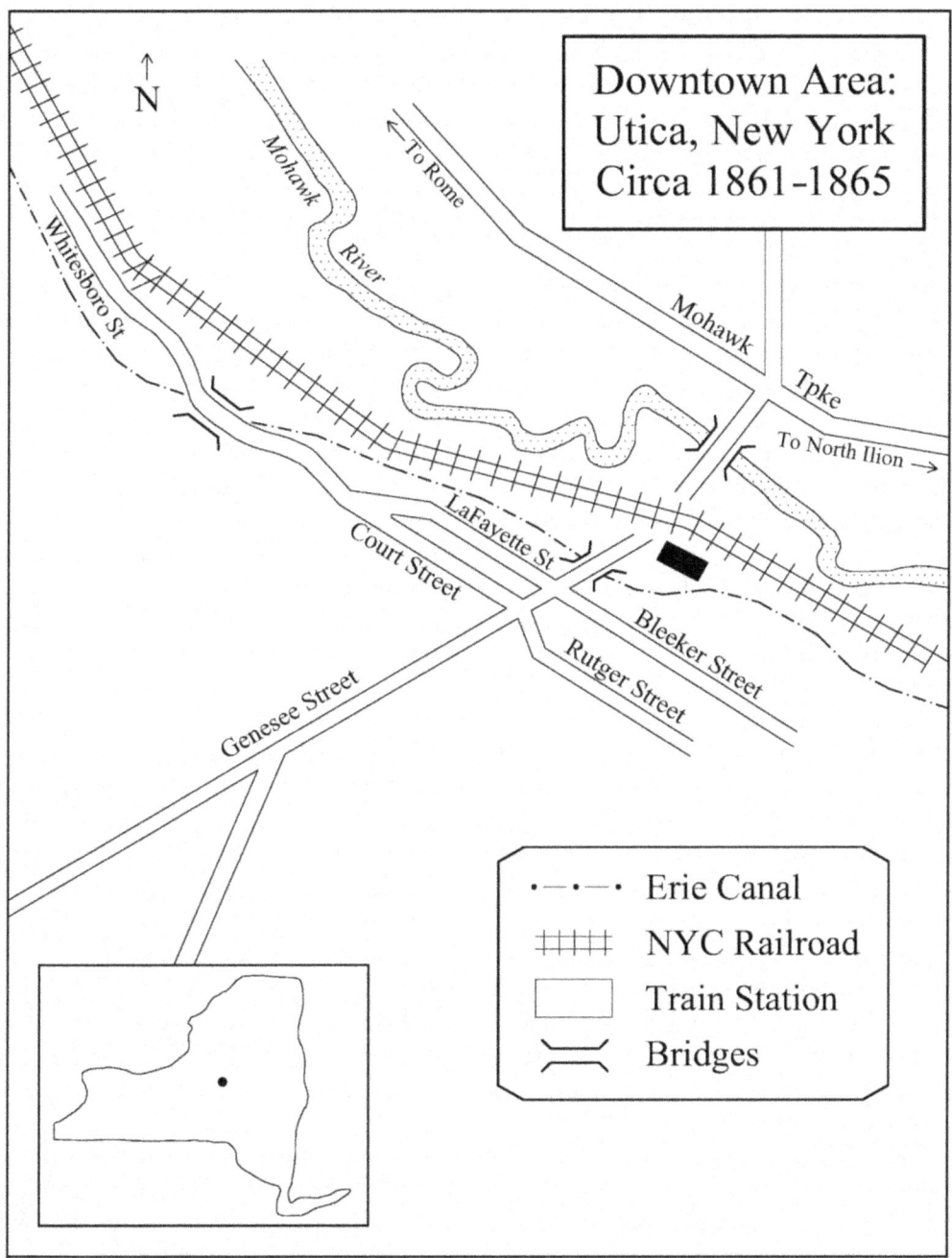

Drawn by Bob Collea.

passing, sharing his belief that "Company A sustained an almost irreparable loss in Captain Bingham."[4] But, after the surrender at Appomattox, the expectation was that such war-related deaths would cease. People almost immediately began to let their guard down, which is why the assassination of the president caught them by surprise.

So, in the wake of this tragedy, a host of mourners was now gathered at the station. For some, this experience was laden with a haunting déjà vu element, for they had been there before to receive the remains of a fallen soldier. Sometimes the deceased hero was youthful lad, with a full life lying before him that would go unfulfilled, brought home over these same tracks to this very location. On this night their past sorrows, never gone but only softened by time, were rekindled and mingled with their current distress. The tears that issued forth did double-duty. One fell for their personal loss, then one for the nation's ... one for their son or husband, one for "Father Abraham" ... one for a boy who died too young, one for a great man taken in his prime. Keeping a stiff upper lip under these circumstances was nigh impossible.

Then, on schedule, the pilot engine had made its appearance, putting the gathering of bereaved countrymen on notice that the funeral train bearing their late president was about to arrive, and, for a few moments at least, providing a welcome distraction from the melancholy thoughts occupying their minds.

The wait for many, especially the number of those arriving early, must have seemed interminable. Yet, as packed as the area around the station became, more people kept arriving. In the hour leading up to this moment, a steady stream of mourners were observed making their way down Genesee Street, the city's main north-south thoroughfare. Undeterred by the precipitation, the mourners took up positions along both sides of the tracks, on the depot grounds, and even spilled back into the adjacent Baggs' Square, an open area ringed with businesses into which Genesee Street emptied prior to reaching the station. While no means existed to take an accurate head count, one estimate claimed that "at least twenty-five thousand were gathered here."[5]

Even if that assessment erred on the high side, the number present appeared substantially greater than those who had gathered for the inaugural stop. Clearly the difference represented the outcome of events as they had unfolded over the last four years. From a previous greeting for an untried and untested president-elect—hallmarked by respect, hope, and curiosity—the reception this was time was for a beloved, revered leader whom they now mourned as the late, lamented savior of the nation. People commandeered every possible vantage point.

For those unable to gain a desirable trackside spot to their liking, they still made do by "occupying every housetop, stationary car [railroad], and roof which offered a chance to view the cortège."[6] Everyone knew that there would be no chance to see the president's remains, but, as one who was present expressed the prevailing feeling, "we all realized the great satisfaction of having seen the train and the car which contained the body of our idolized chief."[7]

Somewhere among the throng of mourners may have been David Wager, Esq., as the depot was only a short walk from his home on Whitesboro Street, a few blocks south of Baggs' Square. What would have motivated the Utica attorney to pay his respects was not a kinship borne out of their common calling. Nor had Wager ever met the president, but his nephew Major General Henry Halleck had and then some. For Henry Halleck, graduate of Union College in Schenectady and then West Point, had been named by Lincoln as "general-in-chief of all Union armies during the early years of the Civil War ... and was one of Lincoln's military advisors throughout the war."[8]

As a boy and one of thirteen children, "the youngster did not enjoy farming, so he was sent to live with his Uncle David in Utica."[9] General Halleck, who had paid his personal respects at the White House funeral on April 19, would be back in Utica come August for a brief visit with his relatives, passing through on his way to California to assume command of Union Army's Division of the Pacific.

If he was one of those amidst the waiting multitude, the elderly gentleman that David Wager was by now need not have worried about his physical well-being. Very much like the behavior exhibited all along the route, the crowd conducted itself with admirable decorum, one in keeping with the solemn nature of the proceedings. Though with such an unusual event as this, authorities were initially not quite sure what to expect, and so they prepared accordingly. To guard against any unwanted outbursts, a contingent of infantry had been ordered out. This took the form of troops from Companies E and I of the 45th New York State National Guard. With fixed bayonets, these veteran troops were drawn up and spaced at set intervals a few feet back from the tracks, providing an element of safety for the crowd from the oncoming train, as well as dissuading any impulsive surge toward the hearse car. However, as it turned out, the military's very presence was sufficient, for

"Old Saratoga," one of the very few relics associated with the passage of the funeral train, faces north about a mile south of the rail bed upon which the Lincoln Special slowly traveled through Utica (courtesy New York State Division of Military and Naval Affairs).

"the temper of the crowd was not of that character which demanded anything more than this mere formality."[10] As interpreted by a local reporter, "each one certainly realized that the body of their late beloved Chief Magistrate was for a time entrusted to their care, and that thought was sufficient to drive from each breast anything like frivolousness or disorder."[11]

While many similarities would exist among the planned tributes offered along the route to Springfield, a decidedly unique stamp was frequently included. For Utica, as the cortège reached the outskirts of the city, a cannon known appropriately as "Old Saratoga"— for the field piece was allegedly taken from the British at the pivotal battle for which it was named—had the distinction of announcing its sighting to those waiting at the station. After this loud overture, now familiar sounds to the onboard mourners began to resonate through the night air. To the accompaniment of church bells, minute guns, and various dirges, the train ground slowly to a halt. Unlike some previous sites, where the casket was removed each time for two processions sandwiched around a period of public viewing, observances at the much shorter stops like Little Falls usually amounted to presentations of wreaths and flowers in various manners. For the little places that dotted the route such as Ilion, the train's passage was met with silence, stares, and supplications.

At Utica, the tribute fell somewhere between those offered by Little Falls and Ilion. While contemporary accounts do not mention the laying of any floral arrangements on the coffin, this makes sense because no one seems to have been allowed access to the hearse car. According to one published report, "a request was here made that the body be exposed to public view, but Gen. Dix was forced to refuse."[12] What Uticans did offer that was distinctively their own were various renditions by two musical groups. On the instrumental side was the Utica Brass Band. Perched precariously overlooking the scene on the wet roof of a nearby boxcar, the bandsmen played dirges such as the "Dead March From Saul," a well-known selection which later was one of the pieces performed at the burial services in Springfield on May 4.[13]

From the throats of a choral group, known as the Mendelssohn Club, came forth other appropriately doleful airs. Named in honor of the well-known composer Felix Mendelssohn who wrote many selections intended for choral singing, the fledgling group's performance was impressive, with "the chant of a hundred voices hymning several songs ... poured upon the car. It was like the passage from one of the grand Operas, in which the intoning voices and dynamic march of the full chorus, alternate with simpler tableaus and sweeter plaints of song."[14]

Once the train had come to a halt, several prominent Uticans were observed stepping down onto the station's platform. Among those in this group of local dignitaries who had traveled from Utica to Albany, accompanying the president's remains through the valley as a show of respect were "Mayor John Butterfield, Horatio Seymour, Roscoe Conkling, and Francis Kernan."[15] An impressive, influential group, this foursome not only contained a local official and founder of a stage line in Butterfield, but also a trio of powerful political potentates in former governor of New York and future presidential candidate Seymour, an eventual United States congressman in Kernan, and in Conkling a past member of the House of Representatives, currently a United States senator, and a man who would one day turn down an appointment to the Supreme Court.

Along with a sea of forlorn faces, those peering out coach windows would have observed mourning drapery at and about the station. One who saw these decorations felt that they were the antithesis of being ostentatious, owing he surmised because those "who had to do with its management cared less for undue display than to reflect by some simple demonstration the general gloom."[16]

Using the customary combinations of black cloth, white rosettes, alternating festoons of black then white, and black-bordered American flags—known as the insignia of mourning—not only the depot but other nearby buildings were all done up in various patterns. Appropriately, all flags on buildings flew at a half-staff. Given the late hour and the enveloping darkness, that so much could be discerned in the area around the terminal at first seems surprising; however, in reality, the immediate vicinity was extremely well-lit, because foresighted planners made sure that "the depot, outside and inside, was well supplied with locomotive and other lamps, rendering it sufficiently light for objects to be discernable at a considerable distance."[17]

While the mourners were focused on the hearse car, up at the head of the train an exchange of engines took place. Since Utica marked the end of the New York Central's administrative division extending west from Albany, this stop represented a break-point in services. For the journey from Utica to Syracuse through what amounted to the Middle Division, a new locomotive would do the honors. Having just participated in the historic run up through the Mohawk Valley, the *Edwin T. Jones* relinquished its place of honor to another machine, the *Major Priest* with Isaac Vroman at the throttle. Not lost on those with better memories, it was recalled that the *Major Priest* was the very iron horse that had brought President-elect Lincoln from Syracuse to Utica in 1861. At the same time, the pilot engine, *Chauncey Vibbard*, was also replaced by a fresh locomotive known only as *No. 4*, with Thomas Harritt as its engineer. In keeping with their forlorn missions, both engines were tastefully decorated with a picture of the late president on the front face of the boiler and flags, festoons, and crepe placed along the sides.

When the pilot engine left at 8:35 p.m., half of the interlude in Utica had ended. The next ten minutes passed altogether too quickly. Soon the station clock registered 8:45 p.m. Yet, even as the *Major Priest's* whistle sounded, signaling its imminent departure, the crowd was still growing. Then, even after the new engine with its special payload in tow had gone, spectators stood watching until the last vestige of the Lincoln Special was swallowed up by the darkness. "Thus Utica has received and honored and sped upon its way the funeral cortège which now hastens to the former house of the late president in the west," a resident reflected on the train's passage through the city. "We received it sadly, tenderly, and turned away from the spectacle only when our eyes could no longer distinguish it in the distance."[18]

The next large city to receive the Lincoln Special lay fifty-four miles beyond Utica. The expectation was that the train would reach Syracuse at 11:05 p.m. Its upcoming passage through western New York between Utica and Buffalo in many ways mirrored the one just completed from Albany, for the way was dotted with many small communities and a limited number of stops scheduled. However, noticeable differences, did exist: the terrain flattened out significantly upon exiting the Mohawk Valley, making the trek less of a strain on the engine; the remaining part of the trip would be made at night; and, in the last three-quarters of the journey, three large communities would get to offer more prolonged tributes.

Throughout the remainder of the night, a steady string of salutes was observed. By virtue of the earth's daily rotation, the land was cloaked in the solitude which night brings.

Had they been snug in their homes, most of the train's inhabitants would have turned in about this time. Some of the riders were able to avail themselves of the comparative luxury that the sleeping cars offered. Exhausted by the day's experiences and the numbing weight of a terrible personal loss, sleep came as a welcomed relief.

But also among the travelers, there existed those who could not sleep. Too keyed up emotionally, they were overtired. For some, the swaying motion of the train and the constant sound of its passage over the rails acted not as soothing rhythms, but rather annoying intrusions into the customary silence of their normal nocturnal environments. Others, however, with a sense of the historic event in which they were participants, stayed awake to take in every nuance of the experience.

To those passengers who maintained an all-night watch, a consistent pattern was observable in the night's trackside vigils—all featured some form of illumination. No sooner was one conflagration passed than the glow of the next pyre was visible up ahead. For those critics who saw only monotony and repetition in this passing montage of local homages, missing was their grasp of the true meaning at the root of this endless string of fiery tableaus. In their pervasiveness, these homespun gestures demonstrated the heartfelt feelings of Lincoln's countrymen. Not one for airs or extravagance, had Lincoln ever manifested his preferences he undoubtedly would have opted for the type of low-keyed farewell more in line with the obsequies specified by Franklin Roosevelt. Though the passing of both men were devastating blows occurring at difficult times, by his dying at the hands of an assassin rather than natural causes made Lincoln's story all the more tragic and compelling. In their desire to establish that the misdeeds of one were not representative of the feelings of the many, public displays helped the people express this sentiment.

For those discerning enough to see beyond the burning torches, beacon fires, bowed heads, kneeling mourners, minute guns, church bells, and decorated buildings, these trackside vignettes could be perceived as manifestations of a collective grief, a national thank-you, a group farewell, and the peoples' love. As the *Geneva Gazette* assessed the various displays, "the funeral obsequies of ex-President Lincoln have been all that a grateful nation could bestow in honor of its lamented head, or skill and ingenuity could suggest, in the way of pageant and outward show."[19]

In 1861, a relative stranger had passed among them. After four difficult years had elapsed, that same man was now viewed as at least a dear friend, and to many, the bond was more akin to being one of a family member. Referencing him as "Father Abraham" and "Uncle Abe" was indicative of these sentiments. In the eyes of those who had been his admirers from the beginning and those who became converts along the way, Lincoln possessed a quality that stayed with him throughout his tenure of office, a trait that many leaders often purported themselves as having but their actions often belied its existence. "No public power, no public care, no public applause could spoil him, he remained ever the same plain man of the people."[20]

While the passage from Utica to Syracuse amounted to only half the distance from Albany to Utica, the level of emotion expressed by mourners along the way was no less intense. Through a dozen little rural communities and the contiguous farmlands and woodlots that connected them, the passengers on the train carried their heavy hearts past equally bereaved countrymen, people they would never meet but with whom they shared a common bond. Through the eyes of one who made the long funeral journey, these shared feelings were consistently omnipresent. Of them, he was moved to share his observation that "on the route millions of people have appeared to manifest every means their deep feeling. All classes spontaneously united in the posthumous honors. All seemed to be as one."[21]

Just outside of Utica, the Lincoln Special went through Oriskany. The little village was already famous in the lore of Revolutionary War, for a pivotal battle fought nearby that helped stopped one of the prongs of General John Burgoyne's ill-fated Three-Point Plan. But on this night, the townsfolk had turned out not make history but rather to watch it pass. While the battle lasted hours, the event for which they waited would be measurable in seconds. Blink ... and it would be missed. In tribute to their country's fallen leader, they had built a huge bonfire that served to illuminate the small station, the train, and their distraught faces.

Between Utica and Syracuse, the largest town along the route was Rome. Just seventeen miles from Utica, a brief stop was made there to top-off the always thirsty engine's water supply. Even though they had to withstand a heavy downpour, the substantial crowd which had gathered at the station was nevertheless grateful for the few extra minutes afforded them to study the train and pay their respects. In anticipation of the funeral consist at least passing through, "the depot and the Railroad house opposite were heavily draped with the weeds of sadness, and the train was received with every demonstration of grief, and sorrow and gloom."[22] As if mesmerized by the presence of the hearse car and all that it implied, the bereaved just stood silently and stared until the train was gone.

In passing through Vernon, the funeral train came within hailing distance of a small cemetery. Ever the appreciative for the service of veterans, not only the commander-in-chief but also the family man in the president would have been interested to know that the graves of three members of the Bingham family—a father who had been in the Revolution, his son a soldier in the War of 1812, and a grandson who had only recently perished in the Civil War—were buried nearby.

Fifteen minutes later, a station appeared with Oneida on its signboard. Along with New York City, Albany, and Buffalo, this little town had a unique distinction, for it was one of the very few places in the Empire State that Abraham Lincoln had spent a night. Thus "Abraham Lincoln slept here" was a proud boast which townsfolk could legitimately make. Traveling east from Illinois in a late-winter snow storm, the Madison Hotel in Oneida provided suitable accommodations at what roughly constituted the halfway point in a pre-nomination journey by Lincoln. At the time, he was an unannounced candidate, though not an altogether unknown commodity in Republican political circles.

In the *Oneida Weekly Herald* of March 6, 1860, its editor discussed the upcoming Republican Convention in Chicago, mentioning the names of Simon Cameron, William Bates, Salmon Chase, Nathaniel Banks, Abraham Lincoln, and William Seward as all being viable candidates for their party's presidential nod. "While Mr. Lincoln of Illinois is not without numerous and influential adherents" was the bare tip of the hat which the paper sparingly gave to the Midwestern politician, no lack of effusive praise was directed William Seward's way when it came to referencing him in the article: "High above all the others he stands out, the very embodiment of the Republican faith ... the Chicago Convention will do well before it dismisses the claim of William H. Seward."[23]

Such support was not surprising, for the former governor of New York and currently one of its United States senators had a substantial base of homegrown support. Furthermore,

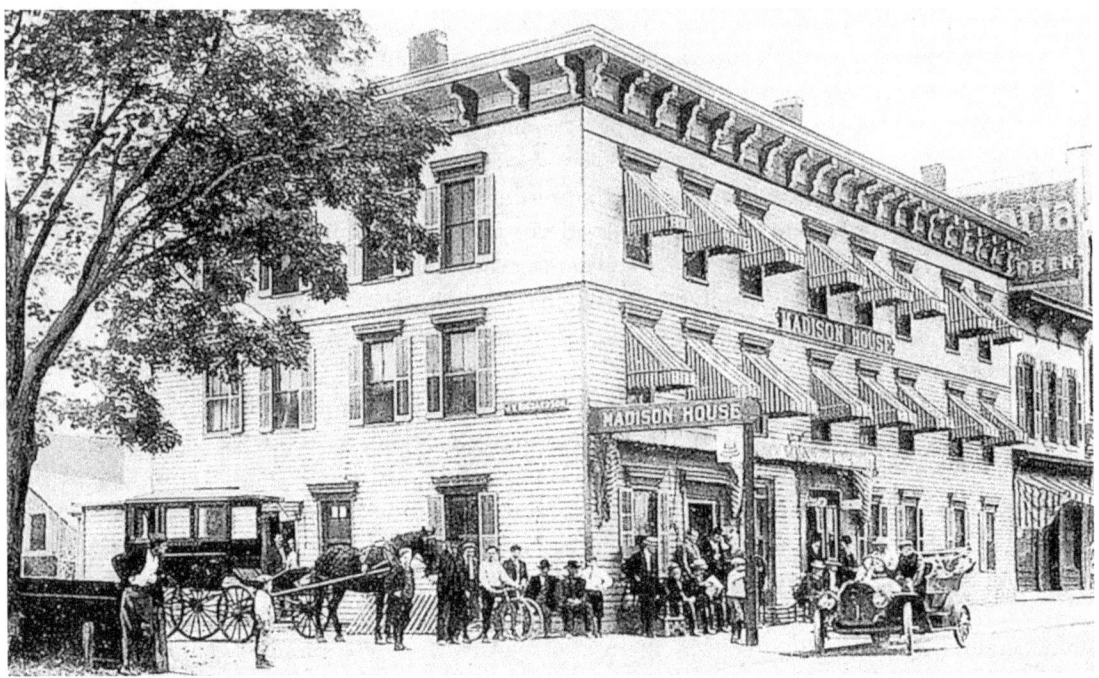

In a later time, the Madison House in Oneida, New York, still retained the small-town, cozy charm that it possessed when Abraham Lincoln stayed for a night in early 1860. From postcard, early 1900s, A.M. Wiggins, Oneida.

the fact that he hailed from Auburn, New York, which lay only fifty-five miles to the southwest of Oneida, made him virtually a homeboy. In these parts, Abraham Lincoln was an interloper in the late winter of 1860. In fact, the local papers contained no announcement of his having been in the community that day. The only tangible record for years, until purloined, was the register of the Madison Hotel, which he signed on February 25, 1860.

Now, slightly more than four years later, Lincoln would pass through Oneida for one last time. Only on this transit, the difference was crushing. Though the train stopped briefly, the president-elect would not be making an appearance and bowing to an enthusiastic crowd as he had done four years ago. No, this time only the crowd would be standing, their posture stooped in mourning and their demeanor somber and silent except for the occasional sobs. The only other sound of significance breaking the stillness of the night was the repeated boom of a solitary cannon.

According to a local boy named J.C. Mitchell, who was present in the crowd at the station, a twelve-pound piece of artillery had been dragged two miles from Durhamville south-southeast to Oneida through the mud created by the rain. Once finally in place, the once formidable weapon became a minute gun, keeping up a rate of discharge which caused young Mitchell to wonder "how the boys ever managed to fire that old gun as many times as they did in the short time the train was there."[24] Upon his arrival at the station, the lad and his friends perched themselves on a pile of railroad ties and waited in the damp night for the train. The reward for their perseverance was "an unobstructed view of the interior of the car ... the casket was draped with flags, the soldiers at each corner standing guard made a lasting impression."[25]

When the express left Oneida at 9:50 p.m., Syracuse lay thirty miles to the west. In covering that distance, the rate of speed was not constant. As the train went through any of the smaller burgs where it was not stopping, the engineer deliberately slackened the speed to twenty miles per hour ... sometimes to even as little as five ... so for the in between stretches the speed of necessity was ramped up a bit to compensate for lost time. This alternating acceleration/deceleration pattern kept the train moving along, past mourners at depots in Wampsville, Canastota, and Chittenango, as well as all the intervening rural pockets of bereaved citizens gathered beside the tracks or at vantage points on hills .and grade crossings. All were equally identifiable to the travelers by the glow from what seemed an almost continuous belt of torches and bonfires across the middle of the state.

These places—along with countless other little enclaves throughout the North—had served the Union cause to the best of their abilities. Like the Mohawk and Hudson Rivers, which could not exist without the many rivulets and streams that fed them, the manpower and foodstuffs that flowed from the rural areas of New York like Oneida, Madison and Cortland Counties eventually merged with like contributions from other parts of the state and country, collectively doing what individually none could ever accomplish alone—that of satisfying the vast supply needs of the voracious Federal war machine. The wheat, corn, and livestock, for which they were paid, represented an agreeable exchange of goods for remuneration.

But the sons, fathers, and husbands who were also sent to the battlefront represented a different type of support. Crops were a renewable resource, but each human life was a one-of-a-kind contribution. While communities proudly watched their recruits march off to fight for a righteous cause, those who were left behind waved goodbye with tears in their eyes and trepidation in their hearts. For they knew, by virtue of the law of averages, that all of them could not possibly return. When the residents of these towns came down to their local station that April night to see the funeral train and pay their respects, feeling the pain of bereavement caused by the war was not a new experience for many them.

One of the worst times had been in the days following the Battle of Gettysburg. The 157th New York Infantry, the unit in which many of their kin had enlisted, took heavy losses in the first day's combat of that bloody three-day ordeal. Then, when the casualty rolls started to appear in area papers, the worst fears of many were realized. Albert Bridge of Wampsville, Timothy Dean of Oneida, Luzerne Johnson of Canastota, and Horace Anguish of Chittenango were just four of almost a score of local boys who would not be marching home, for they were listed as killed in action on July 1, 1863. Other battles like 2nd Bull Run and 3rd Winchester also exacted their tolls, as did Southern prisons at Andersonville, Florence, and Salisbury.

For many, the death of Abraham Lincoln was another soul joining the grieving that had become an on-going experience in a time of war. Like Utica to the east and Syracuse to the west, the "Angel of Death" had also visited homes in these small towns on more than one occasion over the previous four years. All hoped that the president's passing, which brought them together on this dark rainy night, would be the last casualty spawned by the war.

20

On Toward Buffalo
Western New York Offers Parting Tributes

When the Lincoln Special finally reached the terminal in Syracuse, the time was five past eleven. Some folks had been waiting for over three hours. Owing to its urban location amidst businesses and residences lining both sides of Washington Street, space to stand was at a premium. Not only was the station and its immediate vicinity jammed with mourners, but the side streets in both directions were also filled. One estimate of the crowd's numbers suggested that "there must have been a full fifteen thousand people present."[1]

Another eyewitness' description offered that "the crowd was immense, and large delegations came in from Oswego and the surrounding towns."[2] Not only had the regular four o'clock run south from Oswego been packed, but a five-coach special left at six p.m. and brought another load of mourners to Syracuse.

Anticipating of a large turnout, the police department was out in force; however, unlike the excited crowds that greeted the inaugural train, the vigil for the funeral cortège elicited only deafening silence from the thousands now gathered. For those who turned out, the late hour was not the only inconvenience, as precipitation had been alternating in intensity. "The rain came in fits and starts," recalled one spectator, "but rain could not drive the anxious people from the desired sight."[3]

The only moments of anxiety were when the engine started down Washington Street toward the depot. The already narrow thoroughfare was choked with people, clustered in such a solid mass that even the tracks were covered. Moving at a crawl, the train slowly proceeded forward. The crowd, after parting before it, coalesced again and pressed closely in its wake. Here the policemen earned their keep that night, protecting the crowd from its carelessness.

While waiting for the cortège, onlookers had ample opportunity to note the decorative efforts expended to put the surrounding area in the proper mood. Flags with black borders were hung along the length of the depot's outside walls. In front of them, at ten-foot intervals, was added the contrasting touch of evergreen trees. Various surfaces inside and outside the station were decorated with configurations of black and white cloth. Homes and businesses in the vicinity joined in with mourning colors.

Then the long-awaited moment came. On the eastern end of town, the train was sighted as it emerged from an abbreviated tunnel, an underpass that allowed the tracks to pass beneath the Erie Canal. A signal gun was fired. Then, along with the visual tributes, were added what had become the customary aural salutes all along the route. Resounding over everyone's heads were tolling church bells and booming minute guns, while at ground level

Downtown Syracuse witnessed the slow, mournful passage of the second Lincoln Special as the train halted at the city's station for a ten-minute stopover that permitted only a limited viewing of the casket on April 26, 1865 (courtesy Onondaga Historical Society).

a band played dirges and a 100-member chorus offered hymns. Gaslights along the street and in neighboring buildings were lit, but their warm glow provided only limited illumination. In a helpful measure akin that turned the nocturnally dim square into day, "on either end outside were large lights with powerful reflectors which shed a brilliant light for a long distance up and down the railroad [tracks]."[4] Additionally, located ten feet above the ground along both sides of the station were detached locomotive headlights which "gave a fine effect to flags and decorations of mourning."[5]

While the twenty-minute layover afforded an opportunity for mourners to pay their respects, there were other very utilitarian aspects to the stop also. First, the locomotives were switched, with engine *No. 202* assuming the duty of the pilot engine with Robert Simons serving as its engineer, and *No. 248* would now haul the funeral train. Next the necessary replenishments of water and fuel were taken aboard.

Just before the train left the station, "a small bouquet was handed to the delegate from Idaho, upon which were the appropriate words: 'The last tribute of respect from Mary Virginia Raynor, a little girl of three years of age.'"[6] The note was dated April 26, 1865. These offerings were placed upon the coffin by one of the officers on the train. Then, bell tolling, the throttle on Engine *No. 248* was slowly opened by engineer John Brown.

Being at the controls on this run was a multiple source of pride for this native Syracusan and his family. For one, given the assignment's high profile, railroad officials strove to place the responsibility in the hands of their best employees—John Brown was considered one such individual. For engineer Brown, a sense of duty was very much at play; for, not only had he brought Abraham Lincoln to Syracuse in 1861, but he also had answered his president's call for troops, enlisting in the 149th New York Infantry Regiment, in the service of which he was wounded at the Battle of Peach Tree Creek. By these associations, he felt a very personal obligation to help expedite the return of his former commander in chief's remains safely home.

Once he knew that he would be making the journey to Rochester, Brown had asked his wife and mother-in-law to sew flags with which to decorate the engine. Mrs. Brown later shared how "early in the evening of the night that the funeral train passed through Syracuse she and her mother-in-law went to the engine house to see the locomotive with its decoration made possible by their handiwork," professing that "it was one of the proudest days of her life."[7]

As much as his role in transporting the late president meant to John Brown, he was not the only one present who was deeply moved by the momentous occasion. A reporter for the *Syracuse Journal* eloquently expressed what Abraham Lincoln, his death, and the train meant, not just to the people of Syracuse, but to all of those along the route when he wrote: "Last night was a night memorable to every living inhabitant of Syracuse—a night every man and woman and child who shall hereafter be a living inhabitant of Syracuse. For it linked the name of our city with the most marvelous and the most mournful pageant of history.... The route of this national procession, from the political Metropolis of the Republic to that remote Capital of the West, will forever possess a sad charm in the eyes of posterity. The cities that stood in that long and mournful line will forever glow with a melancholy brilliancy—a reflection of the lustrous fame of Abraham Lincoln, shining through the annals of time."[8]

Too soon, the moment came for the funeral train to undertake its sad journey once more. The scene from which the cortège took its leave was by now very familiar to the passengers watching from the windows. The densely packed crowd ... men with their hats off ... tears staining the cheeks of all ages ... heads turning slowly as eyes followed the hearse car until it was swallowed up in the night. A different town, another gathering of mourners, and one more earnest tribute—local in origin but national in scope ... all a part of the massive outpouring of respect grounded in a common sorrow across the North.

To underscore that these feelings existed not just in the larger urban areas, places which possessed the resources to put together a substantive memorial observance, the first tiny locale past Syracuse offered a creative tribute that stood out in its simplicity but was truly moving in its effect as any that had preceded it.

Situated along the tracks thirteen miles to the west was the next station. No stop was scheduled for the tiny hamlet of Warners. However, when he learned that the Lincoln Special would pass through at six minutes to midnight, an area farmer named Francis Nichols organized an informal display of homage to be presented as the train went past. As his daughter, Rachel Nichols, described his next action, "he sent word to all men and boys, far and near, to get an old broom, and come to his barn."[9] There each broom was wound around its bristles with stalks of flax that Mr. Nichols had grown.

Then, on the night when the train passed, all those who possessed the adapted brooms went down to the tracks passing through Warners. Standing two rods apart, they formed lines on both sides that stretched for several miles. "When the train was in the distance," Miss Nichols recalled, "they dipped the brooms in kerosene, and when lighted they made a wonderful illumination."[10] What a dramatic, unforgettable sight this long ribbon of burning beacons leaping into the dark night must have presented to passengers, participants, and onlookers. In addition to the broom-bearers, hundreds of women and children from the surrounding countryside were also present. By the flickering glow, they could see the coffin in the hearse car, its lid bedecked in flowers.

Even though the Engineer Brown slowed the train as it navigated the blazing corridor, the view of the *United States'* interior that spectators had was still at best ephemeral. But the whole scene, one projecting an almost surreal, spectral quality. Whether their viewing posts were up close or distant, the experience was that of "a memorable night, never to be forgotten during the lives of those who were there, a last memorial to a beloved President."

With justifiable filial pride, Miss Nichols shared a quote attributed to the *New York Tribune*. In a subsequent edition, the paper unknowingly praised her father's tribute by observing that "there were many demonstrations along the route of the funeral train in many cities that it passed through, but none exceeded the great illumination seen west of Syracuse, New York."[11]

Pushing irrepressibly forward, the train was next destined for Memphis, followed by Jordan. At the Memphis station, residents had gathered as the train passed at the witching hour. They stood in silence, with the only sounds audible in the damp night air emanating from the train—the tolling bell atop the engine, the hiss of steam escaping from its pistons, and the slow clacking of wheels across rail joints. Holding torches aloft and hats and handkerchiefs in hand, the assembled mourners could say that they had seen the train bearing the late president's remains.

For those onboard who had watched the entire tapestry unfold that night from Albany to Buffalo, they were in the midst of "the most remarkable portion of the whole route for its continuous and hearty demonstrations of respect."[12] For those New Yorkers who constituted the miles of mourners, the transitory sight from trackside constituted an indelible, enduring, and unsurpassed memory for a hard-working people whose existence was often confined to a limited radius and relegated to a fairly predictable cycle of birth, life, and death.

On a night that had already revealed its share of interesting tributes, yet another was about to be unveiled at the little town of Jordan, twenty-one miles beyond Syracuse. As a way of offering a distinctive tribute when the train passed through, a group of furloughed Union soldiers decided to do the honors with a cannon which they had procured locally. Having served as cannoneers in the 3rd New York Artillery, these boys could capably operate the weapon. As the train passed, the crew successfully unleashed salvo. However, no minute gun was this going to be, firing a blank round. No, this performance was going to be the genuine article—real soldiers, real ordinance, and a real ball, with the upside being that a louder report is created when a projectile is released from the barrel.

But the same procedure has a decided downside too, which in this instance amounted to a six-pound iron ball arcing off into the night. Though using live ammunition was probably ill-advised, no harm came to anyone from the discharge of the cannon. However, a living witness of a different species did absorb the full force of the heavy shot. Having

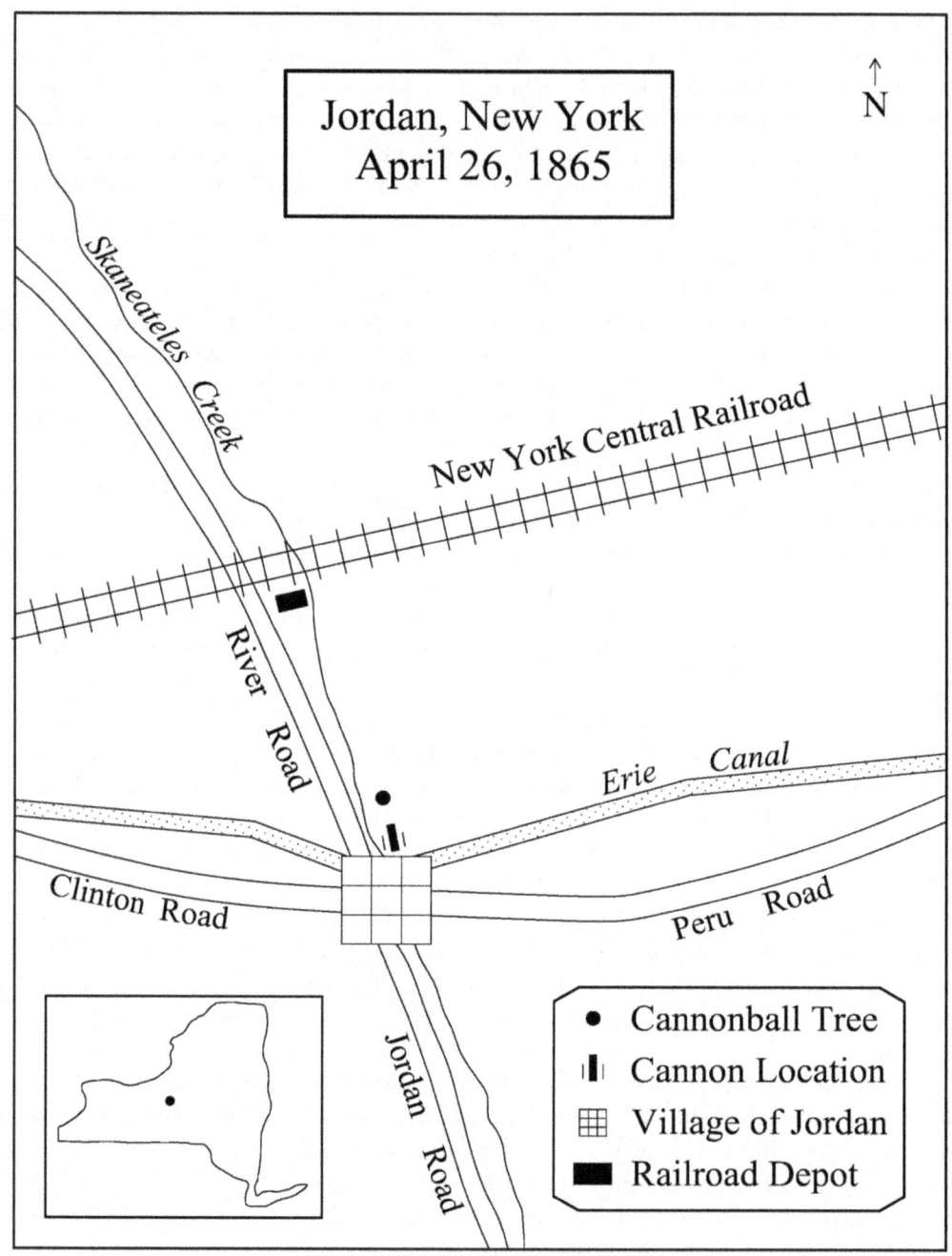

Drawn by Bob Collea.

received approval beforehand with a local farmer, Isaac Otis, to conduct the salute on his property, the cannon had apparently been sighted-in before darkness fell. When the optimum moment came and the piece was discharged, the aim of the artillerymen proved unerring, for "the ball from the cannon lodged in an elm tree on the Otis farm."[13]

Known for years after as the "cannonball tree," the story of the event became a part

With a cannonball lodged where the trunk began sprouting its branches, this stately elm in Jordan lived for many decades beyond the passing of Lincoln's funeral train (courtesy Jordan Historical Society).

of Jordan's oral history, but evidence that the episode was nothing more than local legend did not exist. Then, some six decades or so later, "when the tree had to be taken down, a piece of the tree containing the old cannon ball was saved."[14] The relic now resides in the Jordan Historical Society's Museum, providing tangible proof and a colorful anecdote of the town's link to the passing of Lincoln's funeral train.

Leaving Jordan, the express continued through a rapid succession of little communities, Weedsport and Port Byron among them. As the sameness of the inaugural passage through the core of the Empire State was identifiable as a series of crowds, cannons, and cheers, the funeral run was equally hallmarked by its own proliferation of throngs, torches, and tears.

One significant aspect in which the 1865 crowds differed from those who had gathered four years earlier was the presence of war veterans. The Weedsport area alone saw over 200 men march off to put down the rebellion. While a profound source of community pride, Weedsport did not have a monopoly on men who served in the late war. In traversing New York, it was highly unlikely that the funeral train ever passed a crowd that was not without discharged soldiers standing proud and tall.

Port Byron, like Weedsport, was located miles from any significant water body. However, both towns had picked up their "port" designations from being situated on the Erie Canal. Though neither of the two trains bearing Abraham Lincoln ever stopped in Port Byron, the community had its own unique bond linking it to our 16th president. The story began when a resident, named Amos King, was touched after he read the moving farewell speech that the president-elect gave to his neighbors, just as he was about to leave Springfield in 1861. So deeply affected was Mr. King that he sent a Bible to Washington as a present for the Mr. Lincoln.

A boatman and farmer by trade, Mr. King possessed an admirable ability to express himself in a clear, coherent writing style. This skill allowed him to inscribe a touching note on the Bible's flyleaf, where Mr. King explained his motivation for presenting the gift and concluded with the humble entreaty: "therefore the donor begs leave to present to his Excellency, Abraham Lincoln, President of the United States of America, this Bible as a small token of his high esteem and kind regard in which the giver holds the honored recipient."[15]

While he may have intended it for use in the inaugural ceremony, his offering did not arrive in time. Nevertheless, his gesture was appreciated by the president's descendants who kept the treasured volume among their household items for generations. While Abraham Lincoln no longer has any direct living relatives, the Bible still resides at Hildene, the stately summer home in Manchester, Vermont, that once belonged to Robert Lincoln.

Next in succession were Savannah, Clyde, Lyons, and Newark. At each setting, the respective depot displayed mourning drapery. The now inevitable minute cannons sounded their steady tempo, and conflagrations of differing origins fashioned pyres of dancing light, oases of illumination against the darkness that were at once eerie and yet reassuring. At these little places along the line of the New York Central, distraught Americans had stood patiently for hours in inclement weather, silently bonded by their common desire to pay a few seconds of homage to the man who was seen in a different light by each of them. To some, he was the Great Emancipator. Veterans revered him as their former commander-in-chief. There were others who thought of him as "Father Abraham," President Lincoln, "Honest Abe," or simply Mr. Lincoln. Though small as these villages were, their residents had collectively made significant sacrifices through scores of young men sent off in answer to his repeated calls for troops. Standing in the crowds at the various stations were families whose loved ones would never return, soldiers disabled for life, and veterans recently mustered.

Though not everyone at the station knew it at that time, Savannah had an unusual connection to the death of the president. For, sitting in the audience at Ford's Theater and witnessing events there was Oliver Helmer. A resident of the town, Helmer had enlisted in the 111th New York Infantry. Wounded at Gettysburg and Spotsylvania, he was recuperating at a Washington hospital, when he attended the play on April 14, 1865. Helmer observed that he and a friend who accompanied him "didn't know that that Lincoln was present and probably would have paid little attention to it if we did, since we saw him almost daily in Washington."[16] Like many other theater-goers that night, the two soldiers were at first confused by what they saw. For, as Helmer later described the scene, "when Booth shot him and leaped from the box to the stage, we thought that it was part of the show."[17]

In reaching Clyde, the express did not stop as it had in 1861. Much had happened in the town since then. Many men who had been a part of the community four years ago were off serving in the Union Army. During the war, the little town had produced its share of heroes, with the ranks of Company D of the 90th New York Infantry and the corresponding company in the 67th Infantry being initially filled with recruits from Clyde. Many were still serving, while others were home because they had been discharged. Still others, who had made the supreme sacrifice like their late president, were home for eternity.

Martin Wambsgan was typical of the early recruits, marching off with the 90th in the fall of 1861 and then reenlisting in 1864. He achieved the pinnacle of battlefield bravery when he won the Medal of Honor at the Battle of Cedar Creek, where he saved the regimental colors from the hands of the enemy. Still on duty, Private Wambsgan was unable pay his last respects to the president, but Michael Dwyer was. Wounded in the arm at the Battle of Cold Harbor, he eventually had to have the appendage amputated. This radical surgery led to an honorable discharge and a return home, his empty sleeve as his badge of honor and ever-present reminder of his service to his nation.

For some folks, just being at a train station brought painful memories flooding back. This was surely the case for Manley Stacey's family who lived five miles down the tracks in Lyons. For the Staceys, a spring day in 1862 came vividly to mind, for it was then that the railroad took their young boy off with 111th New York Infantry Regiment. Through his faithful stream of correspondence, the Stacey's were kept abreast of Manley's life as a soldier. Through it, they learned of his capture at Harper's Ferry in the Antietam Campaign, and later his graphic letters told of his being in heavy fighting at Gettysburg, an engagement in which his regiment took the second highest percentage of losses amongst Union troops over the three-day battle. Finally, in January of 1864, a train brought him back. But this time, instead of being seated in a coach, the late Manley Stacey's remains were being transported in the baggage car.

As the Lincoln Special came through Lyons in April of 1865, Sergeant Stacey lay buried in the local cemetery. Having experienced the heat of battle, he had survived its terrible maelstrom only to be accidentally shot and killed by friendly fire the day after Christmas in 1863.

Now closing in on Rochester, the train passed through Palmyra at 2:15 a.m. Even at such a late hour, people of all ages were present to witness an extraordinary moment in time. Not that Palmyra was new to significant events. For members of the Church of Jesus Christ of Latter Day Saints, the area four miles south of the town was sacred ground. On Hill Cumorah in the 1827, Joseph Smith—founder of the Mormon Church—received what would become the tenets of his sect from an angel. Palmyra, like so many communities in the Empire State had faithfully supported the president, first with its ballots in 1860 and then answered his call for troops beginning in 1861, eventually sending over 400 of its sons to fight.

The town's last connection to a living Lincoln was through the chance presence of Dr. Samuel Sabin at Ford's Theater on the night of April 14, 1865. An attendee at the play, Dr. Sabin had rushed to his stricken president's assistance, making him among the first of several medical personnel to reach the box. Immediately assessing the situation, he concluded that the wound was fatal. As he later wrote to his wife, "As soon as I saw the wound, I saw that there was no hope, and another surgeon had stated the same previously."[18] Thirteen days later, the body of the man whom he was powerless to save passed through Palmyra.

After Palmyra came Meriden, Fairport, and Brighton. Typical of the everyday people who were touched by the Civil War were the Caley and Morrill families. Thomas Caley and John Caley were siblings who had immigrated from the Isle of Mann. Thomas and his wife Mary lived in Rochester and had four children, one of whom was Francis Herschel Caley. When the war broke out, like so many other teenagers taken by the romance and glory of war, Francis wished to enlist. But being only fourteen, he needed his parents' permission. Eventually he persuaded them to grant it, and the teenager rode off to battle in the 21st New York Cavalry; however, the family's pride in giving its son to the Union cause was tempered with sorrow when "he was taken prisoner and incarcerated in the prison at Andersonville, [where] he was unable to endure the horrors and privations of that institution and died there in the year 1864."[19] The family lost a son, and, though gaining a hero in the process, the trade-off was difficult to reconcile.

At the same time, the other brother, John Caley, Sr., lived in nearby Brighton with his wife, Katherine, who eventually gave birth to fourteen children. One of the offspring was John, named for his father. For a time as a young adult, John lived with his uncle Tom in Brighton. Eventually John learned his uncle's carriage-making trade, along with the art of blacksmithing. Subsequently, he purchased his uncle's business.

Meanwhile a contemporary of the Caley brothers, living on the outskirts of Brighton, was a dairy farmer named William Morrill. Mr. Morrill had seven children, one of them being Elizabeth Ann. In time this young lady would marry John Caley, Jr., in 1878.

However, in 1865, Elizabeth was a young girl of only thirteen. In the early morning hours of April 26, the Morrill family went down to the New York Central tracks to see the Lincoln funeral train, placing them among the multitudes across New York who saw its passage in the glow of torches, lanterns, and bonfires. Indicative of the powerful impression that witnessing this historic event had, the young girl carried the vivid memory of that night with her for the remainder of her life. The union of John Caley, Jr., and Elizabeth Ann Morrill produced another seven children. One of their daughters was christened Ruth. Eventually she became the wife of Arthur Whitcraft, and together they had a daughter named Roberta.

In time Roberta married Sebastian LaChiusa and in turn a son Thomas was born to them. In a fine exemplar of an oral history strand—one-hundred fifty years later—the now sixty-three-year-old Thomas, great-grandson of the teenaged girl who saw the hearse car remembers how Ann's daughter—his grandmother Ruth—told how her mother had always spoken of having witnessed the funeral train.

While this particular story is a unique part of one family's history across four generations, it is also highly illustrative of the impact that observing the train had on Americans of that era. Every so often an epic event occurs that marks a place in time for those whose lives in some way are touched by it. The lasting effect of such powerful historical events, as a journalist for the *Mohawk Valley Democrat* assessed the passage of the Lincoln Special, was that "it was but a moment that the train tarried, but that moment will forever be remembered."[20]

Later in his life, J.C. Mitchell, the young boy in Oneida who also witnessed the passage of the funeral train, made a similar pronouncement when he said that "long years have passed, but the scene will never leave my memory."[21] Ann Morrill Caley and her descendants could attest to this same enduring power of that momentary experience.

Brighton lay only minutes from Rochester for the westbound train. Soon, the lights of the city could be seen glowing in the distance. After an elapse of eleven and a half hours and the passage of two hundred and twenty-seven miles, the cortege had traveled two-thirds of the way toward its destination at Buffalo. While by no means the end of the night's odyssey, the twenty-minute layover would permit the travelers to stretch their legs. For the patiently waiting mourners, the appearance of the train was a welcomed sight.

More germane to the estimated ten thousand Rochesterians who had forgone a night's sleep, the pause by the train afforded them a longer look at the hearse car and more time to pay their respects. As the gap between the train and the town gradually decreased, the passengers could discern the sounds emitted from minute guns emplaced on the Andrews Street Bridge and church bells across the town, as they filled the night with their measured tempos. Once the engine had come to a halt at 3:20 a.m., a contingent of troops stood at "Present Arms," and all the men in the crowd removed their hats. Newman's Band began playing a dirge, its offerings continuing for the duration of cortège's brief stay.

With the train at the station, passengers could distinguish two distinct groups of mourners. On the north side of the tracks was an eclectic array of military personnel. These units, drawn up in a line, were "the Fifty-Fourth National Guard State troops, first company of veteran reserves ... hospital soldiers ... a battery attached to the Twenty-Fifth Brigade, and the first company of the Union Blues."[22] On the south side was another mixed crowd comprised of "the Mayor with twenty-five members of the Common Council of Rochester, together with General John Williams and his staff, Major A. T. Lee, commander of the post with his corps of assistants, and General J. H. Martindale and his staff."[23] Also perceptible through the coach windows was that the depot "was draped in mourning, and inscriptions and mottoes were displayed, expressive of the sorrow of the people."[24]

After the cars of the train came to a stop, a flurry of activity commenced at the head of the column. There the pilot locomotive *Number 202* was switched out of service, with *Number 79* taking over its run. After a flawless performance, engine *No. 282* was also relieved of its duty pulling the Lincoln Special. Once again, the past and the present came together. For the *Dean Richmond*, the locomotive which was taking over the remainder of the morning's run, had previously held the honor of bringing president-elect Lincoln from Buffalo to Rochester in 1861.

In the hands of experienced crews, the exchange in motive power did not take long. While the fifteen-minute stop was more than enough time to affect the switchover, conversely for the mourners it seemed too little to say goodbye. Regardless, the clock was an

Typical in appearance to the standard locomotives of the era, the *Dean Richmond* had the honor of pulling the Lincoln Special not only on the triumphant inaugural trip but again for the mournful post-assassination run from Rochester to Buffalo (courtesy Edward L. May Memorial collection).

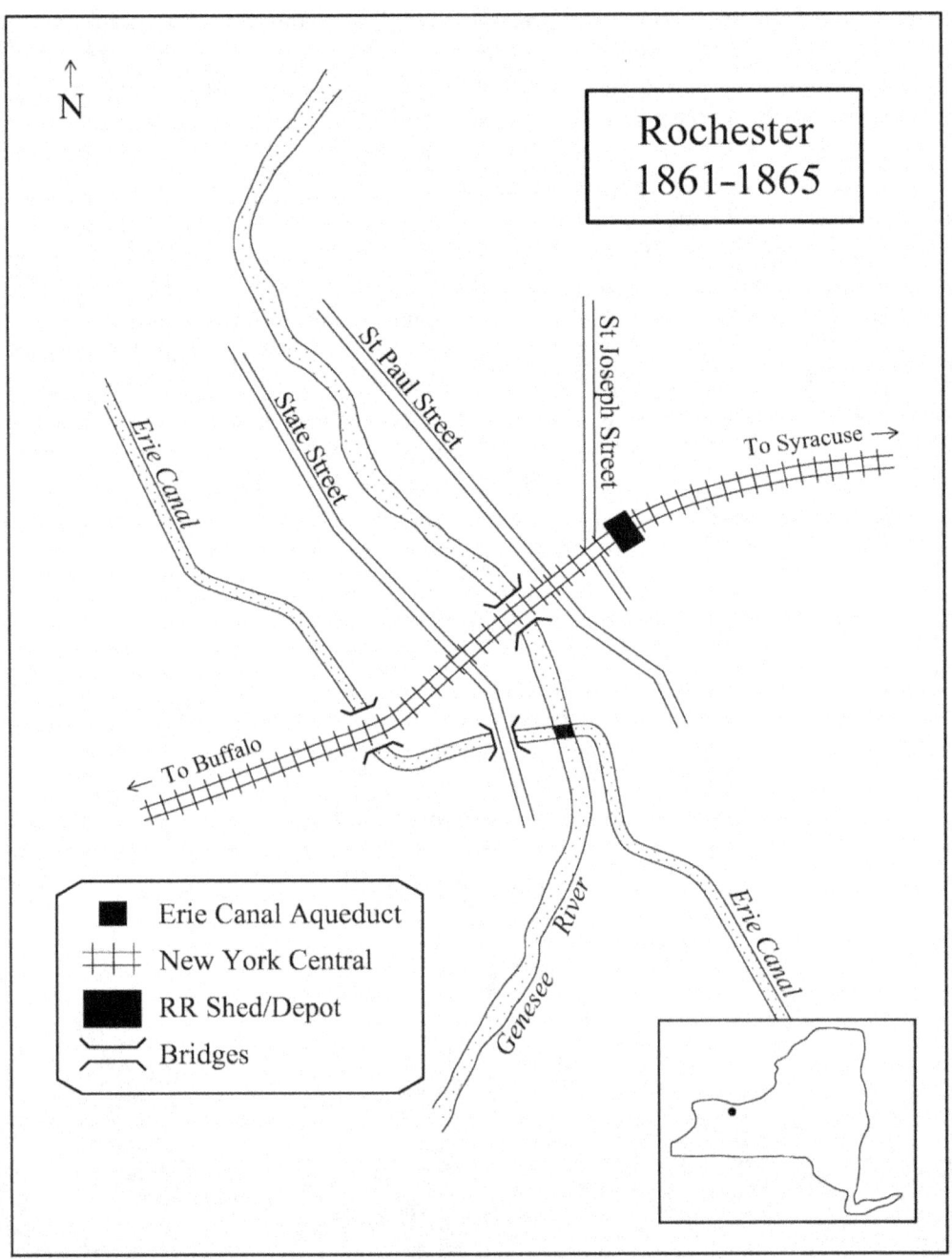

Drawn by Bob Collea.

impervious witness to such human anguish. There was a schedule to which the Lincoln Special was bound to adhere, and 3:35 a.m. was soon upon them. The pilot train, operated by James Day, had been gone for ten minutes. Now Leonard Ham, engineer for the funeral train, was bound to do the same. Slowly his express bore away the mortal remains of the Great Emancipator.

Batavia was last stop before Buffalo. At 5:18, the *Dean Richmond* came to halt for ten minutes at the village's beautifully decorated station. The terminal was in fact so nicely bedecked that those who had been riding the train and "observed the drapery on most of the depots through which the train passed, conceded that the Batavia station was more elaborately finished than any other, with the exception of Syracuse, upon which the extra work had been spent."[25]

What their eyes had beheld was a relatively small building with "the east end ... almost entirely covered by a monster American flag, trimmed with festoons of bunting and white and black crepe."[26] The front featured more festoons of black and white crepe, draped along the wall and dropping down from the projecting roof. An added touch was the wrapping of crepe around a free-standing bell and post at the out of the platform, with several festoons converging from the roof to this point.

With the depot decorated, all that was noticeably missing was an advanced turnout of mourners. For unlike what had been the common practice of residents in other towns along the late evening/early morning's run, Batavians and their neighbors from the immediate hinterlands did not gather at the depot hours ahead of time. While this was a not-to-be-missed event, a sizable number of residents went to bed the night before just as they were accustomed to doing, but they remained secure in the knowledge that the first minute gun would be fired at four a.m., thus affording everyone sufficient time to get down to the station.

Batavia was an important stop, for, in addition to taking on fuel and water to meet the *Dean Richmond's* voracious appetite, a twelve-man delegation from Buffalo was welcomed aboard. Dispatched as an honorary escort, the group was led by ex-president Millard Fillmore. In addition to the superior decorations and a distinguished mourner, Batavia's extra touch was the presence of a vocal group. Situated on a platform constructed in front of the depot, arrangements were made for a large mixed choir to offer suitable dirges.

Then, altogether too soon, it was time to go. With the engine's needs met, its whistle blew at 5:28, and its bell started its slow, rhythmic, and muffled clanging. Slowly the *Dean Richmond* gradually built up speed and left the station and the bereaved behind. After a grueling thirteen-and-a-half-hour odyssey spent riding the rails, the last lengthy stop in New York State was finally within striking distance. The cortège was scheduled to arrive in Buffalo at 7:00 a.m. Here one last parade, one final viewing, and a return procession back to the train were planned. Then, fifty miles down the tracks on the run to Cleveland, Abraham Lincoln would leave the Empire State and pass into Pennsylvania.

21

Leaving the Empire State
The Long Goodbye Is Over

The day dawned clear, as the funeral train arrived in Buffalo at seven o'clock. An immense crowd was on hand at the Exchange Street Station and spilled out into adjacent streets to greet the train. A forewarning that a substantial turnout was in the offing was in evidence as the approach through the eastern suburbs commenced, where the passing scene was described as "animated in the extreme, for nearly a mile along the road, as densely packed as it could conveniently be, and from roof tops, windows, fences and every position commanding a view of the train, might be seen faces in closest proximity."[1]

Once the *Dean Richmond* came to rest, passengers began to detrain. Many headed immediately for the nearby Bloomer's eatery, though some may have later regretted their decision to breakfast at what was viewed as little more than a greasy spoon. In one of the rare instances of negative commentary regarding any aspect of the trek, Bloomer's Dining Hall became the target of reporters' unbridled antipathy—one blasting the food served there as being "the worst cooked, worst served, and most unsatisfactory that was ever the lot of our reporter to see on the table of any establishment of this kind."[2]

While the food may have drawn some subpar ratings, the rest of Buffalo's preparations were worthy of praise and not approbation. As they progressed through the station, members of the traveling party could not help but notice the elaborate decorations that adorned the facility. The by now customary draping of black and white festoons could be observed, in this instance extending along the north wall in double rows, "while the arched windows on the outside, including those of Mr. Bloomer's Dining Saloon, were also heavily draped, miniature flags being suspended from each window."[3] Other buildings in the immediate vicinity of the station were also done up in a corresponding fashion which befitted the solemn occasion.

With the memory still lingering of the uncontrollable crush of spectators that occurred in 1861 when President Lincoln arrived at this very same station, authorities were fully prepared this time around. Even though the crowd was somber, no chances were taken that the situation might suddenly get out of hand. For not only had the Buffalo police been marshaled some three hundred in number, but also during the previous night a restraining barrier was constructed. This safeguard took the form of support posts, a number of which had been driven into the ground and joined by links of a heavy chain in front of the depot and extending some distance in both directions. Also present at the were the 54th Infantry Regiment of the New York National Guard, an artillery battalion, and the Union Blues—all of whom were not just on the scene to provide pageantry but also could be expected to back up to the police if needed.

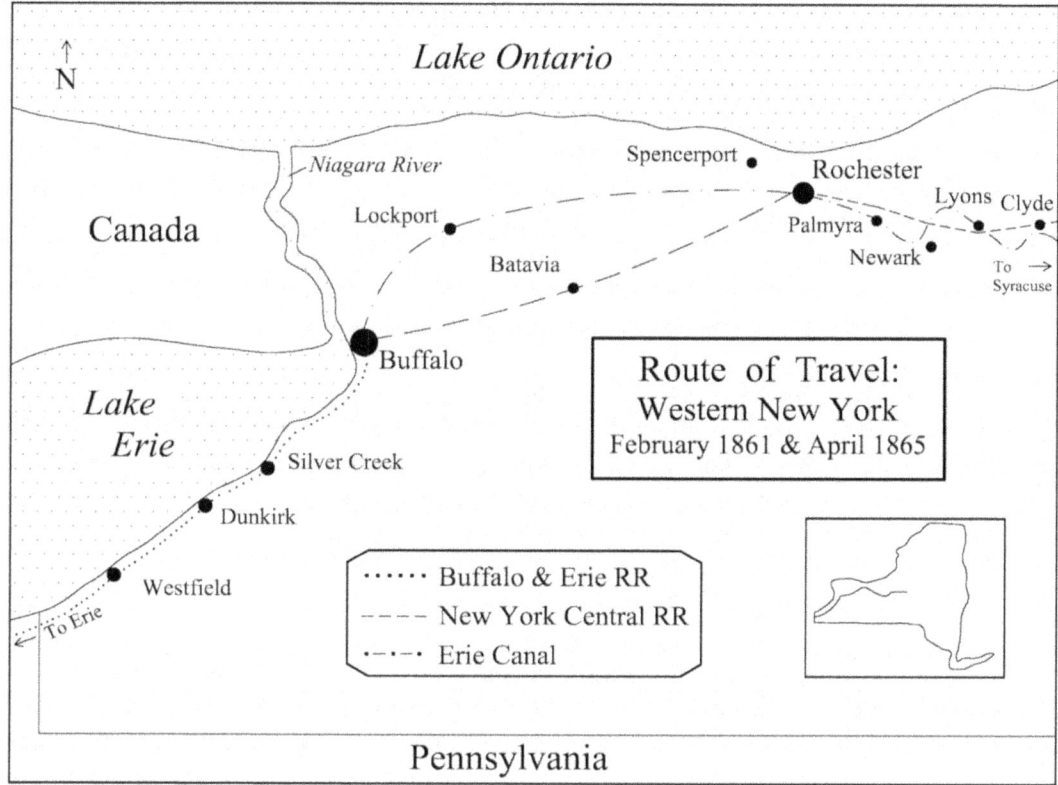

Drawn by Bob Collea.

In the end result, the spectators were well-behaved, more than likely due to the solemnity of the occasion rather than the existence of beefed-up security. Though as is often the case, the presence of a deterrent cannot always be fully measured, but, let something untoward happen, and its absence is quickly singled out as the most obvious cause of the misfortune. So, by functioning in a better safe than sorry mode, chief of police Charles Darcy took the path that insured a smooth arrival. Due kudos for his efforts were sent his way by the *Buffalo Daily Courier*, whose editor tipped his hat to the chief and his men by publicly acknowledging that their effective work at Central Station "kept the immense and almost irrepressible throng that congregated there within their proper limits."[4]

* * *

As the train was disgorging its passengers onto the station platform, 600 miles to the south a concurrent event of monumental proportions was playing out its final moments. Near Port Royal, Virginia, on a farmhouse veranda, John Wilkes Booth lay dying. Having been surrounded in what eventually became a burning barn, he was fatally shot in the neck shot after refusing to surrender. Carried to the front porch, the assassin lingered for almost an hour. Then, fifty-five minutes after being shot, he died. The time was 7:10 a.m. Just as New Yorkers had played a substantial part in the rolling obsequies for the president, so also did they play a significant part in subduing his notorious assailant. For not only was the unit that tracked him down raised in the Empire State—the 16th New York Cavalry—

but the trooper who caused the mortal wound, Sergeant Boston Corbett, was a former resident of Troy, New York.

In the time it took to move the president's remains to the viewing site, word of the successful conclusion of the manhunt was being telegraphed to the nation. Buffalo's *Daily Courier* shared its unabashed elation in a story published the next morning, one in which it proclaimed that "it was a wild and thrilling coincidence which brought the news of the death of the assassin at the very hour when the coffin of his victim was uncovered in our midst."[5] James Munro of Elbridge, New York, probably echoed the feelings of many of his countrymen when he committed to his diary that he had heard the "news of the capture and death of the assassin Booth who was shot in the capture, so he is fairly out of the way."[6]

In one of the peculiarities of the era, Booth's death caused an uptick in the sale of his likeness. They had been readily available for some time, with an advertisement in the *Rochester Daily Express* announcing that a local studio had a current stock of "10,000 Photographs of John Wilkes Booth, The assassin!!"[7] But his demise served to enhance sales. It was therefore possible for citizens to have the odd juxtaposition of daguerreotypes depicting both Lincoln and Booth in their prized parlor albums.

* * *

With the cortège scheduled to leave the city at ten o'clock that evening, time was of the essence in order to maximize the window of opportunity for public viewing. The plan in place called for the casket to be moved several blocks to St. James Hall. This facility had already been rendered safe and secure, with the Union Continentals taking possession at six that morning. At rotating intervals, detachments would function as the Guard of Honor. Furthermore, to avoid confusion when mourners started queuing up to enter the hall, the street in front was placed under the watchful eyes of sentries.

In addition to having obtained a suitable facility in which to lay out the remains, arrangements had also been made to transport them from the station to St. James Hall. By 8:00 o'clock, all was ready for the funeral parade to leave the station. The casket had been transferred from the *United States* to the waiting catafalque, which was hitched to six white horses that had black blankets on their backs and tall black plumes affixed to the top of their heads. Each animal had a soldier assigned as a handler and guide. Marching next to the hearse were a Guard of Honor and eight pallbearers.

The conveyance itself was a classic example of Victorian ornamentation, as it "was heavily covered with black cloth, surmounted with an arched roof, and tastefully trimmed with white satin and silver lace."[8] By virtue of its construction, the coffin rested on an elevated platform and was therefore easily visible as it passed the crowd of mourners.

The hearse was followed first by various military units stationed in the city, then a pair of instrumental groups—known respectively as the Union Cornet Band and Miller's Band—were spaced ahead of and behind the soldiers, next in carriages were those dignitaries who were on board, then local officials also riding, and finally private citizens on foot, among whom was the unassuming ex-president Millard Fillmore.

The presence of Mr. Fillmore among the mourners was not surprising, yet it would have been understandable if he had passed up any highly visible participation. First, the venerable gentleman was sixty-five years old. But, regardless of the walking involved, from a ceremonial perspective a former president honoring a deceased chief executive was most appropriate etiquette for a statesman of Fillmore's caliber. Plus, even though he supported John Bell of the Constitutional Union Party in the 1860 election and became a vocal critic of various aspects of Lincoln's wartime policies, the old politician had put differences aside, befriending the Lincolns and graciously entertaining them when they had stayed overnight on their pre-inaugural trip through Buffalo.

However, these were acts of a cultured, well-mannered individual who intuitively knew how to do what was right. For him not to have been a part of the proceedings would have raised eyebrows. However, had Fillmore chosen to forego any further public participation after an ugly incident befell him on April 15, that stance would have represented an easily defensible decision. While some would still have been critical of his adopting such a posture, for most part his judgment would have been viewed as prudent.

The embarrassing episode that gave Buffalo a black-eye occurred on April 15, the day after President Lincoln's assassination. All across the North, people were putting up mourning displays in the late president's honor. One of more common, outward manifestations of sympathy was to decorate the exterior of homes with some form of mourning drapery.

Despite political differences with Republicans, former-President Millard Fillmore had proven a gracious and amicable host to the Lincolns during their first stay in Buffalo and then stood quietly and humbly among the mourners when the funeral observance was held (Library of Congress).

Much to the surprise of residents across the city, ex-president Fillmore's house stood unadorned, conspicuous in a sea of black crepe all around it. Taking this as deliberate act of disrespect, a mob had wantonly plastered Fillmore's home with black ink. After the damage was done, the truth surfaced—Fillmore, the dutiful husband, had of late been tending to his ailing wife, remaining indoors and oblivious to Lincoln's murder.

In spite of the vandalism and the accompanying insult, Fillmore was not embittered. For shortly thereafter, not only did he have his house appropriately draped, but he was also seen wearing a mourning badge. As Buffalo's first citizen, the man was a class act. But in an era when no official protection was extended to sitting presidents, former leaders of the nation like Fillmore were equally unguarded. As it turned out, whatever anger perpetrated the defacing of his home had dissipated by the time the funeral train arrived. Fillmore suffered no further harm to his home.

With minute guns being fired in

With the hearse moving from left to right down the street, dense crowds—including people perching on windowsills and rooftops—lined both sides of this Buffalo concourse on April 27, 1865 (courtesy Buffalo History Museum).

the distance, the cortège began negotiating the principle streets of Buffalo. As they progressed, the marchers had the opportunity to take in the extent to which townspeople had gone to decorate their homes and businesses in mourning drapery. Commenting favorably on the collective efforts of its citizenry to express appropriate sentiments, a reporter offered his opinion "that our merchants on Main and other business streets acquitted themselves handsomely in the decoration of their establishments, cannot be called into question, while numberless private dwellings displayed the symbols of mourning in such a manner as to speak in unmistakable terms at once the good taste, the patriotism, and the sorrow of their inmates."[9]

As was a frequent form of expression employed in other places, banners with signs and mottoes written on them were prevalent along the route. One in particular that caught the eye and struck a positive chord with many mourners was an inscription displayed on a store that read: "He still lives in the hearts of his countrymen."[10]

Continuing along at a slow, deliberate pace, the procession passed doorways and windows filled with onlookers. At the street level, the crowds were so thick that it gave the appearance of the city's population having doubled. The truth was that "the community had received a tremendous influx from all parts of Western New York, and many from Canada joined with us in the earnest observance of the day; and we may mention en passant that we learn that our Canadian friends immediately across the river, fired minute guns in honor of the occasion during the forenoon."[11]

Finally, the procession reached its goal at 9:35 a.m. Situated at the corner of Washington and Eagle Streets was a cluster of buildings belonging to the Young Men's Association, one of which was called St. James Hall. A large crowd had already gathered. After being brought inside by ten soldiers, the casket was placed on a dais at the center of the room and three-feet off the floor. The head end of the stand was slightly elevated to facilitate ease in viewing the deceased. Above the coffin hung a large chandelier. Also overhead was a black crepe canopy that extended from the floor to the ceiling. Supported underneath by a wooden framework, the effect was to create a circular tent under which the dais rested. Two entrances and two exits existed in order to expedite the movement of two lines of mourners past the bier, one down each side.

Every area of the interior space received some sort treatment. In the central part of the room, "beneath the roof of the tent, and at the upper portion of the walls, beautiful festoons of black and white serge, fringed with bullion, connected by black and white silver cord, and bound up in white rosettes swept around the circle."[12]

The remainder of the facility, outside of the tent, received equally generous attention with crepe draped in various formations, knots of white and black serge, and festoons in black and white. "Altogether," one observer commented, "the temple of mourning was as complete as it could be made."[13] Praise was also received from many traveling with the cortège, foremost among them Major-General John Dix, who "pronounced the arrangement and appearance of the Hall far ahead of anything which had been attempted in any other place through which they had passed."[14]

With ten o'clock designated as the hour for admitting the public, the embalmer had a very small window in which to accomplish his prepping of the body. As in New York City and Albany, Dr. Brown and his assistants removed any accumulated dust that had settled on the late president's corpse and applied whatever makeup they could to keep the face presentable. Since twelve days had elapsed since the deceased had succumbed, concerns arose among many as to how the corpse would appear. With Buffalo being closer to the end of the journey than the beginning, the applications of rouge, powder, and amber could only mask just so much of the natural deterioration that was setting in with each passing day. Too much effort at concealment would produce a clown-like visage, while not enough would make for a startling appearance that could leave mourners more shocked and distraught than they already were.

The possibility of seeing a face that did not look as they remembered caused some individuals to wrestle with a personal dilemma: pay the due respect owed the president's memory and risk seeing him in a deteriorated condition; or stay away from the wake and by so doing preserve intact their own personal memory of how the great man looked in life. Among those who knew Abraham Lincoln well, but who opted to remain with an imbedded memory and forego attending the Washington funeral, was Clara Barton.

The *Rochester Daily Union & Advertiser* described the situation confronting those who had never beheld Lincoln in life by its postulation that "the thousands who seeing our martyred President for the first time, will see him only in his coffin, can gain but a poor idea of his homely, kind, intelligent countenance, as it was when illuminated by vitality, and reflecting the good, generous soul of the living man."[15]

In some ways, the result was not unlike the modern debasement of an individual's appearance created by having altogether one-too-many facelifts. While intentions were good, the results did not always measure up. In spite of the best efforts of Dr. Brown and protestations to the contrary, an element of unavoidable disfiguration was in fact occurring. However, from afar, *The New York Times* listened to their assurances and published a disclaimer "on the authority of the embalmer and undertaker that no perceptible change has taken place in the body we since we left Washington."[16]

This assessment, however, ran counter to the appraisal offered in a Rochester paper which stated that "those who had thought that the embalmer's art would have preserved his features to us almost unchangeable will be disappointed."[17] The ensuing description of the corpse, published first in the *New York Herald*, was less than flattering, picturing as it did a body in which "the eyes of the dead President are sunken, his face is somewhat discolored, sallow about the lower part, dark around the eyes and cheeks; his lips are so tightly compressed that the mouth seems to be a straight sharp line."[18]

The Rochester paper then followed up with a portrayal of the remains that was more corroborative of the *Post's* depiction in stating that once the lid was removed in Buffalo "the color of the face was sort of purple and the skin did not have the appearance of human flesh."[19]

Once the professionals had done what they could to spruce up the corpse's face, St. James Hall was ready to receive the influx of mourners gathered outside. While the early hour of the cortège's arrival at the depot was greeted by a large crowd, the subsequent movements of the body through the streets were not equally watched by overwhelming numbers of people. However, the opposite was true by the time the procession reached the site of the wake. Lines rapidly materialized that saw people standing four abreast as far as the eye could see down the street. Even though quite a show of police and military forces were present in the streets leading up to the hall, "they could not withstand the pressure of the solid mass of humanity filling the street, and the consequence was such a jam as we have never before witnessed."[20] However, by the time the viewing entrance was reached, a semblance of order was restored after the initial crush.

In the ten hours and ten minutes during which the casket was open for the public to pay its respects, a steady stream of mourners made their way into the hall. In the only such stipulation that occurred in New York, women and men would be required to view the remains in separate lines. Furthermore, once inside, the distaff column was kept at a greater distance from the catafalque. This precaution was taken to make it less opportune for women to impulsively touch or kiss the body, as some had been wont to do in other places. At noon, the mayor, city officers, and members of the common council assembled and marched in a body to St. James Hall, followed by the Rochester delegation and the Erie County Board of Supervisors.

Leading this group of dignitaries was an individual of considerable distinction. For along with being mayor of the city since 1862, William Fargo made an outstanding contribution to the war effort by continuing to pay the salaries of employees who had been drafted. However, regardless of any success that he may have enjoyed in the political realm, the world of business was the domain where Mr. Fargo made his greatest mark. For prior to the Civil War, he became a partner in what was known as the Wells Fargo Express Company.

Upon entering the hall and approaching the casket, the first sights and smells greeting the senses of the official party were the proliferation of floral displays placed around the catafalque. One rested at the foot of the coffin. Made of white camellias arranged in the form of an anchor, this array bore the inscription: "Youth crushed to earth will rise again."[21] At the opposite end of the coffin, another floral tribute that was extremely eye-catching took the shape of a harp, with one string symbolically broken. Presented by the ladies of the St. Cecelia Society, this unique, dainty treatment was comprised of interwoven white roses, orange blossoms, and daisies. On top of closed lower two-thirds of the coffin could be seen a white cross fashioned of flowers along with several wreaths.

If the mayoral party was so fortunate, the entourage may have chanced to hear one of the performances of the St. Cecelia Society choir. As the casket was being placed on the dais, these gifted singers offered a poignant rendition of a dirge titled "Rest, Spirit, Rest." Located in a gallery outside and above the tent containing the catafalque, the chorus' voices wafted over the hall, deeply touching the hearts of those present and bringing many to tears. General Dix was so moved that he requested the group to please remain and repeat their performance several times during the course of the day.

Buffalo had certainly turned out in a tremendous show of respect for all that Abraham Lincoln had meant to them. Long-time residents of the community could not recall a time in their city's history when so many people had graced its streets. Available hotel space was at a premium. Estimates placed the number who passed through St. James Hall at between 90,000 and 100,000.[22] The presence of so many mourners insured that a steady stream was constantly entering the hall throughout the day. But 8:10 in the evening came altogether too soon. With the railroad's ten o'clock departure looming as the deadline, the hall doors were shut, and then the casket's lid closed. After the pallbearers retraced their steps with the remains to the waiting hearse, the same units and individuals who had provided the morning's escort were back to assist. The cortège then proceeded to make its way back to the Exchange Street Station, though the New York Central was giving way to the New York and Erie Railroad as the carrier from Buffalo to Cleveland.

By 8:45, everyone was in place. The column shoved off, followed by sizable crowd of citizens. Upon reaching the station, the number of spectators increased dramatically, all hoping for one last look of the casket. The transfer of the remains took place smoothly and without incident. Compared to the chaotic welcome which Buffalo had given him in upon his arrival as president-elect, the city had more than redeemed itself this day with two smoothly run processions and a tasteful, well-attended wake. Now, with the late president's body once more secure in the *United States*, the time had come to leave. With a shrill blast of its whistle, the engine started to gain momentum—all the while its bell clanging a mournful, measured cadence.

Preceded by the pilot engine *Comet*, which its engineer Gus Catlin had set in motion at a 9:50 p.m., the funeral train was led out of the Exchange Street Station ten minutes later by the New York and Erie's *Atlas*, John Hart at its controls. The engine was decorated in typical fashion with flags, crepe, festoons, bouquets, and the large portrait of President Lincoln mounted above the cowcatcher. But, in a unique added touch, "the interior of the cab was concealed from outside view by a monster flag, and the light shining through it produced a fine effect."[23] In time, the New York Central would acquire this line too, eventually extending its run from New York City through to Chicago.

But for now, the Central's role in helping to bring the mortal remains of the late president substantially closer to his final resting place in Springfield was done. The honor of actively participating and the pride of successfully performing a key role in the extended tableau at this time of national tragedy represented a shining moment in the railroad's early history. Now the assignment was passed on to the officials of another carrier.

Traveling southwest through Hamburg, Angola, Farnham, Irving, and Silver Creek, the train passed stations overflowing with local residents. Carrying lanterns, bearing mourning flags, and wearing solemn expressions, they were out late that April evening to pay their respects. With the mourners standing in hushed silence, often the only sounds came from the train, the most haunting being the rhythmic clang produced by the engine's shrouded bell. For years afterward, that distinctive railroad sound would evoke the memory of the Lincoln Special in the minds of those who had heard it ring that sad spring evening.

Next up in the rapidly dwindling itinerary of towns left to pass in New York was Dunkirk. Here, as in all of the other places served by the railroad and visited by the Lincoln Special, a committee had seen to it that the station was fittingly ornamented. For the residents of Dunkirk, this was the second time in less than a year that they had held a special observance. The first one, in the summer of 1864, was a celebration to honor the Dunkirk's returning boys from two companies in the 72nd New York Infantry Regiment. One of its most celebrated hometown enlistees was Thomas Horan. At the Battle of Gettysburg, Sergeant Horan was instrumental in leading a charge of the 72nd which caused at the 8th Florida to give ground. In the process, his aggressive action allowed him to capture the Floridians' regimental colors.

For his bravery, Horan was awarded the Medal of Honor. Subsequently, he was wounded in the leg at the Battle of the Wilderness, leaving him with a limp for the rest of his life. Still he chose to remain in uniform, sergeant's stripes firmly attached, and stay until the war's victorious conclusion. But, others opted to return home at the conclusion of their three-year commitment.

What they left behind was a regimental legacy firmly inscribed in the annals of the Army of the Potomac's war record. But after three years of hard fighting, the fates for some had been tempted often enough. For, of the almost two-hundred who had marched off in 1861, perhaps no more than thirty were present to parade before their grateful townsmen. The vacant chairs in many homes bore out the sad truth, attesting to the reality that war had exacted a terrible toll from the ranks of Dunkirk's volunteers. But even given the understandably mixed emotions among the spectators, the boys who got off the train were treated right. After a five-block procession and variety of speeches at the village park, everyone adjourned to a local eating establishment for a sumptuous meal.

Now on the night of April 27, 1865, another reception after a different kind had been planned. For their efforts, Dunkirk's committee deserved five stars. In the eyes one who viewed the results of their work, "the platform is elaborately decorated, festoons of evergreens extend all along the eaves of the structure, while from the ceiling gracefully droop white and black folds. The background covered with flags, interlaced with crepe, completes the artistic arrangement."[24]

While Dunkirk's tribute also featured the by now standard tolling of bells, firing of minute guns, and playing of dirges, the soft light of glowing lanterns and the warm brilliance of blazing torches served to illuminate a local touch: a group of thirty-six ladies, representing the states in the Union, who were lined up and kneeling along the station's platform. They were described as being "dressed in white, each with a broad black scarf resting on the shoulder and holding in the hand a national flag."[25] The whole effect in the eyes of one observer "created a beautiful tableau."[26]

Departing Dunkirk at 12:10, the mournful express next rolled through Brockton and Portland. Then, at one o'clock in the morning of April 28, 1865, five days after arriving in New York City, the funeral train reached its last stop in the Empire State.

While taking on fuel and water represented the necessity for the halt, this little village was site laden with nostalgia. For it was here in Westfield that President-Elect Lincoln made his first stop on New York soil in 1861. Unlike that visit, filled with joy and exuberance, this occasion was fraught with melancholy. A crowd was once again present, but instead of bright smiles and hearty applause there were only bitter tears and uncontrollable sobs.

While the *Atlas* was being resupplied, five ladies were permitted access to the *United States* in order to lay a cross and a wreath of flowers on the coffin. The cross bore the words: "Ours, the cross, Thine, the crown."[27] As they passed the bier, each woman bent down and with their tears falling liberally in accompaniment kissed the coffin.

Unlike the pre-inaugural visit when Mr. Lincoln singled her out for special recognition

As the Westfield, New York, depot was the first stop to greet the new president on his inaugural tour, so also was it the last to say farewell before the funeral train left the Empire State on April 27, 1861 (Lincoln Insurance Foundation Collection, courtesy Indiana State Museum and the Allen County Public Library).

and everlasting fame, young Grace Bedell—now fifteen years old—was conspicuous only for her absence. But the reason for this was simply that she no longer resided there. In 1862, the family had returned to their permanent home in Albion, New York, which as located about fifteen miles north of Batavia. Since the special had stopped in Batavia, Grace could have been present among the mourners gathered at the station there. However, biographer Fred Trump believed that she probably was not. He based his deduction on "her account years later of all the presidents she had seen—Lincoln, Buchanan, Johnson, Grant, and Benjamin Harrison."[28] Since Millard Fillmore had boarded at Batavia, she would have seen him too had she been there and in turn included him on her list.

Even though Grace had moved from Westfield, her connection to President Lincoln was remembered by at least one individual, for "the private secretary for William Seward sent Grace a macabre memento—a portion of a napkin stained with the blood of the martyred president."[29]

Along with the civic pride that the Bedell-Lincoln story gave the little town, Westfield was also the home of two bona fide war heroes: Thomas Haight of the 72nd New York Infantry and Edwin Goodrich of the 9th New York Cavalry. Both had been awarded Congressional Medals of Honor for performing similar acts of bravery in separate engagements.

In Sergeant Haight's case, he was wounded and captured on My 5, 1862, while rescuing a wounded comrade at the Battle of Williamsburg. Two years later. Lieutenant Goodrich, during a retrograde action by his command at the Battle of Cedar Creek, retuned in the face of the enemy and rescued one of his men who was pinned beneath his fallen horse. Goodrich remained in the service until the summer of 1865. Haight, however, was honorably discharged in the spring of 1863, following his release from a rebel prison. He returned to Westfield, where he quite likely stood in the flickering torchlights as the Lincoln Special passed through the town, bearing the remains of his former commander-in-chief.

Leaving Westfield at 1:00 a.m., the train had precious little time remaining in New York. The last community which it passed through was Ripley, a small hamlet that had contributed forty-two men to the Union forces. After slightly more than four days of traveling north, then west, and finally southwest through the Empire State, the boundary between New York and Pennsylvania was crossed at 1:32 a.m. This transition was marked by a gathering of people at the crossover point.

* * *

Over the course of his fifty-six years on earth, Abraham Lincoln spent approximately three weeks in New York. Two of his visits accounted for ten days, one while among the living and the other after his death. But that pair of passages that bookended his presidency helped endear him to the Empire State's residents in a lasting way like that of no other state save perhaps Illinois, cementing their bond with him forever. Tied vividly to both events were also the images of trains, one eastbound and one westbound. An iron horse brought him, and an iron horse took him away. But in the process, Abraham Lincoln's legacy was indelibly etched into the minds of countless residents who had personally witnessed a small segment of history. Though the man could never return, his memory would never leave.

Appendix A

Presidents and Trains

As distinctive as many aspects of the two Lincoln Specials were, other presidents over the years made frequent use of railroads and had positive experiences. In the early days of railroading, presidents rode in common coaches along with the other passengers. Eventually, for purposes of privacy and safety, they were afforded the luxury of having their own private car attached to the rear of the train. In time, such as when Franklin Roosevelt traveled, an entire train was assembled for his use.

The first president to ride a train was John Quincy Adams, meaning that only the first five chief executives of our nation never had the pleasure. Rutherford B. Hayes gained recognition for traveling coast-to-coast by rail, and in the process, he became the first sitting president to visit Oregon. Trains played highly supportive roles for other presidents too, such as Andrew Johnson, who was transported by rail on his famous Circle Tour of the northeast in 1866 to drum up support for certain policies. On a more personal note, Grover Cleveland and his new bride went on their honeymoon by train.

The concept of using railroads for campaign purposes was initiated by William Henry Harrison in 1836 and continued with varying degrees of electoral success since then, with Harry Truman's famous 28,000-mile, 1948 cross-country campaign tour being perhaps the most famous application of this approach. In more recent times, a bevy of presidents have used trains as nostalgic focal-points for modified whistle-stop tours, thereby adding valuable publicity to their campaigns. Among these more contemporary candidates were Gerald Ford, Jimmy Carter, Ronald Reagan, George H. W. Bush, Bill Clinton, and Barack Obama. There was, of course, Lincoln's long excursion, which has retained a uniqueness all its own, but it qualifies for an asterisk since his unusual outing did not occur until after he was elected.

On the opposite side of the spectrum, trains also were present during some of the grimmer times in the lives of presidents. Perhaps the saddest experience of all befell Franklin Pierce in 1853, when a derailment took the life of his young son just prior to his father's inauguration. Compounding the family's grief was the fact that the boy's death had been preceded by those of his two brothers, sending the Pierces to the White House childless and heavy-hearted.

In 1881, a train gently brought the grievously wounded James Garfield to the Jersey shore, a hopeful, though ultimately futile, humanitarian attempt to aid in his recovery. To facilitate the ease of his movement as much as possible, a special spur of tracks was laid from the mainline right up to the seaside cottage where the dying president's last days were spent.

Then in 1903 a fast-moving express rushed Vice President Theodore Roosevelt from the Adirondack Mountain foothills across New York to Buffalo, where he arrived too late to see the mortally wounded President McKinley but in time to be sworn in as the country's next chief executive.

Warren Harding was engaged in a monumental 15,000-mile train trip across the United States and to Alaska in 1923, when he died unexpectedly in San Francisco.

However, perhaps next to Abraham Lincoln, the president who made the most of rail transportation was Franklin Roosevelt. Frequent excursions took him to Warm Springs, Georgia, for rehabilitation and Hyde Park, New York, for relaxation.

With the passing of Roosevelt in Warm Springs, two separate train trips were required: one to bring FDR's remains to Washington, D.C., for the funeral by way of the Southern Railroad; and a second one on the tracks of the New York Central to bring the casket and mourners to Hyde Park for the burial service.

While in planning FDR's funeral arrangements as they related to railroad procedures, the intent was not to use Lincoln's funeral train as a template, but the reality was that much of what simply evolved was nevertheless striking similar in many ways. Among the most notable parallels between the respective Lincoln and Roosevelt funeral trains were:

- Participating railroads assigned their best personnel and equipment.
- Both trains left from Washington after a White House funeral
- Passage on the funeral trains was by invitation only.
- The speed of the train was purposely kept slow to permit viewing.
- All along the route floral tributes were presented by civic representatives.
- Mourners lined the tracks at stations.
- Military personnel were utilized as guards at stations.
- People stood and waited to see the train through both rural and urban areas.
- The casket was visible in the hearse car.
- The trains ran through the night.
- Bonfires were built for illumination and warmth by mourners waiting along the tracks.
- Both deceased presidents were brought to burial sites near places where they had spent significant portions of their lives.

Appendix B

Special Orders Governing the Safety of the Funeral Train

An original of this document can be found in the archives of the Onondaga County Historical Society.

To safeguard the travel of Lincoln's funeral train across New York State, a set of special orders were issued by Brevet Brigadier General Daniel C. McCallum in his capacity as that of Director and General Manager of the Military Railroads of the United States. Dated April 25, 1865, the document was sent on New York Central Rail Road Company stationary by the assistant superintendent for the Middle Division, W. G. Lapham.

Five stipulations were contained on the list "to be observed during the passage of the Pilot Train and Special Train with Remains" during its passage:

1st. All Telegraph stations shall be kept open during the passage of said trains.

2nd. A man must be stationed at each Highway crossing, with one white and one red light, to remain there and keep the crossing clear until the funeral train has passed.

3rd. The pilot engine and shall not pass any Telegraph station unless one white and one red light are exhibited, which will signify that the funeral train has passed the nearest Telegraph station. In the absence of said signals, the Pilot engine and train will stop until definite information is received in regard to the funeral train.

4th. Where double track is in use, all trains running in opposite directions to funeral trains shall be stopped as soon as the Pilot engine shall have passed, and shall so remain until after the funeral train has passed.

5th. The funeral train shall pass all stations slowly, at which time the bell of the locomotive shall be tolled.

Chapter Notes

Chapter 1

1. *Hartford Daily Courier*, February 14, 1861, p. 1.
2. Larry D. Mansch, *Abraham Lincoln, President-Elect*. Jefferson: McFarland, 2005, p. 142.
3. Ward Hill Lamon, *Recollections of Abraham Lincoln: 1847–1865*. Lincoln: University of Nebraska Press, 1994, p. 345
4. *Albany Journal*, February 23, 1861, p. 2.
5. *Rochester Daily Democrat*, February 18, 1861, p. 2.
6. *Ibid.*
7. Roy P. Basler, *The Collected Works of Abraham Lincoln*, Vol. 4. New Brunswick: Rutgers University Press, 1933, p. 130.
8. *Ibid.*, p. 129.
9. Lamon, *Recollections of Abraham Lincoln*, p. 158
10. Basler, p. 130.
11. *Rochester Daily Democrat*, February 18, 1861, p. 2.
12. John Starr, *Lincoln and the Railroads*. New York: Dodd, Mead, 1927, p. 185.
13. *Westfield Republican*, February 20, 1861, p. 4.
14. *The Brockport Republican*, February 21, 1861, p. 2.
15. *The Centennial History of Chautauqua County*, Volume II. Jamestown: Chautauqua History, 1904, p. 440.
16. *Rochester Daily Democrat*, February 18, 1861, p. 2.
17. *The New York World*, February 18, 1861, p. 2.
18. *Rochester Daily Democrat*, February 18, 1861, p. 2.
19. *Ibid.*
20. *The Centennial History of Chautauqua County*, Vol. II, p. 440.
21. John Fagant, *The Best of the Bargain: Lincoln in Western New York*. Bloomington: Authorhouse, 2010, p. 34.
22. *Cleveland Morning Leader*, February 18, 1861, p. 1.
23. *Buffalo Morning Express*, February 16, 1861, p. 2.
24. *Ibid.*
25. *Ibid.*
26. *Buffalo Morning Express*, February 18, 1861, p. 3.
27. *Ibid.*
28. *Ibid.*

Chapter 2

1. *Buffalo Morning Express*, February 18, 1861, p. 3.
2. *Ibid.*
3. *Daily Ohio Statesman*, February 18, 1861, p. 3.
4. *Buffalo Morning Express*, February 18, 1861, p, 3.
5. *Rochester Daily Democrat*, February 18, 1861, p. 1.
6. *Buffalo Morning Express*, February 18, 1861, p. 3.
7. *Rochester Daily Democrat*, February 18, 1861, p. 1.
8. *Ibid.*, p. 4
9. *Daily Ohio Statesman*, February 18, 1861, p. 1.
10. *Washington Evening Star*, February 18, 1861, p. 2.
11. *Buffalo Morning Express*, February 18, 1861, p. 3.
12. *Buffalo Morning Express*, February 19, 1861, p. 2.
13. *Buffalo Morning Express*, February 20, 1861, p. 8.
14. *Rochester Daily Democrat*, February 18, 1861, p. 1.
15. *Ibid.*
16. *Buffalo Morning Express*, February 18, 1861, p. 3.
17. *The National Republican*, February 18, 1861, p. 3.
18. Milton Stern, *Harriet Lane, America's First Lady*. Washington, D.C.: Self-Published, 2003, p. 54.
19. *New York Herald*, February 21, 1861, p. 1.
20. *Buffalo Morning Express*, February 18, 1861, p. 3.
21. *Ibid.*
22. *Rochester Daily Democrat and American*, February 18, 1861, p. 1.
23. *Ibid.*

Chapter 3

1. *Rochester Daily Democrat*, February 19, 1861, p. 2.
2. *Ibid.*
3. *New York Times*, February 18, 1861, p. 4.
4. Welcoming representatives from Rochester, Syracuse, Utica, and Albany were aboard, along with an escort from Buffalo.
5. *Albany Evening Journal*, February 18, 1861, p. 2.
6. *Douglass Journal*, March 1, 1861, p. 419.
7. *Ibid.*, p. 430.
8. *Ibid.*
9. *Rochester Democrat*, February 19, 1861, p. 1.
10. *The Brockport Republican*, February 21, 1861, p. 3.
11. *Rochester Union and Advertiser*, February 16, 1861, p. 2.
12. *The Brockport Republic*, February 21, 1861, p. 3.
13. *The Brockport Republic*, February 21, 1861, p. 3.
14. *Ibid.*
15. *Rochester Union and Advertiser*, February 16, 1861, p. 2.
16. Starr, p. 192.
17. *Rochester Democrat*, February 19, 1861, p. 1.
18. *The Clyde Weekly Times*, February 23, 1861, p. 2.
19. *The Syracuse Post-Standard*, February 24, 1952, p. 25.
20. *Ibid.*
21. *The Clyde Weekly Times*, February 23, 1861, p. 2.
22. *Ibid.*

23. *Ibid.*
24. *Ibid.*
25. *Ibid.*
26. *The Syracuse Post-Standard*, February 24, 1952, p. 26.
27. *Albany Evening Journal*, February 18, 1861, p. 2.
28. Central New York Chapter of the National Railway Historical Society, *Railroads in the Streets of Syracuse*. Marcellus, Central New York Chapter of the NRHS, 1979.
29. *Syracuse Herald Journal*, September 26, 1947, p. 24.
30. *Albany Evening Journal*, February 18, 1861, p. 2.
31. *Albany Evening Journal*, February 18, 1861, p. 2.
32. *Ibid.*
33. *Syracuse Daily Journal*, February 19, 1861.

Chapter 4

1. *New York Herald*, February 18, 1861, p. 4.
2. *New York Herald*, February 22, 1861, p. 1.
3. *Ibid.*
4. *Albany Evening Journal*, February 18, 1861, p. 2.
5. *Herkimer Democrat*, February 20, 1861, p. 1.
6. *Oneida Weekly Herald*, February 19, 1861, p. 4.
7. *Utica Gazette*, February 19, 1861, p. 3.
8. *Auburn Daily Advertiser,* February 9, 1861, p. 3.
9. *Oneida Weekly Herald*, February 19, 1861, p. 4.
10. Charles Hamlin, *The Life and Times of Hannibal Hamlin*. Cambridge: Riverside Press, 1899, pp. 464–65.
11. *Victoria Advocate* (Texas), February 11, 1948, p. 12.
12. H. Draper Hunt, *Hannibal Hamlin of Maine: Lincoln's First Vice-President*. Syracuse: Syracuse University Press, 1969, p. 118.
13. *Ibid.*
14. William A. Croffut, *An American Procession: 1855–1914*. Boston: Little, Brown, 1931, p. 39.
15. *The New York Times*, February 19, 1861, p. 3.
16. *Ibid.*
17. *Boston Post*, February 19, 1861, p. 2.
18. *Troy Daily Times*, February 21, 1861, p. 2.
19. *Oneida Weekly Herald*, March 5, 1861, p. 2.
20. *Troy Daily Times*, February 21, 1861, p. 2.
21. *Oneida Weekly Herald*, February 19, 1861, p. 5.
22. *Utica Gazette*, February 19, 1861, p. 2.
23. *Ibid.*
24. *Oneida Weekly Herald*, February 19, 1861, p. 4.
25. *The New York Times*, February 19, 1861, p. 1.
26. *Herkimer Democrat*, February 20, 1861, p. 9.
27. *The New York Times*, February 19, 1861, p. 1.
28. *Utica Evening Telegraph*, February 20, 1861, p. 2.
29. *Rochester Daily Union and Advertiser*, February 18, 1861, p. 1.
30. Henry Villard, *Lincoln on the Eve of '61*. New York: Alfred Knopf, 1941, p. 91.

Chapter 5

1. *Utica Weekly Herald*, May 1865, p. 5.
2. *The New York Times*, February 20, 1861, p. 1.
3. Abraham Lincoln to Frances Spinner, Letter of September 24, 1860, Herkimer County Historical Society, Herkimer, New York.
4. After the war, Tryon County, named for colonial British governor, was subdivided and renamed, with Herkimer County being one of the new political entities.
5. Letter of George Collins, March 4, 1864, Herkimer. nygenweb.net.
6. *The New York Times*, February 20, 1861, p. 3.
7. *Little Falls Journal & Courier*, February 11, 1933.
8. *Ibid.*
9. *The Albany Journal*, February 19, 1861, p. 2.
10. *The Albany Journal*, February 18, 1861, p. 2.
11. *The New York Times*, February 19, 1861, p, 1.
12. *Ibid.*
13. *Times*, p. 2.
14. *Douglass' Monthly*, March 1, 1861, p. 430.
15. Ward Hill Lamon, *Recollections of Abraham Lincoln*, p. 33.
16. *Albany Evening Journal.* February 18, 1861, p. 2.
17. *Troy Daily Times*, February 19, 1861, p. 3.
18. *The Evening Post*, February 19, 1861, p. 2.
19. *Ibid.*
20. *Albany Evening Journal*, February 18, 1861, p. 2.
21. *Ibid.*
22. *The New York Times*, February 19, 1861, p. 3.
23. Villard, p. 91.
24. *Ibid.*
25. *The New York Times*, February 19, 1861, p. 1.
26. *The Schenectady Daily News*, February 18, 1861, p. 2.
27. *Ibid.*
28. *Ibid.*

Chapter 6

1. *Rochester Union and Advertiser,* February 14, 1861, p. 4.
2. *New York Times*, February 14, 1861, p. 1.
3. *Ibid.*
4. *Ibid.*
5. *Ibid.*
6. *Rochester Democrat*, February 14, 1861, p. 4.
7. *Rochester Union & Advertiser*, February 18, 1861, p. 2.
8. Starr, pp. 186–187.
9. Peter Hess, www.newyorkhistoryblog.org, June 17, 2015.
10. *New York Herald*, February 19, 1861, p. 1.
11. *Albany Evening Journal*, November 7, 1861, p. 2.
12. *New York Daily Tribune*, February 19, 1861, p. 8.
13. *Albany Daily Advertiser*, February 19, 1861, p. 2.
14. Villard, p. 92.
15. *Troy Daily Times*, February 19, 1861, p. 2.
16. Villard, p. 93.
17. *Ibid.*
18. *Utica Daily Advertiser*, February 19, 1861, p. 2.
19. *New York Times*, February 19, 1861, p. 1861, p. 1.
20. *Troy Daily Times*, February 19, 1861, p. 2.
21. *Utica Daily Advertiser*, February 19, 1861, p. 2.
22. *Ibid.*
23. *Cohoes Cataract*, February 23, 1861, p. 2.
24. *Troy Daily Whig*, February 18, 1861, p. 3.
25. *Ibid.*
26. *New York Herald*, February 19, 1861, p. 1.
27. *Albany Journal*, February 18, 1861, p. 2.
28. Henry E. Pratt, Ed., *Concerning Mr. Lincoln*. Springfield: Abraham Lincoln Association, 1944, p. 55.
29. *New York Daily Tribune*, February 19, 1861, p. 8.

30. Villard, p. 94.
31. *New York Herald*, February 19, 1861, p. 1.
32. *Albany Atlas & Argus*, February 19, 1861, p. 2.
33. *Ibid.*
34. *Ibid.*
35. *New York Times*, February 19, 1861, p. 4.
36. *Albany Atlas & Argus*, February 19, 1861, p. 2.
37. *Albany Atlas & Argus*, February 19, 1861, p. 2.
38. *Ibid.*
39. *Ibid.*
40. *Ibid.*
41. *The New York Times*, February 19, 1861, p. 8.
42. *Cohoes Cataract*, February 23, 1861, p. 3.
43. *New York Times*, February 19, 1861, p. 8.
44. *New York Herald*, February 19, 1861, p. 1.
45. *Ibid.*
46. *Times*, p. 8.
47. *Albany Journal*, February 18, 1861, p. 2.
48. *Utica Morning Herald and Daily Gazette*, February 19, 1861, p. 2.
49. *Ibid.*
50. Lamon, *Recollections of Abraham Lincoln*, p. 34.
51. *New York Times*, February 19, 1861, p. 8.
52. *Ibid.*
53. *Albany Evening Journal*, February 19, 1861, p. 2.
54. *New York Herald*, February 19, 1861, p. 8.
55. Michael Burlingame, *Abraham Lincoln, A Life* (Vol. 2). Baltimore: Johns Hopkins University Press, 2008, p. 25.
56. *Home Journal*, March 16, 1861, p. 29.
57. *New York Herald*, February 19, 1861, p. 1.
58. John Nicolay, Michael Burlingame (Ed.), *An Oral History of Abraham Lincoln*. Carbondale: Southern Illinois University Press, 1996, p. 38.

Chapter 7

1. Nicolay, pp. 117–118.
2. *New York World*, February 21, 1861, p. 3.
3. *New York Herald*, February 20, 1861, p. 1.
4. Villard, p. 96.
5. *New York Herald*, February 20, 1861, p. 1.
6. *New York Daily Tribune*, February 21, 1861, p. 5.
7. Starr, p. 222.
8. *Troy Daily Times*, February 1, 1861, p. 3.
9. *Troy Daily Times*, February 28, 1861, p. 3.
10. *Ibid.*
11. *Albany Argus*, August 11, 1865, p. 2.
12. *Ibid.*
13. *The New York Times*, May 1, 1861, p. 8.
14. *Ibid.*
15. *New York Tribune*, May 1, 1860, p. 2.
16. *Ibid.*
17. *Ibid.*
18. Basler, Vol. I, p. 112.
19. *Cohoes Cataract*, February 23, 1861, p. 3.
20. *The New York Times*, February 20, 1861, p. 1.
21. *Ibid.*
22. *Cohoes Cataract*, February 23, 1861, p. 3.
23. *Waterford Sentinel*, February 23, 1861, p. 3.
24. *Ibid.*
25. *Ibid.*
26. *Ibid.*

27. *Albany Evening Journal*, May 25, 1861, p. 2.
28. *Ibid.*
29. *Ballston Journal*, May 26, 1861, p. 2.
30. *Ballston Journal*, May 28, 1861, p. 2.
31. *Ibid.*
32. *Albany Evening Journal*, May 25, 1861, p. 2.
33. Basler, Vol. 4, p. 386.
34. *New York Daily Tribune*, February 19, 1861, p. 2.
35. Samuel N. Hutchinson, *A History of the Village of Green Island*. Troy: Troy Record, 1934, p. 14.
36. Hutchinson, pp. 12–13.
37. Hutchinson, p. 10.
38. *Troy Daily Times*, February 21, 1861, p. 2.
39. Hutchinson, p. 10.
40. *New York Daily Tribune*, February 19, 1861, p. 8.
41. *Troy Daily Times*, February 20, 1861, p. 3.
42. *New York Daily Tribune*, February 19, 1861, p. 8.
43. *Albany Evening Journal*, February 18, 1861, p. 2.
44. *New York Daily Tribune*, February 19, 1861, p. 8.
45. *Ibid.*
46. Victor Searcher, *Lincoln's Journey to Greatness*. Philadelphia: John T. Winston, 1960, p. 173.

Chapter 8

1. *Troy Daily Times*, February 19, 1861, p. 3.
2. *Troy Daily Whig*, February 18, 1861, p. 3.
3. www.timesunion.com, article by Kenneth C. Crowe II.
4. Don Rittner, *Capital District Civil War Series #9, Troy's Ironclad History*. Blog.
5. *Albany Evening Journal*, February 19, 1861, p. 2.
6. *Troy Daily Times*, February 20, 1861, p. 3.
7. *Daily Whig*, February 20, 1861, p. 3.
8. *Troy Daily Times*, February 20, 1861, p. 3.
9. *Troy Daily Times*, February 19, 1861, p. 3.
10. *Ibid.*
11. *Cohoes Cataract*, February 23, 1861, p. 2.
12. *New York Herald*, February 20, 1861, p. 1.
13. *Ibid.*
14. *Troy Daily Whig*, February 20, 1861, p. 3.
15. *Ibid.*
16. *Troy Daily Times*, February 19, 1861, p. 3.
17. *Ibid.*
18. *Troy Daily Whig*, February 20, 1861, p. 3.

Chapter 9

1. *New York Herald*, February 20, 1861, p. 1.
2. *Ibid.*
3. *Ibid.*
4. *New York Daily Tribune*, February 20, 1861, p. 5.
5. *New York Herald*, February 20, 1861, p. 1.
6. *New York Times*, February 19, 1861, p. 3.
7. *New York Herald*, February 20, 1861, p. 1.
8. *Hudson Weekly Star*, February 2, 1861, p. 2.
9. *Poughkeepsie Daily Eagle*, February 20, 1861, p. 3.
10. *New York Daily Tribune*, February 20, 1861, p. 5.
11. *New York Herald*, February 20, 1861, p. 1.
12. *Hudson Weekly Star*, February 21, 1861, p. 2.
13. *Rockland County Messenger*, February 21, 1861, p. 1.
14. *New York Times*, February 19, 1861, p. 3.
15. *Hudson Weekly Star*, February 21, 1861, p. 2.

16. *New York Daily Tribune*, February 20, 1861, p. 5.
17. *Ibid.*
18. *New York Herald*, February 20, 1861, p. 1.
19. *Ibid.*
20. *New York Times*, February 20, 1861, p. 2.
21. *Ibid.*
22. *New York Daily Tribune*, February 20, 1861, p. 5.
23. *Poughkeepsie Daily Eagle*, February 20, 1861, p. 3.
24. *New York Daily Tribune*, February 20, 1861, p. 2.
25. *Ibid.*
26. Josiah Holland, *The Life of Abraham Lincoln*. Lincoln: University of Nebraska Press, 1998, p. 267.
27. *Poughkeepsie Daily Eagle*, February 20, 1861, p. 3.
28. Richard Lederer, "Lincoln as Jokester." *The Saturday Evening Post*, June 25, 2013.
29. *Hudson Weekly Standard*, February 21, 1861, p. 2.
30. *Ibid.*
31. *New York Times*, February 20, 1861, p. 2.
32. *Ibid.*
33. Ishbel Ross, *The President's Wife: Mary Todd Lincoln*. New York: G.P. Putnam's Sons, 1973, p. 94.
34. *Ibid.*
35. *New York Tribune*, February 20, 1861, p. 8.
36. *Brooklyn Daily Eagle*, February 20, 1861, p. 2.
37. *New York Times*, February 19, 1861, p. 3.
38. Mark M. Boatner, *The Civil War Dictionary*. New York: David MacKay, 1987, p. 165.
39. Ralph Gary, *Following in Lincoln's Footsteps: A Complete Annotated Reference to Hundreds of Historical Sites Visited by Abraham Lincoln*. New York: Carroll & Graf, 2002, p. 273.
40. *New York Times*, February 20, 1861, p. 3.
41. *New York Herald*, February 20, 1861, p. 1.
42. *Ibid.*
43. *Ibid.*
44. Emanuel Hertz, *Lincoln Talks: An Oral Biography*. New York: Bramhall House, 1986, p. 189.
45. *New York Times*, February 20, 1861, p. 1.
46. *Peekskill Highland Democrat*, February 23, 1861, p. 3.
47. *New York Herald*, February 19, 1861, p. 3.
48. Julie Morrisett, "The Civil War Era in Westchester County," *The Westchester Historian*, Vol. 77, # 3 (Summer 2001), pp. 68–69.
49. Anthony Czarnecki, "Mr. Lincoln's Visit to Peekskill: The Sesquicentennial of an Inaugural Journey," Vol. 87, #1 (Winter 2011), pp. 17–18
50. "Letter by Hon. Chauncey M. Depew," September 22, 1922, *Lincoln in Peekskill*, Peekskill: Lincoln Society in Peekskill, 1926, p. 10–11.
51. Norm Macdonald, "Abraham Lincoln's Links to Ossining," *The Westchester Historian*, Vol. 90, #4 (Fall 2014), p.104.
52. *Ibid.*, p. 124.

Chapter 10

1. *New York Daily Tribune*, February 20, 1861, p. 8.
2. *New York Herald*, February 20, 1861, p. 1.
3. *New York Evening Express*, February 20, 1861, p. 4.
4. *New York Times*, February 20, 1861, p. 8.
5. *Albany Evening Times*, February 20, 1861, p. 2.
6. *Poughkeepsie Daily Eagle*, February 20, 1861, p. 2.
7. *New York Tribune*, February 20, 1861, p. 8.
8. *Buffalo Morning Express*, February 18, 1861, p. 3.
9. *New York Sun*, February 20, 1861, p. 1.
10. *Arts & Culture*, "Today in NYC History: President-Elect Abraham Lincoln Comes to Town in 1861," February 19, 2015.
11. *Ibid.*
12. *New York Herald*, February 20, 1861, p. 1.
13. *Ibid.*
14. *New York Tribune*, February 20, 1861, p. 2.
15. *Harper's Weekly*, March 2, 1861, p. 130.
16. *New York Herald*, February 20, 1861, p. 1.
17. *Ibid.*
18. *New York Times*, February 20, 1861, p. 4.
19. *Ibid.*
20. Nicolay, p. 118.
21. Walt Whitman, "Death of Abraham Lincoln," from lecture of April 14, 1879, *Complete Prose Works*, Philadelphia: David McKay Publishers, 1892, p. 308.
22. *Ibid.*
23. *New York Times*, September 27, 2009, p. 8.
24. William Bobo, *Glimpses of New-York City*. Charleston: J.J. McCarter, Pub., 1852, pp. 87–88
25. *Ibid.*
26. *Harper's Weekly*, March 2, 1861, p. 130.
27. *Ibid.*
28. *New York Times*, February 20, 1861, p. 8.
29. *New York Tribune*, February 20, 1861, p. 1.
30. *New York Daily Tribune*, February 21, 2016, p. 8.
31. *The Connecticut Press*, February 23, 1861, p. 2.
32. *New York Daily Tribune*, February 21, 1861, p. 8.
33. Croffut, p. 39.
34. *New York Daily Tribune*, February 21, 1861, p. 8.
35. *Ibid.*
36. *Ibid.*
37. Croffut, p. 39.
38. *Ibid.*
39. *New York Evening Express*, February 21, 1861, p. 4.
40. *New York Herald*, February 21, 1861, p. 8.
41. *Ibid.*
42. *New York Herald*, February 20, 1861, p. 4.
43. Hamlin, Vol. 2, pp. 387–388
44. *New York Herald*, February 20, 1861, p. 8.
45. *New York Evening Express*, February 20, 1861, p. 4.
46. *Ibid.*
47. *New York Times*, February 20, 1861, p. 8.
48. *Ibid.*
49. *Ibid.*
50. *New York Times*, February 20, 1861, p. 8.
51. *Ibid.*
52. *New York Times*, February 20, 1861, p. 4.

Chapter 11

1. *New York Times*, February 29, 1861, p. 4.
2. Edwin Burrows and Mike Wallace, *Gotham: A History of New York City to 1898*. New York: Oxford University Press, 1999, p. 867.
3. *New York Times*, February 21, 1861, p. 4.
4. Mansch, p. 163.
5. *New York Herald*, February 21, 1861, p. 8.
6. *New York Evening Express*, February 21, 1861, p. 4.
7. *New York Herald*, February 21, 1861, p. 8.

8. *New York Times*, February 21, 1861, p. 4.
9. *New York Herald*, February 21, 1861, p. 1.
10. *The Brooklyn Daily Eagle*, February 20, 1861, p. 2.
11. John Pope, "War Reminiscences," *National Tribune*, February 5, 1891, p. 4.
12. *Ibid.*
13. John Lockwood and Charles Lockwood, "First South Carolina. Then New York?" *New York Times*, January 6, 2011, p. 4.
14. *New York Tribune*, December 8, 1860, p. 4.
15. *New York Times*, February 21, 1861, p. 4.
16. *New York Sun*, February 21, 1861, p. 2.
17. *The Brooklyn Daily Eagle*, February 20, 1861, p. 2.
18. *Ibid.*
19. *Ibid.*
20. *New York Times*, February 21, 1861, p. 4.
21. *New York Times*, February 21, 1861, p. 1.
22. *New York Times*, February 21, 1861, p. 4.
23. *New York Evening Express*, February 20, 1861, p. 4.
24. *New York Herald*, February 21, 1861, p. 1.
25. *Ibid.*
26. *Brooklyn Daily Eagle*, February 20, 1861, p. 2.
27. *New York Sun*, February 21, 1861, p. 2.
28. *New York Herald*, February 21, 1861, p. 1.
29. *Ibid.*
30. *Ibid.*
31. *Ibid.*
32. *New York Sun*, February 2, 1861, p. 2.
33. *Ibid.*
34. *New York Herald*, February 21, 1861, p. 8.
35. *Ibid.*
36. *Ibid.*
37. *Ibid.*
38. Stephan Carter, "Lincoln's Top Hat," *Smithsonian Magazine*, November 2013, p. 50.
39. *The New York Evening Post*, September 2, 1839, p. 2.
40. *New York World*, February 21, 1861, p. 4.
41. "Abe Lincoln's Hat," *The Collector*, Vol. 3, # 15 (June 1, 1892): 231.
42. James Carter, "Abraham Lincoln's Top Hat: The Inside Story," *Smithsonian Magazine*, November 2013, pp. 49–50
43. *New York Times*, February 21, 1861, p. 8.
44. *Ibid.*
45. *New York Daily Tribune*, February 21, 1861, p. 8.
46. *Ibid.*
47. *New York Times*, February 21, 1861, p. 8.
48. *New York Evening Express*, February 21, 1861, p. 4.
49. Carl Sandburg, *Abraham Lincoln: The Prairie Years and The War Years*. New York: Harcourt, Brace, & World, 1954, p. 202.
50. Benjamin P. Thomas, *Abraham Lincoln*. New York: Alfred A. Knopf, 1962, p. 241.

Chapter 12

1. *Albany Evening Journal*, May 2, 1865, p. 2.
2. *Ibid.*
3. *Ibid.*
4. *Ibid.*
5. Lamon, *Recollections of Abraham Lincoln*, p. 161.
6. *Troy Daily Times*, April 26, 1865, p. 2.
7. *Ibid.*
8. Harold Holzer (Ed.), *Dear Mr. Lincoln: Letters to the President*. Carbondale: Southern Illinois Press, 1993, p. 341.
9. Holzer, p. 345.
10. Lamon, p. 281.
11. Gary Wills, *Lincoln at Gettysburg: The Words That Remade America*. New York: Simon & Schuster, 1992, p. 60.
12. *Albany Evening Journal*, April 26, 1865, p. 2.
13. *Ibid.*
14. *Washington Evening News*, April 21, 1865, p. 2.
15. *National Tribune*, May 22, 1915, p. 4.
16. *Ibid.*

Chapter 13

1. *Altamont Enterprise*, April 20, 1945, p. 1.
2. *Albany Atlas and Argus*, April 21, 1865, p. 3.
3. Bernadette Loeffel-Atkins, *Widows Weeds and Weeping Veils: Mourning Rituals in 19th Century America*. Gettysburg: Privately Published, 2002, p. 1.
4. *The New York Times*, April 21, 1865, p. 2.
5. *Ibid.*
6. *Poughkeepsie Daily Press*, April 26, 1865, p. 3.
7. *The New York Times*, April 26, 1865, p. 8.
8. *The New York Times*, April 21, 1865, p. 2.
9. *Albany Morning Express*, April 26, 1865, p. 2.
10. *Albany Evening Journal*, April 25, 1865, p. 1.

Chapter 14

1. *The New York Times*, April 27, 1865, p. 4.
2. David Thomas Valentine, *Obsequies of Abraham Lincoln, In the City of New York*. New York: Edmund Jones & Company, 1866, p. 116.
3. *The New York Times*, April 28, 1865, p. 3.
4. William T. Coggeshall, *Lincoln Memorial. The Journeys of Abraham Lincoln: From Springfield to Washington, 1861, as President Elect; and from Washington to Springfield, 1865, as President Martyred: Comprising an Account of Public Ceremonies on the Future Route, and Full Details of Both Journeys*. Columbus: Ohio State Journal, 1865, p. 162.
5. *The New York Times*, April 25, 1865, p. 1.
6. *The New York Sun*, April 25, 1865, p. 1.
7. Valentine, p. 56.
8. *Ibid.*, p. 60.
9. John Carroll Power, *Abraham Lincoln: His Life, Public Services, Death and Great Funeral Cortege: With a History and Description of the National Lincoln Monument, With an Appendix*. Springfield: H. W. Rokker, Printer and Binder, 1882, p. 152.
10. *The New York Herald*, April 25, 1865, p. 2.
11. *The New York Times*, April 26, 1865, p. 1.
12. *Ibid.*
13. Victor Searcher, *The Farewell to Lincoln*. New York: Abington, 1965, p. 132.
14. *The New York Times*, April 26, 1865, p. 1.
15. *Ibid.*
16. *Ibid.*
17. *The New York Times*, April 2, 2014, p. 12.
18. Coggeshall, p. 166.

19. *The New York Times*, April 28, 1865, p. 4.
20. *Ibid.*
21. *The New York Times*, April 25, 1865, p. 1.
22. *Ibid.*
23. Coggeshall, p. 166.
24. Valentine, pp. 127–128.
25. *The New York Times*, April 25, 1865, p. 1.
26. *The New York Times*, April 26, 1865, p. 8.
27. *The New York Times*, April 25, 1865, p. 8.
28. *The New York Times*, April 26, 1865, p. 8.
29. *The New York Times*, April 25, 1865, p. 1.
30. *The New York Sun*, April 26, 1865, p. 1.

Chapter 15

1. *Poughkeepsie Daily Express*, April 26, 1865, p. 2
2. Coggeshall, p. 178.
3. *Schenectady Daily Evening Star*, April 25, 1865, p. 1.
4. Valentine, p. 147.
5. *New York Evening Post*, April 25, 1865, p. 2.
6. *Ibid.*, p. 3.
7. Coggeshall, p. 171.
8. *The New York Times*, April 11, 1965, p. 4.
9. *Rome Citizen*, April 27, 1865, p. 2.
10. Valentine, p. 150.
11. *Ibid.*
12. *The New York Sun*, April 26, 1865, p. 1.
13. *The New York Times*, April 26, 1865, p. 8.
14. *Ibid.*
15. *Ibid.*
16. *Ibid.*
17. Coggeshall, p. 185.
18. *The New York Times*, April 26, 1865, p. 2.
19. *The New York Times*, April 28, 1865, p. 2.

Chapter 16

1. *Rochester Daily Democrat*, April 26, 1865, p. 1.
2. *The New York Times*, April 28, 1865, p. 2.
3. Coggeshall, p. 202.
4. *The Yonkers Statesman*, May 11, 1865, p. 4.
5. *Ibid.*
6. *Ibid.*
7. *The New York Times*, April 26, 1865, p. 2.
8. Gregory Smith, "Farragut and the Lincoln Funeral Train," *Hastings Historian*, Vol. 42, #1 (Winter 2012): 2.
9. "More on the Lincoln Funeral Train," *Hastings Historian* (Spring 2012): 4.
10. *Poughkeepsie Daily Eagle*, April 26, 1865, p. 3.
11. *Ibid.*
12. *Tarrytown Daily News*, January 25, 1934, p. 9.
13. MacDonald, p. 125.
14. *Ibid.*
15. *Poughkeepsie Daily Express*, April 26, 1865, p. 3.
16. MacDonald, p. 124.
17. Coggeshall, p. 202.
18. *Harper's Weekly*, May 20, 1865, p. 1.
19. *Poughkeepsie Daily Express*, April 26, 1865, p. 4.
20. Anthony Czarnecki, "Mr. Lincoln's Visit to Peekskill: The Sesquicentennial of the Inaugural Journey," *The Westchester Historian*, Vol. 87, #1 (Winter 2011): 29.
21. *Rochester Daily Democrat*, April 26, 1865, p. 1.
22. *Ibid.*
23. *Poughkeepsie Daily Press*, April 20, 1865, p. 7.
24. *Poughkeepsie Daily Press*, April 26, 1865, p. 2.
25. *Ibid.*
26. *Poughkeepsie Daily Eagle*, April 28, 1865, p. 3.
27. *Albany Evening Journal*, April 27, 1865, p. 3.
28. *Poughkeepsie Daily Press*, April 28, 1865, p. 3.
29. *Poughkeepsie Daily Eagle*, April 28, 1865, p. 3.
30. *Poughkeepsie Daily Eagle*, April 27, 1865, p. 3.
31. *Albany Morning Express*, April 26, 1865, p. 3.

Chapter 17

1. *Albany Evening Express*, April 28, 1865, p. 2.
2. *Albany Evening Journal*, April 26, 1865, p. 2.
3. *Albany Morning Express*, April 25, 1865, p. 2.
4. *Ibid.*
5. *Washington Evening Star*, April 17, 1865, p. 1.
6. *Ibid.*
7. *Ibid.*
8. *Ibid.*
9. *Albany Evening Journal*, April 26, 1865, p. 2.
10. *Albany Morning Express*, April 26, 1865, p. 2.
11. E. Lawrence Abel, *A Finger in Lincoln's Brain*. Denver: Praeger, 2015, p. 88.
12. *Albany Times and Courier*, April 26, 1865, p. 3.
13. *The New York Herald*, April 27, 1865, p. 2.
14. *Albany Evening Journal*, April 26, 1865, p. 2.
15. *Albany Morning Express*, April 26, 1865, p. 2.
16. *Ibid.*
17. *Ibid.*
18. *Albany Evening Journal*, April 26, 1965, p. 2.
19. *The National Tribune*, May 27, 1915, p. 3.
20. *Albany Atlas & Argus*, April 17, 1865, p. 3.
21. *Washington Evening Star*, April 25, 1865, p. 1.
22. *Ibid.*
23. *Troy Daily Press*, April 28, 1861, p. 3.
24. *Rochester Daily Union & Advertiser*, April 27, 1865, p. 2.
25. *Albany Morning Express*, April 25, 1865, p. 2.
26. *Albany Atlas & Argus*, April 21, 1865, p. 2.
27. *The New York Herald*, April 27, 1865, p. 2.
28. *The New York Times*, April 27, 1865, p. 1.
29. *Poughkeepsie Daily Express*, April 27, 1865, p. 2.
30. *Troy Daily Press*, April 27, 1865, p. 3.
31. *New York Herald*, April 27, 1861, p. 2.
32. *Rochester Daily Union and Advertiser*, April 27, 1865, p. 2.
33. *Albany Atlas & Argus*, April 20, 1865, p.2.
34. *Ibid.*
35. *The New York Times*, April 27, 1865, p. 1.
36. *Albany Atlas & Argus*, April 27, 1865, p. 2.
37. *Albany Evening Journal*, April 27, 1865, p. 2.
38. *Ibid.*
39. *Ibid.*
40. *The New York Times*, April 27, 1865, p. 1.
41. *Albany Times & Courier*, April 27, 1865, p. 3.
42. *Albany Evening Journal*, April 27, 1865, p. 2.
43. *Albany Morning Express*, April 27, 1865, p. 2.
44. *Ibid.*
45. *Ibid.*
46. *Albany Times & Courier*, April 27, 1865, p. 3.
47. *Albany Evening Times*, April 27, 1865, p. 2.
48. *Albany Morning Express*, April 27, 1865, p. 2.

49. *The New York Times*, April 27, 1865, p. 1.
50. *Albany Evening Journal*, April 27, 1865, p. 3.
51. *The New York Times*, April 27, 1865, p. 1.
52. *New York Herald*, April 27, 1865, p. 2.
53. *Rochester Daily Union & Advertiser*, April 27, 1865, p. 2.
54. *Albany Morning Express*, April 27, 1865, p. 2.
55. *The New York Times*, April 27, 1865, p. 1.
56. *Albany Morning Express*, April 27, 1865, p. 2.

Chapter 18

1. *National Tribune*, May 27, 1915, p. 4.
2. *Albany Evening Journal*, April 26, 1865, p. 2.
3. *Ibid.*
4. *Schenectady Evening Star*, April 26, 1865, p. 3.
5. *Albany Evening Journal*, April 27, 1865, p. 2.
6. J. W. Becker and William S. Porter, "The Lincoln Funeral Train." *Journal of the Illinois State Historical Society*, Vol. 9, # 3 (October 1916): 317.
7. *Rochester Evening Express*, April 26, 1865, p. 3.
8. *Batavia Spirit of the Times*, May 6, 1865, p. 2.
9. *New York Times*, April 17, 1865, p. 2.
10. *Ibid.*
11. *Utica Morning Herald*, April 27, 1865, p. 3.
12. *The New York Times*, April 28, 1865, p. 3.
13. Coggeshall, p. 204.
14. Power, p. 159.
15. *Ibid.*
16. *The New York Times*, April 28, 1861, p. 3.
17. *Ibid.*
18. *Ibid.*
19. *Syracuse Herald*, February 12, 1914, p. 17.
20. Power, p. 159.
21. *Syracuse Herald*, February 12, 1914, p. 17.
22. Chauncey Depew, *My Memories of Eighty Years*, New York: Charles Scribner's Sons, 1924, p. 64.
23. *Utica Morning Herald*, April 27, 1865, p. 3.
24. Power, p. 160.
25. *Ibid.*
26. *Little Falls Journal and Courier*, April 27, 1865, p. 2.
27. Power, p. 161.
28. *Herkimer Democrat*, May 3, 1865, p. 2.
29. *Ibid.*
30. Handbill, property of the Ilion Public Library, Ilion, New York.
31. Depew, p. 64–65.
32. Coggeshall, p. 204.

Chapter 19

1. *Utica Weekly Herald*, May 31, 1864, p. 5.
2. *Ibid.*
3. *Ibid.*
4. *Utica Weekly Herald*, May 3, 1864, p. 2.
5. *Utica Weekly Herald*, April 27, 1865, p. 3.
6. *Utica Morning Herald*, April 27, 1865, p. 2.
7. *Utica Weekly Herald*, April 27, 1865, p. 5.
8. *Utica Observer-Dispatch*, August 9, 2015.
9. *Ibid.*
10. *Utica Weekly Herald*, May 3, 1865, p. 5.
11. *Ibid.*
12. *New York Sun*, April 28, 1865, p. 4.
13. *Utica Weekly Herald*, April 27, 1865, p. 5.
14. *Geneva Gazette*, May 5, 1865, p. 2.
15. *Utica Observer-Dispatch*, April 23, 2009, Part B.
16. *Utica Weekly Herald*, May 3, 1865, p. 5.
17. *Ibid.*
18. *Utica Morning Herald*, April 27, 1865, p. 2.
19. *Geneva Gazette*, May 5, 1865, p. 2.
20. *The New York Times*, magazine supplement, April 10, 1915, p. 13.
21. *Geneva Gazette*, May 5, 1865, p. 2.
22. *Utica Morning Herald*, April 27, 1865, p. 2.
23. *Oneida Weekly Herald*, March 6, 1864, p. 6.
24. www.oneidadispatch.com.
25. *Ibid.*

Chapter 20

1. *Syracuse Standard*, April 27, 1865, p. 2.
2. *The New York Times*, April 28, 1865, p. 8.
3. *Syracuse Standard*, April 27, 1865, p. 2.
4. *Oswego Daily Palladium*, April 27, 1865, pp. 2–3.
5. *Syracuse Standard*, April 27, 1865, p. 2.
6. *The New York Times*, April 28, 1865, p. 8.
7. *Syracuse Post-Standard*, February 12, 1914, p. 17.
8. *Syracuse Journal*, April 27, 1865, p. 2.
9. *Baldwinsville Gazette*, February 13, 1864, p. 2.
10. *Ibid.*
11. *Ibid.*
12. Power, p. 160.
13. *Baldwinsville Gazette*, March 12, 1964, p. 2.
14. *Ibid.*
15. *Auburn Citizen*, February 9, 2009, p. 3.
16. *Syracuse Daily Journal*, August 25, 1925, p. 4.
17. *Ibid.*
18. Alfred Seelye Roe, *The Ninth New York Heavy Artillery: A History of its Organization, Services in the Defenses of Washington Marches, Camps, Battles and Muster-Out*. Worcester, MA: Published by the author, 1899, pp. 241–242
19. Elizabeth Caley Copson, *History of Thomas Caley, One of the First Deacons of Brighton Church*. Monograph written for the New York State Historical Society, 1958.
20. *Mohawk Valley Democrat*, April 26, 1865, p. 2.
21. www.OneidaDispatch.com.
22. *The New York Times*, April 28, 1865, p. 8.
23. *Ibid.*
24. Power, p. 163.
25. *Batavia Spirit of the Times*, April 29, 1865, p. 2.
26. *Buffalo Daily Courier*, April 28, 1865, p. 2.

Chapter 21

1. *Buffalo Daily Courier*, April 28, 1865, p. 2.
2. *Rochester Daily Democrat*, April 28, 1865, p. 4.
3. *Ibid.*
4. *Buffalo Daily Courier*, April 28, 1865, p. 3.
5. *Ibid.*, p. 2
6. Diary entry of James Munro, April 27, 1865, Onondaga County Historical Society.
7. *Albany Morning Express*, April 25, 1865, p. 3.
8. *Utica Morning Herald & Daily Gazette*, April 28, 1865, p. 3.

9. *Buffalo Daily Courier*, April 28, 1865, p. 3.
10. *Ibid.*
11. *Buffalo Daily Courier*, April 28, 1865, p. 2.
12. *Buffalo Daily Courier*, April 28, 1865, p. 3.
13. *Ibid.*
14. *Rochester Daily Union & Advertiser*, April 28, 1865, p. 2.
15. *Ibid.*
16. *Ibid.*
17. *Rochester Daily Union & Advertiser*, April 28, 1865, p. 4.
18. *Ibid.*
19. *Ibid.*
20. *Buffalo Daily Express*, April 28, 1865, p. 2.
21. *Buffalo Daily Courier*, April 28, 1865, p. 3.
22. *Buffalo Daily Courier*, April 28, 1865, p. 3.
23. *Rochester Daily Union & Advertiser*, April 28, 1865, p. 2.
24. *Dunkirk Weekly Journal*, May 5, 1865, p. 3.
25. *Ibid.*
26. Power, p. 166.
27. *Utica Morning Herald & Daily Gazette*, April 29, 1865, p. 3.
28. Fred Trump, *Lincoln's Little Girl*. Honesdale, PA: Boyds Mills, 1977, p. 93.
29. *Ibid.*

Bibliography

Periodicals

Albany Argus
Albany Atlas and Argus
Albany Evening Journal
Albany Journal
Albany Morning Express
Albany Times and Courier
Auburn Citizen
Auburn Daily Advertiser
Auburn Daily Advertiser and American Union
Baldwinsville Gazette
Ballston Journal
Batavia Republican Advocate
Batavia Spirit of the Times
Boston Post
Brockport Republican
Brooklyn Eagle
Buffalo Commercial Advertiser
Buffalo Daily Courier
Buffalo Morning Express
Cazenovia Republican
Chatham Courier
Cleveland Morning Leader
Clyde Weekly Times
Cohoes Cataract
The Connecticut Press
Daily Ohio Statesman
Douglass Monthly
Dunkirk Weekly Journal
Elmira Daily Advertiser
Frank Leslie's Illustrated Newspaper
Geneva Gazette
Harper's Weekly
Hartford Courier
Herkimer Democrat
Hudson Weekly Star
Lansingburgh Chronicle
Little Falls Journal and Courier
Mohawk Valley American
Mohawk Valley Democrat
Moore's Rural Journal
The National Republican
National Tribune
New York Daily Tribune
New York Evening Express
New York Herald
New York Sun
New York Times
New York World
Oneida Weekly Herald and Gazette
Oswego Daily Palladium
Poughkeepsie Daily American
Poughkeepsie Daily Eagle
Poughkeepsie Daily Press
Poughkeepsie Eagle
Poughkeepsie Telegraph
Putnam County Courier
Rhinebeck Gazette
Rochester Daily Democrat
Rochester Daily Democrat & American
Rochester Daily Union & Advertiser
Rochester Evening Express
Rome Citizen
Rome Sentinel
Schenectady Daily Times
Schenectady Evening Star and Times
Springfield Republican
Syracuse Central Daily Courier
Syracuse Courier & Union
Syracuse Herald Journal
Syracuse Journal
The Syracuse Post-Standard
Tarrytown Daily News
Troy Daily Press
Troy Daily Times
Troy Daily Whig
Troy Weekly Times
Utica Morning Herald and Daily Gazette
Utica Observer-Dispatch
Washington Evening Star
Waterford Journal
West Troy Advocate
Westfield Republican
Yonkers Statesman

Primary Sources

Basler, Roy. *The Collected Works of Abraham Lincoln*. New Brunswick: Rutgers University Press, 1953.

Coggeshall, William. *Lincoln Memorial. The Journeys of Abraham Lincoln: From Springfield to Washington, 1861, As President Elect; and From Washington to Springfield, 1865, as President Martyred; Comprising an Account of Public Ceremonies on the Entire Route, and Full Details of Both Journeys.* Columbus: Ohio State Journal, 1865.

Croffut, William A. *An American Procession: 1855–1914*. Boston: Little, Brown, 1931.

Herndon, William, and Jesse Wiek. *Life of Lincoln.* New York: Albert & Charles Boni, 1930.
Holzer, Harold (Ed.) *Dear Mr. Lincoln: Letters to the President.* New York: Addison-Wesley, 1995.
Lamon, Ward Hill. *The Life of Abraham Lincoln.* Lincoln: University of Nebraska Press, 1999.
Lamon, Ward Hill. *Recollections of Abraham Lincoln: 1847–1865.* Lincoln: University of Nebraska Press, 1994.
Nicolay, John G. (Ed. Michael Burlingame). *An Oral History of Abraham Lincoln.* Carbondale: Southern Illinois University Press, 1996.
Pratt, Henry E. (Ed.). *Concerning Mr. Lincoln.* Springfield: Abraham Lincoln Association, 1944.
Roe, Alfred Seelye. *The Ninth New York Heavy Artillery: A History of its Organization, Services in the Defenses of Washington, Marches, Camps, Battles and Mustering-Out.* Worcester, MA: Published by the author, 1899.
Villard, Henry. *Lincoln on the Eve of '61.* New York: Alfred Knopf, 1941.
Villard, Henry. *Memoirs of Henry Villard, Journalist and Financier, 1935–1862, Vol. 1.* New York: Houghton, Mifflin, 1904.
Whitman, Walt. *Complete Prose Works.* Philadelphia: David McKay, 1892.

Periodicals

Becker, J. W., and William S. Porter. "The Lincoln Funeral Train." *Journal of the Illinois State Historical Society,* Vol. 9, #3 (October 1916), pp. 315–319.
Candenquist, Arthur. "World's First Military Railroad." *Civil War Times,* Vol. XLIX, #3 (June 2010), p. 36–43
Czarnecki, Andrew. "Mr. Lincoln's Visit to Peekskill: The Sesquicentennial of an Inaugural Journey." *The Westchester Historian,* Vol. 87, #3 (Winter 2011), p. 4–33.
Hankey, John P. "The Railroad War." *Trains,* Vol. 71, #3 (March 2011), p. 24–35.
Hansen, Peter. "The Rail Splitter and the Railroads." *Trains,* Vol. 69, #2 (February 2009), p. 28–41.
Lederer, Richard. "Lincoln as Jokester." *The Saturday Evening Post,* June 25, 2013.
MacDonald, Norm. "Abraham Lincoln's Links to Ossining." *The Westchester Historian,* Vol. 90, #4 (Fall 2014), p. 122–126.
Middleton, William D. "Rails Across the Hudson." *Railroad History,* #186 (Spring 2002).
Morrisett, Julie. "The Civil War Era in Westchester County," *The Westchester Historian,* Vol. 77, #3 (Summer 2001).
Tomaino, Frank. "Lincoln Advisor Visits Utica." *Utica Observer-Dispatch,* August 9, 2015.

Secondary Sources

Abel, E. Lawrence. *A Finger in Lincoln's Brain.* Denver: Praeger, 2015.
Atkins, Bernadette Loeffel. *Widow's Weeds and Weeping Veils: Mourning Rituals In 19th Century America.* Gettysburg: R. C. Atkins, 2002.
Baker, Jean. *Mary Todd Lincoln: A Biography.* New York: W.W. Norton, 1987.
Burlingame, Michael. *Abraham Lincoln: A Life (Vols. One and Two).* Baltimore: Johns Hopkins University Press, 2008.
Central New York Chapter of the National Railway Historical Society. *Railroads in the Streets of Syracuse.* Marcellus: Central New York Chapter NRHS, 1979.
Chautauqua History Company. *The Centennial History of Chautauqua County, Vol. II.* Jamestown: Chautauqua History, 1904.
Fagant John. *The Best of the Bargain: Lincoln in Western New York.* Bloomington: Authorhouse, 2010.
Fox, Richard W. *A Cultural History of Lincoln's Body.* New York: W.W. Norton, 2015.
Gary, Ralph. *Following in Lincoln's Footsteps: A Complete Annotated Reference to Hundreds of Historical Sites Visited by Abraham Lincoln.* New York: Carroll & Graf, 2002.
Hamlin, Charles E. *The Life and Times of Hannibal Hamlin.* (2 vols.) Cambridge: Riverside Press, 1899.
Hislop, Codman. *Rivers of America: The Mohawk River.* New York: J.J. Little and Ives, 1948.
Hodes, Martha. *Mourning Lincoln.* New Haven: Yale University Press, 2015.
Holland, Josiah G. *The Life of Abraham Lincoln.* Lincoln: University of Nebraska Press, 1998.
Holzer, Harold. *Lincoln at Cooper Union: The Speech That Made Abraham Lincoln President.* New York: Simon & Schuster, 2004.
Hunt, H. Draper. *Hannibal Hamlin of Maine: Lincoln's First Vice-President.* Syracuse: Syracuse University Press, 1969.
Klara, Robert. *FDR'S Funeral Train.* Houndmills: Palgrave Macmillan, 2010.
Klein, Aaron. *The History of the New York Central System.* New York: Brompton, 1985.
Leisch, Juanita. *An Introduction to Civil War Civilians.* Gettysburg: Thomas, 1994.
Mansch, Larry D. *Abraham Lincoln, President-Elect: The Four Critical Months from Election to Inauguration.* Jefferson, NC: McFarland, 2005.
May, Trevor. *The Victorian Undertaker.* Buckinghamshire: Shire, 2003.
Meserve, Dorothy Kunhardt, and Philip B. Kunhardt, Jr. *Twenty Days.* Secaucus: Castle, 1965.
Oates, Stephan. *With Malice Toward None: The Life of Abraham Lincoln.* New York: Harper & Row, 1977.
Phelan, Mary K. *Mr. Lincoln's Inaugural Journey.* New York: Thomas Y. Crowell, 1972.
Power, John Carroll. *Abraham Lincoln: His Life, Public Services, Death and Great Funeral Cortege: With a History and Description of the National Lincoln Monument, With an Appendix.* Springfield: H.W. Rokker, Printer and Publisher, 1892.
Ross, Ishbel. *The President's Wife: Mary Todd Lincoln.* New York: G.P. Putnam's Sons, 1973.
Sandburg, Carl. *Abraham Lincoln: The Prairie Years and The War Years.* New York: Harcourt, Brace & World, 1939.
Scarry, Robert J. *Millard Fillmore.* Jefferson, NC: McFarland, 2001.
Searcher, Victor. *The Farewell to Lincoln.* New York: Abington, 1965.
Searcher, Victor. *Lincoln's Journey to Greatness.* Philadelphia: John C. Winston, 1960.
Starr, John W. *Lincoln and the Railroads.* New York: Kessinger, 2010.

Staufer, Alvin F. *New York Central's Early Power: 1831 to 1916*. Privately Published by Alvin Staufer, 1967.

Stern, Milton. *Harriet Lane*. Washington, D.C.: Self-Published, 2003.

Thomas, Benjamin P. *Abraham Lincoln*. New York: Random House, 1968.

Trostel, Scott D. *The Lincoln Funeral Train*. Fletcher: Cam-Tech, 2002.

Trostel, Scott D. *The Lincoln Inaugural Train*. Fletcher: Cam-Tech, 2011.

Trump, Fred. *Lincoln's Little Girl*. Honesdale, PA: Boyds Mills, 1977.

Turner, Justin G., and Linda Leavitt Turner (Ed.). *Mary Todd Lincoln: Her Life and Letters*. New York: Alfred Knopf, 1972.

Wills, Gary. *Lincoln at Gettysburg: The Words That Remade America*. New York: Simon & Schuster, 1992.

Index

Numbers in ***bold italics*** indicate pages with illustrations

Acheron 205
Adams, John Quincey 265
Adirondack Mountains ***55***, 266
Ainsworth, Ira 81
Albany, New York 1, 10, 34, 43, 47, 54, 56, 58, 61, 65, 66, 67, ***71***, 80, 81, 83, 84, 86, ***87***, 90, 96, 98, 107, 111, 116, 122, 123, 142, 145, 165, 168, 180, 186, 192, 193, 194, 198, 199, 200, 202, 203, ***205***, 208, 209, 210, 211, 212, 216, 217, 220, 221, 222, 223, 224, 226, 237, 238, 239, 251
Albany & Northern Railroad 81
Albany & Vermont Railroad 86, 87, 94, 193
Albany Atlas & Argus 73
Albany Burgesses Corps 83, 103, 105
Albany County 68
Albany Evening Journal 37, 79, 93, 101, 158, 213, 222
Albany Herald 89
Albany Morning Express 164, 207
Albany Times and Courier 244
Albion, New York 256
Altamont Enterprise 161
American Hotel ***21***
Amsterdam, New York ***54***, 61, 62, 63, 224
Andersonville Prison 241, 250
Andre, John 116, 121
Andrew, Gov. John 45
Angola 262
Anguish, Horace 241
Aspinwall, William 137
Assembly Chamber 207, 208, 211, 212, 215
Astor, J.J. 137
Astor House 82, 122, 124, 126, 127, 128, ***129***, 133, 134, 137, 146, 147, 148, 170
Atlas 262, 263
Auburn, New York 36, 120
"Auld Lang Syne" 148, 217
Avery, E.W. 51

Babcock, James 132
Bachman, Mayor Samuel 109
Bagg's Square ***49***, 234

Baker, Col. Edwin 151
Ball, H. Chandler 70, 98
Baltimore, Maryland 11, 150, 153, 208, 209
Bangor, Maine 43, 44, 46, 83
Banks, Gen. Nathaniel 239
Barnum, P.T. 143, 144
Barryville, New York 111
Batavia, New York 30, 255, 265
Bates, William 239
Bedell, Grace 13, ***14***, 268
Beecher, Henry Ward 81, 144
Beecher, Lyman 138, 144
Beeson, Father John 28
Bell, John 79, 257
Bellamy, Francis 43
Belmont, Mrs. August 146
Bemis, John 19
Benedict, Erastus 147
Benjamin, William 196
Bible 247
Bigalow, George 144
Bigalow, John 79, 257
Blakely, Adoniram Judson 72
Bloomer's Dining Hall 254
Bobo, William 128
Booth, John Wilkes 80, 153, 212, 248, 255
Boston, Massachusetts 44, 46, 83, 85, 114
Boston & Maine Railroad 44
Brady, Mathew 44, 163, 164
Brandneth, Benjamin 120
Brandneth, Franklin 120
Brandneth Pill Factory 120
Bridgeport, Connecticut 85, 132
Brighton, New York 249, 250
Broadway (Albany) 66, 68, 69, 70, 71, 72, 81, 212, 213, 214, 215, 218
Broadway (NYC) 124, 125, 129, 134, 144, 148, 164, 169, 170, 181, 206
Broadway (Troy) 104
Brockport, New York 32
The Brockport Republican 31
Brockton, New York 263
Brooklyn, New York 114, 125, 137, 145, 164, 178, 181, 190, 191
Brooklyn Daily Eagle 111
Brown, Anson 226

Brown, Dr. Charles 172, 173, 207, 208, 209, 259
Brown, John 243, 244, 245
Brunswick, New Jersey 222
Buchanan, Pres. James 26, ***26***, 31, 51, 79, 146, 264
Buffalo, New York 9, ***12***, 17, ***20***, ***21***, 27, 29–30, 34, 37, 38, 47, 58, 80, 81, 123, 165, 168, 180, 222, 229, 231, 237, 239, 250, 251, 253, 254, 255, 257, ***258***, 259, 261
Buffalo Daily Courier 255, 256
Buffalo Daily Times 255, 256
Burden, Henry 89
Bush, Pres. George 265
Butterfield, John 230

Caley, Ann Morrill 249
Caley, Catherine 250
Caley, Francis 249
Caley, John 249, 250
Caley, Mary 249
Caley, Ruth 250
Cameron, Simon 239
Canajoharie 54, 56, 225
Canastota 241
Cannon's Gallery 163, 200
Capitol building (Albany) 70, 73, ***76***, 79, 103, 104, 203, 206, 210, 212, 214, 215
Capitol building (United States) 151, 154
Capitoline Park 67, 71, 72, 207
Carroll, William 152
casket 164, 168, 170, 172, 173, 175, 176, 177, 179, 180, 181, 183, 186, 189, 190, 194, 200, 202, 203, ***204***, 207, 208, 209, 210, 211, 213, 214, 215, 217, 220, 221, 222, 225, 236, 240, 256, 260, 261, 266
Castleton-on-the-Hudson 193, 195
catafalque 175, 177, 190, 191, 207, 209, 211, 212, 216, 260
Catskill Landing 201
Catskill Mountains ***55***, 116, 120, 199
Cazenovia Convention 36
Central Station Depot 31, ***32***, 68
Charon 205
Chatauqua County 11, 15–16
Chauncey Vibbard 51, 217, ***218***, 237

281

Index

Chicago, Illinois 1, 44, 60, 93, 154, 173, 239, 262
Chiliusa, Robert 250
Chiliusa, Sebastian 250
Chiliusa, Thomas 250
Chittenango 241
City Hall (NYC) 137, 167, 168, 171, 173, 175, 176, 178, *179*, 186
Civil War 2, 57, 58, 61, 77, 88, 94, 95, 99, 115, 162, 170, 196, 222, 225, 235, 239, 249, 261
Clapp, Almon 19
Clark, Myron 141
Claverack Landing, New York 100
Clay, Henry 134, 212
Cleveland, Grover 265
Cleveland, Ohio 30, 154, 253, 261
Clinton, William 265
Clinton, New York 43, 48, 262, 263
Clyde 35–36, 248, 255
The Clyde Weekly Times 35
coffin 158, 170, 173, 176, 177, 179, 183, 184, 190, 203, 204, 205, 207, 216
Coggshall, William 175, 178, 183, 224
Cohoes 87, 88, 89, 216
Cohoes Cataract 71, 75, 91
Cohoes Falls *91*
Cold Spring 115, 129, 198
Collins, Pvt. George 58
Colt, Samuel 86
Colvin, Andrew 75, 76, 77
Comet 26
Congressional Cemetery 154, 156
Connelly, Richard 85, 132
Constitution 96, 97, 112, 113, 119, 120, 121, 186, 187, 201
Cooper Union 121, 128, 129, 145
Cornell, Charles 6, 124, 126
cortège 154, 164, 171, 185, 188, 189, 207, 214, 221, 222, 232, 234, 242, 250, 251, 253, 256, 258, 260, 261
Cozzen's Hotel 115

daguerreotype 35, 163, 174, 256, 258
Davis, David 10, 123
Davis, Jefferson 9, 62
deadhead 34
Dean, Timothy 241
Dean Richmond 29, 34, 251, *251*, 254
DeBrosses Street 106, 167, 169, 170
Delavan House 71, *78*, 79, 81, 82, 98, 142, 211
Democrats 47, 50, 69, 73, 111, 123
DePew, Chauncey 118, 231
DesBrosses Street *167*
Dewey, Joshua 137–138
Dix, Gen. John 168, 169, 174, 178, 179, 181, 182, 183, 207, 209, 237, 259, 261
Dobbs Ferry 121, 193, 195
Dodsworth's Band 217
Doring's Band 98, 102, 205, 217
Douglas, Stephan 5, 64, 79, 111, 123

Douglass, Frederick 31, 34, 60
Douglass Journal 31, 60
Dunkirk 9, 15–16, 33, 34, 221, 255
Dutch 61, 66, 108, 192

E. Remington & Sons 228
Earle, Emma 58
East Albany, New York 67, 87, 97, 108, 193, 202, 203, *205*, 216, 218
East Greenbush, New York 201
East Troy, New York 210
Eastman College Band 199, 200, 206, 217
Edward Jones 218, 222, 224, 226, 231, 237
Edwards, Elizabeth Todd 146
Elbridge, New York 256
Ellsworth, Elmer 10, *92*, 93, 94, 231
embalmer 172, 179, 207, 209, 259, 260
Empire State 11, 12, 36, 55, 61, 75, 77, 97, 106, 107, 110, 124, 146, 148, 149, 165, 166, 168, 182, 210, 221, 239, 247, 249, 253, 263, 269
Engine #57 96
Engine #79 251
Engine #84 34
Engine #202 243, 251
Engine #248 243
Engine #282 251
Erastus Corning 63
Erie, Pennsylvania 11, 57, 253, 255, 264
Erie Canal 30, 36, 37, 40, 47, *49*, 54, 55, 58, 60, 95, 229, 230, 233, 242, 246, 252
The Evening Post 62
Exchange Street Station *12*, 29, 254, 262

Fairport, New York 249
The Farewell to Lincoln 172
Farnham, New York 262
Farragut, David 195
"Father Abraham" 164, 238, 248
Fay, William 261
Fenton, Gov. Reuben 189, 221, 231
Ferdinand Magellan 158
Ferry, Sen. William 70, 76, 77
Filley, Morris 95
Fillmore, Pres. Millard, 27, 28, 47, 253, 256, *257*, 264
Fish, Hamilton 136, 137
Fishkill, New York 114
Fishkill Station, New York 199
Fonda, New York 224
Ford's Theater 80, 131, 145, 153, 205, 249
Fort Crailo 108
Fort Jefferson 89
Fort Moultrie 94
Fort Nassau 66
Fort Orange 66
Fort Pickens 89
Fort Plain 224
Fort Schuyler 47
Fort Stanwix 43

Fort Sumter 69, 94, 99
Fort Washington 192
Frankfort, New York 55, 56
Freeman, William 67
Frémont, Gen. John C. 144
Fugitive Slave Law 36
Fulton County 224
funeral arch 194, 195, 197–198
funeral train 154, 156, 158, 187, 202, 209, 212, 220, 221, 226, 227, 234, 239, 244, 247, 250, 254

Gaiety Theater 80
Garfield, Pres. James 160, 265
Garrison, New York 115, 116, 198, 199
Gary, Ralph 115
Genessee County 30
Genessee River 33, 252
Geneva Gazette 238
Genius of America 121, 200
Germantown, New York 111, 201
Gettysburg Address 70
Gilbert, Vezie, & Eaton 99
Glimpses of New York 128
Godey's Ladies Book 162
Goodrich, Thomas 264
Gould, William Henry Harrison 158, 208, 220
Governor's Room 138, 140, 142, 172, *175*, 190
Grant, Pres. Ulysses S 153, 264
Grates, William 57
Greeley, Horace 139, 147
Green, Seth 203
Green Island, New York 86, 87, 88, 90, 94, 95, 99
Green Island Bridge 99
Grinnell, Moses 136
Groux 95
Grove, Dewitt C. 50
Gunter, Charles 145
Gunter, Godfrey 166
Gurney, Jeremiah 174

Haight, Thomas 264
"Hail Columbia" 58, 109, 146, 148, 149
"Hail to the Chief" 70
Hall, Thomas 178
Halleck, Maj. Gen. Henry 234–235
Hamlin, Ellen 130, 133, 146, 147
Hamlin, Hannibal 44, *44*, *45*, 45, 83, *85*, 86 127, 129, 132, 133, 147, 148 ; *see also* Hamlin, Hannibal; speeches
Hampden, Maine 45
Harding, Pres. Warren 266
Harper, James 141
Harper's Weekly 126, 129, 198
Harris, Sen. Ira 80, 81, 124
Harritt, Thomas 237
Hart, John 262
Harvey, Henry 51, 219
Hastings-on-the-Hudson 193, 194
Hay, John 82, 174
Hayes, Pres. Rutherford B. 205
hearse 168, 170, 172, 186, 188, 189,

Index

190, 203, 209, **210**, 213, 222, 224, 237, 239, 251, 256, **258**
hearse car (train) 156, 157, 166, 179, 180, 183, 188, 200, 202, 221, 225, 227, 228
Helmer, Oliver 249
Henry, William "Jerry" 37
Herkimer, New York 54, 55, 227, 231
Herkimer County 43, 57
Highland CadetCorps 198
Hildene 248
Hoadley, David 136
Hoboken, New Jersey 147
Hogan, James 195
Holzer, Harold 144
Home Journal 82
"Honest Abe" 24
Horan, Thomas 262
hot box 31, 51, 57, 118–119; *see also* journal box
Houdin, Jean Antoine 140
Hubbell, Hon. Albert 50
Hudson 108, 109, 193, 293
Hudson, Joseph 119
Hudson, New York 108, 201
Hudson River 66, 67, 72, 86, 90, 96, **100**, 104, 108 111, 114, 116, 120, 121, 125, 149, 164, 169, 186, 192, 204, **205**, 211, 213, 228, 241
Hudson River Railroad 67, 86, 96, 98, 102, 107, 122, 166, 186, 187, **205**, 221
Hudson Valley 46, 66, 83, 115, 120, 122, 165, 190, 192, **193**, 196, 202
Hunt, Hon. Ward 50
Hunter, Maj. David 10
Hutchinson Cemetery 149
Hutchinson, Samuel 95
Hyde Park, New York 26, 160, 161
Hyer, Tom 141

Ilion 54, 55, 56, 228, **230**, 271
Illinois 64, 77, 92, 131, 150, 153, 156, 170, 182, 229, 239
Invalid Corps 169–170
Iroquois 47, 54, 57
Irving, Henrietta 80
Irving, Washington 121
Irvington, New York 195, 196, 262

Jackson, Pres. Andrew 212
Janeway, Maj. Robert 222
Jay, John 144
Jerry Rescue 37
Jersey Central Railroad 166
Jersey City, New Jersey
John H. Ide 95
John P. Jackson 149
Johnson, Pres. Andrew 265
Johnson, Luzerne 241
Johnson, William 53–54
Jordan, New York 245, **246**, **247**
journal box 31, 51, 57, 118–119; *see also* hot box
Judd, Norman 10

Kelly, Hon. William 110

Kennedy, James 137, 141
Kennedy, Pres. John 160, 161, 162, 165
Ketchem, James 69
Kiernan, Francis 236
Kinderhook, New York 46, 66, 108
King, Amos 247
King's Highway 56, 228
Kingsland, Amos 144
Knox, Charles 144, 145
Knox, Edward 145

Laflin, Col. Bryan 228
Lake Erie 11, 30, 255
Lake Ontario 30, 37
Lamon, Ward Hill 9–10, 13, 50, 60, 79, **152**, 153
Lane, Harriet **26**, 146
Lansingburgh, New York 216, 249
Lapham, Nathaniel 73
Leon, James 145
levee 25–26
L.H. Tupper 83
Lincoln, Edward 150, 151
Lincoln, Mary 5, 25, 28, 30, 48, 78, 79, 82, 107, 110, 113, 122, 124, 133, 143, 145, 146, 153, 154, 155, 159, 160, 167, 173
Lincoln, Robert 30, 36, 113, 124, 132, 143, 153
Lincoln, Tad 28, 30, 51, 114, 124, 143, 150, **151**, 162
Lincoln, Willie 28, 30, 114, 124, 143, 148, 150, **151**, 152, 153, 208
Lincoln and the Railroads 86
Lincoln bell 120
Lincoln pin 151
Lincoln Special 2, 10, 12, 16, 30, **32**, 36, 42, 49, 51, 54, 59, 61, 63, **64**, 67, **88**, 96, 97, 107, 114, 119, 120, 122, **159**, 160, 180, 190, 232, 235, 237, 238, 239, 241, 242, **243**, 244, 249, 250, 251, 252, 264
Lincoln's Journey to Greatness 97
Little Falls, New York 54, 55, 56, 58, 59, 226, 227, 236
Little Falls Journal & Courier 59
Littlejohn, DeWitt Clinton 76, 77
Livingston, Van Brough 121
Lockport, New York 255
Lyons, New York 248, 255

MacAllister 95
MacDonald, Norm 120, 196
Madden, Mary 196
Madison House 239, **240**
Magnolia tree
Major Priest 41, 48, 51
Manhattan Island 114, 124, 125, 168, 190, 194
Manhattanville, New York 192
Martingale, Gen. J.H. 251
McCarihe, Isaac 103, 216
McClellan, Gen. George 102, 115
McCollum, Gen. Daniel 155, 156, 165, 207
McCurdy, Robert 144
McKinley Pres. William 160, 266

Mechanicville, New York 92, 93
Medal of Honor 249, 262, 264
Memphis, New York 245
Mendelssohn Club 236
Meriden, New York 249
Milton Ferry Station, New York 199
Mohawk, New York 57
Mohawk River 47, 54, 55, 60, 61, 87, **91**, 116, 228, 230, 241
Mohawk Turnpike 230, 233
Mohawk Valley 1, 43, **49**, **54**, **55**, 56, 57, 60, 165, 193, 219, 220, 223, 224, 231, 237
Monro, James 256
Montgomery County 224
Morand, Pierre 174, 175
Morgan, Gov. Edwin 73, 74, 75, 82, 126, 203
Morrill, Elizabeth Ann 250
Morrill, William 250
Morse, Samuel 114
Morsett, Julie 118

Nalle, Charles 89
Nast, Thomas 88
National Hotel 79
Nelson, Hon. William 117
New Amsterdam 66
New Hamburg, New York 199
New Haven Palladium 132
New Netherlands 66
New York 11, 51, 54, 62, 66, 67, 81, 82, 83, 85, 86, 93, 95, 97, 103, 106, 107, 114, 115, 118, 120, 121, 122, 123, **125**, 126, 132, 139, 140, 145, 149, 151, 154, 165, 166, **169**, 171, 172, 180, 183, **184**, 186, **188**, 190, 191, 192, 193, 194, 196, 199, 200, 209, 217, 221, 222, 223, 224, 229, 236, 237, 239, 259, 262, 266
New York & Erie Railroad 268
New York Daily Tribune 96
New York Evening Post 144, 182
New York Herald 42, 68, 78, 122, 125, 132, 144, 171, 200
New York State 58, 59, 65, **91**, 95, 100, 132, 135, 148, 178, 228, 253
New York Sun 171
New York Times 53, 54, 60, 63, 96, 136, 168, 172, 212, 214, 260
New York Tribune 139, 231, 245
New York World 16
Newark, New Jersey 241, 250
Newark, New York 250
Nichols, Francis 244
Nichols, Rachel 244, 245
Nicolay, John 127, 174
North Ilion, New York 228, 233
North Star 31

Oak Hill Cemetery 157
Oak Ridge Cemetery 154
Obama, Barack 265
obsequies 153, 160, 161, 165, 178, 180, 190, 191, 199, 217, 229, 238, 255
Officers' Car **156**, 157, 166, 187

Index

"Old Saratoga" **235**, 236
Oneida, New York 47, 241, **240**
Oneida Weekly Herald 48, 239
Oriskany 234
Osgood Hotel 229
Ossining, New York 1, 11, 120, 196
Oswego, New York 37, 242, 246
Otis, Isaac 246

Palatine Bridge, New York 54, 59, 224, 225
Palmyra, New York 249, 255
parade 20–22, 70–72, 122–127, 184, 186, 188, 210, 215–218, 229, 261
Parr, Capt. Harris 203
Parrott, Col. Robert 115
Patterson, George 12
Peekskill, New York 115, 116, 117, 118, 180, 193, 198, 200
Perry, Eli 203
pickpockets 24, 25, 68, 69, 105, 112, 214
Pierce, Franklin 265
pilot engine 30, 33, 107, 186, 194, 197, 201, 219, 222, 223, 234, 237, 243, 251, 252, 261, 265, 267
Pope, Capt. John 10
Port Byron, New York 247
Porter, William 222
Portland, New York 263
Potter, Hon. Platt 63
Poughkeepsie, New York 1, 97, 107, 111, 113, 120, 161, 186, 193, 199, 200, 201, 217
Poughkeepsie Daily Press 197, 200
Poughkeepsie Eagle 200, 201
Power, John Carroll 171, 226
Priest, Maj. Zenas 222, 237

Randall, John 214
Rathbone, Maj. Henry 80
Rathbone, Gen. John 216
Raymond, William 190
Regiments (Artillery): 1st New York Light 33; Light Horse Battalion 216; 3rd New York 245; Washington Artillery 37
Regiments (Cavalry): 9th New York 264; 10th New York 255; 21st New York 249
Regiments (Infantry): 2nd New York 99, 102; 10th New York 81, 206, 216; 21st New York 200; 25th New York 70, 78, 81, 216; 72nd New York 16, 202, 264; 90th New York 248; 97th New York 248; 111th New York 248, 249; 115th New York 224; 117th New York 232–233; 121st New York 57–58; 157th New York 234; 162nd New York 232–233
Regiments (National Guard): 7th New York 168, 169, 170, 175, 179, 189; 45th New York 235; 54th New York 254
Relyea, Peter 183, **185**
Rensselaer, New York 86

Rensselaer & Saratoga Railroad 72, 86, 94, 96, 98, 193
Rhinebeck, New York 110, 111, 193, 201
Richmond, Hon. Seth 59
Rochester, New York 1, 30–**32**, 36, 37, 99, 180, 244, 249, 250, 251, **252**, 255, 260
Rochester Daily Press 256
Rochester Daily Union and Advertiser 32, 34, 51
Rochester Democrat 34, 35
Rochester Union and Advertiser 32, 34, 51
Rocket 9, 11, 18
Rome, New York 239
Roosevelt, Pres. Franklin 158, 160, 161, 164, 165, 238, 267
Roosevelt, Pres. Theodore 265
Russia, New York 58

Sabin, Samuel 249
safety concerns 9, 10, 150, 152–153
St. Cecelia Society 260, 261
St. James Hall 256, 259
St. Johnsville, New York 5, 9, 255
Salisbury Prison 241
Sands, Frederick 179, 207, 215
Sanford, Charles 69
Savannah, New York 248
Schenectady, New York 54, 59, 63, **64**, 80, 87, 97, 186, 216, **223**, 234
The Schenectady Daily Gazette 63
Schneck, Robert 147
Schodack, New York 108, 201
Schreiber's Band 105, 206, 217
Scott, Gen. Winfield 9, 105, 115
Searcher, Victor 97, 172
Secret Service 50, 110
Seward, Sen. William 36, 45, 75, 76, 239
Seymour, Horatio 236
Seymour, Capt. Truman 94–95
Seymour, the Rev. Truman 94
Sherman, Vice-Pres. John Schoolcraft 47
Sickles, Gen. Dan 16
Silver Creek, New York 9, 16, 255, 262
Simons, Robert 243
Sing Sing, New York **119**, 120, 193, 196, **197**, 198
Sloane, Samuel 107, 113, 122
Smith, E. Delafield 134
speeches: Hamlin, Hannibal 46, 84–85, 130–131; Lincoln, Abraham 13, 16, 23, 33, 35, 40, 50, 59, 70, 75, 77, 103, 110, 112, 115, 118, 129, 140, 143
Spencerport, New York 32, 255
Spinner, Gen. Francis 57
Springfield, Illinois 30, 34, 153, 154, 156, 160, 165, 167, 173, 190, 204, 208, 209, 221, 223, 236
Stacey, Manly 249
Stanton, Edward 153, 154, **155**, 182
Starr, John 34, 86
Starr Arms Company 194
Stockport, New York 201

Stowe, Harriett Beecher 138, 144
Stuart, Robert 136
Stuyvesant, New York 108, 193
Styx 205
Sumner, Col. William 10, 82, 105
Swift, Hon. Charles 112
Syracuse, New York 36, 37, **38**, 39, **40**, 99, 237, **243**, 255
Syracuse Journal 244

Taber, E. Randall 225
Taft, Pres. William Howard 47
Tarrytown, New York 121, 143, 195, 196
Taylor, William 144
Taylor, Pres. Zachary 160
Thacher, Mayor George 61, 64, 70
30th Street Station **188**
Tileson, Thomas 136
Tivoli, New York 111
Todd, Lockwood **151**
Tompkins, Albert 120
top hat 53, 144–145, 148
Toucey, James 190
Towle, Elbridge 46
Troy, New York 86, 87, 88, 97, 98, 99, **100**, **101**, 103, **104**, 106, 108, 193, 216, 217
Troy bridge 96, 205
Troy Daily Times 68, 101
Troy Daily Whig 101, 106
Troy Times 104, 105
Truman, Harry S 5, 265
Trump, Fred 264
Tubman, Harriet 36, 89

"Uncle Abe" 238
"Uncle Sam" 88
Underground Railroad 31, 36, 37, 131, 132, 140, 143, 155, 194, 220
undertaker 179, 183, 203, 205, 207, 208, 215, 260
Union 90, 97, 110, 112, 113, 186, 187, 188, 194, 198, 200, 208, 214, 245, 256, 261, 264
Union Station **101**, 108
United States **156**, **227**
Utica, New York 1, 36, 41, 42, 43, 47, 48, **49**, 51, 52, 54, 56, 57, 69, 98, 99, 103, 119, 145, 180, 216, 218, 221, 222, 224, 227, 232, **233**, 234, 235, 237, 238, 239
Utica Gazette 43
Utica Morning Herald 43
Utica Telegram 43

Vail, Thomas 107
Valentine, David 166, 171
Van Buren, John 108
Van Buren, Martin 46, 105, 108
Vandebilt Square
Vasser, William 201
Veteran Reserve Corps 173, 215
Victorian mourning 48, 159, 162, 163, 164, 170, 173, 187, 194, 204, 205, 213, 219, 256
Villard, Henry 52, 63, 69, 72, 83
Vroman, Isaac 237

Index

Wager, David 234, 235
Waldo, Rev. Daniel 40
Wampsville, New York 5
Ward, Gen. Hobart 148
Warners 244–245
Washington, George 40, 47, 121, 137, 140, 180, 213
Washington, D.C. 9, 34, 44, 51, 65, 79, 83, 89, 93, 149, 152, 154, 160, 165, 166, 167, 168, 172, 173, 182, 187, 209, 213, 229, 247, 260
Washington Evening Star 209
Waterford, New York 87, 88, 89, 90, 216
Waterford Junction, New York 86, 87, 94, 98
Waterford Sentinel 92
Watervliet, New York 66, 88, 89, 216

Watervliet Arsenal **88,** 106
Waverly Hotel 32, 33, 34
Webster, Daniel 134, 312
Weed, Thurlow 79, 212
Wendell, Barney 105
West Albany, New York 224
West Point 94, 115, 121, 198, 199
West Troy, New York 87, 88, 90, 216
Westchester County 198
Westcott, Amos 39
Westfield, New York 11–15, **14**, 255, **263**, 264
Whipple, Adam 222
Whitcraft, Arthur 250
Whitcraft, Roberta 250
Whitcraft, Ruth 250
White House 27, 51, 69, 79, 116, 150, 154, 203, 208, 229

Whitman, Walt 128
Whitney, David 178
Wide-Awakes 147
Widows Weeds and Weeping Vails 163Willard Hotel 79
Williams, Honus 222
Williams, Gen. John 251
Wood, Fernando 9, 134, 138, 139, 140, 143
Wood, William 10, 49, 69, 155, 220
Wrightson, George 222

"Yankee Doodle" 108, 148
Yonkers, New York 121
Yosts, New York 60
Young Men's Association 71, 216, 259

Zouave 10, 92, 93, 231

www.ingramcontent.com/pod-product-compliance
Lightning Source LLC
Chambersburg PA
CBHW081543300426
44116CB00015B/2729